BLACK TUNNEL WHITE MAGIC

BLACK TUNNEL WHITE MAGIC

*A murder without motive. A city on the brink.
Sometimes true crime is stranger than fiction...*

RICK JACKSON
AND
MATTHEW McGOUGH

Foreword by Michael Connelly

SEVEN DIALS

First published in Great Britain in 2025 by Seven Dials,
an imprint of The Orion Publishing Group Ltd
Carmelite House, 50 Victoria Embankment
London EC4Y 0DZ

The authorised representative in the EEA is Hachette Ireland, 8 Castlecourt Centre,
Dublin 15, D15 XTP3, Ireland (email: info@hbgi.ie)

An Hachette UK Company

Published simultaneously in the US by Mulholland Books / Little, Brown and Company

1 3 5 7 9 10 8 6 4 2

Copyright © Rick Jackson and Matthew McGough 2025
Foreword Copyright © Michael Connelly 2025

The moral right of Rick Jackson and Matthew McGough to be identified as
the author of this work has been asserted in accordance
with the Copyright, Designs and Patents Act of 1988.

All rights reserved. No part of this publication may be
reproduced, stored in a retrieval system, or transmitted
in any form or by any means, electronic, mechanical,
photocopying, recording, or otherwise, without the
prior permission of both the copyright owner and the
above publisher of this book.

A CIP catalogue record for this book is
available from the British Library.

ISBN (Trade Paperback) 978 1 3996 0161 0
ISBN (eBook) 978 1 3996 0164 1
ISBN (Audio) 978 1 3996 0165 8

Book interior design by Marie Mundaca
Printed in Great Britain by Clays, Ltd. Elcograf S.p.A.

www.orionbooks.co.uk

For Hillary and Megan — the daughters I always hoped for. You've both given me the best reason to love life. You have always been my inspiration.
and
For Debbie — my wife and my love, even after my wait of forty-nine years. Thank you for your steadfast encouragement and support.
—R.J.

For Declan and Hudson — with love and appreciation for the fine young men you have become.
and
For Kathryn — my dazzling, brilliant wife, best friend, and soulmate. Thank you for always being there for me. You brighten every room you walk into and every day of my life.
—M.M.

In memory of Ron Baker and his parents, Gayle and Kay

The smiler with the knife under the cloak.
—GEOFFREY CHAUCER, *The Canterbury Tales*

CONTENTS

Foreword by Michael Connelly   *xiii*

Part I: The Betrayal

1. Holy Terror (June 21 to 22, 1990)   3
2. "Mr. Baker, We Have Your Son" (June 21 to 24, 1990)   13
3. Partners in Crime (June 24, 1990)   21
4. Searching Chatsworth Park (June 24 to 25, 1990)   31
5. "I Always Thought Ron Would Be There" (June 26 to 30, 1990)   45
6. Deception Indicated (July 2 to 6, 1990)   61
7. "The Coolest Motherfucker I've Ever Dealt With" (July 7 to 11, 1990)   83
8. "Not a Flight Risk" (July 12 to 24, 1990)   94
9. On the Run? (July 25 to August 3, 1990)   102
10. The Roller Coaster (August 6 to 22, 1990)   117
11. "Things To Do" (September 4, 1990 to January 21, 1992)   132
12. A Request for Immunity (February 6 to 10, 1992)   145

Part II: The Second Betrayal

13. King for a Day (February 10, 1992)   153
14. Blood Warrant (February 11 to July 6, 1992)   201
15. "Where the Hell Have You Been?" (July 9 to 13, 1992)   224
16. "No Changes, No Edits" (July 18 to October 21, 1992)   247

17. "It's Too Bad We Had to Meet Under These Circumstances"
(October 21, 1992 to January 23, 1993)   267

18. "I Need You for One More Day" (February 9 to 17, 1993)   274

19. "A Hugging Circle" (February 22 to June 10, 1993)   307

20. "A Murder That Someone Else Did" (June 30 to
July 16, 1993)   315

Part III: The Third Betrayal

21. The Burglary (December 13, 1993 to March 4, 1994)   333

22. Deputy D.A. Marcia Clark (May 13 to June 12, 1994)   355

23. Governor's Warrant (June 20 to November 14, 1994)   378

24. The Passport Investigator (November 28, 1994 to
February 26, 1996)   386

25. Judgment Day (March 18 to 29, 1996)   401

26. Equal Justice? (June 3 to August 26, 1996)   425

27. My Return to the Scenes of the Crimes
(1996 to 2020)   436

Part IV: The Final Betrayal

28. "By Virtue of the Authority Vested in Me"
(June 21 to December 7, 2020)   445

29. A Shallow Dive for the Truth (December 8, 2020)   467

30. And in the End, the Life You Take Is Equal to...
(January 25, 2021 to April 26, 2022)   485

Acknowledgments   491
Authors' Note on Sources   495
Selected Bibliography   496
Index   497

FOREWORD BY MICHAEL CONNELLY

PERHAPS MORE THAN ANY other city, Los Angeles has always been a place defined by its murders and its killers. The list is long. The Black Dahlia, the Hillside Stranglers, the Night Stalker, the Grim Sleeper. We can't leave out the O. J. Simpson case, the Manson Family killings, or the assassination of Robert F. Kennedy.

But these citations barely scratch the surface. There are many more. Murder in LA always carries with it something extra. This place is arguably the media and entertainment capital of the world. Murder here sells. It makes headlines that reach across the world in concentric circles that widen and spread.

I came to Los Angeles as a crime reporter. I knew this was a singular place to be in my profession and I wanted to catch a ride on one of those LA murders, write the hell out of it and ride the headlines for all they were worth. When young Ronald Baker, from a good family and good school, was found stabbed to death and with his throat slashed in a railroad tunnel at the edge of town, I thought I had caught my ride. The case had all the ingredients. Good kid, bad end. Throw in the occult pentagrams painted on the walls and all the questions without answers, and I thought I had caught the brass ring as a writer specializing in murder. It was a story that would be hard to shove off the front page.

From the start, the case was steeped in mystery and the unexplainable. But the police were impenetrable. The story eventually died for lack of oxygen. I left journalism and went into the business of fiction. But the investigators, they didn't stop.

It was after I was out that I learned what I didn't know then. About the relentless detectives who pursued the case across many years and many states. Who were undaunted, unafraid, and unstoppable.

And that's the story you have here. You have the inside story told by Rick Jackson, the detective who lived it, and Matthew McGough, the skilled writer he's partnered with to tell it. A perfect combination of storytelling. Ride with them now into this darkness.

This book cuts through the exaggerated newspaper accounts and hysterical headlines. You'll ride with the detectives who never took their eyes off the prize of justice, who worked diligently to decipher what was true and what was not, what was vital and what was clever deflection. You'll find a family whose grief only grew with each passing year. This is a story that doesn't end with convictions and sentences but has waves that draw meaning even today.

They say if you want to get the facts, read a newspaper. If you want to get the truth, read a novel. I think that's true—it's why I made that jump. But it's not true all of the time. Not here, not with this story. This story gives you the truth of character in a pair of relentless detectives, in a damaged family, and in the exploration of a broken system. It offers redemption and hope in those same individuals who persevere despite the obstacles and odds.

This is a book that is surely about killers, but they don't take the spotlight. That belongs to the detectives who worked the case, whose eyes were not jaundiced, and who steadily, methodically closed in. In them you find humanity and hope in a city where killers are often kings.

—*Michael Connelly, Los Angeles*

PART I

THE BETRAYAL

CHAPTER 1

HOLY TERROR
(June 21 to 22, 1990)

IT HAPPENS ONCE A year. That year, it was on a Thursday morning—8:33, to be exact. It set things in motion. It altered lives. None for the better.

It was the summer solstice—the moment when Earth's rotational axis, the imaginary line that runs between the North and South Poles, achieves its maximum tilt toward the sun. From Earth, the sun appears at its highest point in the sky. Not for another year does the Northern Hemisphere receive so much light in a single day.

It passes unnoticed by most, yet the summer solstice has been observed for millennia, since the age of Stonehenge and the pyramids of Giza at least, and likely even earlier. Throughout human history, cultures around the world have granted it spiritual significance. It inspired Shakespeare, who used it for the plot of one of his most famous comedies, *A Midsummer Night's Dream*. In Shakespeare's time, the summer solstice was a celebratory occasion marked by open-air feasts and renowned for its aura of magic and mystery.

That year, 1990, in Los Angeles, the summer solstice figured in a darker plot, one more akin in cruelty to a Shakespearean tragedy. The story begins late on Thursday, June 21, the night of the astronomical solstice.

Four teenagers in the San Fernando Valley, two boys and two girls, wanted a late-night thrill. The boys, Roland and Timo, were already out of high school. Amy and Melissa were younger. Amy was sixteen at the time.

Earlier that evening, they had attended a youth group meeting together. Afterward, Amy asked Roland for a ride home, although she didn't really feel like going home. They piled into Roland's pickup truck and instead drove to Lancers, a nearby restaurant, where they hung out and talked until after midnight.

It was Roland and Timo's idea to go to Chatsworth Park. More specifically, up to the desolate train tunnel in the hills above Chatsworth Park. Roland had ventured into the tunnel two or three times before.

It sounded like a thrill to Amy, the way they described it. You could walk on the tracks into the tunnel, and if you were lucky, a train would pass through while you were inside. Standing tight against the wall, you'd experience an intense rush as the train whooshed past you, just a few feet away. Wait for it to pass and see if you survived.

Amy and Melissa agreed to go along. They arrived at the park around 1 or 1:30 a.m., in the early morning hours of Friday, June 22.

Although it is located within Los Angeles city limits, Chatsworth Park includes terrain that more closely resembles a rugged wilderness than any typical urban playground of sunbaked blacktop. The park is split into two sections, North and South. The railroad tracks run along and above the west side of both sections.

Down below, in Chatsworth Park's lower elevations, are a few dusty baseball fields and picnic tables. But what makes the park so unique and alluring, and defines its landscape, are the rocky hills that loom over it, at the northwest rim of the San Fernando Valley.

The hills above Chatsworth Park are studded with colossal sandstone boulders and, apart from a few trails, covered with scrub and scattered trees. Up close, the jumble of boulders appears almost cartoonish and prehistoric, like a set for a live-action remake of *The Flintstones*, somewhere on the outskirts of Bedrock.

Despite the summer solstice being the day of the year with the latest sunset, it had already been dark for more than four hours by the time the teens got to the park. Compared to denser, glitzier areas of Los Angeles, such as Hollywood or Downtown LA, there was little light pollution in Chatsworth to diminish the night sky. Although the weather that night was fair and mild, it was unusually dark outside. The moon's phase was a waning crescent, providing barely any light to see by.

The only sources of illumination the teenagers had brought on their trek to the tunnel were Roland's and Timo's cigarette lighters. The boys led the way to the unmarked trailhead at the base of the hills. From there, it was a bit of a climb.

Amy had never been to Chatsworth Park before that night. As she followed her friends up into the hills, she realized with some unease that they were not the only ones there. Amy spied some people dressed, strangely, in black capes. Underneath their black capes, all the rest of their clothing was also black. Amy couldn't tell how many there were, or even whether they were male or female. She caught glimpses of the black-caped figures running and darting in the darkness from tree to tree, around and behind them. They never engaged directly or came too close, nor did they run away.

It was only then, on the heels of her brush with the shadowy caped people, that Amy learned another aspect of the tunnel's lore, which her friends had neglected to mention. The tunnel they were about to enter, her friends explained, was very close to "the Manson ranch," where Charles Manson and his "family" of followers lived in the summer of 1969, when they murdered actress Sharon Tate and several other innocent people. The ramshackle property, known as Spahn Movie Ranch at the time Manson lived there, was located just half a mile north of the tunnel.

The notoriety and savagery of the crimes planned at Spahn Ranch stigmatized the property to such a degree that it quickly became better known as "the Manson ranch." The stigma was so powerful that over time the nearby railroad tunnel acquired its own unofficial nickname: "the Manson tunnel." Whether Manson ever set foot inside the tunnel is unknown, a matter of conjecture rather than historical record.

What's more, Amy's friends belatedly informed her, the tunnel's proximity to the Manson ranch had made it a place where "devil worshippers" liked to congregate. Roland had heard "weird stuff" and "Manson-type things" went on up there. This was news to Amy, who hadn't expected to encounter anyone else at the park or the tunnel. Not people in black capes and certainly not devil worshippers. Amy felt afraid, but not enough to turn back. They were almost to the top of the path.

Amy's fears were not unfounded. At the time, in 1990, fear of the occult was palpable and pervasive in American society. The specter of Satanism prompted so much public alarm during the 1980s and 1990s, all over the country, that the period has since been dubbed "the Satanic Panic."

Fears were especially acute in Los Angeles, which had been traumatized by a series of high-profile, purportedly satanic killings, beginning with Manson's in 1969. The randomness of the Manson Family's victims and the ritualized violence he directed against them was a chilling combination that inflicted deep psychic wounds on the city, sowing the seeds for future collective paranoia.

Public fascination with Satanism and satanic possession went national during the 1970s. The 1971 novel *The Exorcist*, by William Peter Blatty, and its subsequent film adaptation gripped mainstream popular culture. The occult and supernatural became the subject of everyday conversation as never before.

In Los Angeles, the trauma the Manson Family inflicted on the local consciousness never healed entirely. Fifteen years later, in 1984, these wounds were reopened when the Night Stalker, eventually identified as the serial killer Richard Ramirez, began murdering people across California, most in the Greater Los Angeles area.

Like Manson, Ramirez appeared to choose his victims at random, and his murders were shockingly brutal and highly ritualized. Unlike Manson, Ramirez committed all his murders himself. At many of his crime scenes, Ramirez left behind symbols of the occult, most commonly an inverted pentagram, which he considered a mark of the devil. At his first court appearance following his arrest in 1985, Ramirez held up his hand in the presence of news photographers to reveal a pentagram he'd drawn on his own palm. Ramirez's trial in 1989 was heavily covered by the media, which only served to stoke public fear of Satan-inspired crimes—and the collective appetite for more such stories. Ramirez was convicted of thirteen counts of murder in September 1989, less than a year before the night of the teenagers' visit to the Manson tunnel.

In 1990, murder and the fear of it were at the forefront of the public's mind in California. This was especially true in Los Angeles. The city had just emerged from the deadliest decade in its history. More than eight thousand people were murdered in LA during the 1980s, a larger toll than the 1960s and 1970s combined. Daily, the local airwaves and newspapers were flush with reports of senseless violence and lives cut tragically short. Amy and her friends had grown up in a culture steeped in attention to evildoers.

The path the teenagers climbed eventually opened onto a flat expanse of gravel and rocky ballast, down the middle of which ran a solitary set of railroad tracks. They had reached their destination: the western portal of the tunnel.

The teens hung out along the tracks outside the tunnel for a few minutes, waiting in vain for a train to pass, before they summoned the nerve to venture inside.

Roland and Timo led the way. Amy and Melissa followed a few feet behind, side by side. There was little artificial lighting at the tunnel's entrance and none whatsoever inside. Both boys held their cigarette lighters out in front of them at arm's length and kept flicking them on to light their way.

It was too dark for the teens to notice the ominous words spray-painted over the arched mouth of the tunnel, as if a warning not to enter: "HOLY TERROR."

LAPD crime scene photo of the western portal of "the Manson tunnel," June 22, 1990 (court exhibit)

Much of the concrete entrance embankment was also covered in graffiti. Among the crudely painted tags and symbols they blindly walked past were multiple inverted pentagrams.

Inside the tunnel it was pitch-black. The tracks between the east and west portals curve slightly, enough that, approaching the midpoint, it becomes impossible to see either entrance. No natural light reaches the middle stretch of the tunnel, even in daytime.

As dark as it was, they kept going, step by tentative step. In those fleeting moments when both Roland's and Timo's lighters stayed lit, Amy could see at most five feet ahead of her, and to her side, one of the tunnel's walls. Whenever the boys' lighters faltered, she could not see anything, not even her own hand in front of her face.

Because they never stopped walking, it took them only a few minutes to make it well into the tunnel. They were more than a hundred feet in when Amy noticed something on the ground ahead of them, off to the side. In the dim flickering light, it looked to her like something or someone wrapped up in a blanket, lying against the base of the wall.

"What is that?" she asked the others. Amy and Melissa hung back while the boys, brandishing their lighters, went to take a closer look.

Timo got closest, within one or two feet, and Roland within five feet, before they realized that it was a body. They couldn't tell whether the person was dead or still alive, but they thought they saw blood on the body. It also appeared to them the body was missing one hand.

"Let's get out of here," yelled Timo. He and Roland took off running, back the way they had come. Amy and Melissa ran after them, terrified, sprinting through total darkness, until they had all made it out of the tunnel.

Timo wanted to go back in and drag the body out, in case the person was still alive, but no one was willing to go with him. Roland had kept on running and was already scrambling down the hill to call an ambulance.

There were some private homes at the bottom of the hill, adjacent to Chatsworth Park. Roland ran to the nearest house and banged on its door. No one answered. At the next house, a woman came to the door but refused to open it. Roland told her that it was an emergency and to call 911, that he thought a person had gotten hit by a train.

Two units from the Los Angeles Fire Department, a fire truck and an ambulance, were first to respond, at 1:42 a.m. Roland waved them down in front of the house the 911 call had been placed from, just outside an entrance to Chatsworth Park. Timo and the girls were also there, having waited with Roland until help arrived.

Inside the tunnel, the firefighters located the bloodied body of a young white male, about twenty years old. LAFD captain Lewis Bressler, the ranking firefighter at the scene, observed that the man's throat was slit. They pronounced him dead at 2:12 a.m.

By the time the firefighters came back from the tunnel, the teenagers were gone. The engineer informed Bressler that the witnesses had hung around for about ten minutes and then left.

The first police to arrive, at 2:25 a.m., were patrol officers from the LAPD's Devonshire Division, the local police precinct with jurisdiction over Chatsworth Park.

As was standard practice upon confirmation of a suspicious death, the first arriving patrol units set up a perimeter within Chatsworth Park, which was now presumed to be a crime scene.

Bressler briefed the officers on his findings inside the tunnel and what the reporting party, Roland, had told him. The LAFD units, having fulfilled all their responsibilities at the scene, left the park at 2:40 a.m.

It was around 3 a.m. when Peggy Moseley, an LAPD detective assigned to the Devonshire Division Homicide unit, was awakened at home by a ringing phone. Her lieutenant, Al Durrer, relayed to her what was known and called her into work. Moseley's detective partner, Ken Crocker, received a similar call from Durrer. After the detectives, Durrer notified the LA County coroner's office.

By 4:40 a.m., Moseley, Crocker, and Durrer had arrived at the park and assumed control of the crime scene and nascent investigation. Also at the scene by then were a photographer from the LAPD's Scientific Investigation Division and a coroner's investigator, Sandra Fitzgerald.

Moseley was familiar with Chatsworth Park and had been there before, although never in the dead of night. When Moseley first approached the tunnel, it was so dark and foggy out that she could not even see the entrance. She had to use her handheld radio to ask officers already at the mouth of the tunnel to flash a couple of light beams just so she could see where they were.

Inside the tunnel, 165 feet from the entrance, they discovered some bloodstained items on the ground: a pair of black sunglasses, an empty pack of cigarettes—Marlboro Gold 100's—and some shards of broken glass, likely from a shattered beer bottle.

A trail of blood droplets, plainly visible with the detectives' flashlights, ran from these items across the tracks to where the body lay, 10 feet farther in. There was a large pool of blood on the gravel railbed just south of the tracks. A few feet away, at the base of the tunnel's south wall, a second, larger pool of blood spread from under the body. Some of the blood was still liquid, but in other areas where it was less dense, it had already begun to dry and flake.

It appeared the struggle had begun on the north side of the tracks, where blood was first drawn. The victim, perhaps attempting to get away, had moved south across the tracks. There he had received additional major wounds that caused him to bleed more profusely, resulting in the pooled blood and, ultimately, his death. Moseley and Crocker found no evidence to indicate that he had been killed somewhere else and then his body dragged or carried into the tunnel and left there.

LAPD photo of crime scene personnel examining the body, dawn on June 22, 1990 (court exhibit)

The victim was slightly built and had curly brown hair. He was dressed in blue jeans, a red short-sleeved shirt with a white undershirt, and white British Knights tennis shoes. His pockets appeared undisturbed. All of his clothing was soaked in blood. He lay on his left side, with his back against the concrete tunnel wall. Both of his legs were bent behind him at the knee, rather unnaturally, with his ankles against the wall. His right ankle appeared possibly fractured. There were also oily, grimy stains on his clothes and skin, consistent with him having come into contact with the nearby tracks and railroad ties.

Fitzgerald observed no obvious trauma to the dead man's face, and his eyes appeared normal and relatively clear. Across his throat, he had an extremely deep open wound that went all the way through his windpipe, leaving it exposed. In his torso were multiple deep open wounds that appeared to be stab wounds. All the injuries would be fully documented later, in an autopsy conducted by the medical examiner, but Fitzgerald noted that the apparent stab wounds were scattered across the victim's chest, back, buttocks, and extremities. A portion of his intestines protruded from one particularly grievous wound to the right side of his abdomen. There were also very severe cuts to his left hand and fingers, likely defensive wounds sustained while attempting to fend off his killer.

When the coroner's personnel turned the victim over, they discovered under his body a second empty pack of Marlboro cigarettes. Two rusty pieces of barbed wire were also found beside the victim, one near his head and another near his feet. Neither were bloodstained or in contact with the body. No marks were observed on the victim's wrists or ankles to indicate that he had been bound at any point with barbed wire. Its presence at the crime scene appeared to be random and unconnected to the present case, detritus that was already at the location before the murder occurred there.

The same could be said for the extensive graffiti behind the body on the south tunnel wall, the backdrop for many of the crime scene photographs taken that night. Even 175 feet inside the tunnel, where ordinarily it was pitch-black and only passing trains were supposed to be, its walls were covered with spray-painted messages. The graffiti was artless, foot-tall block letters applied with white spray paint, which stood out against the dark, sooty concrete wall. The most legible graffiti closest to the body read "DROP ACID NOT BOMBS" and "FUCK REAGAN!!" None of the graffiti appeared fresh.

A thorough search of the tunnel turned up no knife or any other weapons. No wallet was found on the body or nearby. The only item of personal property on the victim was a black string necklace around his neck. The necklace had a circular pendant, made of metal, in the shape of an upright pentagram.

Given the peculiar murder location, the tunnel's well-known association with occult activities, and the deficit of other clues the detectives had to go on, the possibility that the murder was some sort of ritualistic killing or human sacrifice could not be ruled out. The pentagram pendant around the victim's neck did not prove his murder was occult related, but it also hardly disproved it.

The body was removed from the tunnel at 5:45 a.m., shortly after sunrise on Friday morning, June 22, and transported to the morgue downtown. In her report, completed the following day, coroner's investigator Fitzgerald noted, "This tunnel is known to be a location frequented by transients and drug abusers, according to detectives at the scene."

Of the unknown young man, Fitzgerald wrote, "The decedent was not found to be carrying any form of identification... He was assigned John Doe #135 for purposes of identification... His next of kin remains unknown at the time of this report."

CHAPTER 2

"MR. BAKER, WE HAVE YOUR SON"
(June 21 to 24, 1990)

LATE ON THURSDAY NIGHT, June 21, about two hours before the teenagers discovered the body inside the tunnel, the phone rang at the home of Gayle and Kay Baker. The Bakers lived in Woodland Hills, an upper-middle-class area of the San Fernando Valley.

Gayle and Kay had been married for thirty years and had two children, a daughter, Patty, and a son, Ron. At the time, Patty was twenty-five years old and Ron was twenty-one.

The Bakers had lived in this very home since the mid-1970s. The house was located on a steep hillside street. Its backyard boasted impressive views of the Valley and a large in-ground swimming pool. When the Bakers moved in, Patty and Ron were not yet teenagers. Their home became a magnet for the neighborhood's kids. As adolescents, they and their friends had often gathered around the family's dining room table, playing Dungeons & Dragons or working on jigsaw puzzles.

Despite the lovely home, the Bakers were not a wealthy family. They had inherited their house from Kay's father.

Gayle and Kay raised their children there to adulthood. By 1990, both Patty and Ron had flown the nest and were living on their own.

Gayle worked as a writing engineer, proofreading technical plans for the Guidance and Control Systems division of Litton Industries, one of the many aerospace industry companies then flourishing in

*The Baker family on Ron's twentieth birthday, January 1989
(courtesy of Patty Baker Elliott)*

Southern California. Because his job entailed sensitive government defense systems, a security clearance was required. He was unable to share with his family and friends many details about how he spent his workdays.

Kay had been a kindergarten teacher but stopped working after she and Gayle married. Once Patty and Ron were out of elementary school, Kay went back to work part-time.

Gayle and Kay's social life revolved around their church, Woodland Hills United Methodist, of which they were charter members. Kay's part-time job was as the church's secretary. Gayle volunteered as a church trustee and was usually the first to receive a call when something on the premises broke and needed to be repaired fast.

When the phone rang at Gayle and Kay's late that night, close to midnight, the likeliest reason was their church calling with another emergency for him to take care of.

Kay had already gone to bed. Gayle had been dozing in a chair in front of the TV, having fallen asleep while watching the eleven o'clock news. The ringing phone had startled him awake. He glanced at his watch and saw it was ten minutes to midnight. He wondered why anyone would be calling at that hour.

"Hello?" Gayle answered the phone.

He heard a man's voice that he did not recognize. The voice sounded strange and raspy, as if whoever it was, was trying to disguise their true voice.

"Mr. Baker," the caller said. "We have your son. Unless you give us a hundred thousand dollars by five o'clock tomorrow, he will die." The caller's tone of voice was deep and monotone, without inflection or discernible emotion.

Gayle's initial thought was that it was some sort of prank. "Who is this?" he asked.

He received no response to his question. Instead, the caller warned him, in the same odd voice, "Do not go to the police or he will die."

Before Gayle could say anything more, the line went dead.

It was such a shocking and surreal call to receive, almost like a dream while he was dozing.

Gayle was so concerned that he immediately woke Kay and told her what had happened. Then he called Ron's apartment.

Ron's roommate Nathan Blalock answered the phone. Gayle asked him if Ron was there.

Nathan said he wasn't. "We took him to the bus stop at about nine thirty and he hasn't returned," he said. Nathan said he thought Ron was going to meet friends from Mystic's Circle at UCLA, where Ron was completing his junior year. Gayle had never heard of Mystic's Circle previously. Although he knew many of Ron's friends well, he wasn't as familiar with those from UCLA.

Gayle told Nathan about the nature of the call he had received. At the time, Gayle still believed that it was a prank.

"That would be a dirty trick to play on somebody," Nathan responded.

Gayle agreed. He asked Nathan to have Ron call him immediately, whatever time he came home. Nathan said he would.

Gayle decided against calling the police, since he figured it was likely just a prank.

The next morning, around ten thirty on Friday, June 22, the phone rang again at the Bakers' home.

Gayle answered and heard the same raspy, monotone voice as the night before.

This time, the caller said, "Mr. Baker, you had better give us that one hundred thousand by five o'clock or your son will die."

"Who is this?" Gayle asked.

As the night before, his question was ignored, and then the line went dead.

Now Gayle and Kay were deeply concerned.

A short time later, Gayle called Ron's apartment again. Ron's second roommate and close friend, Duncan Martinez, answered. Duncan said that Ron had not come home the previous night. Gayle recounted to Duncan the two anonymous phone calls. They agreed it was unusual for Ron to be out all night. Gayle told Duncan that he was going to notify the police immediately.

Gayle then called 911 and reported his son's possible kidnapping. He spoke with an LAPD detective supervisor in Van Nuys, the location of Ron's apartment and where he was last seen.

The supervisor classified the crime as a "Kidnap for Ransom." The LAPD's Robbery-Homicide Division, its elite detective squad, was notified. RHD detectives are among the department's most experienced and capable investigators—by reputation, the best of the best. The division's caseload is limited to Los Angeles' most high-profile, complex, and heinous crimes.

Given the possibility the Bakers might receive another call, an RHD detective went to their home to set up a phone tap that would enable any future calls to be recorded. The phone tap was a low-tech device, even by 1990 standards. It consisted of a suction cup attached to the phone's receiver. A wire ran from the suction cup to a connected tape recorder placed beside the phone. The Bakers were advised that anytime their phone rang, they were to press the RECORD button on the tape recorder before answering. If the call turned out to be innocuous, they could switch the recorder off.

In case Gayle answered the phone and heard the same eerie voice as before, he was instructed to say the police had not been notified, although that was untrue. Next, he was to confirm the amount of money required to secure Ron's freedom. Gayle was encouraged to ask to speak with Ron, to make sure he had not been harmed. As to how the money would be handed off, Gayle was told to say he was too afraid for his safety to take it someplace remote himself and, for the same reason, unwilling to have it picked up at their home. Gayle would instead have a friend drop the money off wherever the caller specified.

Patty, who lived an hour's drive from her parents, came home to sit vigil with them.

The waiting for a third ransom call or any update on Ron's status was nerve-racking.

Because the Bakers did not have call-waiting, a feature not yet common on home phones, they were counseled to stay off the line as much as possible. Should the kidnapper call again, it was important he get through, rather than get a busy signal. If anyone in the family wanted to place an outgoing call, they had to go to a neighbor's. Patty did just this, using a neighbor's phone to call many of Ron's friends in a desperate effort to locate him.

Despite the LAPD's installation of the recording device on the phone, the coaching Gayle received, and the Baker family's precautions, no additional ransom calls were received.

At 1 p.m. Friday, a robbery detective from the LAPD's Van Nuys Division, Craig Rhudy, visited Ron's apartment on Erwin Street and interviewed his two roommates, Duncan and Nathan. With their consent, Rhudy also took a look around the apartment and Ron's bedroom for any potential clues.

Rhudy's interview of Duncan and Nathan was not tape-recorded, but the detective recounted what was said and the results of his search in a written report.

Duncan and Nathan told Rhudy that Ron had become fascinated with Wicca, which they described as a "metaphysical meditation concept." They said Ron's interest began around October 1989, when he was introduced to it by a friend, Lance Strickler, for whom Ron had worked in a candle-making booth at the local springtime Renaissance Faire.

Rhudy wrote in his report: "Victim has a meditation altar w/ candles etc. set up in his room. Victim has been attending meetings at or near UCLA campus of a group called 'Mystic's Circle.'"

Duncan and Nathan also told Rhudy that they had been receiving numerous phone calls, and calls from the front gate of their apartment building, in which the callers asked for Ron. Upon being told Ron was not there, the callers immediately hung up, the roommates said.

During his search of Ron's bedroom, Rhudy found a flyer for Mystic's Circle, the group Duncan and Nathan had mentioned. Rhudy collected the flyer as evidence.

Mystic's Circle flyer found in Ron's bedroom on June 22, 1990 (court exhibit)

No connection had been made as of yet between Ron's disappearance, the ransom calls to the Bakers' home, and the unidentified young man's body found inside the railroad tunnel.

Moseley and Crocker, the Devonshire homicide detectives, had returned to Chatsworth Park on Friday morning to look for more evidence in the clear light of day. They were unaware that elsewhere inside the LAPD a related investigation was unfolding parallel to their own. They arrived at the tunnel at 10:30 a.m., coincidentally around the same time the second of the two ransom calls was received by the Bakers.

The only additional evidence Moseley and Crocker found at the scene Friday were a few more broken beer bottles on the ground outside the west entrance to the tunnel.

Friday afternoon, they drove to the coroner's office downtown, where they viewed the victim's body and injuries and discussed the same with the coroner's investigator. Fingerprints taken by a coroner's investigator had been sent to the LAPD for comparison with all print records on file. No match was found. Officially, the victim remained John Doe #135.

Word of the grisly discovery in the tunnel had already reached the press. At 3:10 p.m. on Friday, Crocker fielded a call from a *Los Angeles Daily News* reporter.

The news broke in a story that ran in the Saturday edition of the paper. The unidentified male victim was described as "about 20 years old, white, 6 feet, 150 pounds with brown hair that appeared to have been permed into tight ends." The paper reported the victim was stabbed to death and police suspected the motive could have been robbery, because no money was found on him. Anyone with information about the victim or killing was urged to call Devonshire detectives.

Although the Devonshire detectives had told the press that the motive for the murder might have been robbery, that was not the only theory they were exploring. In their "chrono"—the running chronological log kept by LAPD detectives to document all actions taken in an investigation—they noted a possible "devil worship satanic connection due to vict wearing pentagram pendant."

Midday on Saturday, Moseley and Crocker went to the coroner's office to attend the autopsy of John Doe #135. Not surprisingly, the medical examiner who performed the autopsy, Dr. Eva Heuser, determined his cause of death was multiple stab wounds.

Who the victim was, rather than how he died, remained the bigger mystery.

Crocker and Moseley contacted neighboring law enforcement agencies to check whether they had received any missing persons reports that fit the victim's description. They had not.

It was not until Sunday afternoon, almost three days after the body was discovered in the tunnel, that John Doe #135 was finally identified.

RHD detectives investigating the kidnapping of Ron Baker meanwhile had been doing their own due diligence. It was standard protocol in cases with a missing victim for detectives to call local hospitals, to see if anyone matching the victim's description had been admitted. Detectives in such cases would routinely check with the coroner's office as well, regarding recent unidentified decedents. It took only one call to the coroner's office for the dots to be connected that John Doe #135 was Ron Baker.

What had been two separate cases, the murder of John Doe #135 and the kidnapping for ransom of Ron Baker, became one case. The combined case would now be handled by detectives from RHD's Major Crime Investigation Section, which consisted of six teams of two detectives. For shorthand, the unit was referred to as Major Crimes. It had been formed in the 1970s as a top-notch specialized homicide unit with citywide jurisdiction.

With the official transfer of the Baker case, notifications were made to the two on-call detectives assigned to Major Crimes. Ron Baker's murder would now be their responsibility.

CHAPTER 3

PARTNERS IN CRIME
(June 24, 1990)

I WAS RELAXING AT home on Sunday evening, June 24, when my phone rang. We had just finished eating dinner, and I was getting my daughters, then four and nine years old, ready for bed.

My partner, Frank Garcia, and I had been on call all weekend, as the detectives responsible for any homicide between Friday night and Monday morning that came RHD's way. Things had been quiet, though, and it seemed as if our services might not be needed.

I answered and heard the familiar voice of Addison "Bud" Arce, my first partner when I began at Hollywood Homicide in 1981, and now my colleague at Major Crimes.

"Hey, I've got a good one for you, Roy," Arce told me. "Roy" was a term of affection that my former supervisor at Hollywood Homicide, Russ Kuster, called all of his detectives. It was a name he chose to honor his favorite country music star, Roy Acuff. Kuster called his detectives "Roy" so habitually that eventually we began calling one another Roy as well.

Arce relayed the basic details. A murdered John Doe had been found early Friday morning inside a railroad tunnel above Chatsworth Park. That same night and the following morning, a family in the Valley had received two ransom calls suggesting their son had been kidnapped. Earlier on Sunday, a few hours prior, it had been determined that the John Doe was the kidnapping victim. Arce said the body was still at the coroner's office and the family had not yet been notified of their son's death.

I called Garcia, who had received a similar call from Arce.

We were chosen for the case as a matter of chance, as we just happened to be the on-call team that weekend. Had John Doe #135 been identified as Ron Baker on Monday instead of Sunday, the case would have been assigned to another detective team.

Garcia and I enjoyed a simpatico working relationship, although our backgrounds and paths to RHD were markedly different.

Garcia was the senior partner, having been on the job several years longer than me. He was born and raised in El Paso, Texas. Unlike me, Garcia had never planned to become a police officer. As a young man, newly living in Los Angeles, he was working at an aluminum factory that manufactured beer and soda cans. The hours were long and the work dirty, but it was a union job that paid well. His shifts were regularly thirteen or fourteen hours per day, and he would leave work covered in oil from the machinery.

One night when he was driving home from the factory, an LAPD patrol car pulled him over for speeding. Garcia explained to the officer, who looked polished and put together, that he had just finished working a long shift. During their conversation, Garcia asked him if he liked his job. The officer said he loved it and asked Garcia if he liked his. Garcia confessed he could not stand it. The officer asked if he had any college. Garcia said he had three years. The officer told him that if he was interested, the LAPD gave a written test every Tuesday evening at its Harbor Division station.

Garcia replied that he could never be a police officer. As a kid, he had seen cops chase neighborhood troublemakers and thought that wasn't for him. The idea of a police career hadn't crossed his mind in all the years since.

But in the following weeks, Garcia kept thinking about that clean-cut cop and the pride he seemed to take in his work. He didn't just like his job. He *loved* it.

Finally, one Tuesday night, Garcia went in and took the test. He passed. Garcia was clearing an average of $500 a week at the aluminum factory, with all the overtime he worked. The starting salary for the LAPD at the time was $742 per month, before taxes.

At least it was a career, Garcia thought.

Garcia entered the LAPD Academy in December 1969. Upon his graduation, he was selected to work undercover as part of a "buy team," purchasing narcotics on the streets and attempting to identify drug dealers and build cases against them. His unit was known as Administrative Narcotics, "Ad Narc" for short.

He found himself hanging out most days around Theodore Roosevelt High School in Boyle Heights, a neighborhood in East Los Angeles. Garcia discovered he had a good skill set for working undercover and making buys, which entailed a lot of patience and bullshitting. He had a natural gift for conversation with anyone, no matter their background.

One of the dealers he became a steady customer of was a Roosevelt student who went by the nickname "Sluggo." Over a period of weeks, Garcia repeatedly bought weed and pills from Sluggo and other dealers outside the school.

Spending so much time outside the high school, buying drugs, Garcia became a familiar face to some of the Roosevelt students, and vice versa. One particular girl would come out of school every day and, when she saw Garcia, shake her head at him in disgust.

Garcia finally asked her one day, "What's the matter with you? You don't like me?"

"What are you doing here every day?" she asked him.

"Oh, I'm just hanging around," he lied. "I got nothing else to do."

"Why don't you get a job, get a life, make something of yourself?" she chastised.

The end of the school year was approaching, and with it the "roundup," when arrests were to be made. Garcia had just bought some drugs from Sluggo one day after school when the girl walked past. She gave him that look again, but this time she walked right up to him. She held out her yearbook, which had been given out in school that day, and told Garcia she wanted him to sign it.

"You got to be kidding me," he told her.

She insisted she wasn't.

Garcia asked her name and she told him, "Margaret."

He inscribed her yearbook, "Margaret, one of these days I'm going to take your advice and get a job that's worthy of my talents and abilities." He signed it, "Frank."

"I'd like to see that," Margaret said when she read what he had written.

Garcia laughed.

Margaret told him to take care. "We probably won't be seeing each other for a while," she said. She was a senior, and graduation was only a few days away.

A day or two later, on the day of the roundup, Garcia volunteered to personally arrest Sluggo. The LAPD's protocol at the time was to go directly into the classroom to make the arrest. Garcia, accompanied by an Ad Narc detective and three uniformed officers, walked into Sluggo's class. Among the other students in the classroom, coincidentally, was Margaret. Everyone, especially Margaret, was looking at them like *What the hell?*

"Sluggo, stand up," Garcia announced. "You're under arrest for selling narcotics and dangerous drugs." He pulled out his handcuffs and slapped them on Sluggo. As he did, Garcia noticed Margaret staring at him, in shock rather than disgust. Garcia winked at her and said, "I took your advice, Margaret."

Garcia moved up the ranks fast. He was soon promoted to investigate high-quantity narcotics suppliers, including cartel figures and kingpins. After working narcotics for another three years and making detective, he received a call out of the blue to interview for a position at RHD's Homicide Special Section. He was concerned that he lacked homicide experience and pointed that out. He was told there was a need for a Spanish-speaking detective, and his investigative background would be helpful, given that narcotics-related murders were on the rise citywide.

Garcia got the position. The same skill set that had helped him to excel undercover, his gift for talking with people from all walks of life, was also a boon for solving murders. After a few years, he was promoted to Detective II and moved from Homicide Special to its sister unit at RHD, Major Crimes.

Garcia had been in Major Crimes for almost seven years when, in February 1988, he acquired a new junior detective partner: me.

While Garcia fell into his calling by happenstance, I had dreamed of being a detective for as long as I could remember. As a kid, growing up in the Los Angeles suburb of Lakewood, I was obsessed with the Hardy Boys books. I devoured one after another, as fast as I could read them. As I got older, I fell hard for Hitchcock films, particularly *Rear Window*

Detective Frank Garcia, circa late 1980s (courtesy of Frank Garcia)

and *Dial M for Murder*. Seeing how clues were pieced together to solve a case innately appealed to me.

By the time I reached junior high school, I already knew that when I grew up I wanted to be an investigator. I was vocal about my career aspirations. My ninth-grade social studies teacher, Miss Kennedy, signed my yearbook, "Best luck in the detective field." I was fourteen years old.

After college at San Jose State, I applied to the LAPD and was hired in 1976. Upon graduation from the Academy, I was assigned to Hollywood Division patrol.

For a rookie cop, Hollywood was an ideal training ground. It was incredibly diverse, in both its demographics and its geography. The area was world-famous for its association with the entertainment industry as well as its nightlife. Both served as beacons for people from all over the world. The territory was split between the grittier flatlands, which featured well-known commercial boulevards like Sunset, Hollywood, and Melrose, and the wealthier, more rustic Hollywood Hills. It was in the Hollywood flatlands that I spent the bulk of my time, since that was where most of the criminal activity occurred.

Throughout my four years in patrol, I never lost sight of my boyhood dream of becoming a full-fledged detective.

In May 1981, I applied for a detective trainee position at Hollywood.

I was selected and assigned to the juvenile beat. Four months later, to my great surprise, I was informed that I was being loaned to Homicide, effective immediately. That year, 1981, was shaping up to be an especially bloody year in Hollywood. Fifty-five people were murdered between January and August, more than in all of 1980. The Hollywood Homicide unit was swamped with cases and overwhelmed.

The unit consisted of six detectives, three teams of two, plus a detective supervisor, known as the homicide coordinator. The homicide coordinator in Hollywood was Detective Russ Kuster. He had run the unit since the late 1970s and was beloved by the detectives who worked for him.

Kuster's management style and teaching methods were not very hands-on, but he took a lot of pride in his unit and held his detectives to high standards. He demanded they share his attention to detail and work hard at solving cases. If you weren't working overtime on something as important as a murder, that was a problem.

I was excited for the opportunity to live my dream but also a little apprehensive. I had been a detective trainee for only a few months.

Kuster put me with two veteran homicide detectives, Hank Petroski and Bud Arce. Petroski was older and slightly crotchety. Arce, on the other hand, was a born jokester. After my first day, when I went home and took off my suit jacket, I heard something jingle in one of its pockets. Inside was an old room key from a sleazy Hollywood "no-tell" motel. At some point during that day, when I wasn't paying attention, Arce had slipped it into my jacket pocket, hoping to engineer what would have been an awkward, defensive conversation between my wife and me. But I found it before she did.

The first homicide crime scene I ever worked was the October 1981 murder of Wilbur Wright. Wright was a businessman who owned Wil Wright's Ice Cream, a popular chain of upmarket ice cream parlors throughout Southern California. Wright had been beaten to death inside his home in the Hollywood Hills. Unfortunately, his murder was never solved.

During the Wright investigation, I learned that my initial impression of Petroski as prickly was mistaken. Arce was off duty that day so I went with Petroski to the crime scene. He showed me how to document a crime scene with diagrams and detailed notes. Even though I was just learning my new vocation, Petroski made me feel valued, saying things like "What do you think?" and "Give me your thoughts."

A month later, I helped solve a murder case for the first time. A UCLA dean, Phillip Frandson, had been suffocated to death at his Laurel Canyon hillside home that September. Some of his personal property, including his car, was taken. The stolen car was later dumped at an apartment building in Compton, south of Los Angeles. The Frandson case was assigned to Petroski and Arce, but it remained unsolved into November.

Shortly before Thanksgiving, both of my senior partners had a day off. I decided to go interview a potential witness, who lived in the apartment building where Frandson's car had been found. The witness was cooperative but at first denied knowledge of the murder. However, I was able to build a rapport with him, which led to a change of heart. The next day, he identified the killer.

Petroski, Arce, and I arrested the suspect that same night. At Hollywood Station, he confessed and was booked for the murder. I was amazed at how quickly it all came together after my interview with the witness just the previous day.

Once the suspect was booked, I returned to the Hollywood Homicide squad room. My supervisor, Russ Kuster, had drawn a big thumbs-up on the chalkboard behind his desk. It was hard to believe that I had helped solve a real murder.

"I can't believe I'm getting paid to do this," I told Kuster. I joked with him, "This is better than sex."

Of course, the job came with its lows as well. The unsolved cases that frustrated me. The extremely long and inconsistent hours, which meant less time with my family. Seeing the human carnage and the emotional devastation of victims' loved ones.

Despite the challenges, I looked forward to going to work every morning. The job was immensely interesting to me, and I felt lucky to work in Hollywood. While many LAPD divisions were inundated primarily with murders related to the drug trade or gang warfare, Hollywood murders were extraordinarily varied: there were burglary-murders in the Hollywood Hills; robbery-murders on the neon-lit streets of the flatlands; sexually motivated murders, both gay and straight; pimp-versus-prostitute murders; and murders that combined more than one of the above.

In 1983, Arce left Hollywood Homicide for a new assignment within the department, which opened a coveted permanent spot in the unit. Although I was still a detective trainee, I was selected to fill it. My partner was Jerry Stephens, a veteran detective whose investigative instincts and thoroughness were top-notch. I learned more from Jerry about homicide work than anyone else.

I officially made detective the following year. The LAPD's custom at the time was for promoted detective trainees to be reassigned to a new division, for breadth of experience. Kuster, however, wanted to keep me where I was. I loved working there and also wanted to stay put. Kuster went to bat for me and somehow pushed it through. I remained in Hollywood Homicide.

Arce eventually landed a position downtown at Robbery-Homicide Division, one of several detectives to transfer from Hollywood Homicide to RHD through the years. Many credited Kuster, who ran such a tight ship that his unit served as a de facto farm team for RHD.

Until that point in my career, I had not had any contact with RHD, but I knew its reputation as having the LAPD's two foremost homicide units. In August 1984, I caught a new case, the contract murder of a wealthy businessman outside his home in the Hollywood Hills. Within a day, I found the possible motives—personal and work-related—to be so complex that I felt it was a case better suited for RHD. Kuster agreed.

Two detectives from Major Crimes came to Hollywood the next day. I had not met either of them before, but one was Frank Garcia, who would be my future partner when I transferred to RHD a few years later. The other was Garcia's senior partner at the time, Mike Thies. I laid out the case to Thies and Garcia, then took them to the crime scene and walked them through it.

A few months later, Thies called and asked me if I was interested in coming to RHD. He said there was going to be an opening in Major Crimes. I thanked him for the heads-up but told him, "I would love to work RHD, especially Major Crimes, but I'd rather stay in Hollywood a bit longer." I told him I felt I needed to work a few more years where the case volume was higher, to gain more experience, before I took on the more complex cases handled by RHD.

Near the end of 1987, I heard there was going to be a detective opening at Major Crimes. This time, I went for it.

My interview took place in the office of RHD's captain, William O. Gartland, but was conducted by lieutenants Chuck Massey and John Zorn, who oversaw Major Crimes and Homicide Special Section, respectively.

During my interview, I recounted how I'd been invited to apply earlier but declined because I wanted to gain more experience. We discussed some of the homicides I'd handled at Hollywood and my desire to work more involved cases, the type RHD specialized in solving.

Zorn, likely having been tipped off that I was a baseball fanatic, ended my interview with an unusual question.

"Who played first base for the 1964 Rockland County Little League All-Stars?" Zorn asked, deadpan.

I figured such an obscure baseball trivia question probably had an obvious answer. "John Zorn?" I said.

"You're right," Zorn replied. "I think you have a good chance at this job."

The next day, Massey called and told me the position was mine.

My fellow homicide detectives in Hollywood made me an oversized going-away card, fashioned from a manila folder, which they festooned with embarrassing photos and bawdy, affectionately insulting messages. Russ Kuster, my mentor and boss, wrote in the card a poem he had composed:

Roses are red,
vodka has limes,
congratulations,
but fuck Major Crimes!

I officially joined Major Crimes in late February 1988. My new partner, whom I had met once before, on the contract murder case four years earlier, was Frank Garcia.

At the time, I was thirty-five years old, several years younger than Garcia and all the other detectives at Major Crimes. My acclimation was eased by already knowing a few of my new colleagues, fellow alumni of Hollywood Homicide, and by my eagerness to solve cases.

Garcia and I would remain partners for the next five years, until he

At my desk in the RHD squad room, circa early 1990s

retired from the LAPD in 1993. So while Garcia was my first partner at Major Crimes, I would be his last.

To my relief, I found Garcia easy to work with and a lot of fun to be around, which made for an ideal partnership. I admired his charisma and natural ability to talk with people irrespective of their background, a priceless characteristic for a homicide detective in a metropolis like Los Angeles. When I introduced my wife to Garcia for the first time, she marveled at how charming he was. It seemed to me that everyone who met Frank Garcia couldn't help but like him.

Garcia and I had worked together, side by side, for a little more than two years when we were tasked with trying to solve Ron Baker's murder.

Neither of us imagined at the time how many twists and turns the investigation would eventually take, nor how long, even outlasting both of our LAPD careers.

All I knew that night in June 1990 was the little Arce had told me on the phone.

Minutes after Arce's call, both Garcia and I were in our cars and on our way to the coroner's office, our weekend over and our new investigation now in motion.

CHAPTER 4

SEARCHING CHATSWORTH PARK
(June 24 to 25, 1990)

I NEVER LIKED TO linger at the coroner's office. As we walked down the ramp into its drab garage, where day and night lifeless bodies were unloaded from vans, I told myself, once again, that I didn't care if it was the last time I ever visited.

I'd made so many trips there since 1981, the year I started working homicides, I could have navigated my way to the autopsy room blindfolded. Maybe not on a weekend, like that night, when extra gurneys jutted out from the corridors' walls. Weekends often corresponded with surges in violence, and with few doctors working weekends to perform autopsies, the bodies had to wait somewhere.

Along with the visual horror was the unfresh, stagnant odor. The disinfectants could not mask it: that disconcerting smell of death. It was not the putrid smell of decomposing flesh. Those bodies were stored separately in sealed-off rooms. It was more subtle than that. I never forgot that smell. It seemed to remain with me for hours after I left, clinging to my clothing.

Garcia and I were given a report by the coroner's investigator. It stated that other than the victim's clothing, the only property recovered on his body was a metal pendant, in the shape of a circle with a star inside, worn on a necklace of black twine.

Moments later, we were standing over the unclothed body of Ronald Baker, who for the last three days had been referred to only by the very impersonal "John Doe #135." We could see from his stitched-up chest and abdomen that the autopsy had already been completed. An incision we called "the Y-cut," for its likeness to the letter, ran diagonally from each shoulder, meeting in the sternum area, then down past the belly button.

Baker had severe stab wounds all over his body, with the majority to his upper torso, both front and back. It was apparent from their size and shape that a large knife had been used. Defensive wounds were also visible on both of his hands. These were identifiable as slices to his fingers and palms, which indicated he had tried to fend off his attacker or attackers. An especially deep, savage slicing wound ran across the entire front of his neck.

In my opinion, the most vicious action that can be performed with a knife is to slice someone's throat. It was sickening to fathom a person being subjected to such violence, especially inside an isolated, pitch-black tunnel. I found it hard not to shudder.

As Garcia and I left the coroner's office and made our way to his unmarked detective's car, a blue Ford Crown Victoria, I couldn't stop picturing Ron Baker in that tunnel. It was a horrible way to die. I tried to imagine what had been going through his mind in those final moments. Fear? Pain? Helplessness? A desperate realization that his life was ending? He must have felt so alone.

It was always strange to me that I didn't have more nightmares.

The next step in our investigation I consider to be the worst duty of all for a homicide detective. Ron Baker's family still believed, or at least had hope, that their son had been kidnapped and was being held, alive. They had no idea the case was now a murder. We had to inform them.

Making personal notification to strangers that their loved one is dead is traumatic for all involved. This is especially true when the death resulted from murder. What we would tell his family would be the most terrible news they had ever received. Frank and I knew that such shocking news was most compassionately delivered face-to-face. They had lost their son. We would not take much of their time that night. We would tell them the little information we knew and promise to do everything possible to give them answers about what had happened.

Garcia had called ahead to Gayle and Kay Baker to introduce us as the new detectives assigned to Ron's case, and to let them know that we would be stopping by. As we headed up the 101 freeway toward Woodland Hills, I dreaded the conversation awaiting us there.

It was about 10 p.m. when we arrived and knocked on their front door. We were greeted by Mr. Baker, who told us he went by Gayle. He invited us in and introduced us to his wife, Kay. Both were middle-aged. Gayle had silver-white hair and a soft-spoken demeanor. Kay had short blond hair and, like her husband, a kind, quiet manner.

The Bakers led us past their living room, which had a piano with many framed family photos resting on top. We entered their family room, which had comfortable furniture and bookshelves where more photos were displayed. We sat down together.

Garcia explained that we worked out of downtown police headquarters with the other detectives who had come to see them, after they first reported their son's kidnapping. He said that because of some new developments in the case, it had been reassigned to us. He then sensitively told them that their son's body had been found and identified. He added that we had just come from the coroner's office after viewing him. Tears welled up in the Bakers' eyes, but they remained calm. It seemed to me as if they had almost been expecting this news.

Garcia said there was no doubt their son was the victim of a murder. His body, he explained, had been found in a railroad tunnel above Chatsworth Park.

"What was he doing up there?" Kay asked, almost to herself. Gayle offered that Ron had told him that he once was inside a tunnel by Chatsworth Park when a train went through. Gayle said he thought Ron had told him that within the last two months.

It was early in our investigation, but it seemed significant that our victim had frequented the place where his life had ended. I couldn't help but wonder, if the kidnapper was a stranger, how likely would they be to take their victim someplace he was familiar with?

The majority of murder victims are killed by someone in their orbit. Random murders, such as those motivated by robbery, are much less common. This is why it is crucial for detectives to get to know their victim as well as possible, not just from their family members' point of view but also from their friends'. Friends often provide details unknown to the victim's family.

We left the Bakers' home and I shook my arms to release the tension that had built up before we arrived. We knew there was a possibility of a dramatic reaction when we broke the news to them, but outwardly, the Bakers had held their emotions in check. By the time we left, Gayle and Kay seemed totally drained. I knew they'd had no time to fully absorb the news yet, and their grief was just starting.

It was past 2 a.m. by the time I got home. Garcia and I were back at our desks less than five hours later. We wanted to get a head start on what we knew would be a long week working our new case. Even on little sleep, my mind seemed to work best in the early morning. I often scribbled to-do lists and thoughts on my cases while I drove to work.

Among the first questions I wanted an answer to was whether the Bakers' home phone, to which the two ransom calls had been made, was a listed number.

Once at my desk, it did not take long to verify the Bakers' number was indeed listed, under the name Gaylon Baker. The listing also included the Bakers' home address. This meant that their number could have been found in the phone book or via Directory Assistance. It was also possible, however, that the number had been provided by the victim, perhaps under duress while someone held him hostage.

I next called the Devonshire Homicide unit and spoke to Detective Ken Crocker. Crocker and his partner, Detective Peggy Moseley, had handled the crime scene and been responsible for the first three days of the John Doe #135 murder case. Crocker mentioned that one of the teenagers who discovered the body in the tunnel and called 911 was named Roland Karner. He gave me Karner's contact information.

I requested Crocker and Moseley meet Garcia and me at Devonshire Station later that afternoon. We needed to take possession of the murder book compiled thus far on the case. We also wanted them to accompany us to Chatsworth Park and walk us through the scene. Yes, we had their reports, notes, and photographs from the night of the murder, but the perspective of the original detectives was still useful to solicit. They could point out what evidence was found where and other observations they had made. Not everything a detective experiences at a crime scene will make it into a report or the murder book. A walk through might elicit something new from Crocker or Moseley.

In addition to Crocker and Moseley, I reached out to the RHD detectives who had handled the original investigation of Ron Baker's kidnapping. Among the documentation we got from them was the Mystic's Circle flyer Detective Rhudy had found in Ron's bedroom. I noticed at the bottom of the flyer the name Roland as the contact person for the group. The name jumped off the page at me. I remembered learning from the Devonshire detectives that one of the teens who'd discovered Ron's body was also named Roland.

I felt a surge of adrenaline. Roland was a relatively uncommon name. Were both Rolands actually the same person? If the Roland who had found the body also ran Mystic's Circle, why did he not tell the paramedics that he knew the victim? Had the teens in fact been inside the tunnel with Ron, in contrast to what they had said?

My adrenaline rush was short-lived. With a bit more follow-up work, I learned the two Rolands were different people. The Mystic's Circle Roland's last name was Trevino, not Karner. What seemed like a suspicious connection was pure coincidence.

The next question on my list was what happened to Ron Baker's wallet, which was not found on his body or at the crime scene. Nor did Detective Rhudy find it during his search of the apartment. It seemed safe to assume the wallet had been stolen by whoever killed him.

It was important that we report any missing credit or ATM cards right away, in case anyone tried to use them. The use of a victim's credit cards following a murder did not happen in most cases, but we needed to put things in place for prompt notification should it occur. Garcia called all of Ron's financial institutions and requested they enter his accounts into their alert notification systems. Now we just had to hope someone would attempt to use them.

I meanwhile called the security departments for Pacific Bell and GTE, the two phone companies that served the LA metropolitan area. I requested both companies search their data for any billable calls made on June 21 or 22 to the Bakers' home number. If the search returned any results around the time of the two ransom calls, I might be able to learn the phone number of the caller. Back then, obtaining records of past phone calls was much more limited than it is today. Unless a call resulted in a billable charge, it was virtually impossible. I knew it was a long shot that either ransom call was made from a long-distance number, rather than from a local number or a pay phone, but I had to give it a go.

Monday afternoon, Garcia and I drove from Parker Center—the LAPD's downtown headquarters at the time—to Devonshire Station, in the far northwest reaches of Los Angeles County. We knew that during the investigation we would likely be spending a lot of time in that area. Both of us lived with our families on the easternmost edge of the county, often a two-hour drive home in rush-hour traffic. I had two young daughters I often saw too little of whenever I took on a new case. RHD's city-wide jurisdiction meant that, hypothetically, Garcia and I could catch a case one day in San Pedro, in the south part of the city, and the next week a different case in the Valley, forty or more miles away. Longer drives meant more time away from the girls. It was a hard part of the job.

We met with Crocker and Moseley at their desks in the detectives' squad room. They handed over to us the murder book they had compiled to date on the John Doe #135 case.

For each homicide investigated by the LAPD, there is just one murder book, a three-ring binder that holds all the accumulated reports and documentation relevant to that particular case. Section 1 holds the chronological record, section 2 the crime scene log, section 3 the crime report, and so on. Because there is no statute of limitations on murder, it is not uncommon for a murder book to pass through the hands of several teams of detectives over the years, and theoretically even multiple generations of detectives. For that reason, the organization of the murder book is standardized across the department.

Divisional detectives assigned to the LAPD's geographical homicide units sometimes do not take it well when RHD takes over one of their cases. Detectives are by nature protective of their cases. The decision for RHD to take over a case, however, whatever the reason, is always made high above the rank of the involved detectives. Nevertheless, if the original detectives are unhappy to lose the case, it is the RHD detectives who on occasion bear the brunt of the animosity. Thankfully, this did not appear to be the situation here. Neither Crocker nor Moseley appeared annoyed.

We also took custody of all the evidence that was recovered at the crime scene. There was only a handful of items: a pair of bloodstained sunglasses; two bloodstained empty packs of cigarettes; and some broken beer bottles.

Garcia and I wanted to see the tunnel for ourselves. We reconvened with Crocker and Moseley in the park's southernmost parking lot. As we hiked up the steep dirt-and-gravel path to the tunnel, it dawned on me that a suit and leather shoes were not the ideal choice of attire.

Crocker and Moseley led us to the tunnel's western entrance, the same one they used the night the body was found. We had to climb about two hundred feet in elevation to reach our destination. Neither Garcia nor I had been to the park before. Once we were on level ground, I was struck by how beautiful the setting was, with towering rock formations rising around us and Chatsworth Park below.

We carried our flashlights as we walked into the tunnel but did not need to use them at first. However, it got darker quickly the farther we continued in. The air inside the tunnel was damp. The tunnel walls seemed to close in on me as the darkness grew. I shuddered to think I was walking where Ron Baker had taken his final steps a few nights earlier.

We had made it fifty or sixty yards into the tunnel when Crocker and Moseley pointed out the beginning of a blood trail to the left of the tracks. More blood was visible on the railroad ties between the two metal rails. A larger pool of dried blood was just to the right of the tracks, where they said Ron's body had been found. Although it was midafternoon, no daylight could be seen from the opposite end of the tunnel. Garcia and I had to use our flashlights to inspect the area.

We both wanted to explore the tunnel from end to end. We thought it possible that Ron or whoever had killed him entered the tunnel from the other side. As we walked, it became apparent that the tunnel curved to some degree. By the time I spotted daylight at the tunnel's far entrance,

I could no longer see any from the entrance we had used. Garcia and I turned off our flashlights. The tunnel was totally dark, even in the middle of the afternoon. I felt we should return one night to experience just how pitch-black the tunnel became after sundown.

Our walk to the eastern entrance of the tunnel and back turned up no additional evidence.

From Chatsworth Park, we drove to the apartment Ron had shared with his roommates.

We wanted to see where Ron had lived to get a better understanding of him. We would also look for any documentation that could help us piece together his final few days, such as his personal calendar and phone book, as well as any financial records, like his checkbook.

Most importantly, we wanted to speak with Ron's roommates, Duncan Martinez and Nathan Blalock, who were said to be the last people to see Ron, when they dropped him off at the bus stop on Thursday night.

Their apartment was located in Van Nuys, another section of the San Fernando Valley within LA city limits, about fifteen miles from Chatsworth Park.

The apartment building was at 14825 Erwin Street, on the north side of the street. Its appearance was typical for Southern California, with a beige stucco exterior and a terra-cotta tile roof. The building was two stories and had two wings of units, east and west, facing each other across a central driveway that ran between them. Ron and his roommates lived in unit 104, on the first floor of the east wing.

Garcia and I were greeted at the door by Duncan Martinez, an athletic-looking young man with a slim build. He had blue eyes and short blond hair and appeared to be in his early twenties. His demeanor was polite and cordial. He seemed eager to cooperate and displayed no distrust of me or Garcia.

Duncan was not surprised to see us. Garcia had called him from Devonshire Station a few hours earlier to inform him we would be stopping by that afternoon.

Duncan invited us in and introduced us to two female friends of his and Ron's, Lydia Archibald and Kathy Kritzberg, who happened to be visiting and were seated in the living room. Both women also appeared to be in their early twenties. They looked subdued, which was understandable, having just learned of their friend's death.

The apartment was a small two-bedroom unit. It was furnished rather basically, as one would expect of college-aged kids. Scattered around were numerous gray plastic milk crates, being used both for storage and as makeshift end tables. The living room had some seating arranged around a TV, which had a video game system hooked up to it. Both bedrooms were at the rear of the apartment.

We asked Duncan to point out Ron's bedroom. He explained that Ron had his own room, while he and Nathan shared the second bedroom.

I took one look at Ron's bedroom and realized we should call out a photographer to document it exactly as it was. In plain view were several occult-related items. Most strikingly, I saw what appeared to be a small, low makeshift altar in the middle of the room. The surface of the altar was a wood plank resting atop more plastic crates. On the altar were incense holders and a rough-hewn wax candle about the size of a dinner plate. The candle appeared handmade, with a base layer of white wax and multiple overlapping layers of bright red wax on top. At the center of the top layer was a white wax pentagram, starkly visible against the red wax underneath.

LAPD photo of altar and pentagram candle in Ron's bedroom, June 25, 1990 (court exhibit)

Beside the altar, leaning against the wall, I saw a sword that was several feet long. The sword's hilt was wrapped in alternating strips of red and green fabric.

Bookshelves fashioned from cinder blocks and wooden planks lined one full wall of the bedroom. I scanned the shelves and noticed several occult-themed books. One, *Buckland's Complete Book of Witchcraft*, had an upright pentagram on its cover. Another was titled *The Complete Book of Spells, Ceremonies & Magic*. The rest of the decor—various posters of the cast of *Star Trek*, an illustration of the solar system, an oversized world map, and a pale blue United Nations flag—was ordinary by comparison.

I asked Duncan if I could use their landline.

Photography was the responsibility of the Scientific Investigation Division, often referred to within the LAPD as SID, or simply "the crime lab" for short. I called SID and asked for a photographer to meet us at our location.

SID photographer Mike Wilson was in the area and arrived within minutes. I led him to Ron's bedroom and asked him to take some overall shots. I also pointed out a few specific items that I wanted close-ups of. Among them was a scrawled message I had noticed written next to the apartment's phone. Someone had drawn an upright pentagram. Above the pentagram was written the name "Martin" and a phone number.

Garcia and I did not take into evidence any of the occult items from Ron's room that day. We were satisfied that Wilson's photographic preservation of them was sufficient for now.

I did take some items of Ron's that could shed more light on him, and potentially his murder, including his credit card statements and phone bills.

Garcia and I split interview duties with the two young women, Lydia and Kathy. We spoke with them separately, in different areas of the apartment.

Lydia told Garcia she had known Ron for the last six years. She said Ron first mentioned "this witchcraft stuff" after he went to Lance Strickler's house. Lance was someone they all knew.

According to Lydia, Lance had an altar at his house. He had numerous books and had been doing research on witchcraft for years. "That's when Ron got into it. He thought it was real neat. Lance was kind of like Ron's idol," she told Garcia.

Kathy told me she had known Ron for almost three years. She had gotten to know him much better in the last year, due to their mutual interest in Wicca. Kathy said Ron had started getting very involved in Mystic's Circle. Her belief was that the group was "a club at UCLA that was very low-key. It was like white magic—nothing really heavy." Even so, she said, "my gut feeling was that he was getting into something heavier."

Kathy explained that Lance "was teaching real light white magic classes, and both Ron and I were in it." Lance told her he had previously warned Ron "not to get involved in that. I took it to mean darker stuff, like satanic things," she said. She thought this concern had come up even before Ron was found, as there were rumors his disappearance was related. Kathy said Duncan had told her he dropped Ron off at the bus stop to go to a meeting of Mystic's Circle.

Kathy didn't know if Ron ever went to Chatsworth Park with Mystic's Circle, but he did go with the group Lance taught, for a meditation session.

She had no knowledge of Ron's plans Thursday, beyond what Duncan had told her.

She knew June 21 was the summer solstice. She described it as "like a holiday. People like us might have a light celebration." Kathy added, rather ominously, "People into the dark could conceivably celebrate by much more serious actions, including sacrifices."

Meanwhile, Garcia had started to interview Duncan in the bedroom he shared with Nathan.

Duncan told Garcia he had met Ron in 1986 when they both worked at Sears. They had been friends ever since, Duncan said. He and Ron had been roommates previously in an apartment in Hollywood. Later, Duncan and Nathan had lived with Lance Strickler and his daughter, Jenny. Duncan said he and Nathan had been staying with the Stricklers before he and Nathan moved into the Van Nuys apartment with Ron.

Garcia asked Duncan to recount the details of what he did on Thursday, June 21.

Duncan said he was home for most of the day. "Nathan was here with his girlfriend, Diane. Ron came home about five to six p.m. Ron took the bus everywhere he went," he told Garcia. "That evening Ron made dinner for everybody. He cooked spaghetti. Nathan and I were going out to get some beers. Ron said, 'I'm getting together with my Mystic's Circle buddies tonight.' Ron didn't say where. Ron asked, 'What time are you leaving?' and I said about eight thirty to nine. Ron said that's fine and asked if we could drop him off at the bus stop."

Garcia asked what time they left. Duncan said, "We all left the house at approximately eight thirty to nine o'clock and we took Ron to the bus stop at Victory and Van Nuys Boulevards." Duncan assumed Ron was taking the bus to UCLA, since that was where Mystic's Circle generally met.

"What was he wearing?" asked Garcia.

A white T-shirt and jeans, and possibly a long-sleeved shirt, Duncan answered.

Garcia asked how Ron seemed when they dropped him off. Duncan said Ron was in a good mood and didn't seem bothered or worried.

"Was Ron gay?" Garcia asked.

"I don't think Ron was gay, but he didn't have very much luck with women," said Duncan.

The only person Duncan knew from the Mystic's Circle group was a guy named Martin. Duncan provided Martin's phone number, which matched the number I had noticed earlier, written by the apartment's phone. Duncan said Ron had gotten involved with Mystic's Circle about three months ago. "He didn't talk much about what he did with the group. At first, Ron would talk about them. But lately, he didn't discuss it much."

Asked if Ron had a job, Duncan said he worked at the Engineering, Math and Science Library at UCLA. Ron also worked at Lance's candle shop at the Renaissance Faire that spring, Duncan said.

Garcia asked Duncan about Chatsworth Park.

"We used to go to the Chatsworth Park to meditate. The last time we were there was sometime during the first part of the year," Duncan said. Among those who went that night, he said, were Lance, Jenny, Ron, himself, and a few other friends.

Garcia asked when he'd learned of Ron's kidnapping.

Duncan said he and Nathan heard about it Thursday night, when Ron's father called the apartment. On Friday, they talked to Detective Rhudy, who was investigating Ron's disappearance and the ransom calls received by his parents. Duncan said that Rhudy had told them to check areas that Ron frequented. Duncan volunteered to Garcia, "On Saturday at about 10 a.m. Nathan and I went to the park to look for Ron," referring to Chatsworth Park.

Garcia found that strange. "Why would you go there?" he asked Duncan.

"I don't know why... It just seemed like a good idea," Duncan told Garcia. "When we got to the park, Nathan and I went to the north field, then walked up to the railroad tracks that are near the tunnel. We decided the park was too big and we turned back. We were going to go to UCLA to look for him, but we never did."

Duncan said he believed Nathan left for Detroit the following day, Sunday, to attend a long-planned family reunion. Nathan grew up in the Detroit area and was not expected back for about ten days.

An in-person interview with Nathan would have to wait.

Garcia and I left the apartment around 6 p.m. Before we each could go home, we still had to drive to Parker Center to book into evidence the items we had obtained from the Devonshire detectives.

As we drove, we discussed what we'd learned during our first full day on the case. Garcia was bothered by what Duncan had said about him and Nathan going to Chatsworth Park on Saturday to search for Ron. He felt it didn't make sense. A victim at the mercy of their kidnapper would go wherever they were forcibly taken. Why would Duncan and Nathan believe Ron's kidnapper had taken him to Chatsworth Park, a place Ron liked to go?

I agreed. Something else Duncan had divulged to Garcia troubled me as well. I wondered why the two roommates would go to the park to look for Ron, hike all the way up to the railroad tunnel, and then decide to abandon the search. Garcia concurred that it seemed suspect.

Despite the kernel of doubt in my mind, I tried playing devil's advocate with Garcia. I suggested that maybe Duncan and Nathan felt so desperate and helpless, just sitting around, that they decided to take Detective Rhudy's advice to check places Ron liked to go.

It was too early for us to make any conclusions. But we knew how we would find out more: by asking additional questions of people. The answers were somewhere out there, and we were determined to run them down.

CHAPTER 5

"I ALWAYS THOUGHT RON WOULD BE THERE"
(June 26 to 30, 1990)

I RETURNED TO WORK the next morning on little sleep but bursting with questions: Who had killed Ron? Why? Would we be able to get the answers we needed? Would the case go cold?

It was the unsolved murders that affected me most. In my years working homicide I could not forget all the pain I'd seen up close, in family after family. The suffering I witnessed haunted me, but it also fueled my sense of purpose. I could never bring their loved ones back, but I could find answers and try to bring the perpetrators to justice—and, in that way, hopefully give these families some peace.

Ron Baker's murder already had its hooks in me. I could sense the Bakers were a close, loving family. I thought of all the framed photos I had seen in their home, and the loss and grief they were experiencing. I couldn't help but take their devastation to heart.

Ron was an intriguing victim, with his dalliances into the occult. He had been killed on the summer solstice, an occasion that held little meaning to most people but had been of great personal importance to him. The crime scene location was a place Ron had been familiar with, but what had drawn him there that night to his violent death?

Garcia and I had been in the office very little on Monday, our first full day on the case, and with no real direction yet on a suspect, we felt no urgency to get back out on the trail. We decided instead to catch up on some of the basic tasks that come in the early stages of a murder investigation.

We made follow-up calls to Ron's financial institutions about his missing credit cards; to the UCLA police for more information on the founders of Mystic's Circle; and to the telephone company about the ransom calls and whether we needed a search warrant for call records.

Next I contacted our crime lab, SID, to request forensic analysis of several evidence items found at the crime scene. My first call was to the Serology Unit, which dealt with blood evidence. I asked them to retrieve from the coroner's office the clothing Ron was wearing when he was killed, as well as a sample of his blood, which had been collected as a standard part of his autopsy. I wanted them to test for Ron's blood type and compare it to the blood on his clothing and the broken beer bottles found near his body. If any of the blood was of a different type than Ron's, we might be able to use that information to help identify a suspect, or at least narrow our pool of potential suspects.

I asked a different unit at SID, the Chemical Processing Unit, to analyze other evidence from the crime scene for any latent fingerprints. These included the sunglasses and empty cigarette packs that were also found near his body. Again, my hope was that they might find a fingerprint other than Ron's that could help us establish who else was in the tunnel with him.

From the coroner's office I requested copies of all the autopsy photos and the detailed autopsy report as soon as it was completed. We wanted to better understand the nature of the injuries Ron had received. We would have to wait longer—four to six weeks—for the report I was most eager to read, Ron's toxicology screen. It would reveal the presence and levels of any drugs or alcohol in his system at the time of his death. This could help us answer one of our biggest open questions: What had Ron done in the hours between when he was dropped at the bus stop and when his body was discovered inside the tunnel?

Our most immediate investigative priority was piecing together Ron's last days and hours. This meant delving deeper into Mystic's Circle, the group we'd been told Ron planned to meet the night he was killed.

We had two names to go on. The first was Roland Trevino, who was listed on the flyer found in Ron's bedroom. The second was "Martin," whose name and number were written, interestingly, next to a pentagram near the apartment's phone. Duncan had told us he believed Martin was a friend of Ron's from Mystic's Circle.

The UCLA Police Department provided us with Roland's address, an off-campus apartment a block from fraternity row. We drove there, but his roommate told us Roland was living at home for the summer in Altadena. We showed the roommate a photo of Ron. He said he'd seen him at the apartment once, not on June 21 but prior to then.

We called Roland and asked him to meet us at the LA County Sheriff's Altadena Station that night. He agreed.

Roland was cooperative. He explained that he had founded Mystic's Circle in January 1990. To begin with, the group had about ten members, Roland said. All of their meetings were held at UCLA and most featured guest speakers.

Roland denied that the group had anything to do with Satanism. "I hate that," he told us.

He described Ron as a shy, quiet, timid person who seemed to be easily intimidated. Ron seemed more interested in Wicca than other topics the group discussed. In Roland's understanding, Wiccans were basically into witchcraft and nature worship. "They have rituals where they dance around a cauldron and throw pieces of paper into it, with different types of desires written on the paper," he explained. "They usually dance in a clockwise direction. Sometimes they may dance in the nude."

Surprisingly, Roland told us their last meeting had been about eight weeks earlier. Ron and another UCLA classmate, Christine Reyna, were supposed to keep the group going during the summer. The last time Roland had seen Ron was about two weeks ago, at a final exam for their Folklore class.

We asked Roland whether members of Mystic's Circle had planned to meet last Thursday, on the night of the summer solstice. He said no but added that Ron was supposed to attend a Wicca class at Christine's on Wednesday, the night before. Roland said he didn't know if Ron had anything planned for the solstice.

Roland agreed to send us a list of the group's members, as well as a phone number for Christine Reyna, who may have seen Ron the night before his murder. Given their common interest in Wicca, Ron might have discussed with her his plans for the summer solstice.

We resumed our investigation the next morning, meeting with two officers from the Southern California Rapid Transit District police. SCRTD, or RTD, as it is commonly called, provides public bus transportation throughout Greater Los Angeles. Among the 190 or so bus lines RTD ran were several that stopped at the intersection of Victory and Van Nuys Boulevards in Van Nuys, the last known place Ron was seen alive.

Garcia and I explained to the officers that we were only interested in the bus lines that made stops at that particular intersection. They provided us with bus routes, schedules, and the names of the drivers who had worked those lines on the evening of June 21. We hoped one of the drivers might remember seeing Ron board and, if so, tell us where he'd gotten off the bus.

Later that morning, we were back in the office, sorting through our new leads on buses and drivers, when the phone rang on Garcia's desk. He answered.

The caller identified himself as Mike Connelly of the *Los Angeles Times*. He said he was calling to inquire about the status of the Ronald Baker murder.

Up to that point, press coverage of the Baker case had been minimal. Two local newspapers, the *LA Times* and the *Daily News*, had each run only one short, un-bylined story two days after the murder. Both articles had referred to the victim as "an unidentified man." Neither had mentioned anything about the occult or the kidnapping calls received by the Bakers.

Connelly was a young reporter assigned to the crime beat in the San Fernando Valley. He did not say how he had gotten wind of the case. He asked Garcia to verify that the victim was kidnapped and that ransom demands were made.

"No comment," Garcia replied. He suggested Connelly call back the following week.

It was obvious that Connelly thought there was more to the case than had been publicly reported. Although he did not mention the occult angle, we knew it was just a matter of time before that information surfaced as well, which would make the story even more newsworthy.

Once Garcia hung up, he and I discussed the call. To date, the story had been contained, which from an investigative perspective tends to be a good thing. Especially in murder cases, it makes sense to keep specific case details close to the vest, rather than release them for public consumption.

For instance, in a homicide case involving a firearm, a detective would be ill-advised to publicize the number of times the victim was shot, where the gunshot wounds were located on the body, or the caliber of the bullets fired. Details such as these are likely to be known only by the perpetrator of the murder. Should a suspect later be identified and convinced to talk, it's important to know their information comes from their own knowledge, rather than gleaned from media reports.

In the Baker case, we were at a bit of a disadvantage, since we knew Mr. Baker had told Duncan and Nathan about the ransom phone calls. They in turn had told their friends, so that piece of information was out. Garcia telling Connelly "No comment" was an attempt to minimize its spread any further. We decided that once the potential occult connection got out through other sources, and we knew it would, we would explain that it was just one of the possible motives we were looking at for Ron Baker's murder.

Shortly after getting off the phone with Connelly, Garcia tried the phone number for Nathan Blalock that Duncan had given us. Nathan answered and Garcia identified himself. Nathan said he was about to leave for his family reunion in Detroit, but he would be available over the next few days while he was there. He provided a Michigan phone number where he could be reached.

Garcia told Nathan he would like to ask him a few questions now. He asked Nathan what he recalled of the night of June 21, starting from the time Ron got home.

Nathan said Ron came home with groceries, which was odd, because he had never done that before. Nathan's girlfriend, Diane, had come to visit that day. Ron cooked dinner for the four of them, which was also a first, Nathan said.

He and Duncan were going to get some beers and were about to leave when Ron asked them for a ride to the bus stop.

Nathan said they dropped him off around 8 or 8:15 p.m. Ron told them he was going to meet up with some friends. Ron appeared normal when he got out of Duncan's car, Nathan said.

Garcia asked Nathan how long he'd known Ron. Nathan said for a year, after he came back from his Army service in Korea. Nathan told us he'd met Ron through Lance and Jenny Strickler.

Garcia asked about Chatsworth Park and the railroad tunnel. Nathan said a group of them had gone there sometime in November or December 1989. The group had included Lance, Jenny, Ron, Duncan, and a couple of other friends. Then, on the Saturday after Ron disappeared, he and Duncan decided to go to Chatsworth Park to look for Ron. "Duncan said it would be a good area to look," Nathan told Garcia. Nathan had said to Duncan, "We can get a search party," but ultimately just the two of them went to the park. He and Duncan walked up the hill to the railroad tracks. They then decided it was useless because the area to search was too large.

Garcia told Nathan that upon his return to California, he and his partner would need to interview him again in more detail. Nathan said okay.

By then, we'd obtained Christine Reyna's number from Roland.

When Garcia called Christine, she confirmed that Ron had attended a Wicca class at her residence on the evening of June 20. Ron had arrived at the meeting with his friend Martin Carr. We agreed to meet Christine the following morning to interview her in person.

Our contact at the UCLA Police Department, Detective Chuck Burnham, called us and reported that he had received a call from a woman who said she was a friend of Ron Baker's and had seen him at UCLA on the afternoon of June 21. He identified her as Suzi Casement and provided us with her contact information. He added that she worked in the university's Astronomy Department.

I called Suzi immediately. If it was true that she saw Ron the afternoon before he was killed, it was important to speak with her as soon as possible.

Suzi told me she had learned of Ron's murder from a memo sent out by a UCLA astronomy professor. Ron was an astrophysics major. The memo told of his death and talked about him being kidnapped.

Suzi recounted that she saw Ron at work on the afternoon of June 21. Other than their Mystic's Circle meetings, they never socialized together, she told me.

I asked Suzi about her and Ron's involvement in Wicca. She said they had the same interests. "We were both interested in 'high magic' but not necessarily religious stuff," she said.

I asked her whether she knew if Ron had gotten into anything beyond Wicca. She said he never gave her any indication "about being involved in stuff toward the darker side."

The next morning, we met Christine Reyna at her parents' home in Pasadena. Christine had thick dark hair and an artistic aura. She greeted us warmly and told us she was willing to help in any way she could.

Christine told us she didn't know Ron that well, but they shared common interests, in particular Wicca. She also clarified that she was never a member of Mystic's Circle but did attend two of their meetings.

We asked her about the Wicca meeting she reportedly held at her house on Wednesday night, June 20. Ron had arrived at the meeting with Martin Carr, Christine said. She knew Martin, but he had no affiliation with UCLA.

We asked how Ron knew Martin, if not from UCLA.

Christine said Ron and Martin had met in May at a Beltane festival. "We held it at Monrovia Canyon Park. Ron took buses to get there. Martin lives out near Ron, so Martin ended up giving Ron a ride home. The only time I know of that they met again was when Martin gave Ron a ride to my house for our meeting on Wednesday."

We asked her to tell us about the meeting. "I taught what Wicca was and its origins, which is the religion of the ancient goddesses." The meeting was uneventful and broke up at 10:45 p.m., she said.

Garcia asked if she could provide an overview of Wicca.

"Wicca is not an institutionalized religion," she explained. "It deals with old traditions and the philosophy of hunters and gatherers. It deals with living in harmony with Earth. It teaches a give-and-take relationship with nature. Wicca is witchcraft, depending on how you define witchcraft. If you define it as black magic, then that's not it. If you define it as healing art, then yes." Christine exuded a quiet confidence as she spoke. It was striking how knowledgeable she was for a young college student.

We asked what conversations she and Ron had about Wicca.

She said Ron had talked to her about his beliefs and practices. "He mainly did 'solitaire' work, which means he'd do it by himself. He said he would usually go to Chatsworth Park ... Ritual work could be anything that would inspire you. It could be lighting candles, reading poetry, whatever you wanted to do."

We asked whether Ron told her about when he would go to Chatsworth Park.

"He said he'd go to Chatsworth Park on the main Sabbath days, and Thursday would have been one of those," she said, referring to June 21.

We asked what kind of items related to Wicca, if any, Ron would have taken with him to Chatsworth Park.

Christine mentioned several, among them an altar cloth; candles; a staff; a robe; an athame, which was a type of ceremonial dagger; a chalice or cup; and a cauldron. She told us Ron had a blue robe and had been making a new altar cloth. "He described it to me, and I mentioned that it was untraditional. They are usually black with silver writing. I can't recall what colors his new one was, but it was not traditional. I also think he had a pentagram." Even if so, she added, "an inverted pentagram is not necessarily evil. The definitive symbol for Satanism is a pentagram with a goat's head within it."

We asked her to tell us more about the athame.

"An athame is a dagger and is traditionally double-edged," Christine told us. "It is not supposed to touch anything other than the owner's hand. It's used to project force. If it's used to cut anything, it's supposed to be buried." She had seen Ron's athame and believed it was a traditional type, with a wooden handle. An athame's hilt could also be made of horn. She said you could buy them from a cutlery shop. The athame was usually kept in a sheath. She believed Ron's athame had a wooden handle, a brass hilt, and a dark-colored sheath.

"What about wire?" we asked, referencing the loop of barbed wire found near Ron's head and feet in the tunnel.

"Wire is not part of any Wiccan ritual," she said. "If anything was used for tying, Wiccans would use a natural product, like rope... Wire is not a natural product."

"Did Ron ever discuss Satanism with you?"

"Ron was adamantly against Satanism," she said. "He talked badly about Satanists. Satanists and Wiccans do not get along. Their beliefs are completely in contrast."

We asked if there were any sacrificial practices in Wicca.

"The only Western group into sacrifices is the Satanists. Killing anything has no place in Wicca. Wicca only has one law: 'Harm none, love, and do what thou will.'"

We asked if she had ever sensed that Ron might be interested in the darker side of the occult.

"Ron never gave me any indication that he was or was interested in moving toward the darker side."

We asked Christine to describe Ron's personality.

"He was very shy, timid, and introverted." In contrast to what Roland had told us, she had never seen Ron intimidated or manipulated.

We asked what she knew about Ron's drinking and drug habits.

"I've seen him have a few drinks, like he had some ale at the Renaissance Faire. I know he experimented with marijuana, and he mentioned he wanted to try mushrooms. I know he was against cocaine and the synthetic drugs... Drugs are not part of any Wiccan celebration or ritual."

"Did Ron ever mention the names of any of his friends?" we asked.

Christine said no. "Ron did talk about an older guy who was his mentor, to an extent. He said he'd have an infrequent outdoor ritual with his old friends." She also told us, "He did mention once that one of his roommates was in some special military covert deal, in an assassination plot in the Middle East. I don't know which roommate." Garcia and I were taken aback. It was the first time we had heard anything about this.

We asked Christine if Ron was gay. It was important to know. Delving into a victim's background, including their sexuality, can change the focus of an investigation as it progresses.

"I don't think Ron was homosexual," she told us. "He subtly suggested he was interested in me, and he asked me out on a few occasions, so if anything, he would be bisexual."

We asked if Ron had discussed with her his plans for the night of the summer solstice. If it was true that Ron was going to meet friends from UCLA to celebrate the solstice together, she might have heard about it.

Christine said at the meeting at her house on Wednesday, Ron had asked if she was doing anything tomorrow for the solstice. "He said he wanted to do something. Kind of like he had no plans yet. I said I couldn't, so he said he was going to go ahead and do something anyway. No one in our group indicated they wanted to get together, and actually I don't think he mentioned it to anyone else. He didn't know the others very well," she admitted.

Christine returned to the subject of Ron's solitaire work. I sensed that the topic had been bothering her since we'd discussed it earlier in the interview.

"Ron did say he used to like to do solitaire work at night at the park. I told him it was stupid to do that, alone at night, especially when you're in a meditative state when you're not fully aware of what's going on around you. He never said specifically where in the park he went. He never mentioned a railroad tunnel to me."

Before we left, Christine confirmed Martin Carr's phone number.

Christine was sharp. She was the best interview we'd had in terms of developing a better understanding of Wicca.

Later that afternoon, Christine called RHD and spoke again to Garcia. Upon reflection, she did not feel that Ron was homosexual, because he had made comments regarding women, getting married, and having a family.

Christine also told Garcia that in a ritual sacrifice, death is not the ultimate goal. The goal is to obtain blood, considered "the juice of life," she said. We should be aware of any "unaccounted for" blood, as Satanists were known to take the blood away in containers and bury, drink, or burn it. She added that the summer solstice would not be the time to do a sacrifice, however.

By then, it was late Friday afternoon. We reached out to Martin

Carr and Lance Strickler, who was Ron's mentor in Wicca, and set up interviews with them for the next morning.

Friday was also the day of Ron Baker's burial at Forest Lawn Memorial Park in the Hollywood Hills. Garcia and I chose not to attend. Nor did we plan to attend a separate memorial service planned for Saturday at the Woodland Hills United Methodist Church.

Attending a victim's funeral can sometimes be useful, but not in all cases. We opted instead to use the time to continue working the case. We had interviews and follow-up work to do that we hoped could move the investigation forward. Trying to make progress in the early days of a homicide case is just too important.

Friday happened to be my wife's birthday as well. Driving home that day, I pondered the strangeness of working Ron Baker's murder case by day, then taking the evening to celebrate her with our girls. It was going to be a fun and relaxing evening with the people I loved most. Yet earlier that day, the Baker family, riven by grief, had buried their son. I felt so fortunate by comparison. I couldn't wait to see my family and wrap them in my arms.

Garcia and I met Lance Strickler the next morning at Devonshire Station, where the case had begun and close to where Lance lived. From what we had heard in previous interviews, although Lance was much older than his daughter's friends, their affinity for one another was genuine. He enjoyed teaching about Wicca, and most of her circle, all in their twenties, wanted to learn more.

Lance was in his mid-forties and appeared as if he had stepped straight out of the 1960s. He was tall and thin, with long, stringy hair. He had a mild demeanor and the air of an absent-minded professor, which seemed appropriate for someone described to us as Ron's Wicca mentor.

He'd known Ron for about three years, he said. Ron was initially friends with his daughter, Jenny. He thought he last saw Ron in early June at the Renaissance Faire.

Lance explained that he had studied Wicca and had taken to hosting informal classes at his house. Ron attended several of the gatherings, which Lance called "baby circles," since most of the attendees were unfamiliar with Wicca. He said Ron became extremely interested in the subject. Duncan and Nathan came to a couple of classes too, but Lance said, "Duncan had a bullshit view of Wicca. He really wasn't into it."

We asked Lance how he first learned that Ron was missing or had been killed. He told us that late Friday afternoon, June 22, he came home to a message on his answering machine from Duncan. When he called back, Duncan asked him if he had seen Ron. Duncan said Ron had not shown up to work and had not been seen since the night before, when they dropped him at the bus stop in Van Nuys. Lance told Duncan he had no knowledge of Ron's whereabouts. Duncan told him, "If you hear from Ron, call me."

Lance said he and Duncan spoke again later that evening. Duncan told him then that a detective had been to their apartment to investigate Ron's disappearance. Duncan added that Ron's parents had gotten a ransom call. Duncan said he would keep Lance posted. Duncan never mentioned that he had gone to Chatsworth Park to look for Ron.

We asked Lance when he'd learned that Ron was dead. He said it was on Monday. He heard from someone that Ron was found at the park with his face beaten in and his nose cut off. Lance couldn't recall who had told him that. We informed Lance that what he'd heard about Ron's injuries was inaccurate.

After Lance left, I told Garcia that something bugged me about Duncan's first phone call with Lance on Friday, when Duncan inquired about Ron's whereabouts.

We knew Detective Rhudy had visited the apartment and interviewed Duncan and Nathan around 1 p.m. on Friday. Lance had said that his first call with Duncan was in the late afternoon.

We also knew that Mr. Baker had called the apartment on Friday morning, after he'd received the second of the two ransom calls, and had informed Duncan of them. That conversation also took place prior to Duncan's phone call with Lance that afternoon.

I told Garcia that it seemed bizarre to me that Duncan would call Lance about their missing mutual friend and say only that he had not shown up or called into work. Why would Duncan not have mentioned the ransom calls and the police visit immediately, during their first phone conversation? Would it really take a second phone call to remember to relay events of that magnitude?

I posed a hypothetical to Garcia: "Let's say you and I have a mutual friend. I learn our friend has died, but you're unaware. I call you and we have a conversation where we talk about our friend in general terms, but I never mention that our friend is dead. That would never happen."

It felt similar to what Duncan had told us about searching for Ron at Chatsworth Park while he was still believed to be kidnapped. It wasn't necessarily incriminating, but it was strange—the type of thing that promised to gnaw at us as we continued our investigation.

Our next interview, also at Devonshire Station, was with Martin Carr. He was a student at Cal State, Northridge.

Martin had an earnest personality and seemed to be a true believer in Wicca. He told us, "I want to make one thing clear. People in Wicca, and me as well, don't even believe in the devil. Also, there is no blood involved in the practice of Wicca."

Martin had last seen Ron when he gave him a ride to and from Christine Reyna's house on the night before the summer solstice. We asked if Ron had discussed his plans for the solstice. Martin said they did discuss it, during their ride home from Christine's. "I asked him what he was going to do on the summer solstice. He said he was planning on something, and I'm almost sure he said it was by himself. He didn't say what specifically. He didn't ask me to join him, and I didn't think to ask him to join me. He never really talked too much about how he celebrated by himself."

Martin told us he was familiar with Chatsworth Park. We asked him about the park's reputation as a gathering place for occult activities.

"I've never heard of it being a place where people into the occult hold meetings and rituals." Ron once told him about going to Chatsworth Park to celebrate pagan holidays. "I said I didn't think it was a good idea, because it was too dangerous, with the way we celebrate. Some people don't like it. Ron said it was okay because he had this out-of-the-way place in Chatsworth Park that no one really goes to. He didn't say where in the park it was, or describe it, just that people didn't come there much."

Martin said that, as far as he knew, Ron was only into Wicca, not the darker, satanic side of the occult.

We asked Martin when he had learned of Ron's death. He said Christine had called him two days earlier and told him that Ron had been murdered. "She said it was when he was doing a ritual in a park but didn't know exactly." Christine also said she had heard Ron was stabbed.

After the interview, Garcia and I discussed what we'd learned from all of our interviews so far. There were, admittedly, some minor inconsistencies in what witnesses had told us. For instance, one person, Roland Trevino, had said that Ron was easily intimidated. Another person, Christine Reyna, had said the opposite, that she had never seen Ron intimidated. We knew from experience, however, that an investigation is never like a jigsaw puzzle, where every piece of information fits perfectly together. Inconsistencies are natural and routine because witnesses base their statements on their own perceptions of people and events. Recollections of witnesses often vary to some degree and may change over time.

Similarly, Garcia and I were not troubled by the slight variations regarding what time Duncan, Nathan, and Diane told us the three roommates left the apartment. Absent some specific cue that pinpoints the time of day—for example, a favorite TV show coming on or a clock striking the hour—discrepancies among witnesses' time estimates is common and, for detectives, generally not cause for alarm.

We felt good that there were many more consistencies than inconsistencies. All of Ron's friends had described him as a kind and considerate person, if somewhat shy. Several witnesses had told us about the depth and sincerity of Ron's interest in Wicca; that he had been to Chatsworth Park previously; and that he had been interested in doing something to celebrate the summer solstice if he could, even if it was by himself.

That same afternoon, Ron Baker's family and friends gathered in nearby Woodland Hills for a memorial service and celebration of his life. Although we did not attend, we later obtained an audio recording of the entire service.

The service began with a prayer and hymn, which were followed by a series of eulogies from Ron's family and selected friends.

Ron's sister, Patty, was too bereft to speak in front of everyone, so she had her roommate read a remembrance of him she had written. Patty had written of her only sibling, "Ron and I always had a special relationship... He never judged me or anything I did and was always supportive and eager to listen... He was never afraid to speak his mind about anything he felt and always fought for what he believed in. His involvement was always wholehearted in whatever he did."

Next was Mark Johnson, Ron's best friend through high school. Mark recalled a conversation they once had about what they considered to be their own best qualities. "Ron said that his best quality was that he would not let anybody hate him." Mark's voice cracked with emotion as he closed with "I miss him."

Lydia Archibald then came to the microphone. Sniffling through her remarks, she paid tribute to Ron's reliable friendship. She explained, "You call people, and they won't call you back. You make arrangements to meet with people, and they don't show up. Everybody has got an excuse. The best thing about Ron was that you'd call him, and an hour later he'd call you back. And he always wanted to hear from you, and he'd always be there, out of all of our friends."

I had gotten a sense of Ron from the interviews we'd conducted. I was familiar with his interests, his sense of curiosity, and his shy nature. But listening to the recording of his memorial service gave me a deeper appreciation for him. The words coming from the tape recorder showcased Ron's warmth, sensitivity, and desire to make the world a better place. That he had been a good person who wanted to do good for humanity. Ron's chance to live out his dreams would now go unrealized, because of his murder at the hands of a killer or killers unknown.

Duncan was the last of Ron's close friends to address the gathering. He spoke in a soft voice and had to pause several times to hold his emotions in check. He said, "I am Duncan Martinez. I have been Ron's roommate for about the past two and a half years. Mark really hit the nail on the head with the fact about him not having anybody hate him.

He was the most friendliest, sweetest guy there. I mean, he was never real physically strong, or like a lot of the guys I know, but he had it here," Duncan said, touching his chest. "And he would talk to anybody, and be there for anybody, at the drop of a dime."

Duncan paused a long moment to maintain his composure. "I miss him a lot too. And I just hope that it's something I can get over, because I love him. It's just hard to think of a time without Ron—he's always been there. And he is the one friend that I thought I'd know until I was old, until I... I always thought Ron would be there."

CHAPTER 6

DECEPTION INDICATED
(July 2 to 6, 1990)

WE HEARD THAT DUNCAN had been staying at Lydia's family home in Hollywood for the last several days. Garcia reached Duncan at Lydia's and requested he meet us at his apartment that afternoon. Duncan agreed.

We planned to bring with us Detective Pat Metoyer, the LAPD's acknowledged expert on occult-related crimes. We met with Metoyer and walked him through our investigation so far, including Ron's interest in Wicca. We hoped to get Metoyer interested in the case and, ideally, invested enough in it that he would agree to be present later that day, when we searched Ron's bedroom for the second time. On our initial visit to the apartment, the previous week, Garcia and I had observed in Ron's room an array of ceremonial items connected with the occult and Wicca. We wanted Metoyer to explain their potential significance.

Since we knew we needed to be in Van Nuys later, we decided to spend the morning in the Valley, tackling various other tasks, leads, and open questions.

Our first stop was the home of Gayle and Kay Baker. This visit would likely be less fraught than our initial one.

Gayle and Kay welcomed us inside. As on the night we first met them, they were outwardly composed. Internally, it was likely a far different story.

We asked them what they knew of Ron's involvement in Mystic's Circle.

Gayle told us that he had never heard of it before the night of Ron's disappearance. When he called the apartment following the first ransom call, Nathan told him Ron had gone to UCLA to meet friends from Mystic's Circle. Gayle was certain the ransom caller never mentioned Mystic's Circle.

We asked when they had last visited Ron's apartment. Gayle said that he and Kay went on the Wednesday after Ron's murder, to retrieve some clothes for his funeral.

Gayle also told us, "When we went to the apartment on Wednesday, we told Duncan we were concerned because the suspects might have Ron's keys. Duncan said he had Ron's keys and pointed them out on the counter. He said Ron hadn't even taken them."

We asked them if there was anything else they wanted to share with us about Ron. Gayle told us, "Ron was a very curious person. Even though he was brought up as a Christian, and was still involved in UCLA's Methodist youth group, he explored and checked out other things and religions." It seemed important to Gayle that Ron's Christian upbringing was not forgotten, amid all the talk of his involvement with Mystic's Circle.

We asked the Bakers if they had any idea who might've wanted to harm Ron. They said they couldn't think of anyone.

After we left, I told Garcia that something Gayle had said struck me as odd. When they went to the apartment, Duncan had pointed out Ron's keys on the counter, meaning Ron had left the apartment that night without them. "Why would Ron leave his keys behind?" I asked Garcia. If Ron was going alone to UCLA, how could he have been sure his roommates wouldn't be out or sound asleep when he got home? He would've wanted his keys with him, so he wouldn't be locked out upon his return.

Garcia also pointed out that multiple people had told us Ron always took his backpack whenever he went out. Yet the first time we searched his bedroom, we saw his backpack there.

Why would Ron, on the night of his murder, leave home without both his keys and, uncharacteristically, his backpack?

We met Metoyer at the apartment around 1 p.m. Duncan was there and allowed us to view Ron's bedroom. Nathan was still in Detroit for his family's reunion.

Metoyer pointed out various items that related to Ron's interest in the occult and Wicca. No blockbuster insights came from Metoyer's presence, but we felt it was the right thing to have him there, given his far greater expertise on the subject than me or Garcia had.

Garcia and I had noticed many of the items on our initial visit. We decided to take several with us back to RHD for later review and photographing. These included the roughly four-foot-long sword with red and green fabric wrapped around its hilt; a creepy molded candle in the shape of a human hand with long wicks extending from each fingertip; the red and white wax pentagram candle atop Ron's altar; a crystal adjacent to the altar; and a wooden staff, about the length of a pool cue, that Ron had used in his Wiccan observances.

In our search of Ron's bedroom, I also found his checkbook and checkbook register, along with several carbon copies and other assorted blank and canceled checks. I noticed that one of the carbon copies, for check number 702, was made out to Duncan Martinez in the amount of $109.00. The fact that it was written to Duncan sparked my interest. The check was dated June 9, 1990, twelve days before the murder. I decided to take all of the check-related items back to RHD so I could review them more thoroughly.

Garcia, meanwhile, had struck up a conversation with Duncan. Duncan said that he and Nathan both had athames of their own, the double-edged dagger used in the practice of Wicca. Garcia asked if both athames were in the apartment. Duncan took Garcia into the bedroom he shared with Nathan and showed him where they were. Garcia asked if Duncan would consent to us taking both athames. He agreed.

We also asked Duncan if he was willing to come with us to Van Nuys Station for an interview. Again he agreed.

In an interview room at the station, we asked Duncan about his involvement with Wicca. He said he had minimal interest, although he had attended five or six informal classes at Lance Strickler's home.

We next asked Duncan about going to Chatsworth Park with Nathan to look for Ron while he was allegedly kidnapped and still missing. Duncan said it was Detective Rhudy who had suggested to Nathan they put together a search party to look for Ron. He and Nathan only decided to try Chatsworth Park because they knew Ron liked to go there for Wicca activities, both alone and with their group of friends.

We asked Duncan to tell us again about the night they dropped Ron off at the bus stop. He said Ron had mentioned something about meeting with Mystic's Circle but nothing more specific.

Duncan told us that after they dropped Ron at the bus stop, he and Nathan went to nearby Hazeltine Elementary School, where they drank a six-pack of beer. This had been their plan even before Diane, Nathan's girlfriend, decided to come to their apartment. He and Nathan parked in the teachers' parking lot and drank the beer while sitting in their car. Diane remained at their apartment.

Duncan estimated that he and Nathan returned home between 10:30 and 11 p.m. Diane was watching television. Duncan said he and Nathan had been invited to a party by two girls, Tewanda and Vickie, who lived in an apartment upstairs. They decided to stop by the party, again leaving Diane home alone, and stayed there for about thirty minutes, he recalled.

We asked Duncan to tell us his recollection of the call they received that night from Mr. Baker. Duncan said that shortly after they'd returned from the party, their phone rang, and Nathan answered it. After the call, Nathan said Mr. Baker had told him that someone had called and said they were holding Ron and wanted $100,000. Neither Duncan nor Nathan took the story about the ransom call seriously. "I didn't think it could be real," Duncan told us.

I asked Duncan about the check made out to him for $109 that I'd found in Ron's room. Duncan said Ron had written him the check in early June, to reimburse him for various apartment-related expenses, including cable installation, and he had cashed it about a week ago. He added that Ron also owed him $2,800. He explained that Ron had borrowed his car and wrecked it, burning out its engine. They had agreed that Ron could pay him back after he finished college, Duncan said.

At the end of the interview, we asked Duncan if he would agree to submit to a polygraph examination. Up to this point, all of our interactions with him had been non-adversarial and not accusatory. We explained that he and Nathan were the last people known to see Ron alive, and that a polygraph exam could help us eliminate them as suspects. Duncan immediately agreed.

On the spot, Garcia called downtown and scheduled the exam for that Friday afternoon. Duncan said he would meet us at Parker Center.

The time had come, Garcia and I decided, to brief the press on the status of our investigation. We had continued to receive media inquiries, mostly centered on the potential occult angle, but as of yet had not released any information.

Garcia granted interviews to two outlets, the local NBC News affiliate and the *Los Angeles Times*. Our primary goal was to get Ron Baker's photo out to the public on a larger scale, just in case someone might recognize him or know something about the case.

Unsurprisingly, the main focus of the questions Garcia fielded pertained to Ron Baker's interest in the occult. The media's fixation on a satanic motive reflected the public's obsession with the Night Stalker and McMartin preschool cases of the previous decade.

In his remarks to reporters, Garcia was careful not to disclose specific case details that might compromise the ongoing investigation. He conceded that detectives did not yet know how or why Ron Baker had ended up in the remote tunnel where he was killed.

"We don't know if it is an occult-related crime. We are looking at that very hard," he said.

On the subject of Ron Baker, Garcia said, "He was exploring avenues of magic and meditation, metaphysical stuff... We don't know if at some point he graduated from the light to the dark side of that."

The press was already aware the Bakers had received ransom calls, due to a scoop the previous week by *LA Times* reporter Michael Connelly.

"There were ransom demands placed to the family," Garcia acknowledged. "But they are not what we typically expect in a kidnap. There was no effort made to discuss the mechanics of a money drop or anything like that. My opinion is that it was a ruse by the murderer."

Following the press conference, Garcia called Nathan at the number he had for him in Michigan and asked him when he would be back in Southern California to meet. Nathan said he would be returning at the end of the week and would be staying with his girlfriend, Diane, in Riverside County.

While he had Nathan on the phone, Garcia asked a few more questions. He wanted Nathan to tell him again about Duncan and him dropping Ron off on the night of June 21. Nathan repeated the same story as before, that they dropped Ron off at the bus stop between 8 and 8:30 p.m. and then went to drink beers.

"Was Ron carrying anything with him?" asked Garcia.

Nathan said he was not.

Garcia also asked Nathan to recount the call he received later that night from Mr. Baker.

Nathan said Ron's father called close to midnight. He was basing the time on his memory that *The Arsenio Hall Show*, a popular late-night show at the time, was on TV when the phone rang.

Nathan said Ron's father told him that someone had called and said they had Ron. Mr. Baker asked if Ron was there. When Nathan said that Ron hadn't come home yet, Mr. Baker said he hoped it was a joke. Ron's father "seemed disturbed," Nathan told Garcia.

Before they hung up, Garcia also asked Nathan about his involvement with Wicca. Nathan said he had attended a couple of classes but never got into it.

The case was all over the morning papers on Independence Day.

The *Los Angeles Daily News*, the less prominent of the city's two major newspapers, ran a short, un-bylined story that leaned sensationalistic. Below the headline STUDENT KILLED ON SOLSTICE MAY HAVE BEEN SACRIFICED, the story began: "A UCLA student found stabbed to death might have been the victim of a cult sacrifice because he was a member of an occult club and was killed on the summer solstice in a park used by cult members, police said Tuesday."

The *Los Angeles Times* ran a lengthier article, co-written by reporters Michael Connelly and Steve Padilla, that delved deeper into Ron Baker's background. Their story, which spanned two pages in the Metro section of the paper, was headlined MYSTICISM FASCINATED SLAIN MAN, with the subhead, THE INTROSPECTIVE STUDENT MAY HAVE GONE TO A PARK TO MEDITATE. HIS BODY WAS FOUND THERE NEAR A

SITE OF OCCULT OBSERVANCES. The article recounted Ron's involvement in Mystic's Circle and featured quotes from several people who had known him.

I suspected the articles would draw a lot of attention, and most likely tips from the public. Whether or not those tips would produce useful information, only time would tell.

We did not have to wait long. Later that day, Garcia received a call from John Zorn, one of the lieutenants assigned to RHD. Zorn ran the Homicide Special Section, the counterpart to Major Crimes, the section to which Garcia and I belonged.

Zorn told Garcia that he had been notified that a black robe and hood had been left at a church in Chatsworth. The person who found them had called the police. Officers from Devonshire Division had gone to the church and recovered the items, which had been booked into evidence.

Because Zorn supervised a different unit, he was unfamiliar with the details of our case. But he thought we should be informed. I felt that if there had been no news stories laced with suggestions of occult sacrifice, the discovery of the items likely would not have been reported.

In the coming days, we would tally several more calls. All could be traced to the flurry of media attention. Unfortunately, none served to advance our investigation in any meaningful way.

Thursday afternoon, we met Ron's sister, Patty, to interview her.

Patty told us the last time she had seen Ron was in May, when they'd celebrated their father's birthday.

We asked Patty if she knew of any problems between Ron and Duncan. She said she didn't and described their friendship as close. She told us Duncan had visited their family home many times.

The next day, Friday, was the date of Duncan's polygraph exam. Before we had asked him, Garcia and I discussed the pros and cons of offering him a polygraph. I was strongly in favor, even though the results were rarely admissible in court.

In my decade of working homicides, the use of polygraph evidence in court had not occurred once in any of my cases. Nevertheless, I had seen that polygraph exams could be an effective investigative tool. In my experience, if a polygraph subject tested "truthful," it was usually accurate. The "deceptive" results were a bit more circumspect and required additional investigation to corroborate. In more than one of my past cases, a person who tested as deceptive later was determined to have not been involved in the crime. But most of the time, a person who tested as deceptive eventually was tied to the case.

Confronting a subject about a failed polygraph could lead to a confession, or to a partial admission of involvement in the crime. It could also cause a subject to clam up and end the interview.

On the surface, there appeared to be no logical reason to believe that Duncan, or Nathan and Duncan, would have killed Ron. They were longtime friends, and we had not uncovered any hint of acrimony between them.

Still, Duncan and Nathan were the last people known to have seen him alive. There were also two additional issues: the questionable check Duncan had said Ron gave him and the odd story about searching for Ron at Chatsworth Park when he was supposedly a kidnap victim.

It seemed to us a prudent investigative move to ask Duncan to submit to a polygraph exam. Should he follow through on his promise to take the poly, the results would allow us either to move on to other avenues in the case or to tighten our focus on Duncan and Nathan as the suspects.

Friday morning, a few hours before the scheduled polygraph, Garcia called the coroner's office and requested they seal Ron Baker's autopsy report and investigative file. This would help prevent the media or anyone not part of law enforcement from obtaining information that we did not want publicly known, for instance the number of stab wounds Ron had received. The release of such details could compromise witnesses' later accounts and thus the integrity of the investigation.

Garcia also asked the coroner's office, while he had them on the phone, whether the toxicology report had been completed. Fifteen minutes later, the office called back and informed Garcia that Ron's blood-alcohol level was .21, more than double the legal limit to drive.

Garcia immediately called Duncan and asked him if Ron had consumed any alcohol at dinner, prior to them dropping him off at the bus stop. Duncan said he could not recall. Garcia told Duncan he would see him at 1 p.m. for the polygraph appointment.

Garcia then called the Blood Alcohol Unit at SID. The unit was responsible for analyzing blood samples for a wide range of cases, especially suspected DUIs. Garcia explained that his murder victim, who weighed about 160 pounds, had come back with a .21 blood-alcohol level. Garcia asked about how much alcohol he would have consumed to reach that level, if he had started drinking around 9 p.m. and was dead within four hours. Garcia was told the amount of alcohol would've been equivalent to eight and a half beers or eleven ounces of 80-proof liquor.

When Garcia hung up the phone and told me, I recalled that Ron had been described as someone who was generally a light drinker and would not drink alone. It seemed unlikely to us that Ron would have gone to Chatsworth Park to celebrate solo and drink that much. We also agreed that to climb the trails and rocks to reach the tunnel would have been very difficult for a light drinker who was that drunk.

This development added a new factor to the calculus of Duncan and Nathan's possible involvement. The two roommates were the only alibis for each other. They had already admitted to drinking beers that night. We now knew Ron, meanwhile, had been drinking heavily in the few hours before his death.

Duncan arrived at Parker Center on time for his appointment. We had him wait on a bench in the hallway outside the polygraph rooms.

While Duncan waited, Garcia and I met with the polygraph examiner, George Gourley. We briefed Gourley on the details of Ron Baker's murder, including the kidnapping and ransom calls his parents had received. From this information, Gourley would craft several questions he planned to ask Duncan. These questions, which would pertain directly to the case, are known as "relevant" questions. Duncan would also be asked a handful of "control" questions, for instance his name and birthplace—questions that do not involve the crime.

Gourley compiled his list of questions. After he ensured that we had no issues with their exact wording, he was ready to meet Duncan Martinez.

Garcia and I went out to get Duncan, to bring him back to the polygraph area and introduce him to Gourley. About thirty minutes had passed, talking with Gourley, since we'd left Duncan to wait on the bench outside. Part of me wondered whether he might have gotten cold feet and left. But there he was, still sitting on the bench.

Gourley escorted Duncan into one of the very small polygraph examination rooms. Garcia and I left but did not go far. Just across the hall was a monitoring room where we could sit and listen in on the exam as it was administered. All LAPD polygraph exams are also audio-recorded, although Duncan was not informed of that. Under California state law, there was no requirement to tell him.

As was standard procedure, Gourley began by describing how the exam would be conducted and how the polygraph machine worked. He explained to Duncan that the machine would measure and record his body's responses—including, specifically, his blood pressure, pulse, respiration, and skin conductivity—when he was asked various questions and answered them. Gourley's manner was practiced but conversational, an ideal demeanor to put Duncan at ease and elicit information.

Once the tape was rolling, Gourley asked Duncan some basic questions about his educational and work background, information he could use to make final tweaks to questions he would ask during the actual exam.

Duncan's tone was relaxed and matter-of-fact. He mentioned to Gourley that after high school, he went into the Marine Corps.

"You went full through in the Marines?" Gourley asked.

"I was in about two years, a year and a half, something like that."

"Did you get out early?"

"Yeah."

"Got lucky?" asked Gourley.

"George Bush made a cutback and I was one of the few," Duncan said. The more he discussed his military experience, the more confident and animated his voice sounded.

Gourley also asked Duncan if he had ever been convicted of a criminal offense.

Duncan said no.

"Now, of course you know you're here to be asked about a serious crime," said Gourley.

"Right."

"So, what I'm going to do, as I have to with everybody, whether you're a victim, suspect, or simply a witness, I have to advise you of your constitutional rights."

Gourley walked Duncan through his Miranda rights, starting with the right to remain silent and ending with the right to have an attorney present during questioning. Gourley asked Duncan whether he understood his rights.

"Yeah, I can have an attorney if I want one, but I'm not worried, so..."

"Okay," Gourley said. "Knowing these rights, do you want to still talk to me?"

"Yeah, it's fine."

Duncan had mentioned to Gourley earlier that this was not his first polygraph examination.

"You said you had a polygraph test before?" Gourley asked.

"Yeah, I had a quick one in the Marine Corps."

Gourley asked what that involved.

"It was from my MOS," Duncan said, using the acronym for Military Occupational Specialty. "You had to take a polygraph, and they just asked you about drugs and stuff."

Gourley asked Duncan what his MOS was.

"0861 forward observer. It's a derivative of a recon," Duncan said, adding that it was one of the hardest posts to get into. "They don't really want, you know, hotheaded people. They don't want anybody that's going to have problems or anything. They want to make sure they aren't using any drugs and stuff like that."

"Did you have to do extra-long boot camp, or how'd you get in?"

"They have a test, just like recon. You have to do stuff like an eighteen-minute three-mile run in full gear on rough terrain. That's real hard. You have to be able to swim in certain times and do all sorts of climbing stuff. It's pretty fun. It was a fun test day. You get to jump out of an airplane."

"Oh, so you did a little parachuting too?"

"Yeah, it was kind of cool. It was at night."

"Oh?"

"Yeah," Duncan said. "You can't see nothing, just rushing wind going by, and you're out, and you're falling. You're just scared shitless because you can't see anything down below. You don't know when you're going to hit the ground. Right before you get up to it, you start to realize the ground is there, but most of the time when you're falling you have no clue. You could be hitting the ground at any second and you wouldn't know it. It's great."

"It would scare me," said Gourley.

"Yeah, it was definitely a roller coaster."

"They trained you that highly, then they let you go so quick?" asked Gourley.

"Yeah, Bush made some cutbacks and a bunch of people got dropped."

Duncan said that more recently he had been working at a place called Everything Audio, making deliveries.

"What do you know about Ron and what happened to him?" asked Gourley, segueing to matters closer at hand.

"Not much," said Duncan. "They're not telling us much. I heard that he was stabbed multiple times. I heard that his throat was cut … That's about it. I only know where he died from the TV and stuff and from talking to detectives. But that's about it. Kind of weird too. It's hard to deal with."

"What do you think happened?"

"I don't know. Everybody's got a … All my friends and everybody's got a theory. They all make a bit of sense, but none of them just quite click with me. I can't quite come up with something that I really think makes sense. All of this is a pretty unsensible crime. Just nothing seems to work for me. I don't know."

"Was somebody upset with Ron?"

"No. Ron was a good guy. Nobody disliked Ron. That was one good thing he had going for him. Wasn't a real wild guy, wasn't ultra-fun at parties or anything, but nobody disliked Ron. That was, like, his big thing, was that he didn't have any enemies. Everybody else had people that disliked them, and there were conflicts going on between people, and Ron just was always kind of, like, the mediator."

"What were some of his bad qualities?"

"Kind of boring," Duncan said with a laugh. "That's his big bad quality. He couldn't hold alcohol at all, and he used to always try, and that was a bad quality, because that'd usually make him mad, but it was no big deal."

Gourley asked Duncan when he last saw Ron.

Duncan said around eight or nine o'clock on Thursday, June 21, when he dropped him off at the bus stop near their apartment.

"This may sound dumb to you probably, but how come you dropped him off and didn't take him somewhere?"

"I'm not a chauffeur. I didn't really know what was going on too, and it was kind of on the way. He wanted me to drop him off at the bus stop. I didn't like … I was the only one of the three of us that had a car, and I didn't like driving people places because then they'd pass the point where, like, 'Duncan, I need a ride here. Give me a ride,' and you feel bad."

"But you gave him a ride?"

"I gave him a ride to the bus stop. It was four or five blocks."

"Oh."

"It was just to save him a ten-minute walk to the bus stop. Plus, he had made dinner that night. So it was kind of… It would have been pretty cruel to say no."

"Where was he going?"

"I'm not sure. He said something about a Mystic's Circle meeting, which is this group he'd been hanging out with. I didn't know where they were going. I assumed, because he said Victory and Van Nuys, that he was going over the hill to UCLA because the Van Nuys bus goes over the hill. That's what he took every morning to school. But he didn't say … I wish he'd said. I wish I'd asked."

"What's a Mystic … A Mystic what?" asked Gourley.

"Mystic's Circle. It's this group … this witchcraft group that he hangs out with at UCLA, or hung out with at UCLA."

Gourley asked Duncan if he knew what the group advocated or believed.

"I know a little bit about Wicca from last year, but not much. Generally, it's a peaceful … I mean, it is witchcraft stuff, but I mean, it's generally pretty peaceful from what I understand. It's not violent. It's not destructive at all. They just believe in nature or something like that. I don't know. I just wonder if he got mixed up with the wrong people in his group or something. Or if he just got picked up at UCLA or he just got picked up somewhere, the bus stop."

"Did his parents give you a call?"

"Yes."

"What time was that?"

"About eleven, eleven thirty, something like that. They'd just gotten a phone call. They called with a ransom demand or something. I don't know. It just doesn't make any sense. Of all the people I know, there are a lot of people that something like this could happen to. I know this doesn't sound real good, but there are a lot of people who this could happen to, and I can see it. I can say, 'Oh, well. There he goes again, getting mixed up in the wrong group of people.' But not Ron."

Gourley asked if Duncan had ever been upset with Ron before.

"Yeah, we had little spats before but nothing really major. I've been living with him for about two and a half years. I've known him for about five."

"Has he ever done anything to you to make you upset enough to do something? Punch him or—"

"Nah, I couldn't hit Ron. Ron's a real . . . feeble-looking kind of guy. I couldn't even get mad at him, even when he trashed my car."

"Did he owe you money?" asked Gourley.

"He owed me the money for my car, just about twenty-eight hundred bucks."

"Did he owe anybody else money?"

"I don't think so. Not that I know of. But yeah, just a real peaceful guy, total pacifist, totally into recycling and all that, into conservation."

"Sounds like you guys were real friends but, you know, got along real good," said Gourley.

"Yeah, we were real good friends," Duncan said, recounting how he and Ron met while working at Sears and eventually became roommates. "We had a real good time. Yeah, I miss him."

"Do you have any suspicions as to who might have done this?"

"I think it had something to do with the Mystic's Circle. They're the only connection I have at all, and that could be just because, I don't know. You know, he said he was going to meet with Mystic's Circle."

"Is that the same as Wicca?" asked Gourley.

"Yes. The Mystic's Circle is the name of the group, and Wicca is what they practice."

"Oh, I see."

"Yeah, I don't know. There's no one... I've never known anybody to carry a grudge or even dislike Ron for more than a minute, you know, once they got to know him. That's really a shame because that was his true strong point. He was real, real strong in here," said Duncan, indicating his heart.

"On the 21st, the night you dropped him off, did you see him anytime after that?"

"No. I dropped him off at the bus stop and drove off."

"Were you at the park with him that night at any time?"

"No."

"Did he borrow your car to go to the park later on or anything?"

"No, never saw him again," said Duncan.

Gourley was ready to begin the polygraph examination. "What I'm going to do is I'm going to formulate a set of questions here to ask you. I'll be asking questions about your knowledge of this thing," he told Duncan. "It's very, very important to be truthful on these questions."

"Okay," Duncan said.

"You know, we're not talking about a shoplift. What we're talking about here, it's a pretty serious thing."

"Right," Duncan agreed.

Gourley asked if there was anything Duncan hadn't told him.

"Not that I can think of."

"Has anybody told you who has done this thing?"

"No."

"Like I said, I don't want you to hold back about anything, because more than likely what I'm going to end up asking you, more than likely, is if you know who did this. Okay? And do you?"

"No, I don't," said Duncan.

"Okay. The reason I ask you this, not because of anything I suspect or anyone else suspects, is because you're his roommate."

"Right. No, I can understand."

"You were close to him for two and a half years. If anyone would know, you would."

"Yeah," Duncan replied. "You know, that's one of the things that's hard to deal with, too, is I should know, but I don't know. I kind of blame myself sometimes too."

Gourley then proceeded to inform Duncan, in advance, of each of the questions he planned to ask him during the examination. Unlike how polygraph exams are generally depicted on television, it is common practice to reveal up front what questions will be asked. This allows the examiner to see the degree to which the subject's physiological response becomes elevated in anticipation of a feared pertinent question.

"One question I'm going to have to ask you is, do you know who killed Ron?"

"No, I do not."

"Now, do you strongly suspect any particular person?"

"No."

"Were you with Ron when he was killed?"

"No, I was not."

"Obviously, if you were, you would remember that, right?"

"Yeah, I would think so."

"Did you take part in Ron's death?"

"No, I didn't."

"Did you yourself stab Ron?"

"No, I didn't."

"Are you the one that called Ron's parents about the kidnapping?"

"No."

"The only contact you had was that they called you, right?"

"Yes."

"Before 1990, did you ever hurt another person seriously? Have you ever been in a fight and seriously hurt somebody?"

"Not seriously hurt. I've been in fights before."

"Have you ever seriously hurt anybody?"

"No."

"While you were in the Marines, did you ever seriously hurt anybody with a knife or a gun?"

"No."

"Or use your fists at all? Hit them with your fists?"

"No. I got into a couple of fights, but I never seriously hurt anybody."

"Before last year, did you ever consider killing anyone?"

"No," Duncan said.

Gourley said he wanted to make sure that every one of those

questions was clear in Duncan's mind before they began. "Do you have any questions about these questions?" he asked.

"No. I understand."

"Some people sit in the chair and think, *Well, I'll move around, and it'll screw with the test.* It doesn't work... People think, *Oh, I'm going to sit here and memorize a chant or think of something in my head to* ... That doesn't work either, because you don't control what you think."

"Right."

"Then some people think, *Well, I'll just turn my mind off.* You can't turn your mind off. There's no way. So just relax and answer the questions yes or no," Gourley instructed.

Having briefed Duncan on the questions he would have to answer, Gourley proceeded with the actual examination. Duncan was asked the full complement of questions four times. The first two times, the questions were asked in the exact same order. For the third test, Duncan was asked to only think of the answer to each question but not speak it. The final time, Gourley asked the same questions once again but changed their order and asked some of them twice. All the while, the polygraph machine recorded Duncan's physiological responses.

Within a minute of completing the fourth test, the results, in the form of charts of raw data, emerged from a printer attached to the polygraph machine. Gourley tore off the long sheet.

"So how did I do?" Duncan asked him.

Gourley explained that it would take a few minutes for him to review and analyze the charts. Duncan would have to wait.

Gourley brought the charts across the hall into the monitoring room where Garcia and I had been listening intently. We would learn the answer to "So how did I do?" before Duncan.

After Gourley reviewed the charts, he informed us that Duncan showed definite deception in answering several of the relevant questions on the examination. In his professional opinion, Duncan had not been truthful in denying his involvement in Ron Baker's murder.

Gourley said he would return to Duncan and explain the charts showed he had been deceptive. The question Gourley had for us was whether we wanted him to continue his questioning after he told Duncan the results, or if we would rather question Duncan ourselves. I favored Gourley doing the questioning, as he was the polygraph expert and could better explain the intricacies of how Duncan's physiological responses during the question-and-answer session screamed deception. Garcia agreed with that approach.

Gourley headed back to the polygraph exam room while Garcia and I settled in again in the monitoring room. We gave each other a nod, knowing we were about to find out how Duncan would react to being confronted with his results.

"The results have come back," Gourley told Duncan. "Now, there can be three ways these charts can go."

"Okay," said Duncan.

"One is we can't tell the results. They're not readable. That's a very small percentage of cases, and that's not in this case."

"Okay."

"The other is the person's been totally truthful, and this test has benefited them."

"Okay."

"And the third way is the person was not truthful, and this test has hurt them. And in this case ... you have not been truthful," Gourley said.

"With which question?"

"You're involved in this homicide."

"No, I'm not," Duncan protested.

"You are involved in this thing. Now, I'm going to give you some advice here. I can look at these charts and I can see what's inside you. A person cannot deny what's inside them, and you can't deny that ... There's no denying that you're involved."

"I'm not involved," Duncan insisted.

Gourley then deployed a time-tested tactic from the interrogator's handbook, attempting to minimize what had happened. "These things can happen in many, many different ways. Now, you mentioned to me that Ron couldn't hold liquor. People who can't hold liquor sometimes get out of hand. Sometimes disputes happen. Now, there's a difference between a dispute and an out-and-out murder. I don't know what happened that night. I just know that you're involved in this death, and certainly, if an accident happened, if a dispute happened and ended up in a tragedy, that's different than somebody outright killing somebody. But when it gets proven that you're involved in this thing, later on down the way, no one's going to listen to your side of it. Nobody," warned Gourley.

His emphasis on potentially mitigating factors, suggesting that what happened was not intentional murder but spontaneous or accidental, was a gambit to get Duncan to come clean and confess. Gourley told him, "You don't have any big, heavy record. You don't have any problems. This thing is a heavy, heavy thing, the way it sits now, the way it looks now. And what they have to investigate is a homicide. A murder. That somebody would murder for no reason. Now, it's common sense that things happen for a reason, some justifiable, some not justifiable, but things happen. But if we leave it this way, it's going to be—it truly is an out-and-out murder. When this thing comes back to haunt you, it's going to look bad."

"Okay, well, I didn't kill him," Duncan replied. "I thought, even though I've heard these things are bunk a lot of the time, I thought I'd do it to help, you know, to help."

Gourley told Duncan that fingerprints were found on the body, something that was untrue but a legally permissible tactical bluff.

"Okay, that's fine," said Duncan, seemingly unperturbed. He repeated that he didn't have any part in the murder.

Gourley said he was just trying to give Duncan a chance to explain what really happened. "There's no question about the results. If the results weren't accurate, we wouldn't be doing this."

"I think if you're making accusations and stuff, I better talk to a lawyer before I speak to anybody else, and I've got one. My parents wanted me to get this lawyer before I came down here, and I had no worries coming down here because I am innocent, and I had nothing to do with it. It may have shown on your chart that I did, but I didn't."

With that, Gourley acknowledged Duncan had mentioned a desire for an attorney, and the polygraph examination and post-polygraph interview were over.

Garcia and I walked Duncan downstairs one flight to the third floor, which housed RHD. Duncan seemed shaken following his encounter with Gourley and continued to maintain his innocence.

We took Duncan to one of the interview rooms off the RHD squad room. We sat him down and asked him if he would be willing to provide a handwriting sample. We explained our concern about Ron's check number 702, which Duncan had told us Ron wrote and gave to him as reimbursement for bills. He agreed. He also agreed to have his photo taken with a Polaroid camera, for the purpose of documenting his presence and appearance that day.

Duncan Martinez in RHD interview room, July 6, 1990 (court exhibit)

As far as interviewing him more about the case, however, we were done. That door was closed when he invoked his constitutional rights under Miranda, the moment he advised Gourley that he wanted to speak with his attorney.

Garcia and I sat with Duncan while he filled out the various forms we had obtained from the Questioned Documents Unit of SID. The forms prompted Duncan to write a mix of uppercase and lowercase letters, both printed and in cursive, as well as numbers, both in numeral form and written out as words. Duncan also completed a blank check form, which required him to write his own name on the "Pay to the order of" line, followed by the date and amount we dictated to him. At the bottom of the form, he signed the name "Ron Baker." Finally, Duncan was asked to write the name "Ronald S. Baker" on every other line down a sheet of notebook paper. Duncan did everything we asked.

We explained that we would submit his handwriting samples to our examiners, who would compare the writing on check 702 to both his and Ron's known handwriting and signatures.

We had one more request of Duncan. We wanted to search the interior and exterior of Duncan's car and asked his permission. Again, he was agreeable. He completed a vehicle-search consent form, which included the make and license plate number of his car.

Duncan led us to his car, parked in the public lot just outside the entrance to Parker Center. His car was a black 1983 Subaru GL with two doors and a sunroof. Its license plate matched the one he had written on the consent form.

We did not inform Duncan of our specific intent in searching his car, but near the top of our list was whether any bloodstains were visible, inside or out. We knew from the number and severity of the stab wounds Ron had sustained that his killer was likely to have been significantly bloodied. Moreover, Ron's throat had been savagely slit, a wound that could only be inflicted up close and would have increased the amount of blood that left his body.

Two weeks had passed since the murder, more than enough time for the car to have been thoroughly cleaned. Nevertheless, the search still needed to be done. After all, even if the car had been cleaned, it was possible that minute bloodstains could still be found.

Garcia and I looked over the car's exterior and saw nothing out of the ordinary. Inside the car, however, on the right side of the driver's seat, we noticed two reddish spots. We called the crime lab and requested a criminalist from its Serology Unit, which handled blood evidence, be dispatched to our location.

Given the proximity of the crime lab to the Parker Center parking lot, it did not take long for a serology expert to respond. She swabbed several areas inside Duncan's Subaru for the presence of blood, including not only the reddish spots on the driver's seat but also the steering wheel, hand brake, gear shift, and rearview mirror. All tested negative for blood.

Once the analysis of his car was completed, we told Duncan that he could leave.

Garcia and I had one more task to do before we could call it a night. We drove to the intersection of Victory and Van Nuys Boulevards, arriving a few minutes before 8 p.m. This was around the time when Ron was dropped off, according to Duncan and Nathan.

We knew it was a long shot, as over two weeks had passed since the night Ron would have boarded the bus. But we hoped someone might remember seeing him.

Garcia and I split up and took different corners. Over the next two hours, we showed his photo to drivers and passengers on more than twenty buses that stopped there. No one recalled seeing him.

Our canvassing of the bus stop had yielded nothing, but it had still been a productive day. Duncan's polygraph results were a major development and a clear indication of where the investigation needed to go. His failed polygraph corroborated the other troublesome things that had nagged us about Duncan and his actions since Ron's murder.

Duncan, and thus Nathan, were now our primary focus.

Being a die-hard fan of the Dodgers and baseball in general, I often thought in terms of my favorite sport. In light of how the day's events had unfolded, I considered it a tie game, 1 to 1.

Garcia and I had scored a run with Duncan's deceptive polygraph results.

Duncan had scored a run when the search of his car proved negative for blood.

As iconic Dodgers broadcaster Vin Scully used to say in tie games, "Well, folks, pull up a chair. We may be here for a while." And Vin Scully was seldom wrong.

CHAPTER 7

"THE COOLEST MOTHERFUCKER I'VE EVER DEALT WITH"
(July 7 to 11, 1990)

THE MORNING AFTER DUNCAN'S failed polygraph exam, the *Los Angeles Times* ran a new story about Ron Baker's murder. The article carried the eye-catching headline SLAIN MAN FREQUENTLY VISITED SITE OF OCCULTISTS and the byline of reporter Michael Connelly.

Like Connelly's previous stories on the case, it bore the hallmarks of a respectable amount of shoe-leather reporting. He even had persuaded the victim's parents to talk with him on the record. His inquiries about Ron's character and background seemed intended to humanize him.

Reading the story, I sensed that it would likely prompt a new wave of calls and tips from the public. The tunnel where Ron was killed was described as "favored by local teenagers, but recently had also been the scene of occult activities. Pentagrams are painted on its walls, and police have received reports of ritualistic animal killings there."

Ron's father, Gayle, had told the paper, "He and his friends had gone into that tunnel before... It would not have been unusual for him to go there. He may have gone there alone. But who knows what happened after he got there? I feel that someone he didn't know accosted him and attacked him."

The story also went in depth on the two ransom calls the Bakers had received, which it said detectives had discounted as "a ruse by the killer." My partner, Garcia, was also quoted in the article: "My opinion is that they weren't legitimate ... It's a red herring designed to steer us away from the true motive, whatever that may be."

Gayle had said the calls sounded tape-recorded to him. "It was a very strange, raspy voice," he'd told Connelly. "It sounded like a recording ... I thought it was somebody pulling a prank."

Ron's mother, Kay, had said of the ransom calls, "They seemed real ... But if they were real, it seemed that the caller would have followed through. He didn't."

The story concluded that the Bakers believed their son's slaying could have been as simple as Ron being in the wrong place at the wrong time. It closed by quoting Gayle: "Someone found him there at the park ... It could have been drug addicts or transients. It could have been anybody."

Mr. Baker was right. It could have been anybody. But when we returned to work on Monday morning, our investigation was moving in a specific direction.

First thing that morning, Garcia called Diane Henderson, Nathan's girlfriend. She confirmed that Nathan had returned from Detroit and was staying with her in Perris. Perris, a small town twenty miles south of Riverside, was a popular site for skydiving and hot-air ballooning. Diane said they were both available for an interview that afternoon. She suggested we use her parents' home, in nearby Lake Elsinore, for the interviews.

In light of Duncan's deceptive polygraph results, it was increasingly urgent that Garcia and I get across a table from Nathan Blalock and interview him in person. It did not particularly matter whether it was at Diane's parents' house or in a police interview room. We needed to hear what he had to say, and in much more detail than what he'd told Garcia in their two brief phone conversations to date. Most importantly, we wanted to be able to look him in the eye and read his body language when we interviewed him.

Lake Elsinore was a ninety-minute drive from Parker Center. We arrived late on Monday afternoon to meet Nathan Blalock and Diane Henderson for the first time.

Nathan was Black and twenty-two years old. He appeared to be in very good physical shape, over six feet tall, and in the range of two hundred pounds. His demeanor was gracious. He exuded confidence and seemed unconcerned about answering whatever questions we had for him. Diane was white and maybe a few years older than Nathan. She seemed eager to cooperate and genuinely traumatized by what had happened to Ron.

We chose to interview Nathan first and were allowed to use the dining room to do so. Diane waited in another area of the house.

We began by asking Nathan to tell us how he came to know Ron. He said they met at a party at Jenny Strickler's house. Later, Ron came to Wicca classes at Lance's, a couple of which Nathan sat in on. He described the classes as "mainly group discussions dealing with nature."

Nathan said he and Duncan moved into Ron's apartment in January. He and Duncan shared a room, so Ron paid more rent. They all paid for their own phone bills and split the utilities.

We asked Nathan to tell us about his visits to Chatsworth Park. Nathan said the last time he was there was on New Year's Eve. He, Duncan, Ron, Jenny, and a few other friends drove to the park and hiked up to the train tunnel. "We didn't go there to meditate," he told us. "We were just screwing around."

Nathan said that after Ron disappeared, Detective Rhudy came to their apartment. They talked about forming a search party to look for Ron, which Rhudy encouraged. On the Saturday morning after Ron went missing, they dropped off a friend who had stayed at their apartment the night before. On their way home, Duncan suggested they go to Chatsworth Park to look for Ron. "We went up to the railroad tracks. We kept trying to think where Ron may have gone." Nathan said Ron had done things in the past to rebel against his parents. Nathan had heard this from friends. He said he and Duncan stayed at the park for five or ten minutes, then left. "It was too big of an area to cover," he told us.

We asked Nathan, a US Army veteran, what he knew about Duncan's military service with the Marines.

"Duncan did some secret mission for the Marines," Nathan said. "When he got back, he was supposed to get new identification. But he was discharged." Duncan never told him what the secret mission had involved.

Nathan told us that on June 21 Duncan picked him up from work, a sales job at a local video company. They got home at about 3:30

Nathan Blalock US Army photo, circa late 1980s (courtesy of Nathaniel Blalock Sr.)

or 4 p.m. Diane drove up from Perris and came over to the apartment around 5 p.m. "I was getting stressed out because the relationship with Diane was getting serious," he said. He and Diane had been dating since May, when they'd met working at the Renaissance Faire.

Nathan said Ron got home about 5:30 or 6 p.m. He had groceries and told everyone he was going to cook them dinner. Nathan thought this was strange. "Ron never did this before," he told us. Ron made spaghetti and they ate dinner together. Nathan didn't recall anybody drinking any beer at dinner. "We drank Pepsi and Kool-Aid."

Nathan said Ron joked to Diane during dinner, "When are you coming over to fix dinner? If you don't come over, I don't have maid service."

After dinner, Nathan and Duncan had a plan. "I needed to talk to him regarding my relationship with Diane," he said. They told Diane that they had to check on a security job. Then they all took showers and got ready to go out. Ron put his hair in a ponytail and Nathan told him it looked good, he recalled. When Ron was getting ready, Nathan saw him put his wallet in his back pocket. Ron didn't take his backpack.

Ron asked if he and Duncan would give him a ride to the bus stop. Ron had mentioned earlier that he was going to meet some friends from UCLA.

Nathan told us they left home at about 8 or 8:15.

We asked him to describe the route they took to the bus stop. Nathan said from home they made a left turn onto Van Nuys and then another left onto Victory. Ron sat in the front seat. En route to the bus stop, Nathan told Ron he didn't appreciate his comment to Diane during dinner, and Ron apologized. They left Ron at the southeast corner of Victory and Van Nuys, Nathan said.

We asked what he and Duncan did for the rest of their night.

"After we dropped Ron off, we drove to the elementary school where Duncan went as a kid." It took them about fifteen minutes to get there and they got to the school about 8:30 to 8:45. "We talked about my relationship with Diane. I was in a panic state," he told us, referencing his concern over how serious things were getting with her. They drank a six-pack of beer, Miller Genuine Draft, while they walked around the school grounds and talked.

They left the school and went back to their apartment building. Two girls who lived upstairs in #204 were having a party and they decided to stop by. Nathan said they got to the party about 10:30. They drank a couple of beers and played Nintendo. They went down to their apartment a little after 11 p.m. Diane was watching *The Arsenio Hall Show* on television.

Nathan recounted the two phone calls they received from Ron's father. He answered the first call, which he believed was between 11:40 p.m. and midnight. Mr. Baker told him about the kidnapping call he had received. "Ron's dad said he thought it was a practical joke," Nathan told us. "I thought it may be Ron doing his rebellion thing." When Mr. Baker called back the following day, around noon, Duncan answered and spoke with him. After that call, Duncan mentioned the ransom caller had told Mr. Baker something about money. Nathan said he and Duncan then started calling people to inquire if they'd seen Ron.

We asked Nathan about Duncan and Ron's relationship and whether there was any issue about Ron damaging Duncan's car. Nathan said he knew of no problems between them involving Duncan's car. Nathan's understanding was that Ron was going to pay Duncan when he got the money. Nathan told us, "When Duncan was in the Marines, Ron wrecked his car and blew out the engine. Duncan replaced the engine and fixed it up but later found out there was more damage to the frame. This happened about a year and a half ago." Duncan had told Ron to take care of the car or Ron's parents would be responsible.

We asked Nathan to tell us about Ron.

"Ron was the type of guy you couldn't be mad at. You felt sorry for him," he said.

We asked about Ron's drinking habits.

Nathan told us Ron drank beer but did not normally drink hard liquor. At the Renaissance Faire, he would drink more than he usually did. "Ron would buy the forty-ounce bottles of beer, maybe twice a week. Unless we had beer and he would drink ours. Ron drank Olde English 800." Nathan said that on the night they dropped him off, Ron had not been drinking.

"I think Ron got in over his head with this Wicca thing. He was stepping into other areas." Nathan said it bothered him when Ron made the pentagram candle because it was inverted. He also felt bothered by the altar in Ron's room.

We asked Nathan about Ron's other relationships, including with women.

"Ron was not a lady-killer," Nathan said. "He didn't date much at all. He pursued the females but never accomplished the mission."

Nathan said he was glad he wasn't part of the Wicca circle that Ron and some of their mutual friends were in. He didn't know if Ron might have gone to the park by himself, although he did know Ron once went to the park to look for wood for his staff. "He also made a wand, but he didn't like it for some reason, and he took it apart later."

We asked Nathan what he knew about Ron's knife. He said Ron told him he lost his knife at the Renaissance Faire. He described Ron's knife as the same size as Duncan's, with carvings on its handle.

By this time, our interview had passed the two-hour mark. Nathan had fully cooperated and answered every question we had posed to him, without any defensiveness. He showed little emotion but also no hint of evasiveness. Nor had I picked up on any other tells to indicate deception. In my experience, witnesses being asked questions, especially questions they did not anticipate, sometimes telegraph a lack of truthfulness by pausing to think of their answers, rather than speaking them straightaway. Nathan had answered quickly, with no pregnant pauses. His manner throughout the interview was calm, direct, and very matter-of-fact.

We requested Nathan wait in another part of the house while we interviewed Diane. He agreed.

We began by asking Diane to explain how she had met Nathan and, eventually, his friends from the San Fernando Valley.

Diane told us that she had known Nathan for about two months. They met at the Renaissance Faire. She worked at an ale stand, and he worked in security at night. They had seen each other regularly since then, including twice at Nathan's apartment. She met Duncan during the first of those visits, on June 11. She returned to Van Nuys on Friday, June 16, and stayed the weekend at the apartment with Nathan.

Diane next visited on Thursday, June 21. She said Nathan called her that morning and said he wasn't working that day. He invited her to come visit. She said Nathan also mentioned that he had to go out later that night, around 8 p.m., to go someplace with Duncan, but would not be gone for too long. She agreed to drive up. When she arrived at the apartment, at about 2 p.m., both Nathan and Duncan were there.

Diane said Ron got home around 6 p.m. He had groceries and offered to make spaghetti for dinner. While Ron was cooking, Diane asked him what he planned to do that night. Ron told her, "I'm going to a meeting." She did not ask him any more about it. Ron said Nathan and Duncan were going to give him a ride to the bus stop and they were all leaving the apartment at 8 p.m. While the spaghetti sauce was cooking, Ron took a shower, so Diane finished making their dinner.

At 8:15, Diane reminded them of the time and said they better leave, which they did. She did not recall Ron carrying anything when he left. Nor did she hear Ron say anything about UCLA or Mystic's Circle. "I didn't know what the Mystic's Circle was at that time," she told us.

Diane said she did not know where Nathan and Duncan were going, and they did not say what time they would be back.

Diane told us she did not leave the apartment while Nathan and Duncan were gone. They returned to the apartment a few minutes before 11 p.m. Nathan got home first and Duncan shortly after. She asked Nathan to watch *The Arsenio Hall Show* on television with her, which he did. Nathan told her that he and Duncan had been at the party upstairs for the past half hour. Diane thought Nathan and Duncan both seemed normal when they came home that night.

Diane recounted the call from Mr. Baker and overhearing Nathan speak with him. She and Nathan both thought it was a prank. They watched *Arsenio* until midnight and then went to bed.

The next morning, Diane woke up at about 8 a.m. and learned that Ron hadn't come home. An hour or two later, Mr. Baker called again and said the kidnappers had demanded $100,000. "I got worried then," she said. Duncan made a lot of calls to friends to check if anyone had seen Ron, she recalled.

She stayed at the apartment until Saturday. When she woke up that morning, around 9 a.m., Nathan was next to her in bed, sleeping. A few hours later, they drove to Perris, where she lived. Nathan stayed there with her for the next few days.

Once Garcia and I had finished questioning Diane, we conferred and decided we wanted to re-interview Nathan. There were some inconsistencies between the stories he and Diane had told us.

Among the inconsistencies we wanted to reconcile was if Nathan worked on June 21. He had told us that Duncan had picked him up from work. Diane, by contrast, said Nathan called that morning and invited her to come up to Van Nuys and spend the day with him, specifically because he was not working.

Nathan had also told us that he and Duncan went to Chatsworth Park to look for Ron on the Saturday morning after his disappearance. Diane told us that when she woke up that morning, Nathan was asleep in bed beside her, and that a couple of hours later, they drove to Perris. Did Nathan not go to the park with Duncan? Or did he go and return to bed without waking Diane?

When we requested to interview Nathan again, however, Diane's father informed us that he wanted me and Garcia to leave. He said the interviews had gone on for too long and that if his daughter and Nathan wished to continue, we should find another place. To be fair, we had been sitting at his dining room table for nearly three hours. Nathan and Diane both said they were willing to continue with more questioning.

The Riverside County Sheriff's Department had a substation in Lake Elsinore, a short drive from Diane's parents' home. Garcia and I drove there while Nathan and Diane followed in her car. The sheriff's personnel allowed us to use one of their interview rooms.

When we asked Nathan again whether he worked on June 21, he waffled a bit from what he'd told us earlier. "I'm not sure if I worked on the 21st," he said. "I think I did. I'm pretty sure Duncan picked me up."

As for his and Duncan's search of Chatsworth Park, he told us, "On Saturday, I now remember I woke up early. Diane was still asleep... It was early, 7 or 7:30 a.m.... Duncan and I went to Chatsworth Park. We looked up by the tracks and figured the park was too big. We went back home. I went back to bed. Diane was still asleep." He and Diane drove to Lake Elsinore later that day, around 2 p.m., he said.

We then asked Diane to tell us again about what happened Saturday morning. "Nathan could have gotten up earlier in the morning on Saturday and then came back to bed without me remembering," she told us. "Nathan was definitely there when I woke up at about 9 a.m."

We had one final question for Nathan. We brought him back into the interview room and asked him if he would be willing to take a polygraph exam.

Nathan immediately said he would not, citing his lack of confidence in the accuracy of the results. Even after we reiterated that a polygraph was one way that he could help us eliminate him as a suspect in Ron's murder, he declined to change his stance. One thing that Garcia and I did not know was whether Nathan had gotten word about Duncan's failed polygraph a few days prior and if that had influenced his decision.

Driving back from Lake Elsinore that night, Garcia and I discussed what we had learned that day and our impressions of Nathan, upon finally having met him in person.

We agreed that Nathan was very difficult to read. Had he told us the truth or was he lying?

"If he was involved, he's the coolest motherfucker I've ever dealt with," Garcia told me.

I took Garcia's appraisal as quite the backhanded compliment, especially coming from him. I considered my partner to possess one of the most finely tuned bullshit meters around, a sixth sense he'd honed over many years of working homicide cases and, before that, hundreds more cases in undercover narcotics. The fact that Garcia, as perceptive as he was, could not tell whether Nathan was bullshitting us showed how convincing he was.

Over the next few days, we received more occult-related calls and tips, which I attributed to the latest news coverage of the case. All the tips were checked but none proved pertinent to our investigation. Still, it was a reminder of how much information can result from the power of the press. Any story that mixed the subjects of murder and the occult was like catnip to the media, and apparently to the public. I wondered if it was the public interest that drove the media attention or the other way around. I knew that in reality satanic killings were extraordinarily rare.

Late on July 11, Garcia received a call from an attorney named Jim Barnes. Barnes informed Garcia that he was now representing Duncan Martinez in relation to the Ron Baker case. Barnes provided his contact information and made it known that all future inquiries regarding Duncan should be directed through him. Before the call ended, Garcia told Barnes that Duncan had not been eliminated as a suspect in Ron's murder.

Coincidentally, I was already familiar with Barnes. Two other cases I was then handling as a lead investigator, unrelated to the Baker case, were both contract murder cases. One of the defendants in those cases was currently represented by Barnes.

Given that Duncan had asked for an attorney after his polygraph exam five days earlier, and Barnes had called to confirm his representation, there was little doubt that our direct dealings with Duncan were over.

That seemed potentially problematic since Garcia and I had already experienced that Nathan was remarkably cool under pressure. Neither of us, after interviewing him in person, had come away with the sense that Nathan was the type who was likely to break, at least not without some additional leverage.

With respect to case strategy, the fact that we had one white suspect, Duncan, and one Black suspect, Nathan, had not really entered my mind. Assuming they were the killers, it was not uncommon in Los Angeles to have two suspects of different races. I'd investigated several such cases previously. Ron's murder wasn't a racially motivated killing.

Little did we imagine at the time how perceptions about race would enter the equation later. Or that it might affect how potential jurors would look at our investigation.

CHAPTER 8

"NOT A FLIGHT RISK"
(July 12 to 24, 1990)

IN JUST THE PREVIOUS few days, there had been several important developments in the investigation. None proved on their own that Duncan and Nathan were involved in Ron's murder. Collectively, however, they bolstered our suspicions that they probably were.

First, Duncan had failed his polygraph exam.

Second, following his failed polygraph, Duncan had made the decision to secure legal representation. This was, of course, his constitutional right. In my experience as a homicide detective, however, witnesses rarely requested an attorney when they were innocent of the crime about which they were being interviewed.

Finally, although Nathan had cooperated in granting us an interview, when we asked him if he would take a polygraph to help us eliminate him as a suspect, he had declined. Again, this was his right. But it was also my experience that innocent people generally did not refuse polygraphs or pass up the opportunity to exonerate themselves.

A new obstacle was that we could no longer initiate any contact with Duncan except through his attorney, Jim Barnes.

A few days after Garcia spoke with Barnes, we received a letter in the mail from him. The letter was dated July 11, the same day as their phone call.

Dear Detective Garcia,

This letter is to confirm our telephone conversation on today's date during which I advised you that I was retained on behalf of Duncan Martinez to represent him in connection with your investigation into the death of Ronald Baker. Duncan has been cooperating in your investigation up to this point and wishes to continue to cooperate. However, I must insist that any further cooperation on his part be channeled through my office, and that you no longer contact him directly. If you need information from Duncan please feel free to call my office and I will make either Duncan or the information available to you if at all possible.

The letter continued:

Should you determine that you wish to arrest Duncan on this offense I would very much appreciate a call so that I can arrange for him to surrender himself. I believe that his cooperation in your investigation has demonstrated that he is not a flight risk. In any event, please contact me immediately if Duncan is arrested on this case.

Barnes had closed the letter by requesting that his representation of Duncan, and the necessity of contacting him before talking with his client, be recorded in the chronological log of the Baker murder book, to ensure that any and all other LAPD investigators were aware of it.

Barnes's letter struck me as emblematic of a "shotgun" approach intended to cover all the bases. As one might expect, he had stressed the positives, namely Duncan's cooperation, his desire to continue cooperating, and that he was not a risk to flee. Unsurprisingly, he had made no mention of any negatives, including Duncan's failed polygraph exam.

I wondered if Barnes was signaling that Duncan had additional information to advance the investigation. That's how I took it, but it was hard to know for sure. After all, we had no idea if Duncan had told Barnes any more than he had told me and Garcia. If he was involved in Ron's death, had he admitted it to his attorney? Or was he maintaining complete noninvolvement, as he had in his police interviews?

Despite Barnes's apparent concern, Duncan's arrest was not imminent, let alone a foregone conclusion. His failed polygraph ate at me and raised many questions, but it was not sufficient probable cause for an arrest. We had to keep digging for more evidence.

Garcia placed a call to the Naval Criminal Investigative Service, the federal agency that maintains personnel records for the Marine Corps. During Duncan's polygraph, he implied he was a full-time Marine, but he was actually in the Marine Reserves. Garcia spoke to an agent and requested information detailing Duncan's service. He explained that Duncan was being looked at as a possible suspect in a murder case. The agent said it would take a few weeks to obtain the file.

Garcia also called Rita Tisinger, who managed the apartment building where Ron, Duncan, and Nathan had lived. Duncan and Nathan had moved out of the apartment after Ron was killed, since without his share of the rent, they could no longer afford to live there.

Garcia asked Rita about the two young women, Tewanda and Vickie, who lived upstairs in apartment #204 and had hosted a party the night of the summer solstice. Rita gave him both women's names but explained that they too had moved out, having been evicted earlier in the month. Garcia and I would have to track down the two women to ask them about their recollections of Duncan and Nathan that night.

On July 20, I contacted the Serology Unit at SID and spoke to one of its criminalists, Ron Raquel. I requested that Raquel test for the presence of blood on the two athames, or daggers, that belonged to Duncan and Nathan, which we had recovered at their apartment.

A few days later, on Monday, July 23, Garcia returned a call he had received from Gayle Baker, Ron's father. He told Garcia that Ron's final phone bill from the apartment had arrived. Garcia asked him to mail us a copy.

While Garcia had Mr. Baker on the phone, he let him know that we had no new information about Ron's case that we could pass on. Garcia guaranteed him that we were putting in a lot of hours trying to move the investigation forward. It had been our only focus since we were assigned the case. Mr. Baker indicated that he understood. Garcia asked for his family's continued patience.

Little did Garcia and I know that things were about to change in the Baker case. Changes that would alter not just the trajectory of the case but also multiple people's lives.

At 1:30 a.m. on July 24, Garcia was asleep at home when he was awakened by a ringing phone. The call was from Detective Headquarters Division, the entity within the LAPD responsible for coordinating detective services throughout the city. DHD was an around-the-clock operation located on the third floor of Parker Center. It often made notifications, especially during nonbusiness hours, to on-call detectives who needed to respond to crime scenes.

Garcia's notification was not about a new case, however. It was about Ron Baker's case. Fifteen minutes earlier, Lydia Archibald, Ron's and Duncan's friend, had received a frantic phone call from Duncan saying that he had been kidnapped.

Garcia notified me and we agreed to meet at Lydia's house in Hollywood. Minutes after he woke me up, I was in my car and on my way.

Before Garcia got on the road, he called the LAPD's Sound Lab and requested it respond to the location with equipment to record any further calls received about the kidnapping. He also called the security department at Pacific Bell and requested a phone "trap" on the Archibalds' home phone as soon as possible. Once the trap was in place, it would provide the phone numbers, times, and locations from which the calls originated. Due to the exigent circumstances involved, Pac Bell said it would have the trap set up within ten minutes.

Garcia and I got to the residence at about the same time, 3:30 a.m. Lydia told us that the phone had started to ring around 1:15 a.m. She was slow in answering because she had been sound asleep. Lydia said she heard Duncan Martinez's voice, beginning to leave a message, when she picked up. She then had a brief but very alarming conversation with Duncan.

Fortunately, the Archibalds' answering machine had activated just as Lydia picked up the phone. The recorder had captured the entire conversation, from the moment Lydia said her first word.

We crowded around the answering machine and listened to the tape.

"Duncan?" Lydia said at the beginning of the recording.

Duncan spoke in a near whisper and sounded breathless, like he was under duress. "They hit me, Lyd. Four of 'em... They got me in, like, a warehouse in North Hollywood. Get Garcia, let him know what's going on. Oh, fuck. I'm gonna try to get out of here."

"Duncan, call the police," Lydia urged him.

"Holy fu—shit," he replied. His words were followed by a groaning sound, as if he had just been punched or struck in a painful way.

This was followed by a noise that sounded as if the phone had been dropped on Duncan's end. Then the call disconnected.

The entire phone conversation lasted all of twenty-two seconds.

Garcia and I stepped outside to discuss what we had just heard. Both of us felt very skeptical of the call and believed it was highly unlikely that Duncan had in fact been kidnapped.

We were particularly doubtful, knowing what we did about Duncan's history of spinning tall tales. We were certain, for instance, that he had lied to Ron and others about traveling to the Middle East for the Marines and being involved in an assassination plot there.

Despite our suspicions, we nevertheless had to take the possibility of his kidnapping seriously. At least until such time as we could prove it was a false scenario created by Duncan, for whatever reason.

Having learned all we could from Lydia, Garcia and I decided at that point to separate. We could make better use of our time that way, given the number of tasks we still needed to accomplish that night.

I would head to the closest police facility, Hollywood Station, to make additional notifications and calls pertaining to our latest new assignment: the Duncan Martinez Kidnapping Case. Garcia would remain at the house a bit longer, in order to collect the answering machine tape as evidence.

It was a little after 4 a.m. when I arrived at Hollywood Station, my old stomping ground. My first call was to the LAPD's Communications Division, which served as the department's 911 center. I requested they make hourly broadcasts to police patrol units for the next twenty-four hours with a description of Duncan's car. The broadcasts would alert patrol officers citywide that the car might have been stolen in a kidnapping.

Next, I drafted a teletype known as a "felony vehicle stop." By doing this, Duncan's car would be entered in a nationwide database. Should a police officer anywhere in the US run his license plate, the database would show it was the car of a reported kidnapping victim.

At 6:45 a.m., Garcia called Duncan's mother. He informed her of the call her son had made and told her that we were taking it seriously. Garcia asked when she had last seen him. She said Duncan was supposed to come to her home for dinner at 7 p.m. the night before. He had not shown as expected and had not called her. She had no idea where he could be, she told Garcia.

Garcia asked her to call us immediately if she heard from him or learned anything about him from others, which she agreed to do. She provided Garcia with the name of Duncan's girlfriend, Jessica Auerbach, and Jessica's phone number.

Garcia then called Jessica and told her of Duncan's call and reported kidnapping. He asked her when she had last seen Duncan. Jessica said she was supposed to see Duncan the evening before. Their plan had been for him to pick her up at 6 p.m. and then go to Duncan's mother's house for dinner. Duncan had not shown or called her, which she said was unlike him.

I contacted Pac Bell and requested they conduct a search for the call made to the Archibald residence at 1:15 a.m. I could only hope that the kidnapping call from Duncan had been made from a location that would result in a billable call to the Archibalds' home address. If so, the call would likely be traceable.

Garcia meanwhile called Nathan Blalock and asked if he had heard from Duncan since the day before. Nathan said he had not. Garcia told him about Duncan's possible kidnapping. He asked Nathan to call immediately if he heard from Duncan. Nathan said he would.

Garcia was back in the office by midmorning. At 10:40 a.m., he received a call from Lydia. She told him that just a few minutes earlier a call had come in on her home line. She had answered and the caller had immediately hung up.

Garcia promptly called Pac Bell's security department and asked them to check if the call had been captured in their trap. The security official said the call had come in at 10:37 a.m. and been placed from a business called Audio Express, located on Victory Boulevard in Burbank.

Garcia contacted me, and I drove to Audio Express. Upon arriving at the business, I quickly learned that its manager, John Stallings, was Duncan's uncle. He told me that he had called the Archibald home a short while earlier but hung up when he received another call at his business. So much for that clue.

I made some additional inquiries about Duncan. Stallings said he'd last seen his nephew on May 14, well before Ron Baker's murder. He'd last spoken to him on July 20, when Duncan had called him at work. He also reported that on July 22 Duncan had told his grandmother that he was being followed. Stallings said he could not elaborate any further on what Duncan had told her.

Later that afternoon, Garcia spoke to Andrea Auerbach, the mother of Duncan's girlfriend, Jessica. She told him that between 1 and 2 p.m. that day Jessica had received about a dozen hang-up calls. On one of the calls, Jessica heard some background noise and a man laughing. Jessica thought the calls might be in response to her having paged Duncan multiple times.

Andrea Auerbach also informed Garcia that on July 21 Duncan had told Lydia he was being considered as a suspect in a murder case and he believed he was being followed.

The last thing Garcia and I did, at the end of our very long day, was call Jim Barnes, Duncan's attorney. Barnes told Garcia that he was concerned for Duncan's mental welfare and would notify us if he heard from him.

Before we left the office, Garcia and I discussed our perspectives on all of that day's unexpected developments.

Both of us had felt suspicious, from the start, of Duncan's alleged kidnapping. Our doubts were only enhanced when we had listened to the recording of the call. Nothing we had uncovered that day had pushed our beliefs the other way, in favor of it being a legitimate kidnapping. We agreed, however, that until we could disprove that Duncan was a victim and in jeopardy, we had to assume the worst and continue to investigate the kidnapping as real.

Driving home, I couldn't help but go over in my head everything we had been told by the people who were closest to Duncan. A no-show for dinner with his girlfriend and his parents. Telling multiple people that he was being followed. His own attorney sensing that his client's kidnapping claim was false, and possibly the result of some mental health issue.

It seemed very peculiar to me that if Duncan were indeed being held against his will he would call a female friend rather than 911.

Unlike Lydia, 911 could determine the location from which the call was made. If Duncan were truly in peril, he would want his location known, as it would improve his chances of being rescued.

What could Lydia Archibald do? She could contact the police. But that would not quickly benefit Duncan, whose claims could hardly have been more dire. If what he had said was true, his life was on the line.

CHAPTER 9

ON THE RUN?
(July 25 to August 3, 1990)

DRIVING INTO WORK THE next morning, I hoped that we would learn some concrete information soon about Duncan Martinez's mysterious disappearance.

The first call I made when I got to my desk was to the coroner's office. No Duncan Martinez and no unidentified bodies matching his description had come in overnight.

Garcia and I spent the rest of the day working the phones. We called several of Duncan's friends and acquaintances and received calls from several others. No one had heard from him or knew of anyone who had.

We learned from them that Duncan's friends were also calling one another to see if anyone had heard from him. Their many calls back and forth reminded me of an old-fashioned search party, but by telephone.

I was struck by the irony of it. Barely a month earlier, Duncan and Nathan had said they contemplated forming a search party for Ron, although they failed to follow through. Now Duncan's friends were actually searching for him.

As I'd seen happen in my past cases, rumors began to fly. Some of what Duncan's friends had heard and told one another was false. One such rumor was that the police had found the warehouse where Duncan had been held. We had to tell callers it was not true.

Among the people we checked with again, to see if they had heard from Duncan, was Nathan Blalock. He said he still had not.

Even though Duncan's status as a missing person was already in law enforcement databases, I prepared a formal "Missing Persons Investigation Report."

Garcia and I discussed whether a crime report for kidnapping was more appropriate, rather than a missing persons report, but we both rejected the idea. In the time since Duncan had made the call, too many red flags had surfaced that suggested his kidnapping had been staged. We could always make a kidnapping report later if our hunch proved wrong.

Little had changed by the following day. Lydia Archibald had heard nothing from Duncan since the night of his disappearance. Nor had she heard anything about his status from others, she told us. My contact in Pacific Bell's security department, Mark Yelchak, had not yet received any results in his search for more information on Duncan's kidnapping call to Lydia.

I received a call from Chuck Burnham, the UCLA PD officer who had been helpful early in our investigation. Burnham told me UCLA's police chief wanted to know if a reward offer from the university might assist our investigation.

I had been involved in several homicide cases in which rewards had been offered. In my experience, rewards rarely turned unsolved murder cases into solved ones. At the same time, making reward money available did provide an incentive, should someone have information they previously were unwilling to share.

Garcia and I agreed there was no downside. We told Burnham it could be helpful.

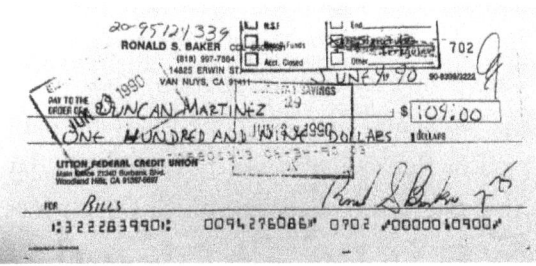

Ron Baker's personal check payable to Duncan Martinez (court exhibit)

That same day, Garcia and I received in the mail an envelope from Gayle Baker. Inside he had placed the final phone bill from Ron's apartment. He'd also enclosed a photocopy of Ron's check number 702, the one payable to Duncan Martinez in the amount of $109.00.

The photocopy showed only the front side of the check. I noticed on the face of the check several stamps, from the various financial institutions it passed through after it was cashed. At the top of the check was a stamp with multiple boxes for check status. The box marked with an X was for "Sig," next to which was a handwritten note, "Signature Irregular." Someone, likely from Ron's credit union, had flagged that the signature on the check did not appear to match Ron's.

We had already planned to request that SID's handwriting experts analyze the writing on the check and compare it to the handwriting samples provided by Duncan on the day of his polygraph. SID's analysis would require us to obtain the original cashed check, which was still in the possession of Litton Federal Credit Union, where Ron had held his checking account.

But in light of the credit union's flag, Garcia and I now had additional reason to believe check number 702 was forged, despite Duncan's claim that Ron had written him the check and given it to him as reimbursement for bills.

It was not the only stamp on the check that caught my eye. As I examined it more closely, I also noticed the check was stamped June 23, 1990, which I took to be the date that Duncan had cashed it.

Duncan had previously told us that the check was written by Ron on June 9 and then given to him.

Ron had disappeared on June 21. Until his body was identified, late in the day on June 24, he was believed to be missing but not dead. On June 24, the only people connected to Ron who were notified of his death were his parents, and that was done very late that night. Duncan was not informed of Ron's death until the following day, June 25. Yet we now knew that Duncan had cashed the check on June 23. The date stamp proved it.

Assuming that the check was a forgery—something I suspected but could not yet say for certain—then the date Duncan had cashed it was potentially very significant, I realized.

Duncan had cashed the check before he should have known that Ron was dead—unless, that is, Duncan was involved in the murder. I asked myself: *Would someone cash a roommate's forged check if they thought the roommate might return and learn of the forgery?* I doubted it.

I showed the check to Garcia and walked him through my thinking. If the check had been forged, why would Duncan cash it before he knew Ron was dead? Only if Duncan already knew Ron was not going to return would it make sense for him to cash it then. Otherwise, he would be taking a huge and irrational risk that the forgery would soon be discovered. In my view, it upped the likelihood that Duncan, and thus Nathan, were involved in Ron's murder. Garcia agreed.

I felt a rush of exhilaration, realizing that we had uncovered another factor pointing to their involvement. In our figurative baseball game against Duncan and Nathan, we had just scored a go-ahead run.

The next morning, Garcia received a call from Gayle Baker. Gayle told him that a few days before Duncan's disappearance, he was at their home to pick up some clothes. The Bakers had agreed to let Duncan store some belongings there after Ron was killed and he and Nathan had to give up the apartment. While Duncan was there, Gayle asked him about two long-distance charges he'd noticed on Ron's final phone bill, which the Bakers were responsible to settle. The two calls to Tempe, Arizona, had been placed on May 17 and June 2. Duncan was reluctant to admit to making the calls but eventually acknowledged he had, Gayle told Garcia.

Garcia, wondering what the calls might have been about, promptly picked up the phone and dialed the area-code-602 number.

A young woman answered. She identified herself as Yasmin Fouda.

Garcia asked her if she knew Duncan Martinez.

Yasmin said she did. She explained she had gone to junior high school with Duncan and they had once been close friends.

Garcia asked if she had recently spoken to Duncan, and she said she had. Garcia gave her the two dates indicated on the phone bill, May 17 and June 2. Yasmin said those dates sounded about right. Prior to Duncan's calls, Yasmin had not spoken with him in about a year and a half.

Garcia asked Yasmin what she and Duncan had discussed.

"We talked about all kinds of things," she said. "Duncan sounded weird. He told me he had some sort of secret mission in the Marine Corps and that some terrorists were after him. He sounded scared and nervous."

According to Yasmin, the last time she spoke to Duncan was in the early part of July, when he called her early one morning. That call lasted three to four hours, she told Garcia.

Later that morning, Garcia received a call from Kathy Kritzberg. Kathy had been at Ron's apartment when we first went there to meet Duncan, but we had not spoken with her since then.

Kathy said she felt the need to call and tell us about her last conversation with Duncan, about two weeks earlier.

Duncan had told Kathy, "There are so many ways I could get screwed." He said that the Marines wanted him to change his identity and that he was "the main suspect in Ron's murder." Duncan claimed the Marines had warned him the people who had killed Ron were after him. "Duncan also told me that he and Nathan had gotten a new job as security guards," Kathy said. "They were going to make about ten thousand dollars a week and get new cars." She also reported, "Duncan told me the Marines wanted him to leave town, but he wouldn't do that because it would make him look suspicious."

After Garcia hung up the phone, he and I discussed the ever-growing list of tall tales that Duncan had told his friends. Many of his stories he had perpetuated just before his alleged kidnapping. His covert mission with the Marines. His need for a new identity because terrorists were after him. His new lucrative security job that would pay him half a million dollars per year. The stories seemed ludicrous to me and Garcia. "Crazy shit," we agreed. I wondered what compelled Duncan to tell such dramatic lies. I knew we had been applying pressure on him recently. But whether that had contributed to his pathological lying, I couldn't say.

I headed home on time that Friday, if not a bit early. It was to be a weekend of youth softball games and a tenth birthday celebration for my older daughter, Hillary. I was relatively good at separating my work and family lives. Of course, I couldn't help but think sometimes, when I was off duty, about my active cases. But I tried not to let it affect my relationships with others, especially my daughters. I had been working homicide for a decade, so I was accustomed to it.

When I returned to the office on Monday morning, the first call I made was to Mark Yelchak. I hoped his search for information on calls received at Lydia's home on July 23 and 24, the time frame when Duncan made his kidnapping call, had been successful.

Yelchak informed me that his search had returned some numbers. One more legal obstacle remained, however. For him to provide the numbers, I needed to obtain a search warrant.

I added the search warrant to one of my always evolving to-do lists, which I religiously maintained to stay organized on the multiple cases I was working simultaneously.

Midmorning, Garcia received a call from Duncan's mother, Jeannie Martinez. She said that Duncan's attorney, Jim Barnes, had advised her to cooperate with us. "What I say to you is in the hope that you find him," she told Garcia. Jeannie was obviously very concerned for her son's well-being. This was also clear from the fact she was cooperating with the police detectives who had her son in the crosshairs on a murder investigation.

Jeannie informed Garcia that Duncan and Ron had a collection of license plates, and that Duncan could have changed the plates on his car.

She also told Garcia that over the past few months Duncan had been telling "bizarre stories." She didn't know whether his behavior might have stemmed from him using drugs.

In early May, she said, Duncan told her and her brother, Duncan's uncle, that he was involved in a bar fight in Culver City. Duncan said the fight involved five guys who were being kicked out of the bar, and during it, one guy's neck was broken. Duncan named two friends he was with, including one he knew from the Marines, Scott McCarty. According to Duncan, they were all taken to the Culver City police station, where they were asked if they wanted to press charges. Duncan told his mother that after he said no, they were released.

Also in early May, she said, Duncan told her his Marine Corps Reserve unit had been deactivated due to defense cuts. Despite that, he said, the Marines had called him in for a secret mission. A team of forward observers, including him, was being assembled for the mission.

Jeannie said that on May 15, Duncan explained the mission was to go to Iran and "take somebody out." He said he was supposed to leave the next day and was scheduled to return in two days, on Friday, May 18.

That Friday morning at eleven, Jeannie received a call from Duncan. He said he was calling from Union Station, the train station in Downtown LA. He had gone on the mission, he told his mother. His girlfriend, Jessica, was supposed to pick him up but had gotten lost en route. He asked if she could come pick him up. She agreed.

Jeannie said when she picked him up, he was very dirty and sunburned, and carrying a duffel bag. Duncan said that he and "four buddies" had gone on the mission, including McCarty and another marine named Stevens.

From Union Station, Jeannie took Duncan to her house. There, he further explained that on the mission, he and his fellow marines "took out" an Iranian general. They had been dropped off in the middle of the desert. During the mission, he claimed, Stevens went crazy and McCarty and a second marine were killed. He said that upon their return to Camp Pendleton, the Marine Corps base north of San Diego, they were briefed by the CIA. The CIA told them the Iranians knew who they were, and they needed new IDs because they were in danger.

Jeannie said she later went through Duncan's duffel bag and found a letter from someone. She did not identify who had written it. The letter talked about friendship and the value of it. "I hope you get through this," the letter said.

On May 20, two days after Duncan's return, Jeannie called the Marine Corps Reserve unit in Long Beach. She spoke with someone who informed her that Duncan was facing an "administrative discharge less than honorable," she said.

Jeannie told Garcia she thought, *Maybe this is what Duncan wanted to get away from*, when he made the kidnapping call and disappeared.

Duncan had done very well in boot camp, Jeannie said, although he did hurt his shoulder. She knew he had completed boot camp because she had attended the graduation ceremony.

Jeannie made an appointment with a psychologist and family counselor for May 25. When she called Duncan and told him, he agreed to go but did not commit 100 percent, she said.

On the day of the appointment, she called him, and he said he couldn't go. She got angry and blew up at him. "I told him he had to take responsibility," she told Garcia. Duncan told her the CIA might change his identity, and if not, he might change it himself.

Jeannie said that in June, on the Saturday before Father's Day, Duncan told her he had been in touch with Camp Pendleton and they were going to relocate him.

Later on, Jeannie said, her husband, Otto—Duncan's stepfather—called the family of McCarty, Duncan's buddy who supposedly was killed on the mission to Iran. The family lived in Michigan. They informed Jeannie's husband that McCarty was alive and stationed in the Philippines on full-time, active-duty status with the Marines.

While Garcia was speaking with Mrs. Martinez, I wrote a search warrant for the Pacific Bell telephone records and got a judge to approve it. I faxed the search warrant to Yelchak and awaited the results, keeping my fingers crossed the results would include the phone number and location from which Duncan had called Lydia.

The next morning, the last day of July, Garcia called a man named Ralph Latham. We'd heard that Latham, Duncan's friend and former high school track coach, had talked with Duncan shortly before he disappeared.

Latham confirmed to Garcia that he was once Duncan's coach. He said he had known Duncan since his tenth-grade year. Garcia asked when they last spoke and the nature of the conversation they had. Latham said he last saw him on July 20 at Santa Monica College. Duncan mentioned nothing to him about leaving town. Duncan did tell him about his roommate's murder. "He said he may get blamed for it," Latham said.

"What would be the motive?" Latham had asked Duncan.

Duncan had answered, "He owed me money, and it's a high-media case. They have to arrest somebody for it."

Garcia asked Latham for his thoughts about Duncan's alleged kidnapping.

"Something inside me tells me he's doing this for attention," Latham said.

Just before lunch, I received a call from Mark Yelchak with the eagerly anticipated phone search results. Yelchak verbally went through the list of almost twenty phone calls captured in his search of July 23 and 24, the day before and the day of Duncan's call to Lydia.

Frustratingly, nothing came back near the time of the kidnapping call, around 1:15 a.m. on the 24th. Multiple calls had been captured on July 23, but only two showed on July 24. One was at 9:01 a.m. and the other at 9:48 a.m., both some eight hours after the crucial call. I badly wanted to learn where Duncan had been when he called Lydia. Yelchak could sense my frustration and promised to continue searching Pac Bell's call records.

Late that afternoon, Garcia and I headed out to the San Fernando Valley. We had an appointment to interview Jeannie and Otto Martinez. Duncan had taken his stepfather's last name after his mother remarried. His birth name had been Duncan Gordon James.

We met Jeannie and Otto at Van Nuys Station a little after 5 p.m. Accompanying them was Duncan's uncle, Jeannie's brother John Stallings.

Garcia and I began by playing for them a recording of the kidnapping call received by Lydia. Otto said it was definitely Duncan's voice. Duncan's mother and uncle said they thought it probably was, but they couldn't say positively. They did not say whether they believed the call was legitimate or a hoax.

I felt for Jeannie and everything she had been put through. First her son was the focus of a murder investigation. There were serious questions even then about his mental state. Next came his bizarre disappearance. Had he really been kidnapped? Was he hurt or in danger? Where was he now? I could only imagine what it must be like as a parent to endure such emotional whiplash.

Jeannie said Nathan had called her earlier that day. He said if Duncan had fled, he had no idea why. Jeannie told us she and Otto spoke with Duncan after his polygraph exam on July 6. They told him he shouldn't have taken it, and he agreed.

Garcia and I had scheduled a second interview at Van Nuys Station, after Jeannie and Otto Martinez. We had located Tewanda Nicholson, one of the two women who lived upstairs from the apartment shared by Ron, Duncan, and Nathan. We wanted to ask Tewanda for her recollections of the party she and her roommate, Vickie Perez, had hosted at their place on the night of the summer solstice. Since then, both apartments had been vacated.

Tewanda explained that her and Vickie's apartment was located directly above Ron, Duncan, and Nathan's.

She recalled that it was on a Wednesday or Thursday night in June that she and Vickie had some friends over. Duncan and Nathan stopped by at about 10:30 p.m. "They came in and drank some beer," she told us. "Everybody was drinking forty-ouncers. Duncan and Nathan were playing Nintendo. Duncan is a pro at it. We ran out of beer and Nathan went to the store to get some more." Tewanda believed they left at about one o'clock in the morning. That was later than Duncan, Nathan, and Diane had told us but not a red flag. Again, discrepancies in time estimates among witnesses are commonplace.

We asked her about Duncan's and Nathan's demeanors that night, and if she noticed anything out of the ordinary about them or their clothing.

"Duncan and Nathan seemed normal, ready to party," she told us. "I knew that they had been drinking earlier. I didn't see anything unusual about them or their clothing."

The weekend after the party, possibly on Saturday, Duncan told her Ron was missing and there was a demand for money, Tewanda recalled.

Tewanda said she had only met Ron twice. She never heard any fighting from their downstairs apartment, only occasional loud noises.

It was later, sometime after Saturday, she recalled, when Duncan informed her that Ron was dead. "Duncan told me Ron had been stabbed several times and his nose had been cut off, and it looked like a sacrifice. He told me that Ron was in some kind of cult." She believed this conversation was on Monday after she got home from work, although it also could have been Tuesday. She told Vickie what had happened that same day.

Tewanda said Duncan usually talked with her about three or four times a week. "After Ron died, Duncan was gone," she told us.

She remembered Duncan and Nathan talking about getting new jobs as "heads of security," she said. "They said they were going to get new cars and they said they were going to make twenty-five hundred dollars a week. They later told me that the boss caught a guy that Duncan and Nathan had hired doing some coke. So they fired Duncan and Nathan too. Duncan was the one that told me this." They never discussed Wicca with her, Tewanda said.

On the afternoon of Wednesday, August 1, the day after we interviewed Duncan's mother and stepfather, and Tewanda, I received a shocking phone call from Duncan James, Duncan's biological father. Duncan and his wife, Shirley, lived in Bowling Green, Kentucky.

Duncan James reported that Duncan, his son, had shown up at their home in Bowling Green two days earlier, on Monday night, July 30. Duncan had come alone to see him, his father indicated. He said Duncan had stayed with them for two nights, July 30 and 31, and had left on August 1, earlier that afternoon. He took Duncan to the Greyhound bus station and Duncan had departed on a bus destined for somewhere in Florida.

We needed to notify Duncan's family and friends that he was safe and had not been kidnapped. My first call was to Duncan's mother, Jeannie, followed by Lydia and Nathan.

I also had to get Duncan removed from the missing persons database. This involved obtaining a copy of the original kidnapping report I had filed on Duncan eight days earlier. At the bottom of the report was an area reserved for case disposition, either "Unfounded," "Arrest," or "Other." I marked "Other." In the comments field, I wrote regarding Duncan, "Missing person traveled on his own volition to Kentucky to visit his natural father (Duncan James)... Detectives have not been able to interview missing person as he has since left Kentucky, possibly en route to Florida. Obviously the kidnapping ploy was just that—a ploy."

Later that same night, shortly after 10 p.m., Garcia received a call at home from the Detective Headquarters Division. The caller, detective and DHD mainstay Rick Dulgarian, apologized to Garcia for the late-night imposition but said he thought it was an emergency. Dulgarian was relaying a message that Jeannie Martinez needed to speak with him as soon as possible.

Garcia promptly called her at home.

Jeannie reported that Shirley James had called her mother, Duncan's grandmother, at about 11 p.m. Kentucky time. "Shirley told my mother she wanted to talk to me, mother to mother," Jeannie said. After Jeannie's mother relayed the message, Jeannie called Shirley in Kentucky.

Shirley told Jeannie that she felt Duncan had "flipped out" or was maybe on acid.

Shirley also said she felt Duncan was responsible for Ron's death. He never admitted to killing Ron but told Shirley "two completely separate stories about being in the park on the night of his death."

According to Shirley, Duncan was going to Frankfort, Kentucky, to get a new ID, then on to Miami "to do a job," which Shirley took to mean a "hit," or contract killing. Shirley said Duncan had hundreds of dollars and a sixty-day Greyhound bus pass, which would let him travel anywhere he wanted.

Duncan told Shirley he had sold his car and was using an alias, "Jake Atkins," because the Iranians were after him. Duncan also made the statement, "If I hadn't left him, this wouldn't have happened." Later, when Garcia briefed me on the call, we agreed this sounded like a reference by Duncan to leaving Ron in the park.

The next day, Garcia and I called Kentucky and spoke directly with Duncan's father and stepmother. Both steadfastly denied that Duncan had made any statements to them about being in the park with Ron on the night of his murder.

After we ended the call, Garcia and I discussed our frustration over the conflicting and changing stories we were hearing. Either Jeannie Martinez had misunderstood the information Shirley told her about Duncan's seemingly incriminating statements or someone was lying.

I wondered if it was Duncan's biological father who was responsible for Shirley's denials.

While we pondered our next steps, I contacted Litton Federal Credit Union, where Ron had had his checking account. I wanted evidence of his true signature, for comparison with the suspicious check. I confirmed its policy was to retain all original checks for its customers' accounts, but only for ninety days, after which they would be destroyed. That meant the original checks Ron wrote in May and June still existed. In order to obtain them, however, I would need a court order or a search warrant, the credit union informed me. I told them a search warrant would be delivered in the next few days.

I decided I would call Shirley again but this time while Duncan's father was at work. I believed she might be more open if he wasn't there. I hoped Shirley might clear up some of the discrepancies between what she had told us and what she supposedly had told Jeannie Martinez.

Shirley cooperated with no hesitation and seemed much less guarded than in our previous conversation, when her husband had also been on the line.

Shirley recalled that Duncan showed up on either a Sunday or Monday night. Duncan told them he did not want them to call his mother and stepfather. He also said he wanted to change his name but didn't say why.

Shirley asked Duncan why he was acting so secretive. "He said the Iranians were after him because he'd done a secret mission for the Marines," she explained in her Southern drawl. Duncan then told them his roommate had been stabbed to death. "He said the Iranians mistook his roommate for him because they look so much alike." They told Duncan the police had called. He instructed them not to call back.

Duncan told them he used to hang out at punk clubs in Los Angeles. Shirley said, "He had a black leather jacket while he was here. He said he used to wear that jacket to these clubs. He said he would put a knife in the back of his jacket in case he needed it." Duncan even showed her the place in the jacket where he had kept the knife. "It was a cut-out spot in the leather on the inside lining area, just above the rear bottom of the jacket. I asked him where the knife was now. He didn't answer me and just immediately walked outside, and just sat on the car staring for a couple hours."

They asked Duncan about the night his roommate died, Shirley told me. "He wouldn't talk about it. All he said was his roommate was stabbed in the park. He said the police probably thought he did it."

Shirley also recalled, "The night before he actually left, Duncan was outside. I told his father that I thought he did it. I think Duncan heard me say this, because he came right in and gave me a real dirty look. He wanted to leave that night, but it was around 11 p.m. and my husband wouldn't take him then. Duncan stayed up all night watching TV."

When Shirley left for work the next morning, at about 6:15 a.m., Duncan was still watching TV. "My husband later told me he took Duncan to the bus station about 2 p.m.," Shirley recalled. "He had told me he had a 2:45 p.m. bus to catch, I think to Miami. I believe it was 2:45 p.m." Duncan said he was going to see a friend named KC or possibly Casey.

Shirley said that while Duncan was staying with them, he walked to a pay phone, telling them that he was calling friends. "He also told us that he had sold his car and that he was using the name of James Lee Atkins."

I pictured Shirley on the phone in Kentucky, spilling the beans on her stepson, whom she hardly knew.

Shirley remembered that when Duncan first arrived, he was unloading his duffel bag and some wigs fell out. "He said he wears costumes," she told me. To me, it tracked with Duncan's paranoid behavior before he disappeared. I thought he might be using the wigs to disguise himself.

"My husband said that Duncan told him he was leaving our house en route to Frankfort to get some new ID," although she never heard Duncan say that herself, she clarified.

Later that afternoon, a few hours after I had spoken to Shirley, I received a call from Mark Yelchak at Pacific Bell. He had good news, he told me. A new batch of search results had captured more calls placed to Lydia's phone on July 24. One very brief phone call had come in at 1:14 a.m., almost the exact time that Lydia had said she received Duncan's kidnapping call.

Yelchak told me the 1:14 a.m. call was made from an area-code-702 phone number in Las Vegas, Nevada. He said the call was paid for by coin and lasted "0.6 minutes," or approximately 36 seconds, from connection to termination. This did not mean the conversation lasted for that entire time, he explained.

Yelchak also informed me that thirty minutes earlier, at 12:44 a.m., someone at the same 702 number called Lydia. That call showed only as an attempt, meaning it was captured but the call did not connect.

Yelchak provided the full number to me. He said he tried to obtain the exact location of the pay phone used to make the calls, but Nevada's Central Telephone security department would not release that information without a search warrant. He promised to fax me the information he had on the Las Vegas phone calls.

I thanked Yelchak for all of his help on the case. I jokingly warned him that I was sure I'd be bothering him again soon.

Garcia and I were elated that Duncan's phone call to Lydia had been captured after all. Although the mystery of whether Duncan was actually kidnapped had already been answered, with his voluntary appearance in Kentucky, the new information was still very significant.

It confirmed for us that Duncan had been lying about where he was when he made the call. He was calling not from a warehouse in North Hollywood, as he claimed to Lydia, but from a pay phone somewhere in Las Vegas. We now had corroboration, in the form of two independent pieces of information, that Duncan had faked his own kidnapping plot.

But where was Duncan now? And why had he fled?

CHAPTER 10

THE ROLLER COASTER
(August 6 to 22, 1990)

PATIENCE IS AN ESSENTIAL quality for a detective. Answers do not always come easily or quickly. Often it pays to wait things out, until a more opportune moment arises.

Sometimes, however, the desire to know now, rather than find out later, is too powerful to resist.

Such was the case when I returned to the office Monday morning, August 6.

I already had obtained the number for the pay phone, located somewhere in Las Vegas, that Duncan had called Lydia from the night he staged his own kidnapping.

I could have gone the official route, as suggested by my Pac Bell contact, Mark Yelchak, writing a search warrant, getting a judge to approve it, and serving it on Nevada's Central Telephone company, which would then reveal the pay phone's precise location.

It did not matter much, factually or legally, where exactly the pay phone was. The knowledge that Duncan placed the call from anywhere in Las Vegas meant that he had not been truthful with Lydia when he claimed he was calling her from North Hollywood.

Even so, I was curious to know the answer and I did not want to wait. I decided to take a more direct approach to finding the pay phone's location.

It was 7:40 a.m. when I dialed the number myself. After many rings, a man finally answered.

I identified myself as a police detective in Los Angeles. I explained to him that I needed to know where the pay phone that he had answered was located.

The man told me it was a phone booth on the "zero level" of Las Vegas' McCarran Airport, where a Greyhound bus stop was located. He said he was happy to help and glad he had picked up the ringing phone. Before he hung up, he told me he was curious if the matter he was assisting on was anything big.

"Just a murder," I replied.

Garcia and I agreed the pay phone's location made sense, given that, according to Shirley, Duncan had arrived in Kentucky with a sixty-day Greyhound bus pass. Regardless of how inconsequential the new information was, it was a satisfying and encouraging feeling, like making progress on a jigsaw puzzle, when facts you only just learned corroborated facts you already knew.

That same morning, Garcia spoke with an investigator at the Naval Criminal Investigative Service, from which we had requested information about Duncan Martinez's military service. She informed Garcia that Duncan had enlisted in the Marine Reserves and started boot camp in May 1989. He had graduated on July 28, 1989. The only discipline or administrative punishment imposed on him was after his graduation, when he failed to report for mandatory drills. In total, he missed twenty-one scheduled drills, she said.

Garcia mentioned Duncan's claims of having participated in covert activities for the Marines in Iran. She chuckled and guaranteed Garcia that Duncan was never sent on any mission to Iran. She confirmed that as a result of Duncan's unsatisfactory participation, he was due to be discharged with the designation "Other than Honorable."

Given all of Duncan's underhanded behavior since Ron's murder, I thought it was a fitting description for him.

Two days later, on August 8, I called the Serology Unit of SID. I requested they analyze Ron Baker's fingernail kit for any trace of foreign materials, including skin, blood, fibers, or hair. The fingernail kit contains clippings and scrapings from under a victim's nails. The evidence is routinely collected prior to a victim's autopsy by criminalists at the coroner's office, at least in certain types of homicide cases. These include sexually motivated homicides as well as murders involving close contact between a victim and a suspect, for instance a stabbing, strangulation, or physical altercation.

There was no telling how long it might take before Ron's fingernail kit was tested. I did not expect the results anytime soon. I knew requests such as this, for an unsolved case, often took a back seat to cases that were already solved. Solved cases, unlike unsolved ones, have upcoming court hearings and deadline dates by when lab results need to be completed.

Thankfully, some of the other requests I had made bore fruit more quickly.

I received from Litton Federal Credit Union the materials I'd sought a few days earlier. Among the records Litton had turned over were originals of eight of Ron's canceled checks, including the suspected forged check, number 702. Litton had also produced Ron's signature card and two pages of an account application he had filled out. All, apart from check 702, were known to have been completed by him and could be used as reference samples of his handwriting and signature.

The same day I obtained them, I delivered the checking account records to the Questioned Documents Unit of SID. Along with the handwriting samples provided by Duncan Martinez in July, they would be used to analyze the validity of check 702. The goal of the analysis I requested was twofold: to determine, if possible, whether the check had been forged, and to determine, if possible, whether it was Duncan who had written it.

The following Monday morning, I received a call from Andrea Auerbach, the mother of Duncan's girlfriend, Jessica. Andrea said that Duncan had called her house on Saturday the 11th at about 5 p.m. He told Andrea that he had been trying to call all day. He said he could not say where he was and asked her not to tell anyone that he'd called. He also said that he was in a hospital but "was okay now." Duncan claimed that he was with the Marines, who were in the process of relocating him. He ended the conversation by saying he would call again.

More extremely bizarre behavior by Duncan.

Wednesday morning, I was informed that SID had completed its analysis of Duncan's and Nathan's athames, their ceremonial daggers we had found in their apartment. I had requested SID test both athames for any traces of blood.

Alison Ochiae, a criminalist in SID's Serology Unit, called me with the results. Ochiae indicated that Duncan's dagger had tested positive for the presence of human blood at the base of the blade, where it met the hilt.

This definitely got my attention.

Ochiae then threw me a changeup. The amount of human blood she had found was insufficient to allow for ABO typing, a test that would tell us the source's blood type. Ochiae said she would continue to work on it by disassembling the knife, in hopes of finding more blood, enough for a sample, within the recesses of its hilt. Blood was sometimes known to seep into a knife's handle.

Ochiae had also obtained results from Nathan's dagger. Again, she had found the presence of blood, but the amount was insufficient even to determine whether its source was human or animal.

Human blood on Duncan's knife was an intriguing turn but also frustrating. We had run up against the limits of what science could tell us, at least at that time. In 1990, DNA analysis required much larger evidence samples to obtain results than needed today. In the case of Duncan's knife, there was too little for a DNA test. Whose blood was it? Had Duncan accidentally cut himself at some point? Or was the blood from someone else, perhaps Ron? We might never know.

Still, in light of the discovery of human blood on Duncan's knife, and some unknown type of blood on Nathan's, Garcia and I agreed it was time for another interview with Nathan.

We called and asked if he would meet us that night in Lake Elsinore, at the same Riverside County Sheriff's station where we'd last interviewed him. Nathan said he was game.

Shortly after we hung up, I received a call from Reymond Bordey, an examiner in SID's Questioned Documents Unit. Bordey informed me that based on his review of Ron Baker's known handwriting exemplars, Ron had not written any of the material on the face of check number 702. In Bordey's expert opinion, all of the markings on the face of the check had been imitations of Ron's writing. Bordey was unable to determine if the person who had imitated Ron's penmanship and forged the check was Duncan Martinez or someone else.

Duncan had repeatedly told us that Ron had made out the check to him and had given it to him. We now knew that was untrue. As Ron's roommate, Duncan had had access to Ron's checkbook. And by Duncan's own admission, he had cashed the check.

Bordey said he also examined the reverse side of the check, where there were "strong indications" that Duncan had written the endorsement signature and phone number. Bordey also said he might be able to upgrade his assessment if he was provided additional samples of Duncan's true signature.

I deemed it unnecessary at that time. After all, Duncan had already admitted to cashing the check.

Garcia and I received one additional lab report from SID that afternoon, before our drive to Lake Elsinore to meet Nathan. SID's Latent Prints Unit informed us that no fingerprints had been found on any of the evidence collected at the crime scene that we had submitted for testing. These included the pair of sunglasses, two packs of Marlboro cigarettes, and the broken remnants of beer bottles found in the tunnel near Ron's body.

Our day thus far had centered on crime lab results, most of which were positive and advanced our investigation. Now it was time to talk some more, face-to-face, with Nathan Blalock.

The Riverside sheriff's deputy who greeted Garcia and me in the lobby of their Lake Elsinore Station showed us to the same interview room we had used five weeks earlier, when we'd first met and questioned Nathan and his girlfriend, Diane.

As always, Nathan was jovial and cooperative. He did not appear irritated or intimidated by our request for another in-person interview.

The first thing Nathan said was that he had not talked to anyone associated with his former life in the San Fernando Valley. "I have not heard from Duncan since he left, not Lydia, not anybody," he told us.

We asked Nathan about Ron's personal check number 702, made out to Duncan, which SID had confirmed was a forgery. Nathan described overhearing a phone call that Duncan had received about a questionable check. Nathan could only recall it had something to do with an irregular signature.

We asked Nathan when that conversation took place.

Nathan recalled it was on a business day the week after he and Duncan found out Ron was dead. "Duncan told me that Ron had given him the check because Ron owed him some money for bills. I know Ron did owe Duncan some money, like for the cable bill. I don't know how much money was owed. And like I've said before, Ron owed money for Duncan's car."

We asked Nathan if he ever saw the questionable check. He said no. He also denied writing the check himself or signing it. Nathan said he had no knowledge that Duncan forged the check or that anyone else did.

Nathan then volunteered that after we last interviewed him, Duncan's mom had called him. "This was two or three weeks ago," he said. "She told me that a marine buddy that Duncan told me got killed is really alive. She said several things that Duncan had told me were lies."

We pressed Nathan on his and Duncan's previous statements about the last time they saw Ron. Had they dropped Ron off at the bus stop or had they taken him someplace else, for instance to a friend's house, or to Chatsworth Park?

"Duncan and I did take Ron to the bus stop that night. We didn't take him to a friend's or to Chatsworth Park," he maintained.

We informed Nathan of the story we had heard via Shirley James, that Duncan had told her he was in the park with Ron the night of his murder.

"I don't know why Duncan would say that, unless he's just saying a lot of things that are flaky," said Nathan. "If someone said we dropped Ron off somewhere else besides the bus stop, then they've gotten some wrong information or else Duncan is flaking out and saying things that weren't true."

We asked Nathan when he'd last spoken with Duncan and what they'd discussed.

"I last talked to him while he was at Lydia's. He was supposedly working at some audio place, dubbing in movie soundtracks."

We asked Nathan if Ron drank any alcohol with him and Duncan, whether during dinner that night, at the elementary school where he and Duncan went drinking later, or at Chatsworth Park.

"No," Nathan said. "Ron did not drink with us that night and he didn't drink anything at dinner. Duncan and I went to his elementary school and drank until we went back to the apartment building. This is all like I told you before."

That much, I had to concede, was true. It was the same account Nathan had given us in our initial interview with him.

We asked when he found out Duncan had surfaced in Kentucky, after his kidnapping call.

"I first learned that Duncan was in Kentucky from you," he replied, indicating Garcia.

We requested Nathan once more talk us through the first few days of the case, from the time he and Duncan dropped Ron off at the bus stop to when he left for his family reunion in Michigan. Again, he retold his story with consistency, unchanged from his prior statements.

Nathan did, however, say one thing that was new and somewhat curious. It came when we asked him, if he knew Duncan had killed Ron, whether he would lie on Duncan's behalf.

"If I knew Duncan did that to Ron, right after it happened I would have lied to you to protect Duncan," Nathan said. "Now I'm not so sure I would, because he's done a lot of crazy things and I guess he's not the kind of person I thought he was."

We asked Nathan about the knives that he and his roommates carried at the Renaissance Faire, and their experience there. Ron's knife was still missing, and we did not tell Nathan that his and Duncan's had tested positive for the presence of blood.

"Ron told me he lost his Faire knife at the Renaissance Faire," Nathan said, before clarifying that actually he had overheard Ron telling that to Duncan. "Duncan only went to the Faire three or four times. He was always in costume. I always went to the Faire on my own."

Nathan said people at the Faire used their knives to eat and cut food. "I never used my knife. Well, I might have used it to carve my name in a wax candle. I never hung out with Ron or Duncan at the Faire. I hung with people I knew from the Northern California Faire. I saw them a couple of times at the Faire. I only dressed in costume once."

Nathan later recalled, "I did use my knife once to eat—that I remember. I had some cheese and a meat roll loaf of some kind."

We showed Nathan photos of his and Duncan's daggers. He identified them and said which one belonged to whom. We asked Nathan if there was any reason he would have blood on the knife he had identified as his own. He said no, and that he had never used his knife to stab anyone or for hunting. He could only recall using it once at the Faire to cut the meat roll loaf, as he said earlier. He told us he had no knowledge of where any blood on Duncan's knife might have come from.

We also asked Nathan to give us his thoughts on Duncan's temperament and his history of getting into fistfights. "Yes, Duncan is cocky and arrogant. Yeah, he was involved in several fights. I was never there at any of the fights he got into. He'd tell me about them later. Yes, Duncan could get pissed off very easily. Once, we were wrestling and I was getting the better of him. All of a sudden he flipped out and started really seriously choking me. Then I resisted a lot and he settled down and apologized."

He went on: "Duncan never talked in detail about the way the Marines taught him to kill. I've seen Duncan really pissed off at Ron before, but he never hit him or anything. He looked at Ron as a wimp, a pussy. He wouldn't talk to Ron while he was mad. He'd wait until he calmed down. I've never seen Duncan drunk enough to get violent. I've known Duncan since November 1989. I never knew him to lie to me until his mom told me all the lies he'd told me."

Nathan recalled Duncan one day got a letter in the mail from the military. "He opened it and said he'd gotten promoted."

We questioned Nathan about Duncan's leather jacket, which Shirley had said Duncan told her had a hidden slot in the lining where he could keep his knife.

"Duncan did have a black leather motorcycle jacket," Nathan confirmed. "It had ties on the sides. They were tied tightly. He wore it a lot. He said nothing about hiding a knife in that jacket or having a slit in it to keep a knife. I wore that jacket once and never noticed anything like that, but I didn't look on the inside lining area."

Nathan said the only knife he knew Duncan to have was the one in the photo we'd shown him. "For a short time he also had a bayonet, but

I think he returned it to the Reserves. I only saw it once, probably in late 1989. I never saw or heard him talking about having a Rambo or survival knife. Duncan never talked about stabbing or cutting anyone."

We asked Nathan to tell us about his, Duncan's, and Ron's drug use.

"After Duncan got out of the Marines, I know he smoked some pot. In early 1990, I know he used speed at least every other weekend. This was while he was at Everything Audio. I did it with him a couple of times. He said he had used acid in his earlier days. Oh, yeah, on New Year's Eve, everyone at the party used acid." Nathan recalled Duncan, Ron, Jenny, Lance, and a few other friends were there. "This was the night we went up to the tunnel. Ron told me he also used acid while at the Faire."

We asked Nathan what he knew about why Duncan had left his job at Everything Audio.

"Duncan quit Everything Audio because he got in an argument with the girl in charge. Then within a week or so of leaving Everything Audio, he packed his bags and said he was leaving for the Middle East. He came back about four days later. He had a real deep tan and there was sand in his bags. He then said he'd been flown to Africa to gear up for a military mission and then went on to do the mission in Iran."

It was dusk by the time Garcia and I left Lake Elsinore. We used the drive back to LA to take stock of everything that we had learned that day.

We were excited to receive the handwriting results, which showed Duncan had lied to us about the check he cashed. At the same time, we felt frustration at the blood results on Duncan's knife, knowing we'd probably never learn whose blood it was. Then there was the seemingly impenetrable roadblock known as Nathan Blalock. He had maintained his composure and total innocence, firmly sticking to the same story he'd told us each time we'd questioned him.

Garcia and I couldn't help but laugh as we discussed Duncan's bizarre array of tall tales: his supposed military missions to Iran and Africa; his story to Shirley that a retaliatory Iranian attack intended to kill him mistakenly resulted in Ron's murder; his desire to adopt a new identity; and of course his faked kidnapping, when he claimed to be held hostage in a North Hollywood warehouse.

Was Duncan's kidnapping ploy, obviously intended to cover his disappearance, also an indication of his consciousness of guilt for Ron's murder? Or had he fled because he felt pressure building from his failed polygraph and our increasing focus on him? Maybe it was both.

No matter how we cut it, Garcia and I knew we had no case yet, despite the circumstantial evidence we had uncovered. Duncan was gone, and who knew when, or even if, he might resurface. What remained was Nathan, but as Garcia once put it, he was "the coolest motherfucker." And so far, he'd shown absolutely no signs of breaking.

August 21 marked two months since Ron Baker was murdered. Garcia and I also had the date circled on our calendar as an important due date. The previous week, we had begun a time-consuming project, one that many homicide detectives dread and consider a chore.

Our task was to write a comprehensive summary of Ron Baker's murder case and where our investigation stood two months in. Formally, the summary was titled an "Unsolved Murder Investigation Progress Report." Informally, LAPD homicide detectives usually referred to it as a "sixty-dayer," because it was due sixty days from the date of any unsolved murder. It was the most thorough, detailed report a detective would need to write on any unsolved case. Often, it was more exhaustive than the "Follow-Up Investigation" report required after a case was solved.

Although the focus of the sixty-dayer was to recount the key facts and investigative actions taken by detectives since the inception of a case, its purpose was forward-looking. Any conscientious homicide detective knows that some percentage of their cases will still be unsolved when it comes time for them to transfer to a new assignment or retire. The sixty-dayer thus served as a "message" to future detectives who might come along years later and review the case. It often contained the personal thoughts, insights, and theories in the minds of the detectives who authored it.

Garcia and I chose to meet at his home and work on our sixty-dayer there. No office distractions meant we could pull it together more quickly.

The format of the report was highly standardized, with numbered sections that pertained to specific aspects of the case. Section 3, for instance, covered the crime scene. Section 11 contained information about the victim, and section 12, about any suspects.

We spent two full days with the contents of the murder book spread out across Garcia's dining room table. The end result was a narrative that spanned eighteen single-spaced typed pages.

Our opening synopsis ended with a paragraph unlike any I'd ever written in a sixty-dayer: "At the time of this report, no suspect has been identified. Additionally, although the victim's property was missing, no motive has been definitively established, as the reader will learn in the following narrative. So sit back for a wild ride and hold on to your hat."

In the section for suspects, we wrote: "Due to some of the actions of the victim's roommates, Duncan Martinez and Nathan Blalock, but particularly Martinez, they have been viewed as <u>possibly</u> having some form of involvement or knowledge about the victim's death."

Our report concluded with a summary of the factors we had uncovered that pointed to their involvement in Ron's murder:

> Detectives are not intending to say that they fully believe that Martinez and Blalock are involved in Baker's death. Detectives have not excluded the possibility that they are not involved and that the killer or killers could be someone other than Martinez and/or Blalock. However, anyone who has read this narrative must agree that the factors pointing to their involvement are extensive.
>
> The below areas are all ones which would tend to make one believe that Martinez and Blalock could well be involved in Ronald Baker's murder, especially when they are considered in viewing the totality of them together.
>
> 1. Human blood was found on Martinez's knife, as well as the possibility of human blood found on Blalock's knife.
> 2. The forgery of Baker's check and the fact Martinez cashed it. This is further evidence in that Martinez cashed it on June 23, before Martinez could have known that Baker was dead unless he was involved in Baker's death... Additionally, Martinez said Baker gave him the check which we know is not true.

3. Duncan Martinez and Nathan Blalock cannot account for their own whereabouts on June 21 for a critical two-hour period, other than their own alibis for each other.

4. A small fact that bothers detectives is that the victim did not take his house key when he left the night of June 21... However, if you left with your roommates and planned to be with them and return with them, you might be less likely to take your own key.

5. Associates of the victim say he always took his backpack with him when he went out. Detectives found his backpack on his bed.

6. The time factors involved on the night of June 21 are a concern to detectives. If the victim left on a bus between 8:30 and 9:00 p.m. and went to the UCLA area first, then drank to the point where he got at least a .21 blood-alcohol level (probably two hours), it might be difficult to believe he could be killed and a ransom call made by 11:50 p.m.... It should be noted here that detectives believe that the victim most likely was already dead when Baker's father received the first phone call... This is in part based on the fact that Baker's body was discovered only 1½ hours after the first ransom demand...

7. The victim obviously had been drinking, which was not something he would do by himself, especially to a .21 level. This is coupled by the fact Martinez and Blalock were out drinking. Were they drinking together?

8. The victim, Martinez and Blalock were all aware of the tunnel location and had been there together before. It is very definitely the kind of location they might all go drink together.

9. The statement made by both Duncan Martinez and Nathan Blalock about going to Chatsworth Park to look for the victim when he was allegedly kidnapped... If someone was supposedly kidnapped, why would you go to one of the victim's hangouts to see if he was there?... Is it possible they went and either decided they didn't want to go

in and possibly see the results of what had happened or did go in and found Baker's body gone? These are just being discussed in a speculative way to give any subsequent reader thoughts that have run through the minds of the current detectives.

10. There is also the ransom demand calls made to the victim's parents... The caller tried to disguise his voice. Would a stranger attempt to disguise his voice?... Could the caller have been Duncan Martinez or Nathan Blalock? It is interesting to view the possibility of Martinez staging these ransom calls when detectives determined he soon afterwards staged a phone call claiming he himself was kidnapped and being held. There is no question he staged this call.

11. Obviously, Martinez's own actions following the killing of Baker must be viewed. He began acting extremely paranoid, even before detectives began indicating that he could not be eliminated as a suspect. Then he stages his own kidnapping and flees the area... Does this mean he doesn't plan on returning? He was also talking about taking on a new identity.

12. Martinez failed the polygraph in all areas and this, along with all other areas of concern, has to make one consider he failed it because he was involved...

This compilation of facts and opinions obviously does list sufficient reasons to make one think strongly of the possibility of involvement of Martinez and Blalock in Baker's killing. Detectives believe it is very possible they are or that one is and the other is covering for him. However, as mentioned before, detectives have not closed their minds to some other explanation on how Ronald Baker met his demise.

We submitted our report on August 22, exactly two months after Detectives Crocker and Moseley were called to the tunnel crime scene. A lot had transpired since then. Garcia and I had significantly moved the case forward.

Nonetheless, we still had insufficient evidence to connect Duncan or Nathan to Ron's murder for the purpose of charging either. They were each other's alibi for the few hours between when they left the apartment with Ron and when they returned home and went to the party upstairs. We could not even put them in the park on the night Ron was killed. Neither Garcia nor I would have felt comfortable trying to charge them with the evidence we had.

For me, despite everything that pointed to the likely involvement of the two roommates, I still could not get past the feeling the Duncan and Nathan angle did not make sense. Granted, many murders do not make sense. In this case, however, Ron Baker and Duncan Martinez had been described by many people as best friends. Other people, including Duncan and Nathan, had described Ron as a gentle and likable soul, someone you could not be mad at. If all three had been drinking together at the tunnel, an argument was possible and could have factored in. But there was no indication of anything brewing between the roommates that might have raised the animosity to such a level as to provoke murder.

Under another theory, that only one roommate had attacked Ron while the other had witnessed it, which roommate was the likely aggressor? If Nathan had attacked Ron because of some spat, wouldn't Duncan have tried to intercede, as a longtime, close friend of Ron's? In the reverse scenario, could Duncan, as a longtime roommate and possibly Ron's closest friend, have reached such a boiling point as to savagely stab Ron multiple times, and then finish by slitting his friend's throat? It was difficult for me to believe either of these scenarios.

Yet despite our best efforts to eliminate Duncan and Nathan as suspects, we were unable to do so. The evidence stubbornly suggested that Duncan and Nathan had had a hand in Ron's killing, whether or not it made sense to me and Garcia.

Around this time, one of my favorite off-duty activities was taking my daughters to local amusement parks, of which there were many in Southern California. My older daughter, then ten years old, especially loved white-knuckle roller coasters, as did I.

It struck me how much working certain homicide cases felt like riding a roller coaster. At the beginning of an investigation, there is a sense of anticipation about what the new case holds, like a coaster leaving the platform. As you move forward on the tracks, and pick up your first promising clues, things ratchet up. Day by day, clue by clue, the coaster climbs until you reach a peak. A major investigative advance feels akin to the adrenaline surge after the coaster's downward whoosh. Inevitably, the tracks level off and the coaster's speed slows. The investigation continues to move forward, but at a more familiar, plodding pace.

Garcia and I did not know when another plunge and rush might come in the Baker case. Weeks? Months? A year? No one could say. I just knew I wanted to stay on the ride until it ended.

CHAPTER 11

"THINGS TO DO"
(September 4, 1990 to January 21, 1992)

WHEN WE RETURNED TO work following Labor Day weekend, Garcia found on his desk an envelope from Kay Baker. Inside was a note from her and a handwritten list titled "Things To Do." Kay's note explained that she and Gayle had discovered the list among the items moved from Ron's apartment and temporarily stored in their garage following his murder. Kay said in her note that the list's handwriting was not Ron's. Garcia and I both thought the handwriting resembled Duncan's.

The list read in full:

Things To Do
1. Set up New ID
2. Sell car (Asap)
3. Set up new work
4. Find out McCarty's parents # (or Johnson's)
5. Check w/ USMC, see what they are pulling
6. Smooth things @ EA
7. Get New Car thru?? (Jessie)

Once we read the list, we had no doubt that Duncan had written it. Each of the seven tasks pertained to subjects he had discussed with family and friends prior to his staged kidnapping. The "EA" in the sixth task appeared to be a reference to Everything Audio, his last job before he skipped town.

We had previously shared with the Bakers our suspicion that Duncan and Nathan were involved in Ron's murder.

Initially, the Bakers' reaction to the idea of Ron's roommates' involvement was total disbelief. They could not wrap their heads around the possibility that Duncan, Ron's best friend and someone they had welcomed into their home, could be capable of killing Ron.

With their discovery of the "Things To Do" list, however, their disbelief about Duncan's possible involvement seemed to thaw. Gayle and Kay both made that known to us when we spoke with them about the list they had come upon.

The discovery of the list was important for a couple of reasons. First, it supported that his disappearance had been a planned scheme. Second, it showed his desire to make himself difficult to locate by assuming an alias and switching cars.

Our options to push the case forward, however, were now very limited. Duncan was in the wind and there was no immediate purpose for more interviews with Nathan. We had requested forensic testing on various items of evidence and were waiting on SID for the results. There was little follow-up investigation that we had not already completed. For the time being, we just had to wait and see.

A few weeks later, on the night of Tuesday, October 9, I had just fallen asleep when the phone rang. I looked and saw it was almost eleven o'clock.

The call was from an officer at Detective Headquarters Division. Garcia and I were the on-call detectives from RHD that week. I knew I was about to get a new case.

The caller informed me an off-duty officer had been involved in a shooting in Hollywood Division and had sustained serious injuries.

I had worked at Hollywood for more than a decade and had left for RHD only three years earlier. I told the caller that I likely knew the wounded officer.

"You definitely know him," he responded. "It's Russ Kuster."

My heart dropped.

Kuster was a close friend and had been my supervisor for the five years I spent in the Hollywood Homicide unit. It was Kuster who had given me my first shot working homicide. I had loved every minute working for him.

I told my wife Russ had been shot and was in serious condition. She was shaken and asked me to call her with updates, no matter what time.

I hurried to my car and drove to Hollywood in a daze. I felt like I was in an episode of *The Twilight Zone*. Russ had always exuded an air of invulnerability. He was the last person I would have expected to hear having been gunned down.

I arrived at the shooting location, the Hilltop Hungarian Restaurant on Barham Boulevard. The restaurant's bar was a known Kuster hangout.

As I exited my car, I saw Bud Arce, another Kuster protégé.

Arce shook his head and advised me that Russ didn't make it. He had been shot multiple times by the suspect. He was transported to the hospital but at 10:30 p.m. succumbed to his injuries. Arce told me the suspect was also dead, having been shot several times with return fire from Kuster. The suspect's body was still inside the restaurant, Arce told me.

I was quickly briefed on what had happened. The suspect, Bela Marko, was a regular. Earlier that evening, he had become drunk and belligerent and was asked to leave by the manager. Marko later returned, with Kuster now sitting at the bar. Marko was armed with a laser-sighted handgun, which he brandished at people inside the establishment. One patron told Marko to put the gun away and identified Kuster as a police officer. Marko pointed the gun at Kuster and fired several shots. Kuster returned fire. Both were shot several times during the exchange of gunfire.

I was only at the scene for a short time before my supervisor ordered me to leave. He told me I did not need to be there, given my close relationship to Kuster. Several other detectives, among them Garcia, had also responded to the location and could handle the crime scene.

Driving home, I thought about the irony of it. Kuster had been a detective and supervisor at Hollywood Homicide for more than fifteen years. Now he would be listed as a murder victim in the same ledgers he had kept for so many years.

Fittingly, through his final actions, Kuster solved and cleared his own murder when he gunned down his killer.

I somehow managed to fall asleep when I got home. I woke again to a ringing phone at 6:30 a.m. It was my father, who minutes earlier had heard a news report about Kuster. He knew we were close and wanted to make sure I knew before I went to work and was caught off guard.

Later, thinking back on my dad's call, I felt so appreciative of him. I knew he did it because he was thinking of me and, in his typical quiet way, hurting for me.

I arrived at Parker Center midmorning and made my way to the RHD squad room. I thought I was good to go.

When I walked into the room, full of detectives, all eyes seemed to fall on me. My coworkers knew I had worked with Kuster for years. I started to walk to my desk on the far side of the room. It hit me that I wasn't good to go. I dropped my head and my eyes filled with tears. I took a seat at my desk, head still down, and wept.

One of the homicide lieutenants, John Zorn, put his arm around my shoulders. "You know you don't have to be here," he told me.

I nodded that I understood and said I would be okay. I knew even then that I'd never forget Zorn's gesture and kindness.

Garcia brought me up to speed. Bela Marko was a career criminal and on parole from prison in Nevada. Marko was also in the United States illegally from Hungary. This meant he should have been subject to an immigration hold upon completion of his Nevada prison sentence. Instead, he had been released, a mistake with deadly consequences.

The night after Kuster's death, my wife and I had tickets, purchased long before, to a James Taylor concert, her favorite singer. I felt drained and didn't know if I would be able to enjoy myself. My wife left it up to me whether to go. We went.

It was a beautiful October night, at an outdoor venue with lawn seats. The music and Taylor's performance were also beautiful. When he got to one of his most popular, classic songs, "Fire and Rain," the lyrics hit me unexpectedly hard, especially the last lines of the verse:

I've seen lonely times when I could not find a friend,
But I always thought that I'd see you again.

Once again, tears flowed uncontrollably. I knew from that moment on I would never be able to listen to that song without thinking of Russ Kuster.

Detective Russell Kuster, circa late 1980s (courtesy of LAPD)

Throughout the fall of 1990, the Baker case remained, for all intents and purposes, dormant.

In early January 1991, we received a report from SID's Serology Unit with their analysis of Ron's fingernail kit, taken prior to his autopsy. We had requested the analysis in August, six months earlier.

The report stated, "Both the right and the left fingernail scrapings contained red material, which gave a positive chemical test indicating the presence of blood." That blood was found under Ron's fingernails was not a surprise. Given the many defensive wounds on his hands, and heavy loss of blood, it would have been more shocking if no blood had been found under his nails.

The obvious question, unanswered in the report, was whose blood it was. Garcia and I contemplated requesting DNA analysis of Ron's fingernail kit at some later point, once testing capabilities had progressed. But according to the DNA training we had received, to obtain a DNA profile it was necessary to have a sample about the size of a quarter. We did not have that.

From time to time, Garcia and I would call various friends of Duncan's, including Nathan, simply to inquire if they had heard from him, or anything about him from someone else. Both questions were always answered, "No."

The roller coaster felt as though it had ground to a halt. Even as the Baker investigation seemed to stall, however, the city and LAPD were barreling toward catastrophe.

In the early morning hours of March 3, 1991, an extremely disturbing encounter with immense and far-reaching consequences occurred in Los Angeles. For years to come, it would reverberate through the LAPD, the city, and throughout the country and world.

That it would alter the public's perception of the LAPD was instantly apparent. But few at the time could have imagined how profoundly it would change society, and Los Angeles itself.

At about 12:30 a.m. that fateful morning, two California Highway Patrol officers went in pursuit of a speeding car on Interstate 210, an east-west freeway through the San Fernando Valley. The car carried three people, all young Black men: two passengers and its driver, twenty-five-year-old Rodney King.

The car pulled off at an exit and eventually stopped at an intersection in Lake View Terrace, within the LAPD's Foothill Division. LAPD units responded to back up the CHP officers. Because the stop was within the city of Los Angeles, the LAPD officers assumed control of the situation. While attempting to take King into custody, three of the LAPD officers at the scene struck him fifty-six times with their batons, leaving him with severe injuries, including multiple facial fractures and a broken leg.

George Holliday, a man whose apartment overlooked the scene, happened to have a camcorder and videotaped the beating. Holliday's recording was soon obtained and broadcast by local TV news stations. The graphic footage sparked a media frenzy and worldwide condemnation.

Within days, the "Rodney King video" was playing seemingly nonstop on TVs across the country and globe. Public outrage about police brutality exploded. The more the video was played, the more condemnation grew. The LAPD was at the center of the turmoil.

The public reaction was understandable. The first time I saw the video, on the TV news like most everyone else, I felt sick. Seeing with your own eyes is so much more visceral and affecting than reading an account. Watching the video, I wished I could somehow turn back the clock and undo it all, for so many reasons. No matter what had led up to it, it hurt to watch another person, any person, being treated so roughly, literally beaten into submission.

In my fifteen years on the job, I had never experienced anything like the intensity of the firestorm prompted by the Rodney King video. As an LAPD officer, I got a taste of what it is like to be judged for the actions of others and to have the worst assumed of me because of my occupation. It felt as if all LAPD officers were being painted with the same broad brush.

I was proud of my service as a police officer and detective. I was proud of the way most of the officers I knew did their jobs. I did have a problem with some officers. Some were lazy. They didn't see police work as a calling and did the minimum, clocking in and out. I didn't like some officers for the way they treated people, whether with indifference or needless disrespect. But most of the officers I worked with cared about their jobs and treated people at least respectfully.

Regardless, there was no question the Rodney King beating had instantly and permanently changed how the LAPD was perceived. In terms of public trust in the police, especially in LA's large Black community, it was a terrible setback. The LAPD and its officers would have to change, and earning back the Black community's trust would not be easy.

Personally, I also knew the backlash to the King beating would negatively affect my work as a detective. Detectives need witnesses. Their cooperation is paramount. Without willing witnesses, it is significantly harder to investigate and solve cases. It is most effective to have witnesses who trust the detectives or even like them. The same is true of victims and victims' families, once again particularly in LA's Black and other minority communities.

My approach with witnesses, whatever their race and background, was always genial and low-key. When I introduced myself on the job, it was "Hi, I'm Rick Jackson." Being called "Detective Jackson" felt too authoritative and didn't suit my personality. The fallout from the Rodney King incident made me resolve to try to be more aware. I needed to continue to treat people with kindness and respect. It was important not just to be a better person but also to be a better detective. I believed my approach helped me be more effective at my job.

Friday morning, March 7, Chief Daryl Gates summoned representatives from RHD to his office. Among the attendees were the two on-call detectives from Major Crimes, Bud Arce and his partner, J. R. Kwock, and Lieutenant John Zorn, who was now our supervisor.

Chief Gates told them our unit was assuming investigative responsibility for any criminal case against the officers. He directed Arce and Kwock to immediately formulate a plan for their investigation. Gates added that he wanted their results presented to the District Attorney's Office as soon as possible.

Upon their return to the RHD squad room, Zorn convened a meeting in Captain Gartland's office. Everyone who was at work that day gathered around the large rectangular table.

It was obvious to everyone that this was not just another LAPD controversy. This went far beyond that. It was a department-altering event, with ripple effects that would continue for years. Although race was not explicitly addressed during the meeting, it was unmistakably an undercurrent. The fact that Rodney King was Black would not materially affect our investigative approach. But it mattered a great deal in terms of the public's perception of the LAPD. In its history, the LAPD had been accused countless times of racial insensitivity, discrimination, and worse. Some of the accusations were justified. Through the years, the department was forced to change, in tune with broader society. But the need remained for the LAPD to demonstrate that it had broken from the regrettable aspects of its past.

Given the prominence and seriousness of the incident, as well as the urgency mandated by Gates, it was an all-hands-on-deck situation. Zorn and Arce delegated assignments to all the detective teams that were present.

Garcia and I were directed to interview the two passengers in the car with King, Freddie Helms and Bryant Allen. Both men lived in Altadena.

Within minutes of leaving the meeting, we called the Helms residence. His mother answered the phone. She told us that her son would not speak to us without his attorney present. She gave us the attorney's contact information. We called and left a message for him.

Because we had only an address for Allen, Garcia and I drove to Altadena and knocked on his door. Allen was polite but also declined to talk to us without his attorney's authorization. The brief interaction confirmed my concerns about the new higher degree of difficulty we would face in trying to persuade witnesses to cooperate.

From Altadena, we drove to Foothill Station and met with a sergeant who was familiar with the officers who had been at the scene. We watched the recording with him, and he made identifications of all the officers he saw on the tape, including bystander officers who would need to be interviewed later. We informed Arce of all of the identifications.

The next day, I returned to Foothill Station to help execute a search warrant that had been granted for the involved officers' lockers. We seized their police uniforms, including their uniform shoes, as well as their batons. These would later be inspected by SID for the presence of King's blood and any other trace evidence.

The following Tuesday, Garcia and I went to County/USC Medical Center, where King had been hospitalized after his arrest. Our task was to retrieve King's medical records and the blood sample that had been taken from him upon admission. It was essential to determine King's blood-alcohol level and if any drugs were present in his system. The results would no doubt be an important issue, for both the prosecution and the defense, in any eventual court proceedings. We booked the blood sample into evidence at the LAPD's Property Division for future laboratory analysis.

The results of the investigation to date were provided to the DA by Arce and Kwock. The DA's Office advised them that instead of filing charges, they would present the evidence to a Los Angeles County grand jury for indictment.

On March 14, the grand jury returned indictments against the three involved officers and their sergeant on multiple felony and misdemeanor charges. I saw the decision by the DA's Office to go to a grand jury, rather than file charges itself, as a political move. It allowed the DA to say the charges had been decided by the public, through a grand jury, instead of by the DA. It also made sense for expediency, since grand jury cases skip the need for the standard, often time-consuming preliminary hearing.

For Arce and Kwock, the lead detectives, the King case would remain their central focus for the foreseeable future. The rest of us at Major Crimes, including me and Garcia, returned to our regular caseloads.

In mid-April, Garcia received a call from a man who identified himself as Will Dorn, a private eye retained by Gayle and Kay Baker.

This was news to us, as the Bakers had never given us any indication that they planned to hire a private eye.

Both of us had, however, sensed some frustration on the Bakers' part, which was understandable. After all, their son had been murdered almost a year earlier, yet they still had not received any definitive answers.

Garcia and I had assured the Bakers that our interest in solving Ron's case remained very strong. We explained that case circumstances sometimes dictated what could be done and how quickly things could progress. We also told them, although it would not have been a surprise to anyone, that some murder cases were never solved. Even in cases in which the suspects were known, there could be a lack of sufficient evidence to move forward with a prosecution. The Bakers had accepted without complaint what we told them.

Dorn provided his contact information to Garcia and said he would be in touch with us should he develop any information.

Garcia did not reciprocate the offer. We both felt it was best to keep any new information close to our vests, informing only those who needed to know.

In late April, I contacted the Serology Unit of SID and spoke to its supervisor, Greg Matheson. I wanted to know if there was a sufficient amount of blood on Duncan's dagger for a sample to be sent out for DNA testing. I advised him of the previous tests done on the dagger, which had revealed traces of blood but too little to determine its source. Matheson said he would have someone check the dagger for the feasibility of DNA analysis.

In early June, I was notified SID would send Duncan's dagger to an outside lab to determine if there was enough blood to obtain a DNA profile. I was glad the lab felt there might be enough blood on the dagger to give testing a shot. Garcia and I badly needed a break in the case or something to shake loose regarding Duncan and his whereabouts.

On June 18, I contacted the FBI in Washington, DC, and requested an "off-line search," FBI-speak for a specific type of database query. The FBI had the ability to search broadly for any contacts that any law enforcement agency nationwide had with a given person. It did not matter if it was for a traffic citation in Idaho Falls, Idaho, a criminal history check in York, Maine, or a warrant check made by an officer in Riverside, Rhode Island.

I thought there was a decent likelihood that Duncan had encountered the police somewhere along his journey over the last eleven months. Less certain was what name Duncan might have used, his own or an alias, in any dealings he may have had with the police.

I asked the FBI to run the two definitive names we had for him, his adopted name, "Duncan Martinez," and his birth name, "Duncan James." The FBI said I could expect the off-line search to be completed within a week.

Meanwhile, I performed my own search of all fifty states' driver's license databases for any recently issued licenses in Duncan's name. No hits were found.

As promised, I heard from the FBI exactly a week later. They had promising news to report. Their off-line search had returned one result. At 8:28 a.m. on January 5, 1991, about five months earlier, a query of some kind was made by the Inyo County Sheriff's Office in California. The search was made in his legal adopted name, Duncan Martinez.

Inyo County was a mostly desolate expanse along the California-Nevada border. The largest city in the county, Bishop, had a population of only a few thousand residents. Inyo attracted vacationers year-round for outdoor recreation, in the winter months to the area's ski resorts and in the summer for fishing and hiking. Duncan Martinez's name had been queried in midwinter.

The same day I received the FBI search results, I called the Inyo County Sheriff's Office in Independence, the county seat. I knew Independence was where Charles Manson was initially jailed in 1969, and subsequently arrested for the seven murders committed at the homes of Sharon Tate and a Los Angeles couple, Leno and Rosemary LaBianca.

I spoke with a records clerk who said she would check for any contacts with Duncan Martinez or any of his known aliases. The search would include all radio logs, traffic citations, and field interview cards for January 5, the date the inquiry was made. She also agreed to ask the deputies who were on duty that day.

The clerk called me back just a few hours later. This time, the news was not so promising. She said she had struck out and found absolutely no contacts with Duncan Martinez in their records. She also inquired of several deputies, none of whom had any recollection of any encounter or making an inquiry about him.

I felt frustrated. Some person with the Inyo County Sheriff's Office had made an inquiry about Duncan Martinez or had had contact with him. Regrettably, the FBI's off-line searches at that time did not provide any information about the identity of the individual who had made the query, only the law enforcement agency from which it had come. Nor could the FBI provide any details or specifics about the query's parameters, beyond the fact that some query had been made.

Had Duncan, after traveling to Kentucky and purportedly Florida, returned to California, specifically Inyo County, over the winter? If so, was he still there?

Or had the query been made by someone who worked at the sheriff's office and knew Duncan, or someone connected to him?

I felt it was very plausible the query was made to check whether an arrest warrant had been issued for Duncan, with regard to Ron Baker's murder. Was the query a bit of intelligence gathering on Duncan's behalf? Maybe someone known to Duncan had an inside contact at the sheriff's office and had requested a favor. But who would admit to that? *No one,* I thought, as performing a search for such an illicit reason could be a fireable offense.

Unfortunately, we likely would never know.

More bad news arrived in early August. The Serology Unit at SID reported that the outside lab had analyzed the blood sample taken from the blade of Duncan's dagger. No DNA profile was obtained from the analysis. Whether the blood was from Duncan, Ron Baker, or some other person would persist as another mystery, as well as how and why it got there.

Without Duncan, there was little we could do to advance our investigation. Several more months passed without notable progress, let alone any investigative breakthroughs. The calendar turned from 1991 to 1992.

Then, on the afternoon of January 21, 1992, Garcia received a call from Jim Barnes, Duncan's attorney.

Barnes wanted to know whether any warrant had been issued for his client.

Garcia countered with a question of his own. Had Barnes been in touch with Duncan?

Barnes stated he was not at liberty to discuss whether or not he and Duncan had spoken.

Garcia told Barnes that we needed desperately to speak with Duncan.

Barnes replied that for that to happen, Duncan would need immunity. Barnes said that Duncan did not commit the murder but may have information as to who did.

Garcia and Barnes agreed to work together to make the interview happen, once Barnes could organize where and when it would take place.

Barnes said he would be back in touch but gave no time estimate as to when that might be.

I was in court that day on a different case, but Garcia later told me about Barnes's call.

Finally, some movement again, I thought.

It appeared the roller coaster was climbing and on the verge of picking up speed once again.

CHAPTER 12

A REQUEST FOR IMMUNITY
(February 6 to 10, 1992)

GARCIA AND I HAD been waiting to talk to Duncan for almost eighteen months. Where had he been? Why had he run? And most importantly, what was he, according to his attorney, Barnes, now ready to tell us about Ron's murder?

Our proposed interview with Duncan, which Barnes was certain to want to be present for, was not scheduled straightaway. As a condition of the interview, Barnes had requested immunity for Duncan, a proposition we told him we would need to discuss with the DA's Office. Garcia and I both knew that without more information about what Duncan could provide, full immunity was a nonstarter.

Barnes had not disclosed where Duncan was. Barnes's calendar was another factor. At the time, he was in the middle of a death penalty trial, defending another client.

Also, despite Barnes's request of immunity for Duncan, it was way too early for anyone to predict how his case might eventually be resolved. Whether Duncan would face charges, and what charges he might face, would ride heavily on what he told us and whether we believed him. Could we trust that Duncan, who had already failed a polygraph and faked his own kidnapping, would give us the straight truth this time?

Given that we did not know where Duncan was, and Barnes would not say, it was left to Barnes to organize when and where the meeting would take place. We decided we would give Barnes a few weeks before we followed up.

In the interim, we could only speculate about what Duncan might say. Would he stick to his original story, that he and Nathan last saw Ron when they dropped him off at the bus stop? That seemed unlikely, in light of Barnes's claim that Duncan had not killed Ron but knew who had.

I expected that for the first time Duncan would place himself at the murder scene but would otherwise attempt to minimize his involvement and culpability. For Garcia and me, it would be a familiar story, one we had heard countless variations of before from other murder suspects: "I admit I was there. Things went sideways and something unforeseeable happened. I didn't say so earlier because I was too scared and/or protecting someone else who was there."

Who would Duncan accuse? Nathan seemed the obvious fall guy. We believed Nathan was likely the only other person at Chatsworth Park with Duncan and Ron, but we couldn't say for sure. Could there have been a fourth person with them that night, someone else whom both Duncan and Nathan had been protecting?

Another X factor we were mindful of was Duncan's history of telling outlandish lies. Would he offer us some bizarre cover story for Ron's murder that only he could dream up?

In truth, there was no telling what Duncan might say. We could only wait and hope to find out soon.

Garcia and I were still waiting to hear back from Barnes about Duncan when, shortly after noon on Thursday, February 6, the phone rang on Garcia's desk.

The caller identified himself as Ken Crook, an FBI agent in Salt Lake City, Utah. Crook informed Garcia that Duncan Martinez had been arrested three days earlier, on February 3, and was in federal custody there.

Crook explained that Duncan had been picked up on an open warrant for making a false statement on a passport application. As it always seemed to go with Duncan, the story was stranger than Garcia and I could have imagined.

The warrant on which Duncan was arrested was not in his name but an alias: "Jonathan Wayne Miller."

A few months earlier, in November 1991, a young man had submitted in Delaware an application for a US passport in Miller's name. Questions about the legitimacy of the application prompted a request for further documentation to verify Miller's identity.

The applicant initially complied and submitted additional personal records, this time to a US passport office in Boston. The second round of documents included a Delaware State ID card, a Social Security card, W-2 tax statements, and an outbound airline ticket to Paris, all in Miller's name. After these were also challenged, the application was voluntarily withdrawn.

Although no passport was ever issued, the unsuccessful attempt led authorities in Boston to seek a federal indictment and warrant in the name of the purported applicant, Jonathan Wayne Miller. The true identity of the person who submitted the application was unknown.

Fast-forward to February 3, when an unsuspecting Utah Highway Patrol trooper pulled over a driver for a traffic violation in Nephi, eighty miles south of Salt Lake City. Asked for his driver's license by the trooper, the driver presented a Delaware ID card in the name of Jonathan Wayne Miller. A computer database search quickly revealed the existence of the warrant. After the driver refused to provide his real name, he was arrested and subsequently taken into federal custody.

In a court appearance on February 4 before a federal magistrate judge, the driver, now a defendant, again refused to tell the judge or anyone else his true identity. The judge ordered the defendant to return to court the next day for a hearing on his continued detention.

At the February 5 hearing, the defendant offered to plead guilty to providing false information on a passport application as Jonathan Wayne Miller but still refused to reveal his real identity. The judge explained that he was not allowed to plead under an assumed name and would not be released until he was positively identified. The judge also warned that if he could not be identified, he would be extradited to Boston, where the federal indictment originated, to face the charges there. The defendant was returned to custody to weigh his options, pending his next court appearance.

Among the spectators in the courtroom at both hearings was FBI agent Crook. After the second hearing, Crook decided to visit the defendant in lockup and try to level with him. Crook told him he did not understand why he wouldn't give up his name, and by refusing, he was only making things more difficult for himself.

Eventually, he admitted to Crook that his real name was Duncan Martinez. Duncan told Crook he was from Los Angeles and had witnessed a murder in a park there. He said he fled LA and had been using an assumed name because he was afraid of the person who had actually killed the victim. Duncan also said he felt the LAPD thought he was involved.

Crook was understandably skeptical. He decided he would call the LAPD to try to determine the veracity of Duncan's story, including whether the new name he had provided was in fact his true identity. That Frank Garcia was the LAPD homicide detective who happened to answer Crook's call was a stroke of pure luck.

Crook ran the story past Garcia, who confirmed that he knew Duncan and that Duncan was indeed a suspect in an unsolved LA murder. Crook asked Garcia for any personal information on Duncan the LAPD could provide, in advance of his next federal court appearance on February 12.

Our investigation into who killed Ron Baker had been stymied for more than a year. Yet in the span of one phone call, the case surged back to life. We finally knew where Duncan was.

Garcia and I wasted no time. Within an hour, Garcia called Crook back and gave him Duncan's date of birth, Social Security number, and other information to confirm his identity. Garcia also informed Crook that we would travel to Salt Lake City on February 10, the following Monday, to interview Duncan face-to-face.

Was Barnes aware that his client had been arrested and was sitting in jail in Salt Lake City? We thought it possible he was not, since Duncan was not yet in custody on January 21, when Barnes had first called Garcia.

We felt we needed to get to Salt Lake City as soon as possible, before Duncan had the opportunity to make bail or was released from federal custody. I doubted that Duncan would get a low bail amount, in light of his deception about his true identity. But given our earlier experiences with him, and the fortunate status of him being in custody, we could not risk him somehow getting out and disappearing on us again.

The strategic decision we had to make was whether or not to tell Barnes.

One option was to call Barnes, inform him of Duncan's arrest, and then work with him, as he had originally proposed, to coordinate the interview.

The other option was to hop on a plane and confront Duncan in person, without telling Barnes. Although Barnes had said he was Duncan's attorney, Duncan had never told us so. Barnes had asked us to go through him if we wanted to talk to Duncan, but we were not obligated to do so. Only if Duncan told us himself, "Hey, I have an attorney. I don't want to talk with you," were we required to comply.

How would Barnes react if, after he had reached out to us, we went behind his back to his client? Not well, we knew. Even if the gambit worked and Duncan decided to talk, Barnes was certain to challenge the admissibility of whatever Duncan told us. Barnes might lose that argument in court eventually, but in the meantime, it would poison our working relationship with him and likely doom any prospect of future cooperation from Duncan. Was it worth taking that risk, only to fly to Salt Lake City and strike out?

Garcia and I ultimately decided it was more advantageous to play it safe and go through Barnes than approach Duncan surreptitiously.

That afternoon, Garcia called Ernie Norris, a veteran prosecutor in the DA's Special Trials unit. Norris was already familiar with the Baker case from previous conversations Garcia and I had had with him. We knew Norris to be a straight shooter and trusted his opinion. Garcia briefed Norris on Duncan's arrest and the possible interview. Norris concurred with us about notifying Barnes.

The following morning, Garcia called Barnes and informed him of our plan to travel to Salt Lake City to interview Duncan. They also discussed the terms of the interview.

Barnes wanted us to take Duncan's statement "outside of Miranda," meaning that whatever he told us could not be used as evidence against him. In theory, interviewing a suspect outside of Miranda allowed them to speak honestly and without fear of criminal exposure, while also providing valuable information that would be difficult to elicit otherwise. Garcia advised Barnes to call Norris to negotiate the legalese.

Ten minutes later, Norris called and reported that Barnes had already contacted him. Barnes had said he needed to speak with Duncan's mother, who had hired him and was paying his fees, to see whether a trip to Utah would be financed.

A few hours after that, midafternoon on Friday, Barnes called Garcia directly and confirmed he would meet us in Salt Lake City on Monday.

The ground rules that Norris and Barnes had agreed would govern Duncan's interview had an informal name: "King for a Day." The conditions guaranteed Duncan a limited form of immunity, in that whatever he told us that day could not be used to prosecute him in the future.

This fell far short of the blanket immunity Barnes had initially sought, prior to Duncan's arrest. Although what Duncan told us could not be used against him, he could still be prosecuted if other incriminating evidence emerged outside the interview. Additionally, Duncan's King for a Day statements were fair game to use as evidence against anyone else besides him.

The way I saw it, there was no downside to King for a Day. We stood to learn new information likely to advance our investigation. Despite all our work on the case to date, we still had not been able to place Duncan or Nathan at the crime scene.

As we flew to Salt Lake City on the morning of February 10, we had reason to hope we were on the verge of a major break in the case.

PART II
THE SECOND BETRAYAL

CHAPTER 13

KING FOR A DAY
(February 10, 1992)

"**PRESENT DURING THIS INTERVIEW** is Jim Barnes, who is your attorney... yourself, Duncan Martinez. And you are in custody here in Salt Lake under the name of Jonathan Wayne Miller... Is that right?" asked Garcia.

"Yes," Duncan said.

We had arranged to interview Duncan at the offices of the US Marshals Service in Salt Lake City, where he was still in federal custody. We met first with Barnes and Robert Booker, a Utah defense lawyer who was representing Duncan in his passport case, then with just Duncan and Barnes for the interview.

Set on the table between us was a briefcase-style tape recorder we had brought with us from Los Angeles. The interview was being recorded as protection for both sides to show exactly what was said. The local time was 4:25 p.m.

Garcia and I had worked together long enough that we didn't need to plan our interview with Duncan to a T. Given my partner's relative seniority, he would take the lead during the interview, with me jumping in as necessary with follow-up questions. Our approach would be to let Duncan talk and for us to listen nonjudgmentally. Generally, it is counterproductive during interviews to show disapproval or make a subject feel ashamed about any of their admissions. We wanted Duncan to be forthright with us and not hold back any important information.

Throughout the interview, I would be reading Duncan for potential tells about his truthfulness. Some tells might be physical, like his facial expressions, eye contact, and body movements, such as squirming or being unable to keep his hands or feet still. I would be listening to his voice as well. Did he sound genuine or come off as rehearsed? When we asked him questions, did he take long pauses before he answered? If there were especially damning moments in the story he told, did he seem to minimize his actions, take responsibility, or a mix of both? Garcia would be looking for the same tells. It's what detectives do.

Garcia stated for the record our names and that we were LAPD Robbery-Homicide detectives. "Duncan, we are here to discuss the murder of Ron Baker. And before we get started, I'm not even going to advise you of your constitutional rights. Okay? Your attorney is present here and I'm telling you right now, in front of your attorney—I have already explained this to your attorney—that nothing you say to us right now can be used against you. Okay? Nothing at all. So with that in mind, and I'm sure you have conferred with your attorney, we would like for you to tell us what happened back in LA."

"Okay," said Duncan. "Do you want me to start at the first conscious knowledge of any of the events, or at the first—"

"The murder went down June the 21st, okay? Of 1990. You remember that day, right?"

"I don't know what the date was. I know it was June. I didn't know—"

"Okay. It was June the 21st. That's the date that Ron was killed. We're talking about Ron Baker," Garcia said. "If you could, pick it up that afternoon when Ron got home and basically run down to us what happened."

"Unless there was something that happened before that that's pertinent," I added.

"Okay. Well, there is," Duncan said.

I suggested he start with the day of Ron's murder and we could circle back later.

"That afternoon, there was plans to go have a few beers between me and Nathan," Duncan began. He said Ron came home, and Nathan's girlfriend at the time, Diane Henderson, was also at their apartment.

"She was staying with us. I don't know exactly how to—there was a hostage plan that had been mentioned before by Nathan, in reference to a TV show, and brought up once after that, I believe... He said something to the effect that he was going to get Ron to go with us tonight, and it was going to be the night where he was going—I'm not sure exactly how he said it, but the gist of it was, he was going to get Ron to come with us. We were going to go drinking, the three of us, and that what was going to go down would go down that night.

"That night Ron came home. He made dinner for all of us, spaghetti. It was kind of a payback for having eaten dinner when Nathan made it a few nights before... Nathan told Ron that we were going to meet some girls up at Chatsworth Park and that if he wanted to come with us, he could. We were going to drink some beer. Ron agreed. We went up to Chatsworth Park later that night and—"

Garcia signaled Duncan to slow down. "I'm sorry, Duncan. I'm just taking notes."

"Yeah, I'm sorry."

"You're going way too fast. Go a little slower," I said.

"It's kind of hard to—"

"I know. I know you are excited and everything," said Garcia.

"Well, excited and scared. I mean, this is a very hard thing for me to talk about."

"I understand that, Duncan. Okay. Nathan told Ron that you guys were going to meet some girls at the Chatsworth Park?"

"Uh-huh, and that was to get Ron to go."

"And that included the three of you, right?"

"Right. And the reason I think that he used the girls was that he didn't want Diane to know. He told Ron, you know, 'Hey, don't say anything to Diane, because I don't want her to know that I'm going to meet some other girls.' Then we sat around the house for a while and played some Nintendo, I believe, and then we drove to the park... I'm not sure what time it was, but it was dark when we got there. I mean, it was dark, dark. It wasn't, you know, just like where it is fading dark."

"Whose car did you go in?"

"Mine. I was the only one with a car... We got to the park. We went up over by the tunnel."

"Let me interrupt you there," said Garcia. "While you are commuting from your apartment to the park, did you stop and buy any booze?"

"No, we bought it earlier... I went out and bought a twelve-pack that morning, or a case that morning."

"How much did you guys take with you?"

"A case."

"Okay. You left your car in the parking lot and you took the beer with you?"

"Uh-huh... You walk up this little trail and you are at the tunnel entrance. We went either over the top or through the tunnel—I don't remember which—to the other side. And that's where we were drinking beer, just on the other side of the tunnel... There was a set of rocks just on the side of the tracks. We were hanging out on those."

"Outside of the tunnel?"

"Outside of the tunnel. Exactly what went on there... what we talked about or anything, I don't really remember... We had been there for probably an hour and had downed a bunch of beers and nobody had shown up. I think Ron said, 'You know, the girls aren't going to show. Let's get out of here. We have been here long enough,' or something like that. And we started to leave. Now, when this whole concoction had been mentioned before, this little rock was where it was going to happen, and nothing happened. And I looked at Nathan and nothing happened, and it didn't—I mean, it didn't faze me... I didn't really believe it was going to happen in the first place and therefore, when it didn't happen, it was, like, no big deal to me. We started walking through the tunnel to go back—"

"Did you go back a different way?" I asked.

"No, we were going back toward the car the same way we came."

"So you had walked through the tunnel?"

"I don't remember if we walked through the tunnel or if we went over the tunnel, because you can go over the rocks there too. There are a bunch of little paths up in there. Um, we were walking back through the tunnel. I was in front. I was carrying the case of beer, and Ron and Nathan were behind me."

"Hang on," Garcia interrupted. "How much of the case of beer was left after an hour and a half?"

"I'm not sure. I mean, we had—I think I probably had at least a six-pack to drink. Um, there was definitely beer left in the case. How much, I don't remember for sure."

"And Ron and Nathan were behind you?"

"Right. Um, we were in the tunnel, and I guess it would be about a third of the way in, Nathan slipped on something and Ron said something, made a comment, you know, kind of a joke about it."

"Like what?"

"Um, I don't remember what he said, and I have been trying to think of this too... I think it had something to do with the fact that Nathan was in the Army and he can't even walk in a dark tunnel, or something like that. It was, like, a stupid little joke, but I don't remember exactly what the joke was. And, like I say, I have been trying to remember what that was. Um, and that's when Nathan jumped him. I heard a fight start. Um, I had the case of beer. I was in shock for a second. I put the case of beer down. Ron was screaming, 'Help me, Duncan,' and I turned around and Nathan was screaming, 'No.'"

"'Help me, Duncan,' and Nathan said, 'No,'" repeated Garcia.

Duncan went on: "I took a couple of steps forward, then I would take a couple of steps back, and I didn't really know what to do. Um, and then Nathan lit a lighter and I could see him sitting on top of Ron with his knees on Ron's arms. And Ron was saying, 'Why are you doing this to me? What did I ever do to deserve this? Why are you doing this to me?' And—"

"What did Nathan have in his hands?"

"He had the knife in one hand and the lighter in the other hand. And the lighter went out and I heard some more noises and the lighter came back on again, and this time Ron was making, like, gurgling sounds and was moving a little bit, but not in any coherent type of manner.

"Nathan's face looked like it was on fire. Nathan then sat there for a second, and I said—I told him to make sure that it was over, because I didn't want Ron to suffer. And I could see that he was probably suffering, if he was still conscious at all.

"And the lighter went out, and I believe Nathan slit his throat a couple of times, because I saw sparks, like, off to the other side, and I could hear the knife hitting something. It sounded like the knife was hitting something and then striking the rocks. I could see the sparks as it hit the rocks.

"The next thing that happened was Nathan walked up in front of me and told me I had to help him move the body. And I said there was no way, I couldn't help him move the body. And so we went back because there was a few beer bottles that we left, and I think we collected the beer bottles up and then went to the car, or maybe he broke the beer bottles or something... I don't remember having the beer bottles when we got back to the car, so I think we left them there. But I think we poured beer from the remaining beer bottles on the beer bottles to, um, wipe off any evidence of us having drank the beer, I think."

"In the tunnel?" I asked.

"No, this is out on the other side of the tunnel, like the side where we were drinking the beer and there had been a few beer bottles that we left behind. And, uh—"

"So Nathan stabs Ron, you guys get your thoughts together, right?" asked Garcia.

"Uh-huh."

"And who decided to go back and pour beer on the empty beer bottles?" asked Garcia.

It was a good question, I thought. The act of pouring beer on the bottles demonstrated an intent to obliterate their fingerprints and destroy evidence of their presence at the scene, which showed consciousness of guilt.

"Um, I don't remember. It could have been me. I was pretty freaked out right then."

"In any event, somebody decides to go back and pour beer on the empty beer bottles to wash the prints off them or what?"

"I guess. I think that's what we did... It's kind of sketchy. I see, like, clips of parts of the—and I remember seeing the beer being poured on the beer bottles, and that is the only thing that would make sense. We went down to the car. I was—I mean, I was Jell-O... I think I fell once walking down the hill, and I never fell there. Um, and I couldn't drive. I made Nathan drive. And he drove to the phone booth on Victory and—the one right around the corner from our house. I don't remember what the street was that we lived off of."

"Lay a time on me, Duncan."

"Well, we got back after—we got to the party at about a little past ten... I think that was the time that we got there... I mean, this is a long time ago now. This is all stuff I have really not thought about, because I try not to."

"And whose idea was it to pull up at the phone booth?"

"Nathan pulled in. He just pulled in."

"To the phone booth?"

"And said, 'Now you have got to make a phone call to his dad.' And I kind of wasn't really in any position to tell him no."

"Explain yourself," I said. "What do you mean when you say that?"

"I was scared shitless and I use that word roughly—and I use that word because I can think of no other word that describes how I felt."

"Hang on. You have to make a call to his father?" asked Garcia.

"Yeah, he told me I had to make the hostage call... So I got out of the car and I went over to the phone and I called his dad."

"Before you got out of the car, was there any discussion of how much money to ask for?" I asked.

"Yeah, there was actually. When it had been brought up originally, a million dollars was what was going to be asked for. And when he brought up making the hostage call, I said, 'There is no way. There is no way. His parents don't have anywhere near that kind of money.' I mean, I knew his parents. I had known them for a long time. And he said, 'One hundred thousand dollars,' and I said, 'There is no way they have that kind of money either.' And then he said, 'Well, call.' And so I went and I called and I asked for one hundred thousand dollars.

"And then we got back to the apartment and we hung out in our apartment for a minute and Ron's dad called and we spoke to Ron's dad. We had just gotten back and then we went upstairs. There was a party going on upstairs at one of the other apartments, and we went up there and hung out up there for a little while... I really couldn't deal with the party so I left and went downstairs. The next day he told me I had to make another call... I don't remember what I said on the call and I have been trying to think of the phone call itself... The first phone call had been made at the liquor store, at the phone booth at the liquor store on Victory and Kester. The second one, there was a pay phone just a block up from our apartment on that street, and I made it there... Then I came back and Nathan was—I mean, he was like Superman. He was higher than life. And then that day Ron's dad called us back, and Ron still hadn't been home. So we all started to worry. And Lydia came over. And a couple of days later, you showed up."

"You started to worry—what do you mean by that?" I asked.

"Well, everybody started to worry about what happened to Ron."

"Well, you weren't worried, were you?" said Garcia.

"Well, I was kind of trying to—I was trying to play games with myself like I didn't know what happened, trying to forget about the whole thing, because I couldn't believe that it happened. But I mean, I knew. When you talked to me that—"

"Let me interrupt you here, Duncan," said Garcia. "It's very crucial that you understand this, and I'm not saying I don't believe you, okay—far from it. We are listening to you right now. We're taking all this down and it's going to be digested completely. But I forgot to tell you prior to starting this interview: Whatever you do today, Duncan, don't lie to us."

"Right."

"Okay? And there is a lot of reasons for not lying to us. You are willing to get this off your chest. You are willing to talk with us at this point. If at a future date, Duncan, we need you to testify in court, or we have to check something and we check it, Duncan, and it comes out that Duncan told us something to this point and we find something else out, it's going to make you look like you are not a believable person."

"Right."

"And Rick and I don't want that problem five, six months or a year from now."

"Right."

"When you get done telling us this, you know Rick is going to have some questions, and I am going to have some questions. But for God's sake, Duncan, don't lie to us."

"Right. I'm not."

"Okay."

"I'm not," Duncan insisted.

"I'm not saying you are, Duncan. And I don't want you to misinterpret that I'm insinuating that, because I'm not. But it's very crucial to you and to us that whenever you tell us something today, be sure you tell us everything you know...And that's for your benefit."

I added, "Even if it's something that you think makes you look worse in this whole thing. It's important that you tell us because your credibility is, like Frank says, should you become a witness, it is of the utmost importance."

Barnes reminded Duncan, "And remember, that's what I told you also...You have got to tell them things...You have got to tell them the truth no matter what."

"Right," said Duncan. "One thing I just thought of, and something I brought up earlier, was in the scuffle, Nathan—and I don't remember which hand it was—but Nathan got a scratch on his hand. There was, like, a couple, but one was decent size and one was kind of small. It looked like someone's fingernails had gone like this across his hand"—demonstrating with a clawing motion on his own hand. "It was good enough that it bled for a while. I mean, it was still bleeding when we got home."

"You are talking about the back of the hand, not the palm?" I asked.

"Right, the very back of the hand. I don't know if it was enough to have scarred. I don't know if it was enough to have left any—"

"You don't know which hand it was?" asked Garcia.

"I'm thinking right hand, but it's too long ago. I mean, I have a glimpse of seeing a cut in my mind."

"Okay. We are talking about Thursday night now. You make the call to Mr. Baker. Nathan tells you to make the call."

"Right."

"Then he tells you to make the call the following day, which is that Friday. What time did you make the second call?"

"I have no clue. I'd say morning, noon-ish...I'm not sure what time it was at all. That was also the same day that—it was also the same day, I believe, that the check was written," referring to Ron's check that Duncan wrote out to himself and deposited after the murder.

"That next morning or the next day?" I asked.

"I believe it was the next morning, yeah."

"This going up to the park—did that have anything at all to do with the summer solstice or Wicca or any of that bullshit?" asked Garcia.

"No."

"So you guys are just going to go up there to drink?"

"Yeah... We used to do it a lot too. We used to do it with other people too, and—"

Garcia cut in. "After the second phone call, Duncan, keep going. What happens then?"

"Okay. I had an interview with you. You came into the apartment and talked to me. Actually I think somebody came in first."

"Let me interrupt you again. From the time Ron Baker is killed to the time that we come to you, what happens to Nathan?"

"Um, he's hanging out with Diane all the time. He went out to Riverside with her. I remember he did that after you guys talked to me, or just before. I think it was just before."

"Do you recall Nathan going back to Chicago, or Detroit, for a family reunion?"

"I think he did that, like, a little while before. Or did he do that after? I remember him going to Detroit. I don't remember if it was right before or right after."

Nathan's family reunion in Detroit was in fact soon after Ron's murder, although we did not tell Duncan we knew that.

"Was that something preplanned?" I asked.

"Yeah, he had been talking to his dad about that for a while. He was trying to get money from his dad to go and do that."

"Okay," said Garcia. "Then at this point Rick and I have already come into the picture, and we start interviewing you."

"Right. The first day you guys interviewed me, I almost told you everything. I remember sitting there and looking at Lydia sitting behind me, and I just couldn't, with Lydia sitting there." Lydia was a friend of Ron's and Duncan's who happened to be at their apartment the first time we met and questioned Duncan, four days after Ron's murder. "Then it seemed like every time, every day that I didn't say something, it was ten times harder, because I was scared to say something because of Nathan. And Nathan wasn't there that day. I was scared to betray, because that is what I felt like I was doing. But on the same token, I felt like I was betraying Ron if I didn't say anything.

"The longer time went on, the more everyone was crying on my shoulder, the more everyone was coming to me for support, and I was giving them all this support, and I know what really happened, and I can't tell anybody because I didn't know what to do. I just—I got really scared... I mean, when I went in that day for the lie detector, and you guys told me it came out negative, it said that I made the phone calls, said that I did this and that, I flipped.

"When I spoke to Mr. Barnes and, you know, the possibility of death row was mentioned, I lost it and I took off. I mean, I didn't take off that same day. I set it up a little bit. I didn't have very much money, so I pawned all my stuff off and then took off... As soon as I got on the plane, I knew that it was a mistake. I went from fits of *This is the stupidest thing I have ever done* to *No, I have got to do this*. I drove back and forth for a long time and then I got to the point where I wanted to come back... This is about a year after, but I couldn't get myself to make the first phone call... And then I did finally."

"Did you call Mr. Barnes here or did you call your mother?" asked Garcia.

"I called my mom first, and then she told me that she still had a retainer for Mr. Barnes. So I then called him, but I didn't get to speak to him."

"This was how long ago?"

"About a month ago."

"Before you were in custody?"

"Oh, yeah. I'd say probably a month before. At least two weeks."

"So prior to you getting picked up on this—whatever it is they got you on—you had started some kind of movement to come back to Los Angeles?"

"Yes."

"Why are you afraid of Nathan, Duncan?"

"Well, he was able to kill Ron. I mean, I play-fought with the guy a hundred times. He knew my weaknesses. He knew what I was bad at."

"What you are saying is, Nathan can kick your ass, or can he?"

"Now, let me answer that fairly. If Nathan were to get the jump on me, I don't think he would have any problem at all. If I were to get the jump on him, it would be an interesting—it would be a very long fight. If we were just to walk at each other and start fighting, it would be a very long fight. I don't know who would win. I mean, because we play-fought so many times. My thing is that if you take out one of my knees, I'm gone. Because I mean, I'm speed. That's the only thing I have, and that's all I have ever had. Nathan is a bigger guy who has got a lot of power. He can take a lot more hits than I can. He knew it and he used to talk about it, that if he ever took out one of my knees, it would be all over."

"Has Nathan ever threatened you?"

"He threatened me when he said—when we went to make the hostage phone call, I believe. I think he said, you know, 'Now you have got to do this.' And I think I said, 'No,' at first. And he says, 'You better do this,' and kind of just looked at me. I don't think he said, 'or else,' or anything like that, but he said, 'You better do this,' and then I did it. I think I did say, 'No,' once in there."

"This was preplanned—that's the inference that I am getting from you?"

"Um, yeah, sort of."

"It was preplanned in the sense that Nathan was going to take Ron out?"

"Yeah."

"Was he going to take him out or just kidnap him?"

"No, he was—from the plan, he was going to kill him."

"When was the first time Nathan Blalock tells you he wants to kill Ron Baker?"

"Well, the first time he ever said anything to the extent of wanting to kill Ron Baker I would say was probably a month before this all happened. Him and Ron got into a little argument and there were a couple of other people at the apartment and Ron left and then Nathan walked in the bedroom and said, 'I'm going to kill him.' And he was just really ticked off."

"Do you remember what that argument was about?" I asked.

"No...As I remember, I don't even think it was that big a deal. And it may have been they had a lot of little things that they had arguments about, like using each other's toiletries, stuff on the Nintendo, you know, not cleaning up after themselves."

"Roommate-type arguments?"

"Right. You know, just generic roommate-type stuff. But before that incident, we—me and Nathan—were sitting around watching a TV show. It was a cop show or something, and on it a kidnapping was done. Nathan said, 'Oh, yeah, we should do that.' Brought it up, and it was definitely in a joking manner. And I brought up a dude that I had known in high school and I didn't like, and I said, 'Oh, yeah, we should do it to John Sands. Yeah, that's it.' And so we called him up and talked to his mom. His mom was like, 'He is off at school. If you want to leave your number, I'll have him call you. But, you know, I don't give his number out.' And I was like, 'Okay.'"

"Who is this? John Sands?" asked Garcia.

"Yeah."

"And you called his mom?"

"Yeah."

"What's her name?"

"I have no idea. His dad is Fred Sands, the realtor in LA... They live up in Beverly Hills."

"You didn't tell her that you had kidnapped John, right?"

"No, no, we just called to get in touch with John."

"Oh, okay."

"And then about—this was probably about, I'd say, two months before the incident, something around that window... Nathan brought it up again and said—and this was after the 'I'm going to kill him' statement."

"How much after?"

"I'd say probably a week or I don't know. It's hard to tell... These are just points of memory now. He said, 'Hey, yeah, we are going to do this kidnapping and we are going to do it with Ron.' And I'm like, 'Yeah, right.' You know, it was about the most ludicrous thing I had ever heard, as far as I was concerned. Then I don't believe we discussed it again until the day of the incident, and he brought it up again. I think me and him were supposed to go drinking."

"Okay. Duncan, on the day of this incident, when was this brought up—morning, noon?"

"Well, I have been trying to work out the series of incidents that day, and I'm not sure, but if I remember right, me and him decided we were going to go drinking, and I went and got beer. Then that afternoon when he talked to Ron, he told Ron that we were going up to Chatsworth Park and all this... I don't remember exactly what he said to me, but I remember that I knew where it was supposed to happen... So I didn't worry. So I knew what was going to happen, and when it was supposed to happen, or where it was going to happen. Um, then we went up there and it happened."

"Had he ever discussed with you how he was going to kill Ron?"

"Um, I don't think he ever said."

"He did tell you that he was going to kill him, though?"

"Well, yeah, when the original plan was brought up that was—"

"That's the original plan which time... a week after?"

"The first time. The very first time."

"With John Sands?" I asked.

"Yeah, when the original plan came up the first time. The original plan, the kidnapping plan was that, you know, we—actually it was Mulholland and not at Chatsworth Park too—it was that, you know, bop the person and then make phony phone calls. And—"

"What was the motive for this?" Garcia asked.

It was another good question. Despite Duncan's explanation about the ransom calls, I still couldn't wrap my head around a motive for victimizing Ron, perhaps his best friend. Whether Duncan realized it or not, it was a win-win question for us. No matter what he cited as a motive, it would further establish premeditation.

"I guess the money, but I mean—"

"He righteously wanted money?"

"Yeah, but I mean, he knew as well as I did that there was no way that it would work."

"Or was it just because he was pissed off at Ron?"

"This is just my assessment—I don't think he had any plans of when we went up into the park of doing it. I don't think he had any—I mean, I don't know for sure. I can't say for sure. I think he knew as well as I did that kidnappings or hostage situation deals don't work. I think he knew as well as I did that this would be a really stupid thing if it ever went through.

"But when we were up there, I think there had just been a bunch of things that Ron had done—I mean, everybody had seen him and Ron get in arguments. Everybody had heard him talking, you know. And I never really put the stuff together because they were both my best friends. You know, and I didn't understand that that didn't automatically make them best friends. Because, you know, I was best friends with both of them.

"Um, and I think he just finally snapped. I mean, like I say, there was a point in which, in the plan, he was supposed to do it and didn't do it. And, you know, he didn't do it and I wasn't surprised. I mean, it wasn't like, *Oh, wow, he didn't do it,* or like, *Whew, he didn't do it.* There was no relief."

"Going up there, Duncan, you knew then that when you guys got over to the west side of the tunnel, where you drank the beer, that was where Nathan was supposed to do Ron in?"

"I don't know. I don't remember if it was the location—I think it was the location that I knew. Or was there a time or something that it was going to be? I think it was the location. I think that's what it was. Yeah, I think it was definitely—like I say, I don't remember that exact part of the conversation, but that's what I think it was. I think it was the location that he said."

"So that was discussed the day of the murder, that afternoon, and then Nathan tells you he is going to do it?"

"Uh-huh."

"Okay. When you guys left the house, did Ron Baker go with you willingly?"

"Oh, yeah, one hundred percent."

"Okay. I have got some questions for you," said Garcia. "Who smokes Marlboro Golds, the 100's?" Among the evidence collected at the crime scene were two packs of cigarettes and a pair of black sunglasses. All were found deep inside the tunnel, about ten feet from Ron's body.

"Ron."

"Ron did?"

"Uh-huh."

"Who else?"

"Just Ron. Ron smoked 100's. Nathan smoked Lights. I smoked Camels, usually. Sometimes I would smoke Marlboro Lights too. And we bummed cigarettes off each other too. But—"

"Which knife did Nathan use?" asked Garcia.

"My KA-BAR. My Marine Corps knife."

"You call it a KA-BAR?"

"Yeah, it's the brand."

"And that's your Marine Corps—is that a survival knife?"

"No. Well, it looks kind of like a survival knife, but it's not."

"Where is that knife now?"

"It was dumped in the dumpster at the apartment next door to ours."

"That night?" I asked.

"Uh-huh."

"How did he get that knife?"

"Um, we used to always take it up there, because there are a lot of weirdos that hang out by the rocks," Duncan said, apparently without irony.

"That night, how did he get the knife?" asked Garcia, referring to Nathan.

"Um, he could borrow it whenever he wanted. He borrowed it from me."

"He took the knife from the house?"

"Yes."

"He had it on him the whole time?"

"Uh-huh."

"In a sheath?" I asked.

"Yes, it had a leather sheath, all black. The knife was black on black also." Duncan described the knife as about seven inches long, from the base of its handle to the tip of the blade. It was the same type he was issued by the Marines during boot camp, although not the same knife. He said he had bought it almost a year earlier, for thirty or thirty-five dollars, at a knife store in a mall.

"After Ron was killed, and you are sitting there with Nathan and you guys are trying to decide what the hell to do with this, what happened to his ID, his wallet, and all that stuff?"

"Um, Nathan grabbed his wallet."

"Was there any discussion there as to what was going to happen?"

"I don't think so."

"What else did you guys take, I mean you guys, you and Nathan? Or if you took anything, or if Nathan took anything?"

"I think all he grabbed was his wallet. I think he just grabbed his wallet and... Um, maybe he grabbed his keys. You know, I think he did grab his keys, because I think Ron had the only mail key, and I think he grabbed the keys because he was expecting a letter. But I'm not sure. Ron could have left his keys at home or something."

Garcia asked Duncan more specifically about what happened in the tunnel. "Now, you hear the fight start?"

"Right."

"Was there anything said prior to Nathan jumping Ron, like 'You motherfucker, I have got you now' or 'This is it'?"

"No."

"Nothing?"

"No. Ron said something as Nathan slipped, and then—boom."

"Nathan went off?"

"Right. Um, I believe—"

"And you knew Nathan had that knife on him?"

"Yes, I did. I knew Nathan had the knife... Now what happened, from the sound of it, is Nathan rushed Ron this way, slammed him against the wall... I think of Nathan having stabbed him right there. And I picture Nathan having stabbed him more than once right there. But I couldn't see, so I didn't know... Oh, jeez, I hate remembering this."

Duncan described what he saw when Nathan next lit his lighter. "I think he had the lighter in his left hand... Nathan had his elbow or knees on Ron's arm and Ron had his hands up like this," Duncan said, flailing his hands in imitation of Ron's motions. "He was going, 'Why are you doing this? Stop. Stop. Why are you doing this to me?' The lighter went out and I heard a couple of blows and the lighter came back on... It didn't look like he was moving coherently... But he was still moving a little bit. I told Nathan to make sure he is dead because I could not deal with that. Jesus. Oh, man, it's been so long."

"So what did Nathan do when you told him, 'Make sure he is dead'?"

"The light went out and that's when, like I said, I think he was cutting his throat because I could see the strikes, the sparks going off to the side."

"Okay. Then you guys sit here in the tunnel for a while?"

"No, then he comes up to me and he stood—I mean, I'm still in the same spot—and he stands right in front of me. And I mean, I could feel the knife, like I couldn't see anything, the lighter was unlit, but the knife was there... He said something about the beer bottles that we left behind. I'm all shaky and we went back. You know, I may have. I don't know. I don't know who said the beer bottles. I may have said that. But the beer bottles were brought up. We went back and I think—I even think I was the one pouring the beer on the beer bottles... Because I remember feeling that it was something I could do, and it made me feel good that I wasn't just thinking about what had just happened. My brain was on something else. And Nathan was just—I mean, he was covered in blood."

"That was going to be my next comment, Duncan," said Garcia. "To do something like this, Nathan had to be covered almost from head to toe with blood."

"Um, he had... I think he was wearing a pair of sweatpants and an old flannel shirt or something, and a T-shirt underneath the flannel. And he had a spray of blood all over his face, and his shirt was pretty much soaked, and he had some on his legs—not as much on his legs as he did on the upper body. And he was bleeding on his hand, but he didn't bring that up until later. Oh, jeez, this is all rushing back."

"Well, you guys... Obviously he didn't drive all the way back to Van Nuys like that, did he?"

"Well, he took the flannel off and he was wearing a T-shirt underneath. And he wiped his face off and he wiped—I guess he wiped himself down a little bit with that. And I guess he kind of pressed everything in. His arms up to here were stained too. I mean, he was a real dark guy and you could see the stains. Um, and then he wrapped the knife up in the flannel, I think. It was some kind of shirt, but I think it was flannel.

"And then we walked back through the—no, I wouldn't go through the tunnel. I refused. I remember this now. I refused to go back through the tunnel, and we had to walk up and around... We got in the car and I told Nathan he had to drive. And then we drove home.

"I just thought of something else too. Um, Nathan had a... I had a little portable tape recorder—I totally flipped out on this—and he had brought it with him. And he told Ron to—he said, 'What would you say if somebody was holding you hostage and you had to call your parents? What would you say?' And we all made little things on the tape recorder. And, jeez, I forgot all about that."

"And that was tape-recorded?"

"That was tape-recorded. Um, and—"

"Where is that tape recorder now?" I asked. The recording would be extremely important evidence, if it still existed and could be found.

"I have no clue. That might even still be in my stuff back at home. It might very well still be in my stuff back at home... Back in LA."

"Okay. Jeannie, your mother, went and picked up the shit from Mrs. Baker, didn't she?" asked Garcia. He was referring to the box that Duncan had dropped off at the Bakers and asked them to store, shortly before he staged his own kidnapping and skipped town.

"Right, she got my—"

"Was it with that?"

"No, it definitely wasn't with that. If it was with anything, it would probably be with the stuff at Lydia's, which I don't think my mom picked up."

Later, after Garcia and I got back to Los Angeles, we would mount an extensive search for the missing tape recorder and the twisted recording of Ron's manipulation by his friends—cruelly tricked into providing a proof-of-life message to his parents, for purposes of their extortion, all the while oblivious to his preplanned, impending murder. We would never find the recorder or the tape.

"Have you been in contact with Lydia?" asked Garcia.

"No, I'm kind of—I really want to talk to Ron's dad, and I really want to talk to Lydia—"

"We don't want you calling anybody, because we are going to have to do some follow-up work after this," I said. "And any calls to anybody could be—"

"Right."

"Yeah, at this point, Duncan, you have come so far in the last few hours, and to call people right now would jeopardize it," said Garcia.

"Oh, I am not—"

"If you are going to talk to anybody, talk to Mr. Barnes there. And I'm sure he will direct you as to who to talk to and who not to talk to."

"I'm sorry. I guess I—when I said I want to talk to Lydia, and I want to talk to Ron's dad... I wouldn't have the cojones to do that now anyway. I mean, I want to. I want Ron's dad to understand what happened. I want Ron's dad to understand that I made a mistake. I didn't catch things that maybe I should have."

"Let us understand what happened first, before you start trying—"

We had been talking with Duncan for almost an hour. We halted the interview for a moment while I flipped the cassette in our tape recorder to the clean side.

Once we were rolling tape again, Garcia said, "Let me ask you something, Duncan, that bothers the hell out of me. Why didn't you tell us?"

"Um, well, like I said, at first I was so scared of Nathan that I didn't know what to do. And I mean, as a kid everybody always tells you, you never snitch. You never tell on a buddy, right? And I was torn between my two best friends. I mean, Nathan and Ron were my two best friends."

"It's not like you caught Nathan stealing." Garcia said.

"Yeah, I know, but I was a little messed up at the time too, I mean. But Nathan—to turn him in meant, you know, condemning him, right? I just—I couldn't get myself to make the final step to do it. Like I said, I almost told you guys. When Lydia was sitting there, I was just saying to myself, *Why is Lydia in the room?* You know, I had the guts to say it. I was ready to say it. I knew that it was going to be a long hard process to deal with, but I was ready to do it. Lydia was sitting right there, and I turned and looked at her, and she gave me this little pouty look of support. And I just, *Jeez, I can't do this in front of her.* I almost asked you if you could have her step out of the room, but then I didn't want her to think that I was trying to hide something from her."

"You had all this time, Duncan, and you run."

"Right," he admitted.

"Okay. And you are running, you were running?"

"Right."

"You staged a phony kidnapping in LA, and we know you called from the Greyhound bus station in Las Vegas," Garcia said, referring to Duncan's fake kidnapping call to Lydia.

"No... I called from the airport."

I clarified that the call came from a pay phone by a Greyhound bus stop at the Las Vegas airport. "You flew in there?" I asked.

"Uh-huh, I flew from Burbank."

"Where did you fly from there?"

"I didn't. I took a bus from there."

"Okay. That's where you called Lydia from?" asked Garcia.

"Yes."

"We checked that, and that's where that call was placed from... You know, I'm not here to analyze why you do what you do. I don't know. You are telling us right now."

"Right."

"But this looks—you know, you were digging a hole for yourself."

"Right, I was."

"When Nathan took the wallet, what did you guys do with that?"

"It went with the knife in the garbage can."

"Okay. You threw the knife away?"

"The knife which was wrapped in Nathan's bloody shirt and Ron's wallet all got thrown into the—"

"The same dumpster in the apartment next to yours, on Erwin Street?"

"Yes."

We did not ask Duncan about what happened with his own clothes, although, in retrospect, we probably should have. Based on his story, Duncan had not been close enough to Ron to get blood on his clothing. Also, given that it was well over a year after the fact, Duncan could have told us anything about his own clothing and we would not have been able to prove it either way.

"Okay," said Garcia. "You get there... Now, you don't remember when the knife and the shirt and everything went in?"

"He went into the apartment."

"Directly into your apartment?" I asked.

"Our apartment. Now, see, he had wiped himself off, right, but you could see the spots where his skin was darkened by the stains. Um, he got there first. I was still in the car or something. I remember because I walked in the apartment and he was there. And I think he ran, like, into the—I think Diane was watching TV, and he just walked back behind. Because remember how that couch was set there, and he just walked back in the bathroom."

"So she didn't see him?" asked Garcia.

"Um, she may have seen him come in and she may have been asleep too."

"But you weren't there?"

"I wasn't much behind him. Then I walked in and I sat at the dining room table, I believe. I think she was sitting on the couch. I think she asked me a couple of questions...You know, 'Oh, how was it? Da, da, da...' And we were like, 'Oh, fine. You know, no big deal.' I'm just trying to—you know, my hands are doing this." Duncan trembled them. "If she turned around, she probably would have seen that and been very curious, but I don't think she did. I think she was watching TV. Then Nathan came out, and I think he came out and went to the party, or went upstairs and found out there was a party, came down, told me there was a party, and I went up with him...We hung out at the party for a little bit. I couldn't deal so I left. I think I came downstairs and went to sleep. I either went to sleep or I sat there and played Nintendo for a little bit. But I think I went to sleep. I don't think I would have been in the mood to play Nintendo...I think I was asleep when Nathan came downstairs."

Duncan explained his decision to flee rather than reveal the truth. "I was scared to come back for two reasons. One, because I didn't want to get blamed for this whole thing, right? The whole reason I ran was because I didn't want to get blamed for it, and I was having trouble saying that Nathan did it. And two, was to face everybody and say, 'I was weak.' You know, I was weak. I should have had the balls to come out and say, 'This is what happened.' Instead, what did I do? I got scared and ran, right? The longer it went, the harder it became, because the longer I made everybody at home suffer. I knew I was putting everybody through torment, and I wanted to stop. When I called my mom, I was ready for her to yell at me and tell me that she hated me and all this stuff. I mean, I expected the worst."

"Okay. Your mom is totally aware of what you know or what your involvement is?"

"Um, no."

"You guys haven't talked about it?"

"My mom has no clue."

"She just thinks the same thing that she thought when you left town?" I asked.

"Well, what did I say to her… She said, 'I don't know if you want to—I don't think you probably want to tell me what happened or tell me anything about it.' And I said to her, 'Well, suffice it to say—because, no, I don't want to get into details—that I know what happened and was just too scared to say anything. That's why I left.'"

Garcia said, "Back to the night of the murder. You're back at your apartment… What was the conversation between you and him at this point?"

"Pretty much whatever he said, I did."

"Were you anything like, 'You crazy fucker, you did it. You killed him'?"

"No, I didn't want to risk calling him a crazy fucker."

"Well, 'Nathan, you killed him,' nothing like that?"

"No, I was shocked, and I was scared… What else do I remember that night? I definitely remember going up to the party. I don't remember getting any beer, any other time but that morning. I guess we could have gone then. I don't think so, though. Maybe we did."

"When did you clean up your car?"

"I didn't really clean it up that much. Probably a week and a half later, two weeks later. It was over at Lydia's house… I don't even think I—"

"So you are telling me, Duncan, that Nathan didn't get any blood on your car?"

"I don't think so. I really don't. I don't think he got any on the car. Because, like I say, he used his shirt to wipe his hands and wipe off his face and wipe his arms off, and all it did was grind the stuff in."

"You remember we tested your car for blood, right?"

"Yeah, I do. I don't—he may have gotten some on there."

"You didn't specifically clean your car, like with peroxide or something, to get the blood out?"

"No, not that I can think of."

"Did he ever ask you to do it?" I said.

"Not that I know of... I mean, it may have been done, but I don't think so."

Garcia said, "Duncan, after something like this, you know, going out and doing something like this, it's not like Rick and I go out and say, 'Hey, do you want to go out and shoot out some streetlights? That would be a lot of fun.' There had to be some conversation days afterward or something like that."

"Okay. Um, we spoke—he was there—"

"He wasn't there very long."

"No, he wasn't. He was gone real quick. And I remember you guys kept trying to talk to him and couldn't talk to him and you had to talk to me."

"I called him in Detroit," said Garcia.

"Oh, did you? I didn't know that. Every time I talked to him, he hadn't talked to you guys, and you guys would ask me questions about him. He wasn't there very long and then I guess he went to Detroit. And then when he got back from Detroit, he moved in with Diane in Riverside, and I saw him once after that. And that was at Lydia's house. He came over with Diane and he brought me outside, out front, and sat me down on the car. At this point I believe I had already spoken to Barnes. I had already pawned most of my stuff and I was ready to fly. I mean, I was gone as far as I knew, right? Um, and I spoke to him."

"Okay. Nathan came to Lydia's house. That's the house that you called up, to tell her that you were being kidnapped?"

"Right."

"What a bullshit story that was."

"Well, you have got to understand. When I left, I was paranoid. I thought you guys were two seconds behind me. When I got off the plane going into Vegas, I thought you guys were going to be standing right there... I'm serious. When I walked through the airport, every time I saw a security guard, I was ready for the dude to walk over to me and say, 'Oh, that's him.' When I was walking—I stayed in Vegas for a day... Every time I saw a police officer, I was ready for him to pull me over. 'Oh, you are the guy, right?' You know, and I was ready for it. I was waiting for it. When I made that phone call, it was just to make everybody think I was still in LA so I could get out of Vegas. I still stayed there for a day. I stayed there all the next day, to figure out what I was doing and to figure out—because I was in this big dilemma. Do I go home or do I bail? Do I go home or do I bail? I was just totally confused. And then I finally left."

"Okay. Nathan comes over to Lydia's house ... He takes you outside, and what did he say to you?"

"I don't remember exactly what he said, but I remember that I knew that I was going to bail. That I was just so scared that I was going to bail. And he talked to me and he told me, 'You know, you aren't about to break, are you? You are not going to say anything, are you?' And I was like, 'Oh, no, I am not going to say anything,' because I was ready to run. You know, running was going to be a lot easier than making a decision here."

"Did he tell you to get out of town?"

"No, he didn't."

"Did he want you to stay?"

"Oh, yeah. He wanted me to stay and he wanted to make sure that I wasn't going to break and rat on him. And like I say, I think everybody knew. Lydia and I think one other person saw us walk out front and have this conversation. And they had this look in their eye like—like they knew. I was just waiting for somebody to say something."

"Did he ever threaten you, Duncan?"

"Um, like I say, I remember this once. Um, and I don't remember if he, you know, verbally said anything beyond that. But I don't think he threatened me that night either. Um, but I was still scared of him. Um, one of the things that scared me the most about him was that it did nothing negative toward him, the incident. All it did was positive. I mean, you know how in comic books when they show somebody, they stand like this, and their chest is out and their back is bent and their arms are in this perfect flex position and they stand there, Captain America or whoever? That's how Nathan stood. I mean, Nathan had been like this for a while. You know, he was all buffed out. And now he was, boom, just this Superman and—"

"What about those other knives that you guys used for the Wicca bullshit?" Garcia asked.

"Those were Renaissance Faire knives. Those were just our eating knives from the Renaissance Faire." Duncan said he was absolutely certain his Renaissance Faire knife was not at the tunnel on the night of Ron's murder.

"Was Nathan's?"

"Nathan didn't have one of those. Ron had one, and I had one. I don't think Nathan had one. And mine definitely wasn't there that night, unless somebody else brought it, and I don't think they did because it was where I left it in my room."

"So all the stab wounds in Ron's body came from your Marine Corps–type knife?"

"Uh-huh."

"And Nathan stabbed him?"

"As far as I know... It was pitch-dark so theoretically, theoretically, he could have used a different knife, but I don't think he did. I am ninety-nine percent sure he didn't. My Renaissance Faire knife wasn't—it was my eating knife. I mean, that's what I used at the Renaissance Faire to eat with. I think I told you guys, when you told me you were going to check it for blood, that I had cut myself with it before, because I had. But it wasn't there that night, at least not anywhere near my knowledge. Like I said, I don't think Nathan had one of those either."

"Let me ask you something, Duncan," said Garcia.

Duncan said okay.

"What if we go to Nathan tomorrow and we are like, 'Guess what, Nathan, here is the story. You killed Ron Baker.'"

"Right."

"And he says, "Oh, no, no, I didn't kill him. Duncan Martinez killed him.' Give us something, Duncan."

"Well... Here are the things that I could think of. I brought up the—on the back of the hand. I mentioned that it looked to me like somebody's hand had done this, right?... Now I was curious as to the fact that maybe some skin had been left under a fingernail. I could see that as being at least likely. Because, like I say, it looked like somebody's hand had done this."

"Did you get any blood on you at all, that you were aware of?" I asked.

"No."

"On your clothing, hands, anything?"

"No, no, I don't believe so. If I did, I got it on there afterwards—after, like, when Nathan was wiping himself off or something. But I don't believe I did. I don't recall having any on me. And if I had, I think I would remember it. Because that would have been something that would have bothered me."

It was surprising to me that Duncan would focus on possibly getting a small amount of blood on him as so disturbing. Minutes earlier, after all, he had just witnessed the slaughter of his closest friend. Was the blood so bad, in comparison to the sight and sounds of Ron being stabbed over and over and his throat slit? It felt to me like an actor's rendition of being horrified, overdramatizing his revulsion to Ron's blood to try to humanize himself.

I asked Duncan, "Did you ever make a list, on paper like this, of the things that you had to do before you got out of town, like dump the car?"

"I don't think so, but I may have. But I'm definitely a list maker."

"Well, you did," Garcia informed him.

"Did I? If I did, I would assume that it would have been left in the hotel room where I stayed that day. And if not—"

"What hotel room?"

"In the Valley."

"That's not where it was."

"Really? Wow... That's the only place that I could sensibly think of where I left it, unless it just totally slipped my mind."

Garcia didn't reveal to him where we had found his incriminating "Things To Do" list, in a box he had asked the Bakers to store for him after Ron's murder.

"Duncan, did you stab Ron?"

"No, I didn't. I can honestly say I did not kill Ron. I did not stab Ron in any way."

"Did Nathan tell you, 'Hey, come here. You give him a hit too. Give him a lick—I did'?"

"No."

"None of that shit happened?"

"No."

"You know we can't use this against you," Garcia reminded Duncan.

"Right, I know you can't and I'm telling—"

"Did you have any part to do with it? Was there one knife that was being jammed into Ron's body?"

"Yes, there was."

"And you had nothing to do with it?"

"I did not stab him."

"Nathan didn't intimidate you or scare you or tell you, 'You have got to give him a lick too'?"

"Nope."

"You stayed away from him?"

"Yes, I did. I refused to touch the body or move it at all."

"After this happened, Duncan, did you tell anybody, confide in anybody, 'You ain't going to believe what happened'? To anybody, did you tell that to?"

"In LA?"

"Anywhere," said Garcia.

We wanted Duncan to tell us everyone he had spoken to about Ron's murder. It was important for us to know. We would likely interview most of them, to learn whether what he told us was consistent with what he had told them. It was crucial in weighing Duncan's credibility, whether it helped him or hurt him. It was also part of his King for a Day agreement that if he told us whom he'd spoken with, all his statements to them could not be used against him in court.

"What about Purpura?" asked Garcia, referring to James Purpura, Duncan's roommate in Utah, whom he had met while on the lam and had lived with in Boston. Garcia and I planned to interview Purpura the next day.

"He knows a little about it."

"What does he know about it?"

"He knows that the incident occurred. He knows that I witnessed the incident. And he knows that that's why I took off."

"When did you run this down to Purpura?"

"When I was in Boston still."

"When?"

Duncan said it was about three months earlier, in late November 1991, when he told Purpura about Ron's murder.

"Did you tell anybody else?"

"Oh, yeah. I talked to a counselor about it and I told her everything."

"Where?"

"Park City."

"Right over here?" asked Garcia, referring to the ski resort town outside of Salt Lake City.

"Uh-huh."

"When did this happen?"

"That started when I got here. Just after I got here I started seeing her."

"I don't know when you got here."

"I got here December 5th or 6th, I believe."

"What is her name?"

"Nancy Bradish. I think I started seeing her a week or two after I got here."

"How much did you tell the counselor, Nancy Bradish?" I asked.

"Um, everything."

"Just as much as you told us or maybe not in as much detail?"

"I don't think I went into as much detail, no. I didn't go into as much detail, no. I didn't go into as much detail on real events around it. She asked me about feelings... How I felt here, how I felt there. And there is a lot of stuff that I told you—"

It looked like Bradish's name rang a bell for Garcia. Then suddenly it seemed to come to him. "Is she a tall...?" he asked.

"Yeah, she is real tall."

"Real thin too?"

"Yeah, pretty thin, curly hair."

"I used to go to high school with a Nancy Bradish."

"It sounds like her. Really cool?... She is good at chess too. I haven't played her yet, but I would like to."

"Did you ever play chess with her, Frank?" I teased Garcia.

"No, we weren't into chess in high school," Garcia replied. "Duncan, is there anything that's important that you haven't told us, any little thing, Duncan?"

"No. Um..."

"Duncan, you know we may have to do this a couple more times... And of course we will contact Mr. Barnes here. There is going to be stuff that comes up... The more people we talk to, the more questions that are going to come up."

"Okay."

"And we want to get this cleared up."

"I do too. I really do."

"There are a lot of people back in Los Angeles that are grieving over this and have suffered a loss over this."

"I know."

"And a lot of the guilt and responsibility is on your ass now."

"I know."

"And I'm sure you know that."

"No, I agree. If I think of anything else that... All I'm going to be able to do tonight is—"

"Do me a favor from now on, if you think of anything about the case... Write it down... And try and keep track of it, okay? What should be checked."

"Okay."

I told Duncan, "There are going to be things that we think of after we leave here that we should have asked. And again, this isn't going to be a one-time thing. We are going to end up talking to you other times." I also had some questions for Duncan. "The kidnapping story that you saw on TV, did you actually see that with Nathan, or did Nathan tell you about it?"

"We watched it together... I think it was, like, an old *Dragnet* or something."

"Okay. Did the person in that story get killed?"

"Oh, jeez, um, I don't think so... I'm not sure, though."

Garcia asked, "How did this story get to the point where whoever the victim was—whether it be John Sands or eventually Ron Baker—how did that come about, as far as he was going to be killed?"

"Well, I believe it was said like, 'Gee, we should do this, but you know, what the hell would we do with somebody? You know, we would have to off them or something like that.' And it was like, 'Oh, yeah.' I mean, at the time we were joking around. I don't think it was—I think that's how it came about. It was just kind of like, 'What would we do with somebody?' You know, we don't have someplace to take them or anything like that. I think we would just have to, you know, kill them... I think Nathan brought up the thing and brought it out a little bit. And I was like, 'Oh, yeah, we should do that to John Sands. I hated that guy in high school,' you know. And I was like, 'Oh, let's call him,' and we called him."

I asked Duncan, "After that one time that you talked to his mom, was there ever any further attempt to contact him, or did you actually contact him, or did he contact you?"

"I left a message I think with his mom. And I may have tried to call back later that afternoon. I remember something about calling back or something."

"Do you remember talking to him?"

"No, I didn't talk to him. I talked to his mom. I think his mom may have said something... I can't remember what it is. Um, but I definitely remember talking to his mom."

"Duncan, the call... We know what time the first call came in, to Mr. Baker. Mr. Baker made a note of it and told us. I'm not going to tell you the specifics, because I don't want to fog up your mind with what Mr. Baker recalls. But I want to go back over that first call. You are positive the first call to Mr. Baker was made while you were driving back from Chatsworth Park and made before you got to your apartment, or could you have gone to your apartment?"

"No, it was definitely before... Definitely."

"Okay. And you were home by, you said by ten or ten thirty?"

"I think so. I'm not one hundred percent positive of when we got home, but I think that's about when we got home... Or got to the party actually... I think it was ten thirty. But, again..."

"Okay. Diane... To your knowledge, does she know anything about what happened?"

"No, no clue, no clue."

"Did Nathan ever tell you he never told her?"

"Nathan wanted to set up—wanted to marry her, wanted to set up a nice life with her and just make things all hunky-dory. There is no way he would have ever told her, I don't think."

"Did Diane, who was there that night, know that Ron was going with you two?"

"No... Well, she knew he was going downstairs with us, but she didn't know he was going to the park with us. She thought we were dropping him off at the bus stop."

"Okay. Why did you tell—because earlier you said Nathan told Ron, 'Don't tell Diane.'"

"Because the excuse he used with Ron was that we were supposed to be meeting some girls up there and Nathan was going out with Diane and he didn't want her to find out."

"Okay. So where did Ron tell Diane he was going or what did anybody say, or do you know?"

"Um, Ron said that he was going to go to a Mystic's Circle meeting and that we were dropping him off at the bus stop, when she asked where he was going. That's where the whole idea came from."

"Do you remember him saying that to her? Or is that something you heard about later?"

"I remember that being said... I'm not sure if I was there when he said that, because I may very well have been, or that if later on it was brought up. Or it may have been said, 'Yeah, you know, he told Diane that he was going to a Mystic's Circle meeting,' or Nathan may have said to Diane, 'We are dropping him off because he is going to a Mystic's Circle meeting.' I'm not sure, but I think Ron said it."

"Where did Diane think you and Nathan were going to?"

"Hazeltine Elementary."

"Who told her that?"

"Me and Nathan. I think that was our original plan for the day."

"That's what you ended up telling us."

"Right."

"That was your alibi."

"Right, because we used to do it all the time."

I asked Duncan, "Did you know the Bakers' phone number by heart?"

"Um, yeah, I think so."

"Do you remember having to look it up or calling information, or whether it was even in the phone book or a listed number?"

"If I looked it up, I looked it up at our apartment beforehand or something."

"Why would you do that?" I asked. Duncan had insisted earlier in the interview that he did not believe the plan to kidnap, kill, and seek a ransom for Ron was real. If the plan wasn't real, why look up the Bakers' phone number beforehand? Both couldn't be true.

"Um, that's a good question, so I don't think I did look it up. That's a very good question," he said. I wondered if Duncan had caught himself and realized mid-answer that it would go against his claim of no premeditation if he had in fact looked up the Bakers' number beforehand.

"Let me ask you this. Ron's your friend?"

"Right."

"All right. Why would you even—and I want to pick your brain, I want you to be honest—why would you even go along to a park where another friend of yours had even talked about doing a hostage thing, and then offing a friend of yours?"

"Um…"

"What was going through your mind?"

"Well, it was such a ludicrous thing to me that I never—it never crossed my mind that it was real to me. At all… Nathan wasn't capable of that in my eyes. There was no reason for it in my eyes. I don't know. They say hindsight is twenty-twenty, and I can see a lot of things now that I didn't notice then.

"I mean, they had arguments a lot, in front of other people too. But at the time I had no—there was no concept of it being real. It was like if somebody was going to tell me that they were going to, you know, rebuild the zeppelin from the parts that were left over—it's just like, that's impossible. There is nothing left. It was totally ludicrous.

"There was no way in my mind that it was possible for Nathan to commit that. There was no way in my mind that it was possible for Nathan to even realistically think about committing that. So when we were going to go to the park, I wasn't looking at it like, *Jeez, you know, I'm going to the park and I'm going to see this happen.* I was looking at it like, *I'm going to the park.* You know, all I was doing it for, all I was in it for, was going to the park and have a few beers.

Um, and no realization that it could in any way be real. It just didn't make sense."

Garcia and I could have pointed out that Duncan's analogy about rebuilding the *Hindenburg* was itself ludicrous and made no sense, but we didn't bother. We were already used to his hyperbole. It was clear that he had a way with words, and a flair for dramatic, vivid descriptions and imagery, such as his comparison of Nathan's aura to Superman's. But there was an out-of-left-field quality to some of what he said, like his zeppelin metaphor, that made you wonder how in the world he came up with what he had said. I believed that Duncan was intelligent and wanted to seem erudite, but he was also prone to overreaching and saying too much, especially once he got talking.

I asked him, "You said earlier, and correct me if I'm wrong... what I got out of your statement was that there was no indication that this was even going to go through, even though it had been talked about, until Nathan fell or tripped and Ron made some kind of a statement."

"Right. Um, yeah, I think that was the time. I guess a lot of stuff had been building up in him. I mean, I have tried to picture what caused this. I tried to go over this in my brain. I mean, I have had a year and a half or two years or however long it has been to work this out.

"And the only thing I can see is, yeah, they had a lot of little arguments. They had a lot of problems around the apartment and I guess it just built up in him, and that remark was the final thing that snapped. Um, because it wasn't him that did that, to me. I mean, it was him, it was physically his person. But it wasn't the Nathan that I knew.

"Because the Nathan I knew, if he saw a cockroach running across the floor and it was just me and him in the apartment, would pick it up and drop it off the railing so it wouldn't die. I mean, if there were a bunch of girls there, he couldn't do it, he had to kill it, to show the girls that he was a big strong guy. But I saw him many times go save bugs just because it was, you know, not that much of a hassle to run it outside. And it wasn't in him. It wasn't the kind of thing that Nathan was capable of, to me.

"I mean, obviously it was, but not in my eyes... He could have sat down for five hours and babbled a plan at me and I would have laughed at him the whole time and not believed it."

I asked Duncan, "Was there anything that happened at the park before then, whether he shook his head or winked at you or anything else, that gave you an indication that he was thinking of this plan, or this thing that had been discussed earlier, regarding the kidnapping, hostage, killing, whatever it was going to be? Was there anything that happened at the park?"

"No, although, I mean, if it had, I don't think I would have noticed. Like I said, I didn't—there was no concept of this being real to me. I mean, if Nathan had looked at me and made some funny look at me, I would have thought he was just getting drunk and made a funny look."

"Was Nathan drunk when this happened?"

"Um, I have been trying to think how much beer we drank and I'm trying to remember. The only way I can think of to try to remember how many beers were left in the case is trying to remember how heavy it was. And that's just totally eluding me. I know we were going about beer for beer... When we went into the tunnel, I think I had a decent buzz going. Um, I'm not—"

"What about Ron?" I asked. I knew from Ron's toxicology report that his blood-alcohol level was 0.21 percent when he was killed, more than double the legal limit to drive.

"I think we were all about the same. I mean, we all used to drink together a lot. Ron couldn't quite keep up in the long run, and he was a smaller guy. But he would drink with us for a while before he would fall behind."

"How about any dope that night?"

"No."

"Any grass, coke, anything?"

"No."

"Before you left?"

"No."

"Had you drank any before you left?"

"No."

"Did Nathan drink before he left, that you saw?"

"No."

"How about Ron? Did Ron drink before he left?"

"No."

"Isn't it true that Ron wasn't a big drinker?"

"Um…"

"Would he go out and drink on his own?"

"Well, Ron would drink with me or Nathan or something, or if a bunch of people were hanging out, but Ron didn't drink every day. Me and Nathan drank just about every day… I would say we probably had at least a six-pack apiece that night from the case."

"What was the discussion afterwards, like, 'Holy shit, this thing really went down. Okay. Let's just get our stories straight one more time'?"

"I don't think we really had much of a discussion like that. And if it was, it would have been a very one-sided discussion, because as far as the whole thing went, I didn't want to talk about it. I mean, once we left the park, once everything had been taken care of as far as the knife and stuff, I just didn't want to think about it. But if we had a discussion, and I think we—I think Nathan probably said, 'Yeah, remember, you know, we went to Hazeltine Elementary tonight and we drank some beers. Then we came back in and that's all we did.' But I don't remember. I don't remember the conversation, though we may have very well had one. But that would have been the extent of what was said."

"Was there any discussion about telling the police that you dropped Ron off at the bus stop?"

"I'm sure that was gone into at the same time."

"Would you have gotten as specific as 'Okay. This was the corner that we dropped him off at'?"

"No, I don't think so. Probably not."

"So looking back on it, is it sort of surprising that you guys got involved in this kind of thing and didn't really—"

"Well, like I say, to me there wasn't anything—nothing was going to happen. I mean, there was no need for an elaborate plan, because nothing was going to be executed. I'm definitely—"

"I'm talking about afterwards, after it was executed."

"Oh, well, to be honest with you, I think I would have been relieved if it had been found out, because then it would have forced me to say what I knew. So I don't think I put any real effort towards anything. Um—"

Garcia interrupted. "I think what Rick is getting at, like after we put you on the polygraph and we told you, 'You are lying to us—'"

"Right."

"'Dammit, we know that you were there. Everything indicates that you were there.' Did you, like, get on the phone and call Nathan and say, 'Hey, man, these motherfuckers are on my ass'?"

"Um, let me think."

"Or did he ever call you and say, 'They have been down here. The cops are down here. You know you better stick to your story,' or anything like that?"

"I don't remember him ever telling me that he spoke with you. I believe he called and said he was coming down the night he came down, and I seem to remember that someone else gave me a message saying Nathan was going to come by tonight. But I also remember talking to him once on the phone. But what I remember—and I talked to him more than once on the phone, but I remember talking to him once on the phone at Lydia's. And of my conversations with him, I don't remember him bringing up having spoken to you guys. I remember him saying, 'No, I haven't talked to them yet.' You know, 'What did they ask you?'"

"He asked you that?"

"Yeah."

"Did you tell him?" I asked.

"I said, you know, 'They just asked me where we were and what we did. And I told them that we went to Hazeltine Elementary and we had some beers and we came back.'"

Garcia said, "Because if I was Nathan, I would be real worried as to what the hell you are going to tell the police and I would be checking with you."

"Right."

"Constantly."

"I don't think he was worried that I was going to say anything."

"Does he trust you that much?"

"We were best friends. I mean, see, that's the thing that screws me up so bad, is that they were both my best friends. They were both really, really close friends to me. Um, and you just assume when you have two people that are your close, close friends, that makes them best friends too. Do you know what I mean? And they weren't, I mean, obviously."

I halted the interview because our recorder was about to run out of tape again. We had been talking with Duncan for about two hours.

"You know as much about me as I do," Duncan said as the interview resumed, with a fresh tape rolling.

Garcia said, "I mean, if it was Rick and I, and I had stabbed somebody or Rick had stabbed somebody, and there was only one person in the world between me…and going to prison for the rest of my life, I mean, shit, I would be real concerned, Duncan, as to who was saying what about me, especially you."

"I understand. I understand completely…I mean, we did talk. I mean, when I was still in Van Nuys after he left…My memory is of him leaving and going straight to Riverside."

"Was there any conversation? 'What have the cops been talking to you about?'"

"I mean, like I say, he asked me, and I said, 'Yeah, they talked to me today.' And he would say, 'What did they say?' and I told him. You know, but I don't think I ever went into any real detail on it. I don't think he—I think he was so convinced that—he was on such a high from the event that I think he was so convinced that there was no way anybody could ever catch him."

"Why did Nathan kill Ron?" Garcia asked. "That still doesn't make sense to me."

"You know, it doesn't completely click with me either. I mean, I would come up with some hypotheses but nothing that would explain it to me."

"It didn't seem like, whatever little arguments they had…I mean—"

"They were petty," Duncan conceded. "I mean, they were all petty."

"Nathan would get pissed off?"

"Yeah, but so would Ron. They would get pissed off for five minutes, then it would be over."

I asked, "What did he tell you afterwards? He had to say something about why he reacted to whatever, or why he did this or why he did that. What do you recall, or did you ask him, 'What did you do that for?'"

"Well, I kind of—you mean as far as their arguments and stuff?"

"No, as far as the killing."

"I didn't... You have to understand that I did not want to talk about the killing. I did not want to talk anything about that.

"I was just so blown away. I mean, I was so freaked by that. And I still—I mean, when I talk about it, I just... It freaks me out. Um, I did not want to speak about the killing. I mean, when I was speaking to you guys, I was just doing my best to control myself. When he would ask me what you said, I would give him a quick, brief thing and I would try to get on to something else immediately, and just try and deal, try and deal with everything else. You know, try to put my brain on something entirely differently, because it just—I didn't want to talk about it.

"Like I said before, I mean I was wrong. I was wrong about Nathan. Um, I believed that Nathan didn't have that in him, and he did. I was wrong. Admitting that I was wrong was a big thing. And admitting it to myself is the hardest part, you know.

"Um, and the more I thought about it, the more I had to think to myself that jeez, I was completely wrong. My judgment of this person was completely wrong. I thought this guy was as harmless as they come and here he goes murdering somebody out of the blue. I mean, it wasn't completely out of the blue, but as far as I was concerned, it was out of the blue."

I asked, "Did he ever say anything to you afterwards, like 'I couldn't believe I did it' or 'The asshole just pushed me too far' or—"

"No."

"Duncan," Garcia said, "this Marine knife and the tunnel and all that shit, that sounds like some of the shit that you would dream up. I'm going back to your CIA missions in Iran, all this bullshit."

"Why was that?"

"No, I'm saying it sounds like something that you would dream up, and not something that Nathan would dream up."

"Um, the tunnel, no. I mean, it's a secluded place, it's a secluded place where we used to go often."

"And you went there to drink?"

"Yeah, we used to... I mean, I had gone there before."

"You were there that night because you heard him talking about it earlier that afternoon, that Nathan was going to take out Ron?"

"Yeah, we were going to go drink and Nathan told me that, and I didn't believe him."

"That he was going to kill Ron?"

"Yeah. Well, he said... What did he say? I don't think he said those words. I think he said, 'Yeah, it's all going to happen tonight' or 'We're going to do it tonight,' and I'm like, 'Yeah, whatever,' because I just didn't believe him at all."

"He took your Marine Corps–type knife?"

"Yeah, we used to take that up there all the time because there are a lot of weirdos that hang out there."

I asked Duncan to go back to Nathan having the knife. "How did that come about?"

"Usually I would be the one that carried the knife up there—not always, but usually. And we always took something up there. Nathan didn't have a knife, as far as I remember. And when we were getting ready to go, he went and strapped on my knife."

"He had it strapped up?" asked Garcia.

"Yeah, it's got a—I had it set with a string so you could put it here on your belt, um, just because it's easier to carry. Because, I mean, with the sheath it's about this long," said Duncan, showing with his hands.

"About a foot long?" I estimated.

"Yeah."

"Where is the sheath now?"

"You know, I don't think the sheath got thrown away with the knife. I could be wrong about that, but I don't think the sheath got thrown... The sheath may have been left up at Chatsworth Park and it may have gotten thrown away with the knife. But I think I remember him just wrapping the knife up in the shirt, and I don't remember the sheath getting wrapped up in it. I'm not positive... Maybe it did get put in the sheath and wrapped up. It was dark."

"Was there any discussion on that night why he was taking it?"

"No."

"Did he say, 'This is how I'm going to do Ron' or—"

"I mean, if I had believed him, if I had believed that this thing was going to go down, I would have just assumed that's why he wanted to carry the knife. But I didn't believe it was going to go down."

"He told you it was going to go down," said Garcia.

"Yeah, but I mean, how many times have you heard somebody say—"

"He told you—"

"Right, he did tell me. But I mean, how many times have you heard somebody say, 'Oh, I'm going to kill him,' and it doesn't happen. And if everybody flipped out every time they heard that, I mean, we would have a lot of people flipping out a lot."

"Why that spot?"

"Um, I don't know. It's a place I had gone with Nathan before. It was a place that was secluded."

"Had you talked about it before at that spot?"

"Um, jeez, I don't remember."

"Like, 'This is a real neat place to kill somebody'?" Garcia asked.

"No, Chatsworth Park was always a real cool—that's where I go to think. That's where I would go when I wanted to be off on my own. Because if you went up in the hills far enough in the back, nobody ever went back there. I mean, it had no graffiti. Nobody ever went that far back. And so that's why I first went up there with a group of people and started doing it a lot. It was to drink. And then when Lance had his little class, we went up there and had a circle there once or twice. Um, then after that I went there to drink."

"Speaking of Lance, did you tell Lance or anybody in that group what happened?"

"No... I didn't confide in anybody before I left."

"How about your real father?"

"I told him something about it, but I don't remember exactly what I told him."

"How about Shirley?" Garcia asked, referring to Duncan's stepmom. "Did you tell Shirley?"

"Shirley was there when I talked to Duncan," Duncan said, calling his father by his first name. "I'm sure you have talked to them. I don't know if you have met them... I know I talked to them about it. I know

I talked about it for a while. They are the ones that drove me over to Kentucky—the University of Kentucky... We went to the library to find out what name I should use. And we looked up a guy who had just turned twenty or was about to turn twenty-one, so I could get a birth certificate and get an ID, and they are the ones who told me about that... And we, uh, just went into the card catalog or they had a computer, I think, and looked up a name."

The initial false identity Duncan had stolen and assumed in Kentucky was James Atkins. Later, he had adopted a different alias, Jonathan Wayne Miller, which he had used until he was arrested in Utah.

I asked Duncan, "The call to Ron's dad... What was the purpose?"

"Um, it was the hostage call or kidnapping call."

"Okay. For your thought or for Nathan's thought, was it to get money?"

"Um, yeah, but I mean—"

"What was—"

"I mean, okay. Nathan knew as well as I knew, right, that kidnappings just don't work. We knew that, and I know he knew that. As a matter of fact, I think even the first time we brought up the kidnapping and we called John Sands and he wasn't there and we couldn't get in touch with him, I think I even turned around and said, 'Well, kidnappings don't work anyway.' And he was like, 'Oh, yeah, that's true.' I mean, I think I said that. I'm not one hundred percent, but I think I said something like that. At least I thought something like that. You know, 'Come on, what are we even thinking about something stupid like this for anyway, because (a) it's really stupid and (b) it's totally illegal and (c) it could never work.' But when—to make the phone call, I think he had this feeling in his brain that since he accomplished that, he could do anything. And that because he was behind it, that we would get money."

"This is your assumption?"

"Right, this is complete assumption. He never said anything like this. But this is just my feeling from having looked at him that night and the next day and everything, because, I mean, he was on top of the world. Nobody could have done anything to him in those couple of days. I mean, he was just—I mean 'Superman' is even a little too little of a word."

"Weren't you guys concerned that you were going to be connected with Baker?" asked Garcia.

"I was. He wasn't."

"Wasn't Nathan?"

"I don't think Nathan had a worry in the world. I don't think Nathan would have worried if it was on video camera and fifty people had seen it. That's how high he was on this. I mean, my initial worry had nothing to do with getting caught. I mean, my brain wasn't going that far in the future. My brain was going, *This minute, what am I supposed to do?* You know, what am I supposed to do? You know, do I—because I wanted to run to the phone and call the police. When I went to make the hostage phone call, I almost dialed 911. And I was like, *Jeez, this is going to be interesting if the police show up and he gets away. What am I going to do?*"

"Where?" I asked. "When you called where? When you went to where?"

"When I went to make the phone call... He stayed in the car and I almost called 911."

"I wish you would have," I said.

"So do I. You know, I have been going back on points in this when I really wish I had turned around and done the opposite thing I did. And, I mean, from the minute the incident occurred, the first thing I wish I had done was dial 911, the very first thing. And before the incident occurred there was a hundred things I would do to change it, a hundred things."

"I'm not trying to put words in your mouth, because this may have nothing to do with it, but was that call made—either in your thoughts or else discussed between you and Nathan—that this may throw the police off? Because obviously they are going to get involved... To think that it was a kidnapping, rather than him being out with a couple of friends, if they find out?"

"No, that was never brought up... I don't think either of us was—I mean, I don't think he would have cared to think something like that. And I don't think I was capable of trying to think of something like that then."

"Was any money kept from Ron's wallet by either you or Nathan?" I asked.

"Um, I think he had a couple of bucks in there and I think Nathan grabbed it."

"Okay. Did he keep any of it?"

"Nah, I think Nathan bought beer with it the next day."

"How about credit cards? Did he have credit cards?"

"He had a credit card, but it was left in there."

"Any other property taken out of his wallet that was kept?" I asked.

"I don't believe so."

"How about a watch?"

"No, he didn't wear one. He had one at home, but he very rarely wore it."

"Okay. What was the purpose of you calling Lydia?"

"From Nevada?" asked Duncan.

"From Nevada and saying, 'They're holding me. Call Garcia.'"

"I was paranoid. I thought that you guys knew that I was running. I thought you guys pretty much knew where I was, were about to figure out where I was. And I did that just to get everybody looking the other direction so I could get out of there, and quick… I was ready for somebody to run around the corner any minute, and it took me about six months to get off of that. I mean, every night I would go to work, and I was ready for somebody to run into work and say, 'Hey, you are under arrest.' And it was completely, I mean, unrealistic but that was what was going through my head… I kind of wish I hadn't made that call too. That was really cruel, but I mean, I wasn't—"

"Why did you cash the check, forge the check?" I interrupted.

"We were broke and Nathan said, 'Why don't we write a check on Ron's account?' and I really wasn't in any shape to disagree. I mean, at this point as far as I was concerned, anything he told me to do I would have done, I mean, just about. If he had kept telling me to do stuff, I guess he would have eventually pushed me over the limit and I would have come to you guys. But—"

"Okay. So it was his idea?"

"Yeah."

"It wasn't your idea?"

"No."

"Okay. You wrote the—"

"I wrote the check."

"You wrote on the whole check?"

"Uh-huh."

"Did he write on any of it?"

"I don't believe so."

"Okay. And you backdated it?"

"Yeah."

"Okay. Obviously you agree that you knew Ron wasn't coming back at that point to catch this check, right?"

"Right."

"Why did you go back to the park, that you told us about?" I asked. "If you did go back."

"We did go back. Um, the purpose was Nathan was ticked off that I wouldn't help him move the body, and he was worried that it was out in the open. And he didn't want it to be found because it would ruin the whole kidnapping deal... I believe that was three or four days later—"

"What was three or four days later?"

"When we went back to the park. Maybe it was—or maybe it was the next day or maybe it was like two days later."

"Okay. We're not going to tell you," I said.

"I don't remember for sure."

"I want you to remember it the way you remember it."

"I am thinking that maybe it was Saturday, because there was a bunch of people there. I mean, there was a bunch of people hanging out, but I'm not sure exactly what day it was. Um, and the point of going back was Nathan wanted to get some gasoline and torch it so that it wouldn't be recognizable."

"Did he have gasoline?"

"Yeah. Brought me along, we stopped at a gas station, um, picked up one of the little things of gasoline, went up there, he walked into the tunnel, came back out, and said he was gone. We had seen a bunch of search-and-rescue people down below, so we figured that's what had happened, they found him, and we left. And I told you guys about that because I thought maybe the search-and-rescue people wrote down the license numbers or something."

"That's why you told us you had gone back there?"

"Yeah."

"And you didn't go into the tunnel then?"

"No, I walked up to the mouth of it and I wouldn't go in."

"Nathan went by himself?"

"Yeah, I'm pretty sure I refused to go in there too."

"Did anything get left behind at the crime scene, that you know of?"

"No, I can't think of anything."

"Did anybody have sunglasses that night?" I asked. I remembered the pair of chunky black plastic sunglasses were found about ten feet from Ron's body.

"Yeah, I think Ron had a pair of... What do you call them? The ones that... What are the ones that the Mexican gangsters wear? You know what I'm talking about?"

"Those wraparound types?" said Garcia.

"Well, not completely wraparound but the square ones that are all black. I think that's what they were... I think Ron had a pair of sunglasses that night. And I think we asked him why he was bringing sunglasses with him, and I don't remember what he said. But I think it was a joke and he was just doing it to be weird."

"Like the ones that the cholos wear?" asked Garcia.

"Yeah. I know he had a pair of those, and I think those are the ones that he had with him that night."

Our interview had passed the three-hour mark. I asked Garcia if he had any further questions.

"Duncan, you had a lot of opportunities to tell us this... You never did it," said Garcia.

"Right."

"And what I want to understand is: We keep asking you if you are afraid of Nathan. We have asked you, and you are saying, 'Well, if I get the jump on him, it will be pretty much even, and if he gets the jump on me, it's over with.' There is an implied or some kind of... that you are afraid of him, and you are implying to us that you are afraid of him."

"Yes, I am very much so."

"And he was your best friend and Ron was your best friend?"

"Uh-huh."

"Are you telling us this now because it's the truth?"

"Yes."

"And you didn't stab Ron?"

"Nope, I did not stab Ron."

"And if we talk to Nathan, he is not going to say you stabbed Ron?"

"Unless he lies... I'm really trying to think of anything I can give you that would—"

"Well, you are going to have a lot of time to think," I told Duncan. "I don't know what is going on with your case here, but you are going to have some time to think. Especially now that you have told us, let it out."

"Right."

"You are going to start thinking about a lot of this anyway... You already have, obviously. But you are going to start thinking and you are going to think of things. What we don't want you to do, and I'm not saying you are going to do this, but we don't want you to just generate something just to try to give us something to make us happy or make us believe this. We want only the truth."

"Okay."

"And I'm sure your attorney has told you to tell us exactly the way you recall it... But if you do think of something, let him know and he will let us know and we will meet back again—"

"Okay."

"What are you looking at here?" Garcia asked.

"The court case here?"

"Yeah."

"From what my attorney said, Mr. Booker, he said that... the FBI guy said that it would probably go on the back burner for this. And my attorney here said that at most I would probably get six months, and more than likely I would probably be on low-range probation. Um, what they were worried about was that I was some big drug lord or something, or wanted in seventeen states for ax murder or something like that. But I don't know. I have a court case on Wednesday, and from what I understand, that is going to pretty much decide what happens."

Garcia asked Duncan about his friend Jim Purpura. "If we go to talk with Jim tomorrow, is he going to clam up on us?"

"I hope not."

"Does he know that you are talking to us?" I asked.

"Yeah, he does, and I will probably call him up tonight and tell him."

"Okay. I was going to suggest that, Duncan," said Garcia. "Call him up and tell him that we will be there tomorrow or call him in the morning. And it's imperative that he tell us the truth."

"Okay. I'll tell him that."

I added, "And do us a favor. We're not going to be there to monitor, but do not discuss any of the things we have discussed with you. We want to talk to him—"

"Okay."

"The least people that know about this, the better off," said Garcia.

Duncan asked, "Is there a number where I can get through to you guys, to contact you if I have to?"

Garcia gave Duncan his card but told him, "Mr. Barnes probably doesn't want you calling us directly at this point…You should probably go through him and we'll get in touch with you somehow…We really appreciate your candor, Duncan. And like I said, it's going to be tough."

"I know, and I'm ready for it."

"You have a lot of work to do," Garcia said, just before we stopped the tape recorder.

Garcia and I had a lot of work to do as well. It had been an extremely illuminating interview. Duncan had given us a multitude of new leads and information we would need to follow up on in the days ahead.

CHAPTER 14

BLOOD WARRANT
(February 11 to July 6, 1992)

FOLLOWING OUR INTERVIEW WITH Duncan, Garcia and I discussed how we thought our investigation should move forward. We decided that we would use the now-willing Duncan to gather evidence against Nathan. This meant that between our two suspects, we would be using the "white guy" to build a case against the "Black guy."

We did not choose that path. That path was chosen for us when Duncan indicated he was willing to cooperate. Had the scenario been reversed, and Nathan the first to assist, we would have used him and gone for Duncan's jugular instead. We also were not precluded from later seeking charges against Duncan if we could gather sufficient admissible evidence.

I knew in my heart that our approach was sound and justified, based on the circumstances. At the same time, I couldn't ignore the optics of this turn in the case and how it might be perceived by some as racial bias.

It was a tense time in Los Angeles. The beating of Rodney King, still less than a year earlier, remained fresh in the public's mind. The demonstration of police brutality immortalized in Holliday's video had stoked racial divisions and resentment of the police. It seemed like those feelings had barely subsided. Los Angeles was on edge as it awaited the upcoming trial of the four LAPD officers charged for their role in King's beating.

Assuming that, with Duncan's help, we amassed enough evidence to charge Nathan, how would our investigative strategy be perceived by the jury? How would those sitting in judgment of Nathan also judge me and Garcia, who had advanced with that strategy?

I knew that any distrust of us or our actions in the case had the potential to alter a juror's vote and the likelihood of the full jury reaching a unanimous verdict.

These were prospective issues, however, not present ones. Also, it was not a matter of choosing between two alternative strategies. We had only one option: try to use Duncan to move us closer to making an arrest in the case.

I kept reflecting on the outlandish motive Duncan had laid out for Ron's murder. His and Nathan's plot seemed unbelievable: a joint attempt to one-up a police TV show they had seen. It was hard to fathom how their plan could have brewed over several weeks without one of them coming to the realization "What the hell are we thinking?" I felt this was especially true of Duncan, with Ron allegedly being his closest friend for the last few years.

Duncan's shocking admission of his and Nathan's plan brought to mind the concept of a "folie à deux" murder, a psychiatric term meaning "madness of two." It refers to a delusion shared between two people. In a homicide context, it means a murder committed by two people that neither of them likely would have committed individually.

There are several significant folie à deux murder cases in the annals of crime. Perhaps the most notorious is the 1959 murder in Kansas of four members of the Clutter family, a case later immortalized by Truman Capote in his book *In Cold Blood*. The killers, Richard Hickock and Perry Smith, together formulated a plan, based on inaccurate information, to rob the family. Finding little of value in the Clutters' home, they decided to massacre them to leave no witnesses.

After hearing Duncan's story, however, the folie à deux murder I immediately thought of was the infamous 1924 kidnapping and murder of fourteen-year-old Bobby Franks, in a wealthy Chicago neighborhood. Franks's killers, Nathan Leopold and Richard Loeb, were themselves only in their late teens. Both came from enormous wealth and had genius-level IQs. Their primary motive was to commit the perfect, unsolvable crime, a feat they believed was possible given their high intellects. By all indications, neither would have had the desire or determination to commit the murder on their own.

I had been familiar with the story of Leopold and Loeb since high school, when I first read a book about the case and was inspired to look up old newspaper accounts of the trial.

I began to call Ron Baker's murder, due to its similarities to the historic case, "my blue-collar Leopold and Loeb case," a reference to Duncan's and Nathan's lack of wealth compared to the killers of Bobby Franks.

The morning after our interview with Duncan, Garcia and I drove east from Salt Lake City and into the mountains. Our destination was the ski resort town of Park City, where until his arrest Duncan lived with his friend Jim Purpura.

The day before, we did not know Purpura's name. Now, in light of what Duncan had told us about the new friend he had met while in Boston, Purpura would be an important interview. The key thing was for us to hear, as best as he could recall, exactly what Duncan had told him about the murder. What he said would either corroborate or contradict, or a combination of both, the story Duncan had told us.

We met Jim at his and Duncan's apartment. Duncan had called ahead at our request and let him know we needed to interview him, so he was expecting us. Jim was athletic-looking and seemed to be about the same age as Duncan. His demeanor was cooperative, which was no surprise, considering Duncan had asked him to talk with us.

We began by asking him to tell us how he had met Duncan.

Jim recounted that he first met James Atkins, the name Duncan was using then, about a year and a half earlier, during the summer of 1990. They both worked at a pizzeria in Boston. Even though Duncan told him his name was James Atkins, he went by "Jake," which is what everyone called him. "We became good friends, and part of the time he stayed with me," Jim said.

"We planned to travel to Europe," Jim also told us, "and he said he'd have to change his name to get a passport. He explained it was something to do with his military background."

Jim said they traveled to Delaware and stayed there with Jim's parents. Jake went back and forth between Delaware and Boston a few times. At some point, Jake got a Delaware identification card in the name of "Jonathan Miller." It was while they were in Delaware that they mailed their passport applications, because they still wanted to go to Europe.

We asked Jim if they ever talked about the murder of Duncan's roommate. Jim said he and Jake were on the phone sometime in November 1991. He was in Delaware and Jake was in Boston. Jim believed this was the first time Jake told him the whole story about his roommate's death. It was also when Jim learned that Jake's real name was Duncan Martinez. "Since then he and I have talked this over hundreds of times."

Jim said of Duncan, "He has always told me the same story. He told me that Nathan, Ron, and himself were in the park bullshitting and drinking. He said Ron and Nathan were arguing a little bit, but that was nothing unusual. He said it was nothing out of the ordinary. He said Nathan had the knife they usually took up there. He said it was a KA-BAR knife. They had finished drinking and were going through a tunnel back to the car. Duncan was first and Ron and Nathan were behind him. Something was said between Ron and Nathan, and Nathan snapped. He said it was dark and he could hear a struggle. He said Ron was screaming, 'Duncan, help me.' He said it didn't last long and the struggle was over. Duncan said he was very scared and he couldn't believe Nathan would do this. Nathan had blood on his hand and on the knife... I think Duncan said he didn't get blood on him."

Duncan never discussed going back to the park later, that Jim could recall.

We asked Jim if he knew whether Ron's killing involved any advance planning.

"Yes," Jim told us. "He told me that he and Nathan had seen something about a kidnapping on TV and discussed kidnapping in general. Somehow Ron's name eventually came into this as being kidnapped. Duncan told me he never took this whole thing seriously. He said this was never a definite thing when they went to the park that night. Like I said, he never even took this seriously, including the part where Nathan said they could kidnap Ron and kill him and call for a ransom. I honestly believe he was telling me the truth, that he didn't know this was going to happen."

Jim continued: "When they were on their way home after the killing, they stopped at a phone booth, and Nathan told Duncan to go make the call. He said they made the call close to home and Duncan said he used his best 'Grover from *Sesame Street*' voice. He said he told Ron's dad they had his son and wanted a ransom, and they'd call back.

"He said they went back to the apartment, and Ron's dad called right away, asking where Ron was. When he told Ron's dad that Ron wasn't home, I think Duncan said he told Ron's dad to ignore it, it was probably no big deal. Duncan said he placed one other call, but I don't know how much later it was. Duncan said he was upset but scared of Nathan and confused. I don't recall what was said in the second call.

"He told me numerous times that he doesn't know why he just didn't tell you guys and that he wanted to," Jim said, referring to me and Garcia. "Duncan and I have discussed him coming forward with what he knew." Jim also recalled that Duncan wanted to call his parents.

Jim said he and Duncan flew to Utah on December 5 with plans to live there and ski.

In Jim's understanding, Duncan decided he wanted to come forward about a month to a month and a half ago, which was late December to early January. "Duncan talked to his mother in January, and she said she still had Mr. Barnes on retainer. Once he talked to Mr. Barnes, it got set up," Jim said, referring to our interview with Duncan. All of this had happened before Duncan was arrested for the passport fraud.

Duncan admitted to him that he had made some mistakes. "Duncan told me he knew he did some things wrong," Jim said, "like making the calls and knowing what happened and not telling."

Following our interview with Jim Purpura, Garcia called Duncan's therapist, Nancy Bradish, who was also located in Park City. Garcia first confirmed she was the same Nancy Bradish who had been his high school classmate in El Paso, Texas. Garcia then explained why he was calling, not knowing whether Duncan had given her a heads-up after our interview with him the day before. Garcia said he needed to interview her regarding the statements Duncan had made to her in counseling about his roommate's murder.

We expected that we would need a release form signed by Duncan, a requirement Bradish confirmed. She provided her office address and directions. Garcia said we would be there shortly to get the form.

On our way over, Garcia and I discussed the randomness of the coincidence. He and Bradish had known each other as teenagers and had been in the same graduating class. He remembered her as smart and could picture her face, but they had never been close friends. After high school, Garcia had left El Paso and moved to Southern California, some eight hundred miles to the west. Nancy Bradish at some point had also left El Paso and relocated to Park City, more than eight hundred miles north, where she'd set up her practice as a licensed clinical social worker.

Twenty-six years after they'd graduated, Bradish received a call out of the blue from someone who wanted to see her as a new client. That person was Jonathan Miller, an alias for Duncan Martinez. A bizarre overlap in their professional lives had brought Garcia and Bradish back together a quarter century later. Garcia and I agreed it was a small, small world.

At Bradish's office, she and Garcia couldn't help reminiscing about their adolescence in El Paso, their classmates from years before, and remarking on the strange circumstances that had brought them back in touch.

Bradish gave Garcia a release form that she said Duncan would need to sign before she could discuss things they had talked about in their counseling sessions. Bradish had typed both of Duncan's names on the form: "Duncan Martinez," followed by "Alias, Jonathan Miller." By signing the form, Duncan would authorize Bradish to discuss with us "any and all information that I have shared during the therapy sessions," whether psychological, medical, or social.

Garcia informed Bradish that we wouldn't interview her on our current trip but at a later date when we would return to Utah.

It was midday when we arrived at the jail where Duncan had been housed since his arrest on the federal warrant. Duncan signed the release next to each of the two names Bradish had listed for him on the form. We then flew home from Utah to plan our next steps.

Our primary focus was Nathan. First of all, we wanted to get a sample of his blood. Second, and most importantly, we wanted to set up a conversation between Nathan and Duncan, whether by telephone or face-to-face. We knew we needed more evidence before anyone could be charged with Ron's murder.

Soon after we returned to Los Angeles, Garcia called the Serology Unit at SID. He requested that Ron Baker's fingernail clippings, taken at his autopsy, be reanalyzed for the possibility of blood foreign to the victim's type A blood. SID had previously tested the clippings and found traces of blood but had not determined the blood type. Garcia explained that one of the suspects had been scratched during his struggle with the victim, based on what a second suspect had told us. SID agreed to reexamine the evidence.

On February 27, we spoke with Duncan Martinez by phone. He indicated that he was out of custody. He had pled guilty to the fraudulent passport application charge and had been released pending his sentencing on April 22. Duncan also said he remembered one other thing he had forgotten to tell us in his interview. After Ron's killing, Nathan washed his hands off with beer at the scene, Duncan told us. I thought this might explain why, when we inspected Duncan's car for evidence, no blood traces were found on the steering wheel.

The following week, in early March, we discovered some new, surprising information about Nathan and what he had been up to since our last meeting with him in August 1990, a year and a half earlier.

We learned that at 4 p.m. on October 29, 1991, two Black men entered a Bank of America in the city of Moreno Valley, approached different tellers, then pulled handguns and demanded money. The tellers handed over cash, including bait money with recorded, traceable serial numbers. The men fled the bank and, according to a witness, drove off in a black Nissan sedan.

The Riverside County Sheriff's Department, which policed Moreno

Valley, responded to the scene. The deputies broadcast a description of the suspects' vehicle.

An hour and a half later, a deputy on patrol spotted a car that matched the description. The deputy saw only one Black male in the car, but based on the vehicle description, he initiated a stop.

The deputy took that man, later identified as James Lowery, into custody. He found over $5,000 in cash in Lowery's possession, including bills that matched the serial numbers on the bait money. On the car's floorboard was a driver's license of another Black man. The name on the license was Nathaniel Blalock.

Later that night, Lowery was identified in a lineup by two of the bank's employees. Lowery was also on parole for robbery.

Riverside sheriff's deputies went to the address listed on Nathan's driver's license. Diane Henderson was there, but Nathan was not. Diane told the deputies that Nathan used to be her boyfriend, but they had broken up about a month earlier. She said she hadn't seen him since. Diane consented to a search of the property, but no evidence of the robbery was found.

The detectives assigned to investigate the Bank of America robbery focused on Nathan Blalock as the second suspect. Not until about two and a half months later, on January 11, 1992, was he located and arrested, in an apartment complex in Moreno Valley.

Garcia and I also learned that Nathan had been held since his arrest at Riverside County Jail, and he was still in custody there.

Garcia drafted a search warrant for Nathan and got it approved by a judge. The warrant authorized us to obtain a sample of Nathan's blood, for purposes of comparison to the results of any future blood or DNA analysis performed on Ron Baker's fingernail kit, which Garcia had already requested.

We also had a second motive for seeking the warrant. Garcia and I needed to devise a strategy and plan of attack, in hopes of building the evidence necessary to move forward on the Baker case. Serving the search warrant on Nathan would be an opportunity to help set the stage for what might come next in our game plan.

On March 10, Garcia and I drove to Riverside County Jail to meet Nathan and get his blood. We had called ahead and arranged for a medical assistant from a local contract laboratory to be on hand to draw the blood sample. We also had informed jail officials that we did not want Nathan alerted to our pending visit. Garcia and I wanted to see his reaction when we served the blood warrant on him in person. Would there be a tell in his behavior upon hearing that news, especially if it was true that he had been scratched by Ron?

At the jail, Garcia and I were escorted to an interview room for the sample to be taken. Nathan was brought there from his cell. We had the medical assistant wait outside while Garcia and I explained our purpose.

We had not seen Nathan for more than a year. As always, he was congenial. He greeted us with his usual "What's up, guys?" or something similar.

Garcia and I told Nathan a few things before we informed him of the search warrant.

We advised him that the LAPD crime lab had recently tested the fingernail scrapings that were taken from Ron Baker's body. This was true.

We then told him that based on those tests, foreign blood had been found under the nails. This was not true, as we had not yet received any results from the crime lab. It is legal to lie to a suspect, as long as it does not involve their constitutional rights or false promises of leniency.

This was all part of our strategy. If the information Duncan had told us about Nathan being scratched that night inside the tunnel was true, there was no doubt our crime lab update would cause Nathan stress and concern. Nathan knew whether he had been scratched by Ron.

We next informed Nathan that we needed to obtain a blood sample from him to compare to the evidence results. We emphasized, as we had many times before, that he and Duncan were the last people known to have been with Ron. His blood sample was needed to assist in either eliminating or including him and Duncan as suspects.

After we told Nathan this information, and added that we had a search warrant authorizing us to obtain his blood, his attitude and demeanor changed completely. For the first time, he seemed to lose his cool in our presence. He became irritated and antagonistic. He said he was tired of still being a part of this investigation. He said he had always been agreeable to meeting with us and had always provided truthful answers to our questions. He was pissed off because he felt we should have known he would cooperate, as he always had.

The explanation we gave Nathan about our reason for the search warrant was that it was hard for us to assume he would voluntarily provide a blood sample. We had driven a long way to see him. If he chose not to cooperate, it would mean a drive back to LA, followed by another drive out with a search warrant. We said we had erred on the side of caution to save us from having to make two trips to Riverside. It was nothing personal.

Nathan seemed to accept that explanation. He settled down a little bit after that. His blood was drawn. The two tubes containing the sample were given to us by the medical assistant. We advised Nathan that the results might take some time, but he would be notified.

On our drive back to Los Angeles, Garcia and I discussed Nathan's angry reaction to the warrant and the dramatic change in his demeanor. I thought Nathan's reaction was significant. He had kept harping on the issue of us not trusting him enough to assume he would cooperate. I saw his focus on that as a front. He had been acting as if his feelings were hurt, but my sense was he was actually very concerned. I thought Nathan was probably thinking, *Holy shit. I can't believe they have foreign blood.* He had known right away it was going to be his because he was the one who had struggled with Ron. It was just a gut feeling I had, but that was my read on the situation.

Once we got back to Los Angeles, we had the two blood vials booked into evidence at the LAPD's Property Division.

Later, Garcia called the Serology Unit and requested to have Nathan's blood sample analyzed for ABO blood type. He also requested their report indicate if any foreign blood that might be found in Ron's fingernail kit could have come from Nathan, given his blood type.

On April 22, Duncan appeared in federal court in Salt Lake City for sentencing on his felony passport charge. For providing false information on a passport application, he was sentenced to two years of probation and fined $300.

We received the report on Ron's fingernail kit and Nathan's blood type on the morning of April 29, about a month after our request.

The crime lab had found the presence of foreign blood in its analysis of the fingernail scrapings from Ron Baker's left hand. Ron's blood was already known to be type A. The foreign blood had come back type AB, the rarest of the four blood types. AB was found in only 4 percent of the population.

Finally, the report indicated Nathan Blalock's blood type: AB.

From our perspective, the news could hardly have been better. Granted, we did not yet have Duncan Martinez's blood type, but we would get it on our next trip to Utah or upon his return to LA. The odds were on our side that Duncan would, with a high probability, not have AB blood. After all, 96 percent of people did not.

The results supported what Duncan had told us in his interview. Barring him also having AB blood, Nathan was the attacker who stabbed Ron and was scratched by him during the struggle.

Late on the afternoon of April 29, the same day we received the promising lab report, major news broke in Los Angeles. The jury in the case of the four LAPD officers charged in Rodney King's beating had reached its verdict. The trial was being held in Simi Valley, a predominantly white community. The majority-white jury acquitted the four officers of all the charges except one. On that sole remaining charge, against one officer, the jury deadlocked.

I was shocked by the almost complete acquittal. I knew a lot of people would be infuriated by the verdict. The Rodney King case was already an emotional tinderbox. The verdict seemed certain to fuel the flames of fury. I could understand why it would, considering how bad the video looked and that no officers were held accountable at trial.

Later that night, my family and I were out at a restaurant having dinner when my pager beeped. I excused myself and called the office. I was told that major violence had erupted in parts of Los Angeles, in reaction to the verdict. In response, the LAPD was officially mobilizing and dividing all personnel into two twelve-hour shifts. I was assigned "A" watch, which ran from 6 a.m. to 6 p.m. There would be no days off until further notice.

When I arrived at work early the next day, the "B" watch detectives who were going off duty looked exhausted. They had worked a full day the day before, then were kept on for the next twelve hours, which meant they had been awake for more than twenty-four hours straight. Garcia was one of them. He and I would be on different watches until further notice. Once things settled down, we could resume our case work and usual schedule.

It was unbelievable to see the devastation in the inner-city communities south of downtown, which was almost exclusively the area where my squad and I were sent. Charred buildings and smashed store windows were everywhere I looked. So was graffiti like "FUCK LAPD" and "LAPD 187," the California Penal Code for murder. The B watch squads, in contrast, seemed to spend the majority of their overnight shifts in the San Fernando Valley, where significantly less rioting had occurred. The detectives on the two shifts would trade stories when one watch relieved the other, every twelve hours.

Not until almost a week later did the violence finally subside. The repercussions of the LA Riots of 1992 would last years, even decades, longer. So would the scars to the city's landscape, and more invisibly, the scars on the psyches of its inhabitants, collectively and individually, as a result of the traumas witnessed and what many people believed was a miscarriage of justice.

Things had changed, palpably and permanently. This included perceptions of the LAPD and its relationship with the city. Within weeks, Chief Daryl Gates, who had run the department since 1978, was forced to step down.

Even Gates's departure did not ameliorate the situation. Popular resentment of the police was badly inflamed by the officers' not-guilty verdicts. Raw feelings, and racial tensions in particular, persisted and would continue to fester.

Our assignments to A and B watches and alternating twelve-hour shifts eventually ended. My fellow RHD detectives and I resumed our normal partnerships and work schedules.

The first new information we received on the Baker case, following the riots, came on May 20, when Greg Matheson, the Serology Unit supervisor, returned my call. I had inquired how much remained of the blood sample used to obtain the AB blood result from Ron's fingernail clippings. Matheson reported that the blood sample had been fully consumed in the latest round of testing.

This was not unexpected news but still disappointing. It meant there was no possibility of doing any further lab tests on the blood sample. We had to accept the AB blood results were the best we would get. Given the blood type's rarity, it was still compelling evidence.

The following morning, I called Riverside County Jail to check on Nathan Blalock. Garcia and I hoped to put our game plan into action the next week, when we would make a return trip to Utah.

A clerk informed me that Nathan was no longer in custody.

When I asked about his status on the pending bank robbery charge, I was told he was released on his own recognizance on April 21.

I was shocked. A release on an armed bank robbery without posting any bail, with just his promise to appear?

The clerk checked Nathan's booking sheet, which showed he had given no home address or any emergency contact information.

This further bewildered me. I could not fathom a judge would agree to release a suspect on such a serious charge, bank robbery, on his own recognizance and without a documented address.

The investigating agency in Nathan's case was the Moreno Valley Police Department, the clerk told me. I called and spoke to a robbery detective, Mike Jordan, who agreed to look into the case.

Jordan did some digging and reported back that Nathan had pled guilty to the bank robbery charge on April 21. He was given an OR (own-recognizance) release, meaning he had to post no bail, only promise to return for his sentencing on April 29. The judge had warned Nathan that if he failed to appear, his negotiated sentence of four years would be vacated. The judge would then have the option to impose a longer sentence, up to a maximum of sixteen years. Nathan's partner in crime, James Lowery, had already been sentenced to sixteen years.

According to Jordan, Nathan had appeared for his sentencing on April 29, but the hearing was rescheduled. A new date for the sentencing was set for May 4. On May 4, however, Nathan was a no-show. The judge had issued a warrant for his arrest.

I checked the status of the warrant and discovered it was still active. This told me that in the two-plus weeks since the warrant was issued, he had not been found. Now it was Nathan's turn to be "on the run."

Garcia and I flew to Salt Lake City a week later, on Wednesday, May 27. Our original intent was to use the trip to launch the game plan we had developed, in hopes of making headway on the case. With Nathan out of custody and his whereabouts unknown, we knew that might have to wait. We decided to go ahead with the trip anyway, as there were other necessary tasks we could accomplish while in Utah. There were also some avenues we thought we could pursue there in an attempt to locate Nathan.

We met Duncan at his apartment in Park City that evening. He had been out of custody for three months. Duncan seemed himself, talkative, cooperative, and at ease with Garcia and me.

We told Duncan we wanted him to make a call to Diane Henderson and attempt to find out where Nathan might be. Duncan had not spoken with Diane since before his disappearance, almost two years earlier. He would tell her he needed desperately to get in touch with Nathan about something very important, and she was the only person he knew who might be able to help him.

We had Duncan use his landline, on which we had set up recording equipment.

At about 10 p.m.—9 p.m. in California—Duncan dialed the last number he had for Diane. It was disconnected. He then called Diane's family, the other phone number he had for her. Duncan told Diane's father that it was very important she call him.

Diane called Duncan back within twenty minutes. She was obviously surprised to hear from him.

Duncan explained he was out of state and needed to talk with Nathan.

Diane told him, "Nathan and I broke up in August. Since then he's been in Riverside County Jail, since September or October sometime, and the only way you can get ahold of him is through writing."

"How come he's in jail?" Duncan asked.

"He got mixed up with the wrong people," Diane said. "These people might have been connected with a bank robbery, and Nathan's ID was found in the vehicle used. So they arrested Nathan and they thought that he might be involved, or he might know something… He says he doesn't know anything, so I don't know. The last time I heard from Nathan was on March 18th, when he wrote me a letter. So, that's all I know." She gave Duncan the last address she had for Nathan, a post office box in Riverside. Then she asked, "Duncan, have you heard of anything about Ron?"

"Well, that's kind of what I'm calling about," Duncan said.

Diane said she saw a TV program, five or six months earlier, that had profiled Duncan. "That's the only thing I know of. Detective Garcia called me about the same time that was aired. He asked me if I'd heard from you and all this stuff." Diane asked if he had spoken to Garcia at all.

"No, no, I'm doing my best not to," Duncan said. "There's definitely some stuff going down, and I really want to talk to him because I want to let him know what's going on. So I can do my best to help him out."

"Are they trying to prosecute you too?"

"I think so."

"Duncan, how do you know if they are if you're not in contact with anybody?"

"Well, I wasn't in contact… Let's just say this: I wasn't in contact for a long time and I just got in contact with somebody again. And found that they recently started asking a lot of questions again."

Diane said she heard the detectives were at the Renaissance Faire. "Not Detective Garcia but the other character," she said, meaning me. "He was there and Nathan saw him. I didn't see him, but Nathan and I were both working at the Faire."

I had in fact visited the Faire the previous June, following up on a possible Duncan sighting that proved false. Until I heard Diane say that, I was unaware Nathan had also been there and had spotted me.

Diane continued: "They were probing around there. They haven't let it die. So it's not like it's all this new evidence."

"Well, I heard, from what I understand, there's some people who they stopped asking questions to, and gone back and started harassing them," Duncan said. "From what I also understand, they found something and they got something. So if you hear from him at all."

Diane said she could write to Nathan and give him a phone number where he could call her back, but that was it.

Duncan asked for her phone number and she gave it to him.

"I don't know, Duncan. I think they're pressuring you because they want to talk to you. I personally don't think they have anything, unless you and Nathan did do something. I'm not accusing you. I'm just saying, if you and Nathan have something to hide, then I'd be worried. But if you don't, they're just trying—that's their game. They try to scare you and say they have something and they don't."

"Right," Duncan said. "Whatever you do, don't tell them that you talked to me, okay? It would be probably in both of our best interests if you didn't. I mean, if they find out or whatever, then that's your thing, but just try to keep that on the—"

"Okay. Well, I mean, I'm not going to be sending up any flags, but Duncan, my life has changed."

"I know what you mean."

"And if they flat-out ask me, 'Have you heard from Duncan?'—"

"Right, I'm not going to ask you to lie, but..."

"But I'll pray for you, because you need it. You need to get this straightened out. You need to... Whatever has happened, it needs to be taken care of... You know, I was at the apartment, and I know nothing of what you and Nathan did in that time."

"Right."

Diane told Duncan it was in her best interests to tell the detectives the truth.

"Right," he replied. "Like I said, I don't want to ask you to lie either. I'm just saying, it probably wouldn't be good if you ran back and called them right after you talked to me."

"I won't. As far as I'm concerned, if Detective Garcia finds me, fine... The only advice I can give you, Duncan, if you guys are clear, then come home. If you guys have something that you don't want really revealed, then do what you feel is best. I still care for you guys a lot, especially you and Nathan. I mean, what we went through was traumatic and, I mean, we weren't friends for very long."

"Right."

"This will make us friends for life."

"Absolutely," said Duncan.

"But what happened to Ron, I didn't really see you guys becoming a part of that. But I don't know, because we haven't been friends for years. Do you understand what I'm saying?"

"Right."

"I want to believe one thing. I have no evidence to make me believe otherwise, but I'm just scared for you guys."

"Right. Like I say, if he talks to you or gets in touch with you, please give him the message to call me... Do you know when he's supposed to get out of jail?"

"No. I don't know anything about that. They were holding him for a while. He was supposed to go to court February 5th or something like that. And that was the last time I actually spoke to him. Then the last two letters I got were basically, 'Hi, how are you? I care about you.' And nothing about court."

"Okay."

"All right, sweetie. You take care of yourself."

"You too."

"I will," said Diane.

"Okay, one last question," said Duncan. "What did he say to you about everything?"

"Garcia?"

"No. Nathan. As far as what went on with Ron."

"Nathan just said that you guys dropped him off. You guys went and had a few beers in the parking lot at the elementary school and you guys came home. That's all he said..."

"Right."

"I just, I don't know... I just hope for the best for you, Duncan. It was like you said: They're going to catch up with you sooner or later. Nathan, they've already—if they want to speak to him, they know where he's at. The life that you're leading is not good. So you just be careful. I'll pray for you," Diane said again, before they ended the call, which had lasted about fifteen minutes.

Garcia and I were still in Utah the following night when we received a call from our coworker Bud Arce. Arce explained that he had taken a call at the office from Diane Henderson, who said she wanted to reach us. After Arce told her we weren't there, Diane asked him to let us know that she had gotten a call from Duncan Martinez. She asked for one of us to call her back and left her number.

Garcia called Diane back that night. She recounted that Duncan had called her out of the blue the night before, urgently trying to reach Nathan. She told him that Nathan was in Riverside County Jail, she said. She also said that Duncan, just based on things he had said, had caused her to believe he and Nathan might have been involved in Ron's death. She gave Garcia the Utah phone number at which she had called Duncan.

Garcia and I of course already knew the content of her recorded phone call with Duncan. Still, we thought it was significant that Diane had called us at all. Duncan had asked her not to, and she had told him she wouldn't. But here she was, calling us the very next day to report it. That alone showed that she considered his call fishy. Garcia and I agreed that Diane had seemed to be telling the truth when she told Duncan that Nathan had said nothing to her about that night, other than dropping Ron off at the bus stop. Diane's comment casting suspicion on Duncan and Nathan and their possible involvement in Ron's murder was another indication to us of her truthfulness. She had been honest with Duncan, not knowing we were listening in, and honest with us in recounting what had been said.

Although Duncan's call with Diane did not achieve its primary objective, locating Nathan, it demonstrated to us that Diane could be trusted and was not protecting either of them.

The next morning, Garcia and I drove from our Salt Lake City hotel back to Park City. We had scheduled an interview with Nancy Bradish.

We gave Bradish the release form that Duncan had signed with both his true name and his alias. The release permitted Bradish to talk with us about what Duncan had told her during their counseling sessions.

We asked her to take us through their sessions chronologically.

Bradish said her first appointment with him was on January 9, 1992.

Although she knew now that his real name was Duncan Martinez, she knew him initially as Jonathan Miller.

She described his demeanor and appearance when he came in as nervous, pale, and unkempt. He told her that he had trust issues discussing his main problem with her. It took him about twenty minutes before he told her that he had been a witness to a murder. He said he had been on the run for two years, living in Boston for most of that time. He said he felt anxiety and a lot of guilt, so much so that he was not sleeping or eating.

Duncan told Bradish about Nathan. He said Nathan at some point started talking about killing Ron. Duncan said he just blew it off. He and Nathan had been drinking and Duncan just figured "that's how you talk when you're mad at someone." But Nathan kept talking more and more about the plan, Duncan said.

Duncan explained to Bradish that Nathan planned to get Ron drunk. They would go to the top of some hill. After Ron got drunk, Nathan was going to kill him. Duncan said he went along with it but thought it was "BS."

Duncan told Bradish that when it didn't happen when Nathan said it would, he was relieved. Duncan said they were in a tunnel, with him walking in front of Ron. He heard fighting, and Ron started screaming for help. Ron also screamed, "Why are you doing this, Nathan?" Duncan saw Nathan holding a lighter to Ron's face and waving the knife around. Duncan said he saw blood and just watched. He heard Ron yell, "Don't do that! What are you doing?" Then Nathan killed Ron.

Duncan told Bradish he was in shock and feared for his own life. He was also drunk and did nothing to help. He said he thought Nathan would turn on him. He described Ron and Nathan to Bradish as "his two best friends."

Duncan never described Ron's body. He told Bradish he was in a hurry to get out of the tunnel.

Bradish said Duncan seemed to feel relief after their first session. She advised him he needed to call his mother. She also referred him to legal aid.

At their second session, Duncan broke down and cried, Bradish recalled. He told her he had gotten a lawyer and planned to face the consequences. He had spoken with the lawyer and his mother. He also told Bradish that he would testify.

Bradish said that at one point she asked Duncan why he did not help the police. Duncan replied that it was a "pact with friends" and that "you stand by your buddy."

Duncan never mentioned anything to her about making any ransom calls.

Bradish told us she believed Duncan and felt he was consistent in what he told her during their sessions. Duncan talked about having to lie while he was on the run. He said he had been blocking it all out emotionally and had not been showing emotion for a long time. He also had nightmares of Ron being bloody. Duncan said he grieved but tried to be strong, as he felt showing emotion was a weakness.

At the conclusion of our interview with Bradish, Garcia told her we would be in touch if we needed anything else. If not, he joked, he would see her at their next high school reunion.

Garcia and I flew home to Los Angeles that same afternoon. Although we had not achieved our primary objective, locating Nathan, the trip had not been totally fruitless. We had gotten a better feel for Diane Henderson's reliability, thanks to her call to us about Duncan. Also, our interview with Bradish had corroborated most of the story Duncan had told us. One discrepancy jumped out at me, though. Duncan had seemed to play down to Bradish that Ron's murder was planned, more so than he had with us.

Everything was primed for us to put our game plan in motion. There was just one piece missing, but it was essential to the plan: access to Nathan Blalock.

Garcia and I simply needed to be patient and wait for Nathan to be found. Once he was arrested and booked for the active Riverside County warrant, we would be ready to roll.

We had asked Duncan before we left Utah to try to get in touch with Nathan's father in Michigan. We thought he might know of Nathan's whereabouts. We left a tape recorder with Duncan so he could record any calls he made to Nathan's father and just in case he received a call from Nathan himself.

Duncan had to call a few times before he reached Mr. Blalock.

"I'm an old friend of Nathan's. I used to live with him in Van Nuys," Duncan said.

"Oh, he's not here," Mr. Blalock said.

"I know. I was wondering if you know how to get in touch with him."

"No, I sure don't. I haven't heard from him."

Duncan provided his phone number and said, "It's real important that I talk to him. I tried to get in touch with him through his girlfriend, or his ex-girlfriend, I should say. She gave me one place where he was and he wasn't there. Yeah, it's real important that I talk to him."

"Right," Mr. Blalock said.

"So if you talk to him, I'd appreciate it," said Duncan.

Despite his efforts, Duncan did not receive a call back from Nathan.

The month of June, and with it the second anniversary of Ron Baker's murder, passed without notable progress in the investigation. As we entered the summer of 1992, Duncan and Nathan had switched roles. Duncan was now accounted for and "in pocket," while Nathan remained incommunicado in parts unknown.

Then, on July 6, the Monday after the Fourth of July weekend, there was a break in the case. I checked the database of active warrants and learned that Nathan's warrant was no longer in the system. This meant, almost assuredly, that he had been arrested.

With some additional checking, I determined that Nathan had been arrested in the LAPD's Rampart Division, just west of Downtown LA, on June 26. He was booked for the warrant in the Jail Division at Parker Center, two floors below our offices. Four days later, he was transferred to Riverside County Jail.

I obtained Nathan's booking photo from his June 26 arrest. I was shocked by how different he looked, compared to just three months earlier, when we had served the blood warrant on him in March. In the two months Nathan had been on the run, he appeared to have lost twenty-five to thirty pounds. He had always been in good physical condition and looked healthy. Now he looked gaunt and almost malnourished. Based on his appearance, I surmised he had been using a lot of drugs. To sum it up, Nathan looked terrible.

I called Riverside County Jail and spoke to a sheriff's deputy, asking him to check Nathan's status.

The deputy informed me that Nathan had already been sentenced. On July 2, two days after he was transferred to Riverside, Nathan appeared before the judge on his bank robbery case. For Nathan's earlier failure to appear for his sentencing, the judge tacked on an extra year in prison. The promised four-year sentence Nathan had previously agreed to became a five-year stint. Still, it was a far cry from the sixteen years the judge had warned him about if he did not appear for his sentencing.

The deputy also said Nathan was still in custody there in Riverside but would not be for much longer. He was only waiting on his prison commitment papers, which would then result in his transfer to one of California's state prisons.

Based on my own experience with county jail inmates being transferred to state prison upon conviction, I figured we had at least a week to put our plan in action.

Later that afternoon, after conferring with Garcia, I called Riverside County Jail again. I spoke to a supervisor, a Sergeant Cleary, and asked about the jail's policies and procedures. Specifically, I wanted to know whether inmates were permitted to make calls during the evening hours. I also asked if there were any policies that regulated a private citizen visiting the jail and wearing a body wire, if that visitor was assisting another law enforcement agency. Cleary told me both could be done, with prior approval and coordination with jail personnel.

I had one additional question for Cleary. I explained that my partner and I wanted to have jail personnel pass a note to inmate Nathan Blalock. The note would advise Nathan that there was a family emergency and he needed to make a call immediately to his family member. Could that be done?

Cleary told me yes, it could be.

I asked if that would be such an unusual action, in a jail setting, that it might cause an inmate to become suspicious.

Cleary said he did not feel it would alert them to the point where the inmate would have any reservations about receiving such a note, assuming the inmate knew the person who was requesting the callback.

I told Cleary we would likely request to have this passed note and phone call scenario initiated the following week, and that it would be during the evening hours.

Cleary instructed me to call back on the appointed evening.

Garcia and I called Duncan in Utah and told him he would need to travel to Los Angeles. We had already discussed with Duncan what we wanted him to do, and he had agreed.

We made Duncan's travel arrangements the next day. It would be his first trip back home in two years, at least that we were aware of. Duncan would likely stay a minimum of five to six days. We wanted him to do several things while he was here.

Our plan would get underway the following week. Both of the two missing pieces of the puzzle, Duncan and Nathan, were now in place.

CHAPTER 15

"WHERE THE HELL HAVE YOU BEEN?"
(July 9 to 13, 1992)

THE CIRCUMSTANCES WERE RISKY and far from ideal.

A phone call premised on a lie, the passed note, solicited by a known liar, Duncan.

Placing our trust in someone who had demonstrated himself to be untrustworthy.

But it was our only chance to get what we needed, if there was any hope of securing justice for Ron Baker.

Should the call go well, it had the potential to break the case wide open. The best-case scenario was that Nathan would receive the message and call Duncan. They would have an unguarded conversation, during which Nathan would make incriminating statements, on tape, that later could be used against him. Nathan would never contemplate, let alone suspect, that he was being set up and that Duncan, his one-time close friend, was actively betraying him as they spoke.

If anything went wrong—a distinct possibility—it would leave our case hanging by the thinnest of threads: Duncan's credibility. Without some incriminating statements by Nathan on tape that we could present as evidence against him, we would be stuck with Duncan as the lone witness. A lone witness to tell a jury about the plan they'd hatched and what had happened in the tunnel.

Garcia and I were not lawyers, but we knew that Duncan, by virtue of his past actions and lies, would be a terrible witness. So bad that it was difficult to imagine a prosecutor being willing to stake a case on him and his word. Even worse, I believed any jury was likely to despise him, given his earlier betrayal of his other closest friend, Ron.

In the event of that worst-case scenario, the DA's Office would have to make a choice. Either file a case against Nathan using Duncan as a witness or decline to file a case at all.

Duncan and Nathan had not spoken in almost two years, ever since Duncan fled Los Angeles a month after Ron's murder. Would Nathan take the bait and buy Duncan's note asking him to call? Or would he smell a rat? If Nathan did call, would he be wary of discussing anything about Ron's murder on a jailhouse phone line, knowing it could be monitored? If Nathan was willing to discuss those details, would he sense at any point that something was off, become suspicious, and shut down the conversation?

How it would go was anyone's guess. One thing was certain: If the call went sideways and Duncan for any reason lost Nathan's trust, it would deal our case a blow from which it was unlikely to recover.

Garcia and I set the date for Thursday, July 9. We did not want to wait, since Nathan was due to be transferred any day to state prison.

We had Duncan fly in from Utah a few days before. We put him up in a hotel along Interstate 5 in the area of Santa Clarita, thirty-five miles northwest of Downtown Los Angeles.

From a strategic point of view, the visit had to be on the Q.T. We gave Duncan strict instructions to contact absolutely no one, especially his local friends and acquaintances, while he was here. Should anyone in his old group become aware of his visit, the news would spread quickly. Garcia and I did not want to field a ton of calls informing us of what we already knew, namely that Duncan was back in LA.

On the appointed night, Garcia and I brought Duncan to Parker Center and up to RHD on the third floor. We would make the call not from the open squad room, where our desks were, but from the office of our captain, William Gartland.

The captain's office occupied the southeast corner of the building and had a large picture window that looked out over the city. The phone on his desk had multiple lines for him to make calls. Most were internal LAPD lines, but one was an "outside" line, used when the caller did not want it known that a call was coming from within an LAPD facility. This would be the phone line we would use for our gambit with Nathan.

We set up the recording device on the captain's phone. A little after 7:30 p.m., I dialed Riverside County Jail and spoke to a Sergeant McPherson, who had been told to expect our call. I walked McPherson through what we needed him to do and dictated what we wanted the note to say, which would be passed directly to Nathan. I asked him to take down my words verbatim: "Nathan—Diane told me where you were. Please call me collect as soon as you get this. There's an emergency in our family. I'll only be here for an hour or so—Duncan." The return phone number for the outside line at RHD was written after Duncan's name.

I hung up the phone with McPherson at 7:40 p.m. All we could do now was sit and wait.

Garcia and I had prepared Duncan by suggesting some topics he could bring up during the conversation, should Nathan call. These included talking about their plan to kidnap and kill Ron; being at the park that night and what happened inside the tunnel; their destruction of evidence after the murder; their ransom calls to Ron's parents; and the scratch Nathan supposedly received on his hand while struggling with Ron.

We stopped well short, however, of telling Duncan what to say specifically. We did not want the call to feel scripted in any way.

The best approach, Garcia and I believed, was just to let things flow between the two friends. Duncan knew Nathan far better than we did. He also knew better than us how they talked with each other normally.

The major unknowns were on Nathan's side of the equation. Would jail personnel be able to locate him in a timely manner and pass him the note? If he called, would he have a suspicious mindset? Or would he opt not to call?

We did not have to wait long to find out.

The phone on Captain Gartland's desk rang at 8:08 p.m. The light on the phone that lit up was for the outside line.

Garcia hit the button to start recording. Duncan picked up the phone and answered.

"Pacific Bell with a collect call from Nathan," an operator announced. Duncan agreed to accept the charges.

"Hello?" Duncan said.

"Yeah," came Nathan's voice through the receiver.

"Bud!" Duncan said.

"What's up, man?"

"Dude, what are you doing, man?"

"Where the hell have you been?" Nathan asked.

"Uh, everywhere. I ended up in Boston for a while. Was down in Kentucky."

"Yeah?"

"How about you?" Duncan asked. "I heard about you being in a lot of trouble."

"You could say that," said Nathan. "How the hell did you get in touch with Diane?" he asked, in reference to the note passed to him in the jail.

Duncan told him he still had the number for Diane's father and left a message asking her to call. Nathan seemed to accept Duncan's explanation.

"I just got back in here a week ago, man," said Nathan, of being in jail.

"Really? You were out?"

"Out for fucking three months."

"Dude, I called her, like, a month ago and she said you were in," said Duncan.

"No, see, she didn't know. No one knew. I got out on a seven-day stay of execution," explained Nathan, referring to when he was given an OR release to get his affairs in order before sentencing. "And for seven days I was out... I jetted to LA, dude. I've been partying in LA for the longest. LA, Hollywood, Van Nuys. I've been all over that whole area, man. Just kicking it and partying. And then a week ago yesterday, Metro, LA Metro, came through and picked me up. They found out I had a warrant. I had a no-bail warrant out here. So they brought me back."

"Fuck," said Duncan. "What are you looking at, time-wise?"

"About two years."

"Fuck. Well—"

"It's nothing, though, dude. My sentence is five years, right? But I'm only going to do, like, two and a half of it. And it's a bank robbery. What do you expect?"

"Dude, listen to this," Duncan said, his first attempt to shift the conversation. "I just got in touch with my mom."

"Okay."

"She says that they've been over to her house. Giving her, like, serious shit about my blood type and stuff." It was not necessary for Duncan to identify Garcia and me by name. Nathan understood who he meant.

"Yeah, they came here and got mine," said Nathan.

"Okay. Remember you got your hand scratched?"

"Yeah."

"Do you remember that?"

"Yeah," Nathan repeated.

"Maybe it's something to do with that."

"I thought about that," said Nathan. "And I thought about, like, when you guys would—when we were wrestling and stuff?"

"Uh-huh."

"There's so many possibilities, dude," said Nathan. He seemed to be suggesting that there was more than one way he might have picked up a scratch, including roughhousing between the roommates. The implication was that this would be his explanation if he were questioned about how his type blood was detected on Ron's body.

"Yeah, because you guys did wrestle for a while."

"Yeah, and vice versa," said Nathan. "But they never came back."

"Okay, well, maybe they don't know then. But, dude, if this comes down … I mean, it's not just you. It's me too, you know."

"Yeah, I know," acknowledged Nathan.

"I mean, I may not have been an executioner, but I'm still going to get pegged," ventured Duncan. "What are you going to say if they do come back?"

"I have—I have nothing to say about that. I'm—I don't know if this line's secure or not. Don't forget where I am."

Garcia and I realized that Nathan's concern about the phone line not being secure, while they discussed the murder, was evidence of consciousness of guilt. Nathan would raise the same concern several more times later in the conversation. Garcia and I similarly took note that when Duncan called Nathan an "executioner," Nathan did not deny it, argue, or ask what in the world Duncan was talking about.

"I know where you're at," said Duncan. "I've got a buddy who's a lawyer, and I know they cannot tap those lines."

"Well, I'm on an outside phone. But there's also a microphone in front of me. I'm in an attorney room."

"Right, but in the attorney booths, they can't do that."

"Okay, well, I don't know that. Like I said, they came down. Detective what's-his-face? The both of them who were initially in on that—on that thing?"

"Right," said Duncan.

"Came, and they took my blood type. Not only did they take my blood type, they didn't ask me if I ever wanted to give it up. They came with a warrant for my blood type. They took my blood type and they said, 'We should know...' He told me they should know the results in a month or so. A month and a half went by. They never came back and said anything to me about it. So I didn't worry about it. I'm not even giving it thought, really."

"Okay. Well, apparently they've been giving my mom, like, a lot of problems. Like, they think she knows something, or something. And from what I understand, something's up. I wouldn't be real secure being where I was if I was you. Being where you're at. That's why I got worried about it. Because I wanted to see if there was any way we could get you out or something."

"Not really. Because it would have to be, like, a jailbreak, if anything," Nathan said, laughing. "I've already been sentenced, dude. I've already gone to court... I'm waiting to catch the train to Chino now," referring to the state prison in Chino, California, east of Los Angeles.

"Fuck."

"I think where I am, if there had been anything, when they picked me up in LA, it would have came up then."

"Yeah, but you know, going from department to department has got to take a long time to figure stuff out."

"I don't know... Like I said, they knew I was in custody, man. I was in custody a hundred and something days, dude. Like a hundred thirty something days I was in custody here. You know? They knew where I was. And like I say, they came and took my blood. They said, 'Within a month, we'll know,' you know, and like I said, a month and a half, almost two months went by. And I was sweating the whole time."

"Right," said Duncan.

Garcia and I recognized it as another incriminating statement that Duncan had elicited. If Nathan was not present and had no contact with Ron in the tunnel, why would he be sweating?

Nathan seemed to sense that Duncan was more concerned than he was. He reassured Duncan: "They never came back and said anything. And I'm pretty sure, at that point in time, if something would have been extremely positive, they would have slapped another warrant... When they found out I was not in custody, they would have put a warrant out. And when LA picked me up, that warrant probably would have came through. The only warrant I have is the one from here."

"Right."

"You know, I think they're just sweating to be sweating." Nathan then speculated on why he believed the investigation was still ongoing: "I think there's someone kicking a lot of finance down in this situation. That's the only reason why they're sweating."

"The only thing I can't see is, I mean, they've left my mom alone for, you know, a year and eleven months. And then all of—"

"All of a sudden, bam," said Nathan.

"Boom, they're talking to her just about every day. You know, and she does not want to deal with it anymore. She's talking about trying to get a restraining order for the police, you know, so that they won't bother her anymore."

Nathan advised Duncan, "Tell her to go through and do that... I just think, like I said, there's another party kicking in a lot of finances here. And it's pushing, it's pushing the police to do that. If there's anything else really positive, they would have came back either way."

"What do you mean there's another party kicking in a lot of finances?"

"Well, there's someone paying, somewhere. Because normal police investigations don't go like this. You understand what I'm saying? Either that or there's something up somewhere."

"Okay."

"You know?"

"Yeah, there's definitely something going on," Duncan said. "I'm going to be in town for, probably, I don't know, probably another week. Um, I'm at a friend's house right now."

Nathan urged Duncan to visit him in jail. "Come to Riverside. Check me out, dude."

"I will," said Duncan. Before the call, Garcia and I had discussed with him the possibility of a jailhouse visit, as a next step to obtain more potentially incriminating statements from Nathan.

Nathan explained the jail's visiting hours and procedures.

"Okay. Let me see what I can do," said Duncan.

Nathan asked Duncan how long ago he talked with Diane. Duncan said about a month.

"Wow. Because, dude, I've been out and in... It's just a fluke that you actually called. I've only been here a week, man."

"That's funny," Duncan said with a chuckle.

"It's a fluke that I'm actually here."

"Well, it's good to talk to you. And I got to talk to you."

"Yeah, it is, dude," Nathan agreed. "You want to write? I don't know the address here."

"Well, we got to talk too. So let me see if I can't come out, deal with it that way."

"You could probably come out now. What time is it?" Nathan asked. It was apparent that he was eager for Duncan to visit him and to catch up with his friend in person, after so long.

"I can't do it tonight," said Duncan. He made another effort to steer the conversation back to the real purpose of the call. "Because yeah, I'm just getting real flipped out. I was feeling pretty secure about things, and I'm getting real worried. And I mean, I got flipped out before. But I'm getting worried again. And we got to deal with this."

"Yeah?"

"You know, I mean, I've been on the run for almost two years. And, uh—"

"Look who's talking," said Nathan. "You know what, it's funny, though. You didn't even have to, like, leave, dude."

"Well, dude, I didn't know that though, man. I mean...I'm sitting here and they're about to arrest me for something I didn't do."

"They weren't going to arrest you. It just seemed that way."

"Well, dude, it seemed like it. I mean, fuck, man. I sit there and I watch somebody get stabbed, and then I'm going to get arrested and go to jail for it? Dude, that's not cool, you know."

As earlier in their conversation, when Duncan called him an "executioner," Nathan did not deny, contest, or question Duncan's statement about having witnessed a stabbing.

Duncan went on: "I'm getting all this info now, and I'm finding out that they—what they're telling my mom is that they know we were there...They can't prove that, you know, they don't know that anybody stabbed him. They can't say that, you know, 'Yes, Nathan did it,' right? But they know we were there."

"They can't say that anyone did it. And I wish you'd quit using my name on such an unsecure line."

"Sorry, I'm just—I'm really freaked about this."

"About what you're saying, dude, I, you know, you say these lines are secure. I can't swallow that...As far as I'm concerned, this is an unsecure line."

"Right, I'm just—I mean, I've been nervous for the last two years. I'm still real nervous, you know, and I guess I should be nervous about that too."

"You should have, like, dropped a line at Diane's, dude...I could have came, flew to wherever the hell you were. Picked you up, dude. I mean, I know people out here now...All you had to do is drop a line. Like I said, I've been out for the last three months, running the streets in LA...You know, I'm not no big hard criminal. Or no big gangster or mobster. Nothing like that. But I have pulls and connections, man. And like I said, I could have came and got you from wherever you were. We could have, like, hit Hawaii or whatever, man."

"Right."

"You know, but you bailed out. And you didn't say nothing to nobody."

"Dude, I was too scared, man. I was convinced that I was going to—"

"And then the big thing... the big story before you left, about the job and car and all of that stuff. What was all that?"

"I don't know, you know, I mean, you were around for all that. That was all—"

"Yeah, but I didn't even know. Like, all I know, one day you told me you got a job. And I'm like, 'Okay, cool.'"

"No, dude, you knew about all that. We were talking about all of that."

"No, no, no, no, no—about some Mustang."

"Oh, that was just—that was how I covered myself leaving."

"Yeah, see, I didn't know all of that. And all of a sudden, bam, you were gone," Nathan said.

They had been talking on the phone for ten minutes. Duncan started to wrap up the call. "Well, here's my deal. I'm at a buddy's house. And, you know, I don't want to let him know that I'm having people call collect over here."

"Yeah."

"And they should be back in a little bit. So I got to bail."

"Okay."

"I'll try and stop by... Let me see if I can come down. We can rap."

"Yeah, I'm in Riverside County Jail, dude... Look, relax, man... And like I say, be careful what you say on unsecure lines. Hey, you're a soldier, dude. You know?"

"Yeah, like I say, I talk to a lawyer and he tells me something, I usually take it as the word of God. Because those people are God sometimes."

"Yeah, well, you know, lawyers—I see lawyers in court in action, you know, hey—"

"Well, I got some good connections with one too. Let me see what I can do."

"Yeah, okay, but look, with this family emergency. They're not going to let me out again," Nathan said, laughing.

"Let's just leave it at this. Let me see what I can do on my end."

"Okay."

"And I'll try and come stop by, like Monday or Tuesday or something."

"Get a lawyer to come down here and, you know, verify this family emergency to some point where I might be able to step out a day with escort service or under house arrest or something. It'd be cool."

"Yeah."

"You know, because I don't have a lawyer. I don't have any of that kind of pull. But now, once I do hit this house-arrest thing, believe me, we could hit whatever country you want to hit."

"Cool."

"All right?"

"Yeah, so I'll talk to you soon," said Duncan, before they said goodbye and hung up.

The way the call ended perfectly teed up what we wanted to happen next: a face-to-face meeting between the two. During that meeting, unbeknownst to Nathan, Duncan would be wearing a body wire to record everything that was said.

The next day, I called Riverside County Jail and requested their assistance in arranging a visit from Duncan and us. A lieutenant at the jail told us we could do it the following Monday, July 13. He said he would hold an attorney visiting room for Duncan and Nathan to meet in, so they would have a private setting to talk.

On that morning, before our drive out to Riverside, Garcia and I met with Duncan at Parker Center. He voluntarily provided us with a blood sample for subsequent lab analysis. It would be tested for ABO blood type to confirm what Duncan had told us, that he had type A blood. If so, it would rule him out as a possible source of the AB blood found under Ron's fingernails.

We arrived at Riverside County Jail around noon. The wire Duncan wore consisted of a microcassette recorder and an attached body mic concealed under his clothing. Garcia stated for the record, "The date is July 13th, 1992. It is now 1236 hours. And we are situated in the Riverside County Jail. Duncan Martinez is getting ready to go into the interview with Nathan Blalock."

This time, unlike Duncan's phone call with Nathan a few days prior,

Garcia and I would be unable to eavesdrop on their conversation as it unfolded. For obvious reasons, we needed to remain well out of sight, and the jail's attorney visiting rooms had no capabilities for real-time monitoring. Garcia and I would have to remain behind in our hideaway and wait until the meeting was over to find out what had been said. Duncan would know before us the extent of the information he elicited from Nathan. Garcia and I would not learn the details until we got to listen to the tape later that day.

I told Duncan, "All right, we'll talk to you when you get back, okay?"

"Okay," he said.

A deputy then escorted Duncan toward the attorney room that had been reserved for the meeting. Duncan carried with him a folder with some papers inside, legal documents ostensibly provided by the lawyer friend he had mentioned previously to Nathan. The folder was a prop to support his cover story about how he was authorized to visit a restricted area of the jail.

"I hope this works," Duncan said. It was impossible for me to tell, later listening to the tape, whether Duncan said it aloud for his own encouragement in that moment, or performatively, since he knew he was being recorded and we would hear it later.

The attorney room was empty when Duncan arrived. While he waited, a deputy in the background called out to him, "You're visiting an inmate?"

"Yup," replied Duncan.

"You an attorney or just visiting?"

"Legal clerk."

Nathan arrived within a few minutes. He and Duncan had not seen each other in two years. Much had transpired and changed in that time. But they greeted each other as old friends.

"What's up, bud?" said Duncan.

"How's it going, guy?" asked Nathan.

"Good."

"You're looking good."

"Thanks," said Duncan. Taking on an exaggerated businesslike tone, he told Nathan, "I am officially here as a legal clerk to sign power of attorney and stuff, so they think that I'm working with a lawyer."

"Right," Nathan replied.

"So what's up, man?"

"Nothing. I just got out of the shower. Getting ready to leave soon... So what you been up to? Tell me about your, uh, vacation," Nathan said, referring to Duncan's return to Los Angeles.

"Thanks, man, I'm having a good time. Just going around. Went down to Melrose yesterday. Hung out up in Hollywood. Having a good time. Keeping it low, you know?" He asked Nathan, "So, what's it like in here?"

"It's not bad. It's kind of like boot camp, but you don't have to run around outside and shoot shit, you know?" Nathan said, referencing their common military experiences.

"Fuck," said Duncan. They both chuckled at Nathan's analogy. "That's what I liked about boot camp, was being able to run around and shoot shit."

"You know what I'm in for, right?" asked Nathan.

"Yeah, bank robbery."

"Yeah. See, my partner got caught. And one thing led to another. They recovered part of the money. They didn't recover all the money... I'm going to go for about twenty-two months, probably. That's under two years. That's not bad." Nathan said he was going to a "level 2" prison, which offered amenities other prisons did not. "They have golf courses, bowling alleys. Oh, yeah, it's like the Richard Nixon Center." Both of them laughed.

"Dude, how do I go?" asked Duncan.

"In fact, I'll be right in Chino, right here in California, in Chino."

"That's not far."

"I know... And you got open-yard visits, contact visits, where I can actually—people can actually come and, 'Hey, what's happening, man? You bring me some food?' Stuff like that."

"Cool," said Duncan.

"Yeah, so it's not bad. I mean, I'm just going to boot camp again. Basically I'm just going to a 'get your body in shape' program."

"Right. Yeah, that's true. Twenty-two months of—"

"Of Club, um... Club Chino," said Nathan.

"Right."

"I just went on a spree, man. Like, me and Diane broke up. Just went balls to the wall, man. Like, pulled out all my underworld contacts that I knew. Just went balls to the wall, man. Made a lot of money, met a lot of people, did a lot of things. And, you know, had I not fooled around with one careless person, I wouldn't be here now."

"It happens," said Duncan.

"But about this other thing," Nathan said, acknowledging the elephant in the room, Ron's murder. Surprisingly, it was him who brought up the subject first, not Duncan.

"Yeah, go ahead."

"Well, I guess, while you're on vacation, you know, the way you're sweating, you and yours now, me and mine were sweating the same way for the whole time. Renaissance Faire, they'd pop up anywhere, anytime. Like, 'Bam, whoa! What are you guys doing here?' They out at Ren Faire."

"Right."

"They came here with a warrant and drew my blood. In case I said no, they had a warrant." Nathan mimicked the conversation for Duncan. "'Well, you got to give it to us,'" he said, playing me and Garcia. "'Screw you, man... I would have gave it to you anyway,'" he said as himself, then continued: "But nothing ever came back on it. I think they're just pushing for something that's... Pushing for something that's not really there, you know what I'm saying?"

"Well, I talked to my buddy. And that's how I got in here too. I got in here like this, so this is a little more secure... Um, and what he said is, he's got a buddy in the DA's Office... And they've, like, for the past two weeks, they've been pushing for a warrant, for you, in the DA's Office. They've got something," Duncan said ominously.

He asked Nathan, "Did you talk to Diane? Did you tell her anything? Did you talk to anybody? Fuck. Because I mean, I told this guy a little bit. I said, 'Look, here's the deal. I need advice. I need to know,' right? Because they're bothering my mom, and they stopped bothering her for a year and a half. You know?... He went down and he talked to his buddy at the DA's Office. And he's been kind of trying to inquire without anybody, you know, knowing he's talking to me. And, uh, he says they got something. Right? He says they've got to have something, that they can almost do it. What he said is, the key thing would be validity.

If they find out that something's going on, and come up to you and say, 'Look, pal. We know you did it. We know, you know, blah, blah, blah, blah, blah,' and you come out and say, 'Okay, I did it, blah, blah, blah.' And say one story, and then they catch up to me and I say something completely different."

"Well, see this—I'm not saying nothing. But, uh, the original thing was—"

"Yeah," Duncan said, lowering his voice to a whisper, although they were in the room alone, "but Nathan—"

"Remember that—"

"But Nathan, if they find out that you did it—"

"If it goes to trial, dude. It's not going to trial," Nathan said, now whispering as well.

"Dude, if they've got something—"

"I don't think they have. The most they can have is fucking skin or DNA underneath his nails. We were roommates. We wrestled, we played."

"Yeah, but dude—"

"We wrestled, we played, we're roommates. All right? That could have been there for fucking hours before anything happened."

"Right."

"All right? Diane's a witness that the three of us were wrestling, before we even left. Remember?"

"Yeah, maybe they got something different... I mean, I heard they were looking for my car so long—"

"Yeah, but you took off," Nathan reminded him.

"Well, yeah, but apparently they were looking—they weren't looking for my car, because they thought I took off. Because I told everybody I was selling my car."

"Well, personally, I'm not going to lose any sleep over that, because like I said, if it goes to trial—that's not the standard for trial."

"I don't know, man. I just, I been talking to this guy—"

"Well, if he told someone or somebody or something—"

"I talked to one guy. Like I said, my attorney. And—"

"I'm denying everything and I'll take it to trial," declared Nathan.

"What if they found the clothes?"

"What clothes?"

"Remember the fucking clothes wrapped in the knife? Or the knife wrapped in the clothes?" Duncan said, correcting himself.

"In the dumpster. The trash truck came that morning."

"Hmm... I'm just trying to think of things they could have come up with. Because it's got to have been something, if they figured it out. Because they stopped for so long. They stopped harassing everybody for so long."

"Like I said, I'm not going to lose sleep over it. I'm not going to worry about it. They go to trial, they can't prove it."

"They've got to have something," Duncan insisted.

"If they did prove it, it's in LA. LA is easier than shit like that. LA will throw shit out like this," said Nathan, snapping his fingers. "I've seen people come in here with 187s"—the California Penal Code for murder—"and it's, like, the evidence was so weak, they kicked it right out. You don't have to worry about it, dude. It's not worth losing sleep over it."

"From what he said—all he said was, if they do figure it out, right? And he said they've got to have something—"

"You told this guy a lot more than—"

"Dude, nah, I didn't even say that much. I said, 'Look, I was involved in something. I'm not going to say what happened,' you know, I didn't tell him you did it. I didn't say anything like that. I just said, you know, 'I'm involved in something. I want to find out what the deal is.' And I explained the circumstances. I explained that Ron was killed, right? I didn't say you did it. I didn't say anything. I just said that Ron was killed. And that I want to figure out what the deal is, you know, and I threw hypotheticals. And I threw a couple that were completely untrue. And I threw a couple that were kind of right on. To see what his different advice is, because I told him, 'I don't want to say anything,' you know, because that's not cool."

"The whole thing was a conspiracy," said Nathan. "We both go down."

"Yeah, but dude, I didn't think it was fucking real. I mean, honestly?"

"That's reality, though, isn't it?"

"Dude, when that happened, man, when you fucking—dude, that

was the scariest moment of my life when you did that. Dude, I was so fucking shit scared, I think about it now, and I still fucking flip out. Dude, I mean, people just don't go and fucking stab people like that."

"What did you think was the whole plan, though?"

"Yeah, but, I don't know."

"That's reality, though. It happened. I'm sorry, dude. That's the military. I don't mean, you know, I could push a button, and this or that."

"Yeah, but how could you do that? I don't know. I mean, it was never real to me because it just didn't make sense. It didn't make sense at all. I mean, again, you guys have little arguments once in a while. But nothing to that."

"Yeah, well, you know, like I say, it was a plan. We both know what the plan was."

"Yeah. I don't know. Until that moment when you first slammed him against the wall. Until that very fucking moment, it was bullshit to me. There was no concept that it would ever happen."

"Well—"

"It was just a fucking plan we dreamed up while we were drunk. And then those few fucking moments when he was fucking screaming my name to help him out. Dude, I thought I was fucking going to die, man. I was so fucking scared. You know, and that's hard for me to admit. You know that. You know? I'm just being honest."

"I hear you," Nathan responded.

At times, the recording was too muffled to make out their exact words, although the essence could be discerned from the context. For instance, Nathan next said something about the two ransom calls Duncan made to the Bakers, reminding him of his complicity in carrying out the plan.

Duncan responded, "Yeah, I did make the phone calls. I was fucking shit scared of you... You don't believe me? Why didn't I drive home? Huh? Who always drove when it was with me and you in my car? I did. I couldn't drive. Dude, I could barely walk. Why wouldn't I walk through the train tunnel again? Remember how I made you walk over the top? Dude, I had no legs. Dude, I was so fucking scared, man."

"Well—"

"I mean, dude, think about it. Think about it from my perspective."

"Uh, they don't know where you are?" asked Nathan, seemingly referring to Duncan's attorney friend.

"No."

"Well, whoever you're talking to, don't talk to him anymore."

"Uh, he's a—"

"Don't talk to him anymore."

"Okay."

"You're jeopardizing me a lot. Listen to what I say here. I'm really being fucking—I see a noose going around my neck... I'll say it like this. I won't really say, you know, who else was involved or nothing like that, or anything else, if it does come out on me. You know? But I will take it to trial, because I honestly believe that they don't have anything. Maybe a skin sample."

"Right."

"A skin sample's not—it doesn't prove shit until you—"

"Unless they found it there."

"Found what there?"

"Part of you on the wall."

"No, there's no part of me on the wall."

"Dude, you fucking had scratches on your arms and stuff from smashing Ron against the fucking walls of the train tunnel."

"It was from him."

"Oh, well, okay, but it was—"

"It was fucking—it's his nails."

"Yeah, I was worried that maybe, like, you know, you'd been—"

"I never touched the wall. I never touched anything except—you know."

"Right. I couldn't tell that, because I couldn't see until you fucking lit the lighter."

"Believe me, it doesn't prove shit, except we were roommates, and, um, wrestled or something. And those witnesses are saying we've always wrestled... About this warrant thing, I don't know nothing about it."

"Well, I'm going off what I heard."

"He said they're trying to get a warrant for me? For my arrest?"

"To connect you with this."

"In connection with—"

"They're trying to put a warrant out for your arrest. First-degree murder of Ronald Baker. That's what they're trying to do. And he said they're this close to getting it."

"Then what's stopping them?"

"I don't know. They've got to be one piece behind. He can't get everything without making it obvious that he's talking to me."

"Well, like I said, I'm not going to worry about it."

"I've always—I mean, I wish we weren't here, because this isn't completely secure, but it is. I've always wanted to ask you why."

"It just happened... It happened," said Nathan. He asked Duncan about his folder of papers. "What is that? What do you got in there?"

"All sorts of fun stuff. Power-of-attorney paperwork. That's what I'm officially here to do, is get you to fill out power-of-attorney paperwork. A legal pad."

"Understand, though... I don't know nothing, and, um, they can try to pin it on me, but it's not going to stick, you know?"

"Right, well, what he said to me is 'Make sure if he does go down, and he starts saying something, you know what he's going to say.' You know what I mean? I mean, if it goes down, I mean, are you going to say exactly what happened, because that's going to be first degree?"

Duncan seemed to be suggesting something contrary to what he had always told us, that he never believed the kidnap-murder-ransom plan was a real, serious plot. Yet his question implied that if Nathan told the truth about what happened, it would reveal premeditation and thus be first-degree murder.

"I don't remember what happened," Nathan emphasized.

"Okay."

"All I know is he was dropped off. That was it."

My interpretation of this exchange was that Nathan was reiterating that he was going to stick to his story if he was ever questioned again by the police.

Duncan raised the possibility there may have been other people that night in the park who had seen or heard them with Ron and could identify them to the police. Nathan doubted it.

Duncan told him, "Fuck, if you listen... if you think about what was said that night. I don't know if you do. Fuck, man. It goes in my fucking head every fucking night when I try and go to sleep. You know, 'Fucking help me, Duncan. Help me, Duncan. Nathan, why the hell are you doing this to me?' And that's Ron screaming—dude—both our names. Right there."

Once again, Nathan did not deny or contest any of Duncan's graphic descriptions of what took place in the tunnel. Nathan calmly advised Duncan, "Like I say, you know, don't sweat it. If it happens, it happens. You know?"

"Right."

Nathan urged Duncan to remain calm. "There's no evidence, no weapon, no fingerprints... My skin underneath his nails? We were roommates, we used the same fucking soap... You understand what I'm saying?"

"Yeah, right... Good point."

"You know? I had nothing to do with the 187—187 is murder. I had nothing to do with 187... I'm not going to worry about it, I'm not going to lose sleep over it... This shit, don't worry about it, man. Just don't think about it... I guess you can't blank it out or erase it. But, you know, I wouldn't do anything... You know what I'm saying?"

"Right."

"I was hurt... I was fucking hurt by you taking off, you know? You understand what I'm saying?"

"Yeah."

"Okay. I wouldn't do anything... You know, you don't have to worry about me doing anything either."

"Right. I was too scared. I had to take off. I couldn't sit around anybody. You know, Lydia and all of them, and have them fucking cry all day about something that I knew about and not tell them. And I couldn't tell them."

"Well, at least you could have, like—you should have told me something earlier. Now I guess you're afraid that, you know, I don't know. But like I said—"

"I was afraid to tell anybody," said Duncan. He checked the time. "I got two more minutes."

Nathan confided, "In the last year or so, especially the end, I had a real bad paranoia streak. I don't trust anybody, for nothing, except myself, man. And I'm in a situation where it's a damn good thing I felt that way, because it took me myself a while to get me out of there. I mean, it's like fucking I'm going out in a blaze of glory type of shit... But, um, you know, I didn't trust anybody... My dad doesn't even know where I am."

"Yeah, I called him too, when I called Diane."

"You did? What did he say?"

"He said, 'I don't know where he is.' I said, 'Oh, okay.'"

"Yeah. He doesn't even know where I am. So I'm going to have to call him soon and give him—let him know I'm incarcerated."

"My buddy is picking me up at quarter after, and it's ten past," Duncan said.

"Peace out," Nathan told Duncan as they parted.

"Peace," replied Duncan.

The tape continued to roll while Duncan walked back to the room where Garcia and I were waiting.

"Well?" Garcia asked him.

"I think it worked," Duncan told us.

Garcia ended the recording: "The time is now 1311 hours and we're now shutting the tape off." Duncan's surreptitiously recorded conversation with Nathan was thirty minutes long.

Garcia and I listened to the full recording later that night. In general, we agreed with Duncan's assessment. He managed to elicit some solidly incriminating statements from Nathan. As in their earlier phone call, there were also several damning nonresponses, when Nathan did not deny or contest statements Duncan made about Ron's murder and what had happened inside the tunnel.

Although Nathan never explicitly admitted to stabbing Ron, some of his nonresponses bolstered our sense that he, not Duncan, had wielded the knife. For instance, when Duncan mentioned that he never told his attorney friend that Nathan "did it" and killed Ron, Nathan did not object or say anything like "What the hell are you talking about, me doing it?" To me, however, this information did nothing to diminish Duncan's complicity in Ron's murder, legally or morally.

Crucially, there was no indication that Nathan was suspicious of Duncan or wise to his buddy's continuing betrayal of him.

The absence of hiccups in obtaining the recording was a major relief to me and Garcia. Our roller coaster of an investigation had picked up speed and appeared primed to continue barreling down the tracks.

The excitement I felt while listening to the tape was tempered, however, by how disturbing I found it, in both tone and content. It was shocking to hear two friends so casually discuss an act of evil incarnate: the unprovoked murder of their own friend by their own hands.

Factually speaking, I understood everything Duncan had told us. The plot was hatched after he and Nathan happened to watch an episode of *Dragnet* about a botched kidnapping-for-ransom. The ostensible motive was money, the $100,000 demanded twice of the Bakers, first on the night of Ron's murder and again the following morning. That Ron was lured, under false pretenses, by two people he trusted and considered his friends, to a pitch-black tunnel where he was stabbed and left for dead.

Even so, despite the considerable progress we had made in piecing together what happened, it still made no sense to me. I could not fathom how two friends could conspire to kill another of their friends, their own roommate, and then carry out the devious plan. How could someone, or in this case two people, go from watching an old TV show to deciding it was okay to commit a cold-blooded murder, with the goal of making it impossible to solve?

Prior to the murder, neither Duncan nor Nathan had any significant criminal history, let alone any record of criminal violence. In our interactions with them, both came off as personable, even friendly. Both fully cooperated with our investigation, made themselves available to answer our questions, and submitted to repeated interviews, all with no apparent resentment. The only exception had been when Nathan's anger briefly flared after we told him we had a warrant to obtain his blood sample.

And yet somehow the dynamic between their two personalities had led them to do something that Garcia and I felt neither of them would have been capable of individually. I kept thinking: *How could this have been planned and carried out without either of them, especially Duncan, saying, "Wait a minute. What the hell are we talking about? We can't do this." How could things get to the point they did without someone stopping it?* This was the most troubling and bewildering aspect of the case.

Beyond these curiosities, which Garcia and I had been discussing off and on for months, we knew there was a more practical and immediate question that we needed answered:

Was this new tape, along with all the other evidence we had previously amassed, sufficient to now charge Nathan with Ron's murder?

Garcia and I felt it was. But we also knew that it was the DA's call to make and not ours.

Shortly after their face-to-face meeting, Nathan was transferred to state prison to begin serving his sentence for bank robbery. Duncan flew back to Utah as a free man, at least for the foreseeable future.

CHAPTER 16

"NO CHANGES, NO EDITS"
(July 18 to October 21, 1992)

GARCIA AND I PREPPED for what we knew would be a pivotal meeting with Deputy DA Ernie Norris.

Norris would decide what happened next in the case. Would he agree with Garcia and me that we now had sufficient evidence to charge Nathan with Ron's murder? Or would he demur and insist more was needed before he would take that step?

We met on July 18 in his office at the DA's Special Trials unit. We walked him through the two conversations, the first over the phone on July 9 and then the face-to-face at Riverside County Jail four days later. To highlight some of the more incriminating statements that Duncan had elicited from Nathan, we played him key portions of the tape.

Norris seemed favorable about moving forward but said he could not give us a definitive answer just yet. He told us he wanted to review everything before he made a decision and would get back to us soon.

In the meantime, Garcia and I set out to tie up a few loose ends.

On July 20, we received the results of SID's analysis of Duncan's blood sample. The report indicated Duncan had type A blood. This meant the blood found under Ron's fingernails could not have come from Duncan. It also meant that, of the three roommates in the tunnel that night, only Nathan's blood was consistent with the type AB under Ron's nails.

SID's report additionally noted that blood on the broken beer bottle pieces at the crime scene, previously tested as type A, could only have come from Ron. Although Ron and Duncan were both type A, the blood on the broken glass contained a specific protein that excluded Duncan's blood and was consistent with Ron's.

The lab results supported Duncan's story that only Nathan, not Duncan, physically struggled with Ron inside the tunnel. If Duncan had lied to us about that, we had no evidence to prove him wrong.

Later that same day, I called the parents of John Sands, Duncan's former classmate and the original target of his and Nathan's kidnap and ransom plan. Duncan had admitted to us during his King for a Day interview that he had called the Sands home, looking for John, but was told John was away at school. Neither parent had any recollection of Duncan's call, they told me.

Naturally, they were shocked to learn their son's name had come up in a murder investigation. I reassured them that John was in no danger and the one suspect who knew him was now cooperating with the police.

Although the parents of John Sands were unable to corroborate Duncan's story, it was important I made the effort. If they had been able to remember Duncan calling for John, it would have served as additional strong evidence of premeditation.

We heard back from Deputy DA Norris within a week or so of our meeting. Norris felt there was enough evidence to charge Nathan with Ron's murder, but he wanted us to go for one more conversation between Duncan and Nathan, in a final shot to elicit even more incriminating statements. Whether it was on the phone or another face-to-face meeting was up to us, he said.

I had some reservations. We had made it through the first two conversations seemingly without raising any suspicions from Nathan. Would Duncan contacting him a third time, especially in quick succession, strike Nathan as strange and cause him to question what Duncan was up to?

What if during the third conversation Nathan did become suspicious and tried to recant things he had said earlier? For instance, by challenging Duncan and saying that there had been no plan between them, or that Duncan was actually the stabber, shifting blame from himself.

I asked Norris about this. If Nathan did in fact recant his prior statements, would Norris opt not to charge him, despite what already seemed like a strong case?

Norris said he would still be inclined to charge Nathan, regardless of how the third conversation fared. Based on that assurance from Norris, we agreed to have Duncan contact Nathan once more. If the call was successful and we gathered more incriminating statements, it would further strengthen the prosecution's case.

Garcia and I felt it would be prudent to wait for some time to pass before Duncan reached out to Nathan again. After the recent initial call between the two, and the Riverside County Jail visit just a few days later, we did not want to rush their next call or meeting.

Nathan was serving his prison sentence and was going nowhere. We could afford to let the dust settle a bit from their last meeting. Waiting a period of time, we believed, might make Nathan less likely to clam up or refuse another overture from Duncan to talk.

In mid-October, a little more than three months after the face-to-face meeting, Garcia and I felt that enough time had passed. The timing seemed right for Duncan to make contact again.

By then, Nathan had been transferred from Chino to a different state prison, the California Correctional Institution in Tehachapi, in the high desert about 120 miles north of LA.

Garcia and I debated whether the third conversation should be in person or over the phone.

We ultimately settled on the latter, for several reasons. We knew from the two recordings we had already made that the sound quality of a phone call would be far superior to a conversation recorded with a body wire. Moreover, Garcia and I could be present for the call and monitor what was said in real time, an impossibility during a face-to-face meeting.

We opted against flying Duncan to Los Angeles, as we had done for his first call with Nathan. He would call instead from Utah. Garcia and I would travel to be there when the call took place. Bringing Duncan back to LA posed a risk of him running into someone from his old circle of friends. Doing the call from Utah would also avoid the risks associated with a new cover story for what he was doing back in California should Nathan inquire. Nathan knew Duncan was living in Utah, so it would be only natural for him to call from a Utah phone number. There was one other consideration. In the months since we had last seen Duncan, he had enrolled in classes at the University of Utah. As of the fall semester of 1992, he was officially a college student. For all of these reasons, Garcia and I felt making Duncan come to Los Angeles would be more logistically complicated than us going to see him.

Garcia and I made our travel arrangements. One thing we needed to do was find somewhere Nathan could place a collect call to reach Duncan. We did not want Duncan to use his actual phone number, given the eventuality that Nathan would learn of Duncan's cooperation.

I called a Marriott hotel in Salt Lake City and spoke with the hotel's director of security, Richard Boden. I asked if there was a room available where a collect call could be received directly, rather than through the hotel switchboard. Boden said there was: a penthouse suite on the twelfth floor.

I also called the state prison in Tehachapi. As I'd done with Riverside County Jail, where a note had been passed to Nathan before the first call in July, I explained what Garcia and I needed them to do. We wanted to have prison staff pass a note to Nathan in the early evening hours of October 21. I was told it would not be a problem.

Garcia and I flew to Salt Lake City on October 20. The following day, a Wednesday, we picked up Duncan and drove with him to the Marriott hotel. We had already made test calls to the hotel room's outside number, to verify it could be dialed directly and did not go through a switchboard operator or the front desk. As far as Nathan would know, it was just a direct line to reach Duncan. Assuming, that is, that Nathan took the bait and called back.

A little before 6 p.m., I called the prison and dictated the note we wanted passed to Nathan as soon as possible: "Nathan Blalock—Please call collect as soon as you get this. Family emergency. Call collect to Duncan," followed by the 801-area-code number for the hotel room.

We had already set up the recording device on the hotel phone. As with their first call in July, we would only be able to hear Duncan's side of the conversation while the call took place. Other than what we might overhear coming through the phone's receiver, we would not learn what Nathan said until we listened to the tape.

I felt some tension build as we waited. We had discussed with Duncan some possible scenarios to guide their conversation, but only generally. Like before, we did not want the call to feel scripted or contrived. We trusted Duncan would know how to talk with Nathan in a way that felt comfortable to both of them. Duncan had already proven himself in their prior recorded conversations to be adept at ad-libbing.

Our advice to Duncan to get Nathan talking was to create some pressure by upping the ante a little. One possibility we mentioned to Duncan was that he'd heard a warrant had been issued for his arrest. By and large, however, where the conversation went from there would be up to Duncan, Nathan, and the dynamic between them.

We encouraged Duncan not to give up if Nathan seemed reluctant to open up. We knew that when they'd first spoken on the phone, Nathan had had a concern about the lines not being secure at the Riverside County Jail. We assumed he would have the same concern on a call from state prison.

At five minutes past six, the phone in our hotel room rang. Would it be Nathan? Or prison staff alerting us that Nathan could not be located immediately or had refused to accept the note?

We hit the RECORD button and Duncan answered. An operator announced it was a collect call from Nathan. Duncan agreed to accept the charges.

"Hey, bro," said Duncan.

"Hey, what's up, dude?" replied Nathan.

"What's up, man?"

"Nothing much."

"Oh, man. Um, I got a problem," said Duncan.

"Talk to me."

"They went to my mom's house this morning with a warrant for my arrest."

"And..."

"Well, they wouldn't—they weren't able to get a warrant two years ago. They weren't able to get a warrant a year ago. How come they can get one now?" Duncan asked. He appeared to be setting Nathan up for their conversation to go well beyond what Nathan seemed ready for.

"I have no idea," said Nathan.

"Well, I don't know what I want to do. I was thinking about starting to try and straighten my life out. And, you know, my mom's flipped out. And when they talked to her, they said that it's death penalty for sure."

"What—what?"

"They're going for murder one. They're saying that the body was tortured and that they're going for murder one. And that's DP." Duncan's allusions to torture and the death penalty were talking points he had come up with on his own, not fed to him by me or Garcia.

"So, what's the—what evidence do they have on you?"

"They didn't say that. They don't have to say that. I don't know what they've got. But I'm flipped, man. I mean, I've been running for over two years. And I was finally thinking I had my life where I could, you know—"

"Where you at?"

"I'm still in Utah."

"How do you know this? You talked to your mom today?"

"Yeah, she called me flipped out. So I'm pretty freaked. I mean, they said it was torture. That's why they can go for this. They said it was because the—it had been stabbed so many times. I mean, how many times did you stick him? I mean…"

Listening in the hotel room, I winced when I heard Duncan ask Nathan this. It felt to me a little too blatant and early in their call to ask that over a potentially monitored prison phone. I thought Nathan might have a suspicious reaction or verbally shut down. But the conversation continued.

"I don't know really nothing about all that stuff, man. I'm just trying to figure out how they could put a warrant on you."

"I don't know either. All I know is that I'm flipped, and I don't know what to do. And I don't know what I'm going to tell them if I do go down. I mean, what should I tell them? What should I say?"

"That you didn't do it."

"Yeah, and—"

"And you don't know who did."

"Well, what if they've got, like, some evidence that they didn't have before? What if they've got something that ties me there?"

"I don't see how."

"I don't either, but they've got to have something if they've got a warrant out."

"Not necessarily. They could have heard you were back in the state. You know, you've been gone for two years, dude."

"Yes, I came back for a couple of days."

"Maybe they heard. Maybe they found out."

"How are they going to hear?"

"I don't know," said Nathan, sounding a bit exasperated, his tone of voice rising.

"I mean, the only people I saw were you and my mom, really, you know."

"Well, now, your mom could have said something."

"My mom wouldn't. There's no way."

"And I didn't," said Nathan. "I mean, as far as I'm concerned, it's like there's nothing there."

"Yeah, well, the way they put it, they made it sound like, that with the amount of damage done—"

"They always hype up situations, dude... I listen to millions of stories every week. They always hype up stuff to be what it's not."

"Well, then how come they've got a first-degree warrant?"

"Because they always try to go for the max, because they know it's going to get broken down in court to something of a lesser charge."

"Well, they've got to have something. That's how I see it."

"Not necessarily. They could be reaching, man. They could just want you because, you know, maybe your mom did say something. I mean, you say she wouldn't, but maybe she did."

"Well, part of it too is, they mentioned that they knew that you were there too."

"Huh?"

"They mentioned you too to my mom."

"What did they say about me to her?"

"They said that they knew you were there too."

"That's drama, dude, because—"

"It can't be drama."

"If anything they would have sent me a—how long ago was this? Today?"

"This morning. What they told my mom is that they weren't worried about you because they knew you were in custody. That's how I knew where you were."

"Uh-huh."

"But they wanted to find me. And they were telling her that she can go down too, for harboring a fugitive, if they find out that she knew where I was at."

"Does she know where you are?"

"Well, she's got my phone number."

"Dude, I don't know nothing about it. And I'm gonna, you know—this is, like, what? Three years old now?"

"Two."

"And, uh, I don't even remember what happened that day. You know what I'm saying?"

"Oh, come on. You can't say you don't remember what happened that day."

"All I remember—I don't even remember what happened that day. That's three years ago. I don't know any details from three years ago of any specific day."

"I think you'd remember that day. I mean, that's me. I mean, that was a pretty major day."

"What?"

"That was a pretty major day for me. I mean, it's not every day that something like that happens right in front of you. And I would think from your position it would be a pretty major day. And I think the fact that, you know, I don't know. I basically gave up two years of my life to cover for you. And—"

"To cover for me?" asked Nathan, incredulous.

"Hell yes. I mean, don't bullshit me, Nathan. That's not cool."

"I'm not bullshitting you. All I know is that, you know, neither one of us was there. We don't know what happened. They don't really know what happened. They want you because you've been running for two years. You know, I'm not saying turn yourself over neither. But you're in another state, man. As long as you don't break any laws, you can't get picked up for anything."

"Yeah, well, I don't know. I can't see how you can be so indifferent."

"What?"

"I can't see how you can be so indifferent."

"I can barely hear you," said Nathan.

"I can't see how you can be so indifferent. It doesn't make sense to me. It doesn't make sense to me because this is something that's screwed with me for the past two years. And I don't know. I don't know. I mean, I just ... I don't understand."

"Well, if you're, you know—if you feel really bad about it, and thinking about turning yourself in ... I don't know what you're going to do. I can't really give you any advice. All I can say is that, you know, I hear hundreds of stories all the time about how they hype up something, and people wind up beating things right and left. You know? There is no concrete evidence, um, about the thing that happened. When they came and gave me a blood test about skin under the fingernails. We were all roommates. We wrestled and played. We wore the same clothes. We took showers in the same shower. Used the same soap."

"Yeah, but Nathan, they can time stuff like that too. I'm wondering about that and, you know—"

"How can they time anything like that?"

"You can take a blood sample and figure out how old it is. If they figure out that the blood sample that they got under his fingernails is from the same time period as when he was offed—"

"I remember within that, within that same eight-hour time period, we were all wrestling in the living room."

"Well ..."

"So what difference does it make?"

"I don't know ... I don't know what it could be, okay? All I know is I'm flipped. And I don't know what to do. Okay?"

"Like I said, I suggest you get a legit job and just stay where you're at. And continue to live your life, man. And put that behind you. There's nothing that—I mean, as far I'm concerned, you know, I wasn't there and I had nothing to do with it...As far as I can say, you know, it's done, it's over...The most they could try to do is say...There's not even a weapon!"

"Yeah, well..."

"They don't know who did what. They don't know who did it."

"Well, I wish I could be as confident as you about that. Because I'm not."

"If there was even...Who's that Black guy he used to hang out with anyway? The big guy that they could never find on campus...You know, so Ron hung around with too many people who were into too many shifty things anyway."

"Not really. I mean, it was us. It was our group of friends. The heaviest thing—"

"There was the people he hung out with on campus too, who none of us know anything about. And the police can't find none of them."

"No, they've talked to them."

"Not all of them."

"Well, they pretty much had consistent alibis, if you remember from way back when."

"The few they talked to, yeah, those were his close people on campus he hung out with. A bunch of people from that group he hung out with, they couldn't even be found."

"Well, that's not what I heard. What I heard is that they had had, like, a party or something. All of them were there. And they all vouched for each other."

"Just like we vouch for each other."

"Yeah, but that was twenty people. This is two."

"Well, we had more than—we have more than two...We still got three vouching for us."

"Who?"

"Diane."

"Yeah, but Diane was passed out on the couch."

"No, she wasn't. She was awake watching *Arsenio Hall*. She was watching TV when I came in... And she told the police that. While you were gone, they came all the way out to Elsinore just looking for me or whatever, and talking to me on a regular basis. She already told the police that, and everything else."

"Well—"

"And she's a good Christian person."

"Well, then maybe we're covered as far as that goes."

"So I understand, you know, the warrant—if you're missing from the scene of a crime and you can't be found, man, then of course they're going to issue a warrant."

"No, the warrant's not—it's not, like, that they want—"

"It's for 'suspect of'—right or wrong?"

"They have to have serious evidence to get a warrant."

"They didn't have serious evidence against me, for what I did, what I'm in here now for, but the warrant said 'suspect.' I was a suspect. Period. Anytime you're wanted for questioning, you're a suspect."

"So basically what you want me to say is, you want me to say I have absolutely no idea what the hell they're talking about. Is that what you're saying?"

"Basically, you don't. You're confused. You don't really know."

"Okay. So then—"

"Do you really know?"

"Let me ask you a question. Say I say, okay, I don't know anything about it, I wasn't there, you know, and then they pull something out and say, 'Look, this shows you were there,' okay? What do I do then?"

"What they—it would have to be within a certain time frame."

"Not on this."

"We'll just have to see what they have, man. I don't think there's anything that says either one of us was there. The last thing I remember was dropping him off at the bus stop. Period."

"Dude, you—that's so bogus... That's so bogus."

"Huh?"

"That's bogus, man," repeated Duncan.

"It's not bogus. Think about the situation. I'm in here now. And when I get out, I don't want to come back for anything. For anything."

"That's right. I don't want to go for anything."

"That's right. So the last thing you remember is dropping him off at the bus stop. Whatever happens, if anything happens, don't say a word until you speak to the lawyer. Remember your Miranda rights. Don't say a word until you speak to the lawyer."

"I don't know."

"And your lawyer and my lawyer's going to have to get together sooner or later. And then we'll go from there, if they want to try to put it on us. If not, then, you know, you get a job. Go to church. Get a religion. And live out the rest of your life."

"Yeah."

"You're going to have to put it in the hands of God, man. Ask for repentance."

"I don't believe in God."

"If you feel guilty about something, ask for repentance. Ask the Lord for repentance and be serious about it. I admit, I know that sounds like a joke but—"

"You know how I believe about God," said Duncan.

"Well, you can—maybe it's time for a change, man."

"Yeah."

"Maybe the things you're believing in hasn't been working for you. Maybe now is the time to try something different. You know what I'm saying?"

"I don't know. I don't know what to do. I don't know what to do at all."

"Until you're in custody, don't worry about it."

"How can I not worry about it?"

"Because you have to worry about other things that are more important at the point in time. Like living every day. Getting a job. Oh, you have a job yet?"

"Yeah, I got a job."

"And is it—it's not your name, is it?"

"No. Fuck. Is there any way Diane could have told them anything? I mean, did she know anything, other than the fact that we went to the school?"

"No, they're going on the blood test, man. That's all they can go on."

"Well—"

"And the blood test doesn't prove anything because we wrestled... Everyone knows that. And anyone would vouch for that."

"Yeah."

"Lydia, Lance, all of them know we all wrestled. We all went down to the parking lot, we did the nunchucks... We were physical people, the three of us."

"Doesn't this bother you?"

"I don't have time for it to bother me right now. I have, like, two years of something else that's bothering me."

"I don't understand how you can do that. I don't see how you can be in jail and not spend half your time thinking about this."

"Because I have other things to think about."

"Yeah, but Nathan, this isn't, you know, like going to the store and, you know."

"And the police are a lot of hype too. I find that out every day. They're a lot of hype."

"Well, they may be a lot of hype, but this is something you did that's fucking me up. And I don't know what to do about it. That's why I wanted to talk to you about it."

"And I'm telling you what to do about it."

"You're telling me to—"

"Get a job, change your, you know, do what you've done already. Get a religion, man, and ask God for forgiveness. That's what I've done."

"How can you ask for forgiveness for something like this?"

"I've asked God for forgiveness."

"I don't understand. So that makes it better?"

"It's hard to—it doesn't make it better. It doesn't make it worse. But it makes me able to function and continue to do what I have to do."

"Wow, I couldn't do that. I couldn't do that."

"Right now, where I'm at, I could—someone could kill me any minute. I could get stuck right here talking to you on the telephone."

"So that makes it better? Because you're in that—"

"I have to look at my immediate surroundings. I can't look at what happened three years ago."

"I have to every day. I have to think about it every day. I have to—"

"And I don't?"

"Huh?"

"And I don't?" Nathan repeated.

"Well, that's what you're saying. You're saying you don't have to think about it."

"I have choices to make though, man."

"Huh?"

"I have choices to make. I have to look at things that are more important for right this minute, and the next hour, and tomorrow."

"So you just blow this off?"

"Right now, I have to."

"I couldn't do that. See, I can't do that. I did that for a while. I pretended like it didn't exist for a while."

"You're going to have to. It's not a fact of pretending that it didn't happen."

"Well, he was my friend, bro."

"I understand that."

"He was your friend too, I thought."

"It's not that it didn't happen. You accept it and you deal with it. And sooner or later it'll stop bothering you."

"So I just have to deal with it."

"You've dealt with it. And dealing with it doesn't mean that you have to come in for something you didn't do. Because the worst thing the police could do... There's nothing they can really hold... They don't have anything. Keep telling yourself that. They don't have anything. They're making threats. And they're trying to get something. If they had something, they would have acted a long time ago."

"Well..."

"And it's just peculiar... It's strange how they happen to come up with this warrant right around the time when you're in town."

"No, they didn't. I've been out of town for three months."

"They don't know that."

"I mean, that's assuming that they knew I went to town. I've been out of town for three months."

"You know, I know that. But they don't know that."

"But they don't even know I was in town. See, I can't—"

"You don't know that they know or that they don't know."

"Okay. Well, let me put it this way. I can't blow this off. I can't blow this whole thing off. Just like I can't blow you off. I can't pretend like you don't exist and say, 'Screw that.' I can't. You guys were both my friends, you know, and it put me in such a situation that I just didn't know what to do. I mean, you doing that to him just—it threw me a curve. It totally threw me a curve. And I don't know. I don't know what to do now."

"Well, okay, look. This is a penitentiary, and these lines, they may not be totally secure."

"Well, what am I supposed to do? I can't come see you."

"I'm just saying watch what you say."

"Okay."

"Because these are not secure lines... All I can say is let me do the worrying and you just go on and keep on working."

"I come home at night—"

"What?"

"I come home at night. And if I'm alone at home, I sit and I think about it."

"Why? You can't find anything better to do?"

"I try to. Play Nintendo or something. And then I end up thinking about it."

"You got a girlfriend?"

"Yeah, but when she's not over... I mean, she doesn't spend the night every night."

"You got to occupy your mind with something else, man."

"It's hard to."

"Get a religion, man. Get a new religion."

"I... I can't do that."

"That'll help, for starters."

"I can't do that. You know that. You know what I believe about that."

"You can if you want to."

"Yeah, but I can't, because I don't believe in it logically. And you've known that."

"Look into different religions, man. I'm serious. That's for starters."

"I can't go to religion ... I couldn't ask for forgiveness for this. I did—well, I didn't do anything."

"You didn't do anything."

"No, but I did, okay? You know what I didn't do? And this is what I beat myself up on a lot."

"What?"

"When I think about it? I didn't say anything, okay? He was my best friend and you were my best friend, okay? What was I supposed to do, okay? Was I supposed to stick on your side or his? I stuck on yours, okay? And I'm still—oh, man, I'm still there. But I'm losing it. I mean, I keep thinking about what I heard that night. I keep hurting about what I saw that night, when you lit the lighter, you know? And I don't know if you can picture what that did to me, but—I don't know if you can at all. I mean, it sounds like you've got it tucked away like it never happened. And I can't see how you could do that. I mean ..."

"Because I have to live my life. I have to go on."

"Yeah."

"It happened. It was a mistake. And it's, you know, but I still, I have to—I cannot live three years ago. I have to live for the time that's coming up. Do you understand what I'm saying?"

"It was two years ago, by the way. But—"

"Almost three."

"No, well, two and a quarter. And I—"

"Okay. Two and a quarter."

"And I think about that all the time too."

"There's a lot of people out there who have done worse or seen worse, man. And they live with it and deal with it every day."

"Well, it's hard for me. It's hard for me because there's a part of me that wants to think of you in a really negative light, because of that night, okay? And I can't. Because—"

"I can understand that."

"Because you're my friend. And you were always my friend. And, at the same token, so was he. And when I think about him not being around anymore ... I don't know what to do about it, you know, and I mean—the way he died wasn't cool. And the way things have happened since, you know, haven't been cool. I have had no support. It wasn't like I had Diane sitting there to be able to help me through this. I was out on my own. You know? And all it's done is screw me up. All it's done is screw me up. And yeah, maybe it was my mistake for taking off. But I was too damn scared. You know, I could cover, but I—"

"Yeah, well, she wasn't much help when the police were questioning me... In fact, she actually applied more pressure. And her family didn't help neither."

"Well, at least you had somebody there. You didn't end up in another city, all alone, knowing nobody. Trying to find a life. And, yeah, maybe it was—"

"Yeah, I did. When I moved to Elsinore I didn't know nobody but her."

"Well, at least you could call people. I couldn't. And maybe it was a mistake I took off. But there was no way I was going down for something I didn't do. There was no way, you know, I'd cover—"

"What has changed that thought now? How you going to go down for something you didn't do now?"

"What happens if tomorrow I get picked up for a speeding ticket, right? Or what happens if I happen to have a warrant out for my arrest for a speeding ticket, right? And I get put in jail."

"See, here it is right now—"

"Okay."

"A chance to live your life and be a good citizen."

"Yeah, but Nathan—"

"Don't speed. Don't break the law, period."

"Yeah, but come on. Let's be realistic. You know how I drive."

"Well, it's time, like I said, it's time to change then."

"So I can't ever do anything that even breaks the law minusculely again, for the rest of my life?"

"Not if you don't want to get caught for it."

"That's pretty restricting."

"But not really."

"Yeah, it is."

"It's what you should have been doing anyway. We shouldn't be law-breaking citizens anyway."

"No, we shouldn't. But we are, I guess."

"So here's the chance to become... well, you don't want to find God. But here's a chance to become a productive citizen, period."

"Do you still have my address?" asked Duncan.

"No. I don't even have a pen on me. I lost my phone book, man, when I first got here."

"That's why I was—I was just wondering why you never wrote me."

"Or else I would have wrote. Believe me, I would have wrote... I would have wrote at least one letter. But I lost my phone book. I got another one now."

"Do you want to go grab a pen?"

"No, let me see if I can't get one. Hang on."

Nathan put the phone down for a moment, then came back on the line. "All right," he said.

Duncan told Nathan to write to him under the name James Atkins. For his address, he provided a post office box in Park City, Utah.

After Duncan gave him his contact information, Nathan told him, "You know, we've been on the phone for half an hour now."

"I don't care. This is important to me."

"Okay, um..."

"There's two things I need to know. Or there's one thing I got to tell you, one thing I got to know. I'm thinking about—I might not be here that much longer."

"Okay."

"Write me a letter so I have your address—"

"Okay."

"For when I bail. Because I can't afford to call like this all the time."

"Yeah, I know."

"And second is, I need to know you'll stand behind me if I get snagged."

"Stand behind you how?"

"You know what I mean."

"I'm sticking to the original story, man," said Nathan.

"Okay. No changes, no edits," replied Duncan.

"No changes, no edits," Nathan repeated, as if in agreement.

"Okay."

"Is that what you want to hear?" asked Nathan.

"Yeah, I guess. I mean, I don't know."

"I'm sticking to the original story. And I would advise you to do the same thing. Because, um, you know, there's a lot of things in our favor that I can see that you don't. You understand what I'm saying? By being where I'm at right now. Because this is nothing but another branch of the law. There is a very extensive law library here. And I'll do a little research."

"Is it possible—I mean, I don't know. I don't know."

"What did the warrant say they were going to try to get you on? First degree?"

"First degree."

"All right."

"I mean, they said some stuff that really flipped out my mom."

"Like what?"

"Like they said it was torture. They said that, um, it looked like that they tried to cut the head off. And, I mean, stuff like that. They said that by the number of times that the body had been, you know, that, uh, how many times it'd been stabbed, that it made it look like, um, he was tortured before he died. And I mean—"

"That's hard to prove in court, man, torture ... I'll see what the law library has. I'll drop you a letter sometime between—before next week. Before next Wednesday, it'll be in the mail."

"Okay."

"It's good to hear from you, though. Even though it's not the best of news."

"Yeah, well, maybe things will lighten up one of these days. Maybe things will be cool."

"Okay."

"But I'll look for your letter."

"All right, dude."

"Talk to you soon."

"Talk to you," Nathan signed off before they hung up the phone.

Garcia stated for the record, "Okay. The time is now 1835 hours. And Duncan has just terminated the conversation."

Contrary to their parting words, it was the last time Duncan and Nathan ever spoke.

Two years after Ron's murder, Duncan's second betrayal, his double-crossing of Nathan, was complete.

CHAPTER 17

"IT'S TOO BAD WE HAD TO MEET UNDER THESE CIRCUMSTANCES"
(October 21, 1992 to January 23, 1993)

WE HAD GOTTEN WHAT we needed from the call. Nathan had made several more incriminating statements that would be very difficult to explain away. Additionally, when Duncan had brought up damning allegations, such as Ron's wounds constituting torture, Nathan had said nothing to challenge or deny it. He had responded instead that torture is "hard to prove in court," and he would research the issue in the prison's law library.

After the call, Duncan asked if Garcia and I would drop him off at a location on the University of Utah campus, on the east side of Salt Lake City. We agreed.

When we reached his destination on campus, Garcia and I got out of the car to say goodbye and thank him for his efforts. Duncan then made a comment to us that I will never forget.

"It's too bad we had to meet under these circumstances, because you guys would be a lot of fun to hang out with," he told us, seemingly with utter sincerity.

Left unsaid was that "these circumstances" were the murder of a close friend—one he had helped plan, had witnessed, and had tried to cover up—and the selling out of another close friend, just minutes earlier, in order to save his own hide. Duncan's demeanor betrayed no discomfort with having called Nathan under the guise of being distressed and seeking his advice, while actually paving the way for Nathan's arrest for murder.

That night, Garcia and I went to dinner at Mulboons, a steak-and-seafood restaurant in Salt Lake City where Duncan had mentioned he once worked as a waiter. We discussed where we were in the case and where things might lead. Neither of us had any idea how Duncan would fare in this whole investigation.

Would he be used as a trial witness and take some type of plea bargain for his cooperation? Or was his credibility so suspect, and ripe for attack in court, that his testifying would be more harmful than helpful in the case?

If he took a plea, what charges would he plead guilty to? How much of a break would he receive on his sentence? How much of a sentence reduction, if any, did he deserve?

All of these questions were out of our hands. Garcia and I would give our opinions, but the DA's Office would make the ultimate decision.

Garcia and I were well aware that we did not have enough admissible evidence even to put Duncan in the park that night, let alone prove beyond a reasonable doubt that he was guilty of Ron's murder.

According to the terms of our King for a Day deal, nothing he told us could be used against him, including his statements to Nathan in their three monitored conversations. The remaining evidence against Duncan made for a fairly weak circumstantial case. Absent any new evidence, it seemed doubtful the DA would consider filing a case against him.

Nathan, between his statements to Duncan and the AB-type blood under Ron's fingernails, was a completely different story. We knew Nathan would be charged when the time was right. The DA's Office would determine when. There was no rush since he still had a couple of years to serve on his current prison sentence. Time would tell.

A few weeks after we returned from Utah, Garcia and I met again with Deputy DA Ernie Norris. This time, Norris's supervisor, a senior prosecutor named Michael Montagna, also sat in on the meeting. Garcia and I both knew Montagna well from working with him on prior cases. Montagna had been the deputy DA on the criminal homicide of comedian John Belushi, a case in which I was involved.

Because of Montagna's presence, and his relative unfamiliarity with the case, Garcia and I started at square one and ran through our entire investigation. We concluded our presentation with a summary of the final surreptitiously recorded phone call between Duncan and Nathan.

Both prosecutors agreed there was sufficient evidence to charge Nathan. All in attendance also agreed that no filing would take place until Garcia and I had made a run at interviewing Nathan, to see if we could obtain a confession. A confession would be icing on the cake, as even without one there was no doubt we had put together a strong case against Nathan.

Whether Duncan should be used as a witness was more complicated and could not be answered, at least not yet. Much depended on what would happen next with Nathan. If he confessed, then Duncan's importance as a witness would be significantly lessened. If he refused to confess, then Norris and Montagna would have to make a difficult decision.

Garcia and I felt using Duncan would be ill-advised and told the prosecutors so. Yes, much of what Duncan had told us about Ron's murder was corroborated by Nathan's own statements. Duncan's story had also been bolstered by Nathan's conspicuous failure, at multiple points during their three conversations, to deny the various allegations Duncan had confronted him with.

In our opinion, however, those factors were outweighed by how vehemently a jury would dislike Duncan, knowing not only of his extreme culpability in his friend Ron's murder but also that he was testifying against his friend Nathan to get some beneficial plea agreement. Then there was the issue of Duncan's wild tales of covert military assassination missions to the Middle East, lucrative security jobs that did not exist, his faked kidnapping and false identities, and so on. All of these lies were certain to be brought up at trial and exploited by the defense to destroy his already shaky credibility.

Norris nevertheless said he wanted to use Duncan as a witness. Montagna seemed to be on the fence. He requested we bring Duncan in for an interview with him and Norris. He said he felt he could more easily weigh the pros and cons by talking with Duncan in person. It was agreed we would have Duncan flown to Los Angeles for a meeting at the DA's Office on the Monday of Thanksgiving week.

On the morning of November 23, Garcia and I escorted Duncan to the Criminal Courts Building. We took the elevator up to the eighteenth floor, where the DA's Special Trials unit had its offices. Garcia and I looked on while Norris and Montagna asked Duncan question after question. At their request, he recounted the entire evening of June 21, 1990, as well as his earlier discussions with Nathan about Ron becoming their future victim. The interview lasted a couple of hours. At the end, the two prosecutors said they would discuss their thoughts with us later.

My sense leaving the interview was that Norris still wanted to use Duncan as a witness. Montagna, on the other hand, seemed inclined to err on the side of caution and wait to see what happened during our interview with Nathan. That was the course Garcia and I favored. At this point, why rush into any decision now that time in this case was finally on our side?

After our meeting at the DA's Office, Garcia and I drove Duncan to Van Nuys. He directed us to an apartment building at 14845 Erwin Street, just west of where he once lived with Ron and Nathan. At the rear of the building, Duncan showed us a trash dumpster. He said this was where he and Nathan had tossed the murder weapon, Nathan's bloodied clothing, and Ron's wallet.

Next, Duncan showed us the locations of the phone booths, both a short walk from their apartment, where he had made the two ransom calls to Mr. Baker.

Our final stop was a military supply store in nearby Tarzana. Duncan identified an exact duplicate of the knife, "KA-BAR USMC," that Nathan had used to stab Ron. Garcia and I purchased one. It would be an impressive court exhibit to show a future jury.

Our long day with Duncan was done. Before he flew back to Salt Lake City to resume college classes, Duncan told us he had received a letter in the mail from Nathan, as Nathan had promised in their October phone call. Duncan gave us the letter and the envelope it was mailed in.

The letter was addressed to "James Atkin," a misspelling of the alias that Duncan had given Nathan during their last call. The letter was handwritten and one page long. It read in full:

Hey, How goes it!

Bad opening, but its common which is what you have to be, common. The loss of your friend is felt by us both and many others. I understand the police have little info and no weapon. No matter what they say unless someone tells them something their going to have a hard time convicting anyone of murder of any degree. I can't do much to help you right now. But I can keep you in my prayers to Allah. I'll also ask you to find God. He alone can ease the pain you feel inside. Now is the time to try God and find the peace your looking for.

Write soon take care
Your friend.

I imagined Nathan's letter was an effort to soothe Duncan's angst and guilty feelings, which Duncan had repeatedly voiced in their call. It was also a reminder from Nathan to Duncan that if they stuck together and to their story, there was nothing to fear.

Garcia and I booked into evidence the knife we had purchased and the original letter from Nathan.

On the morning of December 16, I received a telephone call from an officer with the University of Utah Police Department. The officer, Sherri Barnes, said she was calling regarding a rumor about a student named Duncan Martinez.

Barnes explained that she had been contacted by an advisor to one of the fraternities on campus, Phi Delta Theta. She said the advisor, Doug Christiansen, told her that Duncan had been talking about his involvement, and subsequent cooperation with the LAPD, in a Los Angeles murder investigation. According to Christiansen, Duncan had told people that "he might get arrested for voluntary manslaughter." The information eventually had made its way into conversations among the fraternity brothers at Phi Delta Theta, which was how Christiansen had heard about it. Barnes was calling to ask if there was any truth to the rumor.

I recalled that Duncan had mentioned to us, at some point that fall, that he had decided to pledge a fraternity.

I told Barnes I couldn't discuss too many details but could confirm that Duncan was working with us and the District Attorney's Office in relation to an ongoing murder investigation. I also informed her there was no indication, at this point in time, that Duncan was going to be arrested for anything.

The fact that Duncan's involvement and cooperation in the Baker case was being gossiped about on the University of Utah campus was unwelcome news to me and Garcia.

The terms of Duncan's cooperation agreement with us, struck prior to his King for a Day interview, was that he could not discuss Ron Baker's murder with anyone but us and the District Attorney's Office. Any future statements he made to other people about the planning and details of Ron's murder could be admissible evidence against him. His limited immunity covered only his ongoing conversations with us and the District Attorney's Office, as we had explained to him at the time.

First of all, whatever Duncan had said on campus violated that agreement. Second, no final decision had been made yet about whether or not he would be used as a witness. The more he discussed with others what he might need to testify about, the more perilous his potential testimony would be.

Garcia and I promptly called Duncan and told him what we had heard. We reminded him, and warned him, that talking with anyone else about the case was technically a violation of the original agreement we had made with him when he began his cooperation. We reiterated that any grist he supplied to the rumor mill was bad for him and bad for the investigation. We both told him not to do anything like that again.

Duncan apologized and said he understood where we were coming from. He seemed to feel a little bad about it and appreciative of our advice.

That warning to Duncan was the last action we took on the Baker case in 1992. It also turned out to be Garcia's final action as a police detective on the Baker investigation, a case that had consumed so much of his time over the past two and a half years.

Just before the holidays, Garcia was offered a position by an investigative firm in the private sector. One of his former detective partners, Mike Thies, already worked there and convinced him to accept.

January 23, 1993, marked the end of an era. After twenty-three years on the job, Frank Garcia officially retired from the LAPD.

CHAPTER 18

"I NEED YOU FOR ONE MORE DAY"
(February 9 to 17, 1993)

THE TIME HAD COME to reveal our hand to Nathan and lay our cards on the table.

How would he react when confronted with the case we'd built against him? Faced with the evidence, would he stick with the same story he had told us every time we had spoken with him previously, since the early days of the case? Or would he, in spite of his unflappable demeanor, finally break and admit what we believed to be true, that he had stabbed Ron to death inside the tunnel?

It had been a collaborative effort by Garcia and me to reach this delicate and critical stage in the case. Over his final few years as a detective, leading up to his official retirement that January, he and I had spent more time digging into and discussing Ron Baker's murder than any other case.

Nevertheless, it appeared I would be without Garcia's assistance and presence in the room with me when I went to visit Nathan.

I had yet to be assigned a new partner after Garcia retired, so for the time being, I was working on my own.

For an interview this important, there was no way I would meet with Nathan alone. The main reason is that it's easier for a suspect to stonewall one detective than two. In case I said something that inadvertently caused Nathan to shut down, I wanted someone else there who could jump in and try to get the interview back on track.

Also, even though I knew the interview would be tape-recorded, having an additional witness in the room would serve as an insurance policy of sorts, just in case the recording equipment failed. The nightmare scenario, in the middle of taking a confession by yourself, would be to look down and see that your recorder's batteries had died or there was some other malfunction. In that event, it would be your word alone against the suspect's as to what exactly was said, a situation to avoid.

One option I had was to approach another Major Crimes detective and ask them to come with me to the state prison in Tehachapi, where Nathan remained incarcerated. I had no doubt that one of my colleagues would agree.

Whoever it was, however, would have limited knowledge of the case. They also would have no history or rapport with Nathan.

What if Nathan shut down on me for one reason or another? Who could jump in to try to carry the conversation forward? Not someone who was unfamiliar with the details of the case and only meeting Nathan for the first time.

I wanted Garcia to be there.

I called him at home on February 9, eight days before my target date to interview Nathan. Garcia had been retired for exactly seventeen days.

"I need you for one more day," I told him.

Garcia agreed without hesitation.

Although I was unaware of any department policy prohibiting it, it was unusual to have a retired detective perform official police business. I felt I needed to obtain authorization from Captain Gartland.

I told Gartland that Garcia and I had developed the case together and established a rapport with both suspects. I explained that for the good of the case, Garcia being there with me gave us our best chance at eliciting a confession from Nathan. Gartland signed off on it but also told me, "Let's not make a habit of this."

I picked up Garcia early on the morning of February 17. It would take us a few hours to make the drive to Tehachapi, enough time to talk over the plan I had come up with for the interview.

I would read Nathan his Miranda rights, I told Garcia, since I would be the only sworn officer in the room. I would explain to Nathan this was necessary because unlike all of our prior interviews with him, he was in custody.

I had brought two tape recorders. One was fitted and wired inside a briefcase and would record the interview. It would be switched on before Nathan even walked into the room. The second recorder would be used, when the timing was right, to play key excerpts of the recorded conversations between Nathan and Duncan.

I had chosen several highly incriminating exchanges to play for Nathan. The first one was already cued up, set to play at the push of a button. For the others, I had documented the tape counter numbers of their start points, so I could fast-forward or reverse between them quickly.

Of course, this was all dependent on Nathan agreeing to waive his rights and speak with us. To that end, we also strategized about how best to begin the interview and break the ice.

I told Garcia I would start on a very low-key, nonconfrontational note. I planned to ask Nathan to recount to us, one more time, the night he and Duncan had dropped Ron off at the bus stop. "Maybe we are missing something," I would tell him. It would be an easy request for me to make and for Nathan to comply with.

We arrived near 11 a.m., the time we had arranged with the prison. After we completed some paperwork, went through security, and were shown to the interview room we would use, it was close to 11:30 a.m.

The room was small but sufficient for our purposes, with just enough space for a table and chairs. It was situated off a corridor through which prison employees and inmates walked from time to time. We decided to seat Nathan with his back to the door, which had a small window that looked out on the hallway. This would minimize any potential distractions for him. I would sit across from Nathan and Garcia to his side, all around a table that was only about four by three feet.

Both tape recorders were placed on the floor by my side. They likely would not be visible to Nathan when he entered the room and sat down. Unlike reading him his Miranda rights, we had no legal obligation to alert him that the interview was being recorded.

Once we were settled, we requested the prison officer bring Nathan to us. I felt nervous. A lot was on the line, both for the case and, unbeknownst to Nathan, for him and his future. We believed we had enough evidence to prosecute him successfully, but there was no guarantee a jury would see it the same way. It is always preferable to secure a confession.

The last time we had seen Nathan, we had collected his blood sample at Riverside County Jail. He had been imprisoned in the state system now for several months. Would his acclimation to prison life cause him now to balk at speaking with us? What about the information Duncan had conveyed to him in their last call, about a warrant being issued for Duncan's arrest? Would that affect his willingness to talk? It was impossible to know, but we were about to find out.

Within a few minutes, Nathan was escorted through the door of the interview room. He seemed a bit surprised to see us again but greeted us in an unconcerned manner, at least outwardly.

"What's happening, Nathan?" Garcia asked him.

"What's up, guys?" he replied. "What's going on?"

We exchanged a little small talk. Garcia told Nathan he looked like he'd lost some weight.

"No, I'm kind of just trimming down a little bit."

"Are you?" Garcia asked.

"Yeah. I still weigh about two twenty. I gained weight, actually."

"So they feed you good?"

"Food here sucks, man."

"Really?"

"Yeah, it sucks real bad." Nathan said he went to the prison store on a regular basis. He could buy canned goods there, he told us.

I began by explaining why we were there. "It was almost a year ago we came and took your blood. And obviously we didn't come back. I'll be right up front with you. There wasn't enough for DNA," referring to the blood evidence under Ron's fingernails. "We're still kind of in the same boat that we were in back then. We haven't really done much with your case since then because we've had other cases and stuff."

"It's good you guys are keeping busy," Nathan said with a laugh.

"Anyway, what we're trying to do, we were looking through your statements. A couple of things in your statements, they've always been consistent. We've never been able to break what you told us. I mean, not that there is anything definitely to break. But what we want to do, maybe there's something right under our noses that we're missing, whether it has something to do with you or whether it has something to do with somebody else that was involved in it. We don't know. We still are in the same boat. So what we want to do is, we want to go over your statement again. See if there's anything else—try to think of anything else you can think of. Granted, it's been a long time."

"Shit, we're talking two years here," said Nathan.

"I know it. But maybe there's something, if we go over the statement again, that is going to mean something to us. Maybe not. I don't know. And the other thing is, and it's kind of ironic, in going through the notes, I've never point-blank asked you... Did you kill Ron, or were you present? I want to ask those questions. I mean, just to have them on the record. I don't think we've ever asked those questions."

"I think you asked me that before."

"Yeah, but we're looking through our notes, so—"

"But maybe it wasn't written down," said Nathan.

Garcia spoke up. "Nathan, the thing is, when all the bullshit is said and done on this thing, you and Duncan were the last ones to be seen with Ron."

"True," said Nathan.

"And you know, from our standpoint, that's important. It's critical. Okay?"

"Mm-hmm," he said.

"Have you heard from Duncan?"

"No."

I told Nathan, "Okay. Let me tell you something I do have to do. You're in custody now. You were never in custody when we talked to you before. And I'm going to ask you point-blank, like I said, 'Nathan, did you kill Ron?' And, 'Nathan, were you present when Ron was killed?'"

"No."

"Okay. I'm going to ask you those. But since you're in custody, I'm going to read you your rights... I do want to go over the story again, or you can just tell us. We don't have to necessarily read through the statement or we can read through it or whatever. However you want to do it.

It doesn't matter. You may want to refresh your memory. You may not. I don't know. But also, I'm going to ask you, did you kill, or were you there—"

"No," answered Nathan, before I could finish.

"Or do you know—"

"No."

"Let me read your rights before I ask you those."

Nathan chuckled at having jumped the gun in answering. "Does it really make a difference that I'm already in custody? I mean—"

"Yeah, it does, because you're in a custodial setting. The way Miranda goes is, if you're in a custodial setting—which obviously, in here, you are—and I'm going to ask you any question like that, I've got to read you your rights."

"Okay," he said.

"I mean, it's the way it is. So I'm going to read them right from the card." I always carried with me a wallet-sized card with the text of the Miranda warning printed on it, for just such situations. I no doubt could have recited it from memory, but it was always safer to read it verbatim. Deviating from the script by even a word risked inviting legal challenges later, in court.

I advised Nathan of his constitutional rights, including his rights to remain silent and to have an attorney present during questioning. "All right. First of all, do you understand each of the rights I've explained to you?"

"Yes."

"Okay. Do you wish to give up the right to remain silent? In other words, do you want to talk to us?"

"Yeah. I'll talk and give you the best of my recollection of what happened, I suppose."

"Okay. Do you wish to give up the right to have an attorney present during questioning?"

"I don't think I need an attorney at this point. It's the same line of questioning."

"All right... Let me get to the questions that I want to at least start with right up front. Nathan, did you kill Ron?"

"No."

"Okay. Were you present when Ron was killed?"

"No."

"Do you have any knowledge of how Ron got killed or know who was involved in it?"

"Only from what I've read and heard."

"Okay. But you don't know who killed Ron?"

"No."

"Okay. You're sure?"

"Yes."

Garcia said, "Nathan, we talked to you a couple of times. You remember that?"

"Yeah."

"We talked to you July the 9th of 1990, and that was at Diane's father's house, I believe. Remember when he got pissed off and kicked us out? We had to finish the interview at the Riverside Sheriff's?"

"Yeah."

"That's probably the first official interview we had with you. Then we went back and talked to you August the 15th, which is roughly a month and a week later."

Garcia and I asked Nathan several questions about his whereabouts in the first few weeks after Ron's murder, including his trip to Detroit for a family reunion. Nathan said that trip was preplanned. "The tickets were bought, essentially by my father, way in advance, before any of this even occurred... I was gone a week, a week or two, something like that."

I asked Garcia, "Should we just let him run by what he recalls?"

"Do you want to tell us what you remember?" Garcia asked Nathan.

"At this point in time, it's getting hazier and hazier. It is something that I don't sit and dwell upon. Right now I'm looking forward to completing the term I'm doing now."

"How much longer do you have?" I asked.

Nathan said he had twenty-two more months to serve, at "halftime." Back then, California inmates who worked in prison and had clean disciplinary records qualified to have their sentence cut in half, even for violent crimes like bank robbery. "So I don't sit and think about what happened years ago. I'm thinking about what I'm going to do with my life when I get out. Really, I just remember, like, bits and pieces of it... Because, I mean, it's something—why would you want to remember the night your friend died, you know?"

"Well, do you remember what you did that night?" Garcia asked.

Nathan told us the same story as he had before. He and Duncan dropped Ron off at the bus stop in Van Nuys, went to the store and bought some beer, swung by Duncan's old school, and then went back home.

"What time did you drop him off?"

"That I really can't say now... I really don't know what time it was."

"Do you have any independent recollection of what you told us?"

"No."

"Who was with you?"

"The three of us... Duncan, Ron, and myself."

"Whose car were you in?"

"Duncan's car."

We asked Nathan some more questions about his and Duncan's activities that night.

Nathan said he was pretty sure that it was after sunset when they dropped Ron off. He couldn't recall whether Ron told them where he was going that night.

Garcia asked what time they got back to the apartment.

"I remember when I walked through the door *Arsenio Hall* was on, so it was somewhere around eleven... We didn't go straight back to our apartment. There was two girls that lived upstairs."

"Do you remember their names?"

"No, I don't."

"What if I said Vickie and Tewanda?"

"I would say maybe, maybe not."

"Nathan, do you recall what time you went to their apartment? They're in the same apartment building, right?"

"Right. Right upstairs."

"Do you recall, basically, what time you got back from the school after drinking beer?"

"Not really. I can't really recall."

"Do you remember how long you were at the school?"

"Not long at all—that I remember. I don't think we were there that long."

"How long would you say you were there?"

"I don't know. Long enough to down a couple beers maybe."

"Okay. In your first statement, Nathan, you said you got there about eight thirty, eight forty-five, and you got to Vickie's apartment at about ten thirty."

"Okay."

"We're talking roughly two hours, right? Eight thirty to ten thirty more or less, right? And these are a critical two hours to us."

"I understand that," said Nathan.

"Were you at the school the whole time?"

"We naturally, in that two-hour time, we had to buy beer and drive around to the school... I don't remember where the school was," he said. "I don't know how far it was..."

"It was Duncan's school, right?" I asked.

"It was his school. See, I'm not from here. So, you know, naturally, I guess, it was one of those times, those male-bonding moments, I guess... That sort of thing."

"So does maybe an hour and a half sound about right, at the school, that you maybe were there?"

"I wouldn't say a whole hour and a half there."

"An hour?" asked Garcia.

"Maybe forty, forty-five minutes, I guess. I don't know. It's really hard to recall now. You know, I've done a lot since then," he said with a chuckle.

"So basically once you dropped Ron off, you never saw him again?" I asked.

"No, I never saw him again."

"You dropped him off at the bus stop and then he just never showed up."

"That was it."

Garcia said, "You know one thing that bothers us, Nathan... Rick and I have kicked this thing around forever, since it happened. One of the biggest things that bothers us is the Saturday morning... You told us that you went to the park, to Chatsworth Park, to look for Ron."

"That was a spot where he and a lot of other people who were in that clique went to often. We had all gone there before... We've all gone there at one time or another together. When you're looking for someone, you go to the places they hang out in. You go to the places you know they might be in."

"See, the thing that bothers us is, when Ron's father talked to you guys, he didn't tell you Ron was missing. He told you Ron was kidnapped."

"But it wasn't like Ron not to come home either," said Nathan.

"I mean, he always came home, right?" asked Garcia.

"Yeah, he would come home, so it wasn't like him not to come home."

"But see, it's like, if they tell you, you know, Rick's been kidnapped, it's not like, 'Hey, Rick didn't come home. He's out screwing around or he's pissed off or something.'"

"From what I understand, and this is all second- and thirdhand information, there was a few problems between their family anyway," Nathan said, referring to the Bakers. "I have no personal recollection of this. I can't tell you this is firsthand information. This is second- and thirdhand information."

"Did you talk to Mr. Baker when he called?"

"That I can't remember."

"Okay. Because in your statement, again... You can look at this," said Garcia, showing Nathan his statement from his initial interview. Garcia read aloud what Nathan had told us then, about the call he had gotten that night from Mr. Baker: "'Ron's dad called later. It must've been eleven forty to midnight. Ron's dad asked if Ron was there. I said, "No." He wanted to know if I knew where he was, and I said, "No." I told him we dropped Ron off at the bus stop. Ron's dad said he had received a phone call. He said they had taken Ron or Ron had been kidnapped. Ron's dad said he thought it was a practical joke... I thought it may be Ron doing his rebellion thing.'"

"Okay," said Nathan.

I asked, "So what you're saying is that you thought maybe this whole kidnapping thing was a hoax on Ron's part and that he was trying to get back at his parents, for whatever reason, that he might be hiding out."

"I guess at that point in time, yeah, I did. Yeah."

"And you haven't heard from Duncan at all, or have no idea where he might be? Have you heard from anybody that—"

"I have not heard from anybody in that group at all, since the last Renaissance Faire, when you guys went to the Renaissance Faire," referring to my visit in 1991.

"You haven't heard where Duncan might be from anybody? Would you tell us if you had?"

"Yeah, but it'd be kind of hard for me, getting in contact with him here."

"No, I'm not talking about him. But if somebody had told you… Like, have you talked to Diane at all?"

"No, we don't even talk at all. She got back with her ex-husband, so, you know, we don't speak at all."

We asked Nathan where he thought Duncan could be. Nathan said he knew Duncan had family back east, in Kentucky, and they spoke a few times about Florida. "Other than that, I really can't tell you."

Garcia asked, "Did you and Duncan ever talk about, either seriously or jokingly, about kidnapping somebody?"

"No," said Nathan.

"You never talked to Duncan about taking somebody hostage or doing a kidnapping?"

Nathan indicated no.

I looked over at Garcia. "What do you think?" I asked him.

Garcia asked Nathan, "Well, you know that sample we got from your blood?"

"Mm-hmm."

"Okay. Like Rick said, there wasn't enough there to do DNA."

"I don't see why not," said Nathan.

"Well, it all depends on how much of a sample," I explained.

"The sample we got from you, there was plenty there to do DNA," said Garcia.

"Oh, so you got two pints," said Nathan.

"What I'm talking about is, in Ron Baker's fingernails, we got some tissue… The blood we got under Ron Baker's fingernails, Rick wasn't lying to you. There wasn't enough there for DNA, but it's enough to tell us that it's human blood. And it's enough to tell us the blood type."

"Okay, what's the blood type?" asked Nathan.

"It's your blood type."

"It's my blood type?"

"Uh-huh," said Garcia.

"Well, I don't—"

"AB blood, which is only four percent of the population," I said.

"Do you know your blood type?" asked Garcia.

"Yeah, my blood is AB positive."

"Yeah, well, that's what this blood is—AB positive. And like Rick says, Nathan, it narrows it down to four percent of the population."

"And Ron's not AB," I added. "Ron's A and Duncan—"

"—is something else," Garcia interrupted, likely so Nathan would not wonder how we knew Duncan's blood type.

"Unless Duncan's AB," I said, to further cover.

"I don't know," said Nathan.

"Well, we have military records," I said, referring to Duncan's service in the Marines. "What does his military record show?" I asked Garcia.

Before Garcia could respond, Nathan said, "It should. Even then, I would have to say that's a real thin line, because as it was in your reports and other witnesses, I'm pretty sure that the three of us did wrestle a lot and play around in the apartment. So we could've wrestled that day and he could've scratched me. It could've been there from that."

"Did you?" asked Garcia.

"That's a good question. I'm pretty sure we did... We used to sword fight and pole fight and stuff... So that really to me—"

"In none of your statements, Nathan, do you ever mention anything about wrestling or fighting. You mentioned fighting with Duncan, or wrestling."

"Ron did indulge sometimes too. I didn't mention it. I didn't feel it was necessary." Nathan said the apartment building's manager saw them wrestling and could tell us she had.

I asked Nathan to let me have a look at his hands. "Do you have any scars?" I asked him. I did not see any. But it had been a couple of years, and I knew not all scratches left scars.

Garcia asked Nathan, "So you're saying that if Ron Baker had tissue under his fingernail and that tissue belongs to you—"

"I'm saying it didn't come because I killed him. That's what I'm saying."

"You're saying—"

"I'm saying it could've came—it should have—it should come from us wrestling or something. That's the only way possible."

"But you don't recall whether you wrestled that day."

"I think we did wrestle that day."

"You do?"

"But don't take my word for it."

"In the tunnel?" I asked.

"No."

"You didn't wrestle with Ron in the tunnel?"

"No, I'm talking about at the apartment. Don't take my word for it. Talk to Diane. She was there the whole day. You can take statements from the manager, who will tell you, like I said, we used to take—"

"Well, we're concerned about that day, though," said Garcia.

"I'm talking about that day."

"Because for you to wind up, or for Ron to wind up with your tissue under his fingernails, it would've had to have been probably that day."

"Well, like I say, I have no idea—"

Garcia again pointed out that, until now, Nathan had never told us anything about wrestling with Ron.

"Evidently, I didn't feel it to be necessary, but if, like I said, the tissue is mine, that's the only way possible. That's the only way possible."

"The tissue could've got there because you killed him."

"No."

"And he struggled with you."

"No."

"Could've been that way," said Garcia.

"You can understand our concerns of this," I said.

"Yes, I can. Yes, I can. And once again I say no."

Garcia said, "Because it's very common, Nathan, in situations where people are stabbed to death, that there's a fight. There's a struggle. People are fighting for their lives. They claw—"

"If it was a fight or a struggle, wouldn't my clothes or something have been torn? Wouldn't it have been noticed by someone else who—"

"Where are your clothes that you had on that day? Do we know where your clothes are?"

"Do you know where they are?" I asked.

"I don't know where none of my stuff is now."

"No, I mean at that point, or on July 9th, 1990"—the date we first interviewed Nathan—"did you say, 'Look Garcia, Jackson, here's the clothes I had on that day.' We wouldn't have known the clothes you had on that day."

"No, I'm sure I didn't do that."

"But there's no way of us telling either. You could have—"

"Well, I left and came back with the same outfit on. I mean, it's pretty obvious. And that I'm pretty sure Diane can testify to."

"Well, she can't testify to it."

"Why?"

"Because Diane was on the couch...And she says that you guys came right in and went to the bathroom and the bedroom, and then you came out."

"No, she had to see when I walked through the door. She would have had to see me walk through the door."

"Well, see, Rick and I were at the house. And the way I remember it is, the couch—you could walk right behind the couch, when somebody is laying on the couch watching TV, and you wouldn't even really see them."

"That's true too, but when the door opens and a key goes in the door, you're going to look to see who's at the door."

We had been talking with Nathan for almost thirty minutes. We had established what we needed to, regarding his prior statements. It was time to drop the hammer.

"Well, Nathan, the thing is," said Garcia, "what if we tell you that somebody's telling us you killed Ron Baker?"

"I'm telling you they're lying."

"Okay. That's what we're confronted with, Nathan. Somebody's telling us that you killed Ron Baker."

"Well, once again, I'm telling you they're lying."

"Do you know who that someone could possibly be, that's telling us this?"

"No, I don't."

I reached down to get the cued-up tape recorder and placed it on the table. I told Nathan, "We'll let you listen to a tape of an interview and then you can tell us."

Garcia said, "Because, you know, we're here to give you the benefit of the doubt, Nathan. We want you to tell us and explain to us what's happening, okay?"

I checked that the tape recorder was ready to play and signaled to Garcia it was.

"So, Nathan, whoever's telling us that you killed Ron Baker is lying?" asked Garcia.

"Yes."

"Okay," I said. "We'll let you listen to this. And there's other things we're going to play too. This is just a start."

"Is it all right if I smoke in here?" asked Nathan.

There were no signs in view prohibiting smoking. Garcia said he would have one too, then.

"Go ahead. We'll let you," I told Nathan. He laughed. In reference to the tape I was about to play, I said, "This may not be the exact spot, but it's pretty darn close, though."

"Well, let's just listen to the whole thing," said Nathan. "I have nothing but time on my hands."

I hit PLAY. From the recorder's speaker came Duncan's voice, midway through his second, most recent phone call with Nathan: "I can't go to religion... I keep thinking about what I heard that night... what I saw that night, when you lit the lighter,... It sounds like you've got it tucked away like it never happened. And I can't see how you could do that."

Then Nathan's voice came from the recorder: "Because I have to live my life. I have to go on... It happened. It was a mistake... I cannot live three years ago. I have to live for the time that's coming up."

As the recording played, and it dawned on Nathan what he was hearing, he dropped his head, eyes to the floor. He realized that he had been betrayed... and by whom. His body language conveyed total defeat. I almost felt sorry for him, not for the situation he was in, which was of his own making, but for how trapped he must have felt at that moment. Nathan looked like he was in the loneliest, most hopeless place imaginable.

Garcia, repeating what we had just heard on tape, quoted him, "'It happened. It was a mistake.' What'd you mean by that, Nathan?"

"That Ron was killed."

"Who killed him?"

"I don't know."

"Well, it sounds like Duncan's telling you, 'Man, how can you just brush this under the carpet and go on living?' You say, 'Hey, it happened. It was a mistake.'"

"My uncle died and he was a police officer. I mean, I'm not sitting here dwelling upon that, but it's still going on," Nathan said, as if to explain the stoicism Duncan had described on the tape.

"You want to hear more?" I asked.

Nathan did not say yes or no.

I hit PLAY. Duncan's voice again came from the recorder: "It's hard for me because there's a part of me that wants to think of you in a really negative light, because of that night, okay? And I can't. Because—" Nathan's voice responded on the tape: "I can understand that." I again paused the recording.

"You can understand that he's thinking of you in a negative light," I said, quoting Duncan. "There's all kinds of things here, Nathan."

"You know who's saying you killed Ron, right?" asked Garcia.

"The person on that tape."

"Who's the person on the tape?"

"Duncan's voice."

"Who's the other person?" pressed Garcia.

"It sounds like me."

"Do you remember those conversations?" I asked.

"Yeah."

I hit PLAY again. Again, we heard Duncan's voice: "I can't blow this whole thing off...You guys were both my friends...I mean, you doing that to him...It totally threw me a curve..."

Followed by Nathan's voice on the tape, replying to what Duncan had just told him: "Look. This is a penitentiary, and these lines, they may not be totally secure."

Duncan: "Well, what am I supposed—"

I hit the PAUSE button on the recorder.

"No denial," I said. "You just say, 'Hey, don't use—'"

"But I think somewhere I did deny it."

"No, no, you didn't. We have everything...We have several tapes, three conversations, including the face-to-face one."

Garcia said, "All you were worried about is the lines not being secure, Nathan."

"We have the face-to-face conversation you had with him in Riverside County Jail, which, by the way, I can play it for you. Let me tell you what you said exactly," I said, paging through the transcript, a copy of which we'd brought with us. I paraphrased, "He talks about it. You talk about it being reality. 'That's reality, man. It happened.' Duncan talked about 'That's the scariest thing that's ever happened to me. I couldn't fucking believe it.' And you say, 'That's reality. It happened. I'm sorry it did.'...You say right there, 'I'm sorry I did it.'"

Garcia also paraphrased, "Then you go on, in another part, and you say, 'Hey, it was a plan. Once the plan was in action, we carried out the plan,' or 'I carried out the plan.'"

I pointed toward another passage in the transcript: "'You knew the plan. And I knew the plan.' And then Duncan: 'What if they found the clothes?' You say, 'What clothes?' Duncan: 'The fucking clothes wrapped in the knife? Or the knife wrapped in the clothes?' You said, 'In the dumpster. The trash truck came that morning.'"

"Do you remember saying that, Nathan?" asked Garcia.

"No."

"You want me to play it for you?" I asked.

"Go ahead," said Nathan.

While I readied the tape, Garcia said, "Nathan, what we're here for, too, is if something happened in the tunnel between you and Ron, you can tell us about it. We don't know what happened up there. And you know, there's a lot of difference between killing somebody and *killing* somebody. There's all degrees of killing."

I said, "There's a lot of talk about knowing it's the plan... Duncan laid the whole thing out. The plan, the kidnapping, and everything. He laid the whole thing out. And the thing is, if that was the whole plan, that's one thing. But if something happened in that tunnel that made you snap, or you snapped and did something to Ron, that's a different story. From listening to these tapes, your own words, there is no doubt in my mind that you were the stabber. No doubt at all. And the blood in the fingernails is another thing. But if you listen to all these tapes, there's no doubt in our minds at all. And there's not going to be a doubt in anybody's mind if you hear these tapes... You're saying, 'Don't talk on an unsecure line,' all that kind of stuff. But you say a lot of things."

Garcia added, "You say, 'Whoever you're talking to, don't talk to him anymore.' You got to do this. You got to do that."

I quoted another example. "'You're jeopardizing me... I see a noose going around my neck.' These are all things that are in this tape, Nathan."

Garcia said, "A jury's going to listen to that, Nathan. A judge is going to listen to it. Rick and I aren't mind readers. We don't know what's going through your mind. We don't know if you had a reason to do what you did. And if you did, we want you to tell us now."

Nathan said nothing.

"Nathan, did something happen up there to set you off? Was there a fight?" asked Garcia.

More than twenty seconds passed in silence before Nathan said, "I don't know what happened."

"Talk to us, Nathan."

"I don't know what happened."

"Did Ron piss you off?"

"I don't know what happened."

"Were you in the tunnel that night?"

Nathan didn't answer.

I played the portion of the tape I'd read earlier, then repeated aloud Nathan's last line: "'In the dumpster. The trash truck came that morning.'"

Nathan said nothing.

"Nathan, what happened in that tunnel, man?" said Garcia.

"I don't know."

"Were you in the tunnel with Ron?"

"I don't remember."

"You got to remember, Nathan. You know, there's two sides to every story, Nathan."

"Does it matter?"

"Sure," said Garcia.

"Yeah, it does," I said.

"It does to us, Nathan," said Garcia.

I said, "Nathan, you're a smart man. You know it matters."

Garcia told him, "You know we've never gotten out of hand with you. We've always treated you like a gentleman. You've always treated us like a gentleman. And we're here treating you like a gentleman right now. We want to know what your side of the story is. There's two sides to every damn story, Nathan."

Five seconds passed in silence.

Garcia went on: "We know, Nathan. Rick and I know by listening to this, by the evidence that was left at the scene... All we want to know is what the hell happened in the tunnel, Nathan. You know as well as Rick and I know that you were in the tunnel with Ron and Duncan. You guys didn't drop him off at the bus stop. You know, you say you don't remember what happened in the tunnel. I don't know. Do you remember? Did you black out?"

"I don't remember."

"You remember going up to the tunnel with Ron and Duncan?"

"No. I remember going to the park the next day."

"You don't remember anything about the night before, at all?"

"No."

I asked, "Did you go to the school?"

"I think so."

"You think anybody is going to believe that, when you hear this tape, Nathan? You laid out things that we didn't even know, that corroborate what Duncan told us before you guys had any conversations."

"So is he in custody?" asked Nathan.

"What's it matter?"

"Just curious."

"Obviously we know where he is, and obviously we've been dealing with him."

"Duncan is going to have to go to court, Nathan," said Garcia. "He's going to have to take the witness stand, and he's going to have to testify to everything that's on these tapes. You know that. We know that. Duncan knows that."

"And the jury is going to have to hear these tapes," I said.

I sensed Nathan felt the walls closing in on him. What was important to Garcia and me was to keep the conversation going. We wanted to drive home to him not only how obvious it was to us that he was involved but also how obvious it would be to a jury.

Garcia told him, "They're going to hear the tapes, Nathan, and it's going to be up to them to say, 'Okay, Duncan's telling the truth' or 'We don't believe Duncan' or 'You're telling the truth' or 'We don't believe you.' The point is, Nathan, you're probably going to have to take the stand. That's going to be up to you. It's going to be up to a lot of other people besides Rick and me. We just investigate the damn thing. That's why we're asking you right now what the hell happened in that tunnel... We got a place on this tape, Nathan, that makes you look real bad."

Garcia continued, paraphrasing the recording, "When Duncan tells you, 'Hey, man, they're going after special circumstances because it's torture, because of the number of stab wounds.' And you know what your answer to that was, Nathan? 'Torture's hard to prove in court.' That is your answer to that statement. I want you to tell us what the hell happened in that tunnel, Nathan. You know, it's better for you to tell us now, than for you to go to court six months from now, or two months from now, whatever it is, and say, 'Hey, here's what happened. Ron came at me. He jumped me in the tunnel. He pissed me off. He said something about Diane that pissed me off.' Whatever."

I said, "First thing they're going to want to know is, why the hell didn't you tell us there were mitigating circumstances? Why didn't you tell the police at the time? Now you've had time to think about it and come up with a bullshit story, and we ain't going to buy it, because they're going to listen to these tapes. Several times Duncan says something about you stabbing or 'How can you forget? How could you not be bothered by that? How could you do this? How could you do that?' And you never say, 'Wait a minute, what are you talking about? Huh? What? I didn't do shit.' It's always, 'Hey, man, don't be using my name on the phone. I wish you'd quit using my name on the phone.' We can play another one... You never say anything like 'What are you talking about? You're full of shit. I didn't do anything.' Never. We can play that too."

"Nathan, is there something that happened up there that set you off?" asked Garcia.

"I really don't remember what happened up there."

"You remember being there with Duncan and Ron?" I asked.

"I remember being in the park, yeah."

"The night of the murder?"

"Yeah."

"Do you remember drinking beer up there?"

"Yeah."

"Do you remember going there specifically to kill Ron?"

"Not specifically, no."

"Do you remember—"

"It wasn't—" Nathan started to say, then stopped and laughed. "Should I talk to my lawyer now or something here?"

"That's up to you... That's up to you, Nathan," said Garcia.

"Because, you know—"

I reiterated, "That's up to you. We're here to hear your side of the story. But you're in control as far as whether you don't want to talk to us or you do want to talk to us. We're just trying to get everybody's stories."

Garcia said, "You just brought it up, 'Should I talk to my lawyer right now?' Are we to take that, that you're invoking the right, that you don't want to talk about this anymore?"

"I don't know what to do anymore. Period, point-blank," said Nathan.

"Think about it for a second. Let us know," I said.

Garcia said, "You know, Nathan, you can terminate this interview right now. You can say you don't want to."

Nathan said, "It's not going to prove anything. I mean—"

"Well, but do you understand that you have a right to have an attorney?"

"I understand all my rights, believe me. Yes, I understand my rights."

"The thing is," Garcia said, "we're trying to get at the truth of the matter here. We didn't come in here going, 'Oh, man, this and that, this and that.' We never jammed you. Like I said, we've always treated you like a gentleman, Nathan. Rick and I want to find out what the truth is here. And we're asking you to tell us the truth." Almost ten seconds passed. Then Garcia asked, "Did you have Duncan's knife that night?"

"Duncan had his knife."

"How did you get the knife? Did he give it to you?"

"I took it from him."

"You took it from him? Is that while you guys are drinking beer?"

"That's when we were drinking beer."

"When you were drinking beer? All three of you were drinking beer." Five seconds passed. "What happened in the tunnel, Nathan?" asked Garcia.

"That's real blurry. I will say, I wasn't the only one who did anything to Ron. I will say that."

"Talk to us. Like I said, Nathan, there's two sides to every damn story."

"The blood under the nails did not come from the tunnel, that I'll tell you. That I know for a fact."

"It didn't come from wrestling," said Garcia.

"It didn't come from the tunnel either," Nathan insisted.

"Where'd it come from?"

"That I can't tell you, but it didn't come from the tunnel."

"Did he scratch you while you guys struggled in the tunnel?"

"No, he did not scratch me."

"Okay."

"I was never scratched then, that I felt. I mean, the only thing that was exposed was hands and face... I don't have any deep scratches on my hands or face."

"Well, those could have healed."

"Even so, it would still leave a scar, if it was that deep. I mean—"

"Not necessarily," I said. "But go ahead."

"I still have scars on my hands from years ago. But anyway."

Garcia asked, "What happened in the tunnel?"

"There was a hassle, a tussle," said Nathan.

"With you and Ron?"

"Yeah."

"What brought it on, Nathan?"

"That's a good question. Being drunk. Just—I don't know. I really don't know. I really don't know what brought it on. It just happened."

"But you already had Duncan's knife."

"Yeah, I had took it earlier. But it just…" His voice trailed off.

"Did you take it with the intent to do anything to Ron, Nathan?"

"Not when I took it, no. Not when I took it, no, I did not have intent on doing anything to anyone. But it happened, so that's that."

"So you stabbed him?"

"Yeah."

"Now you said you weren't the only one doing anything. Are you saying—"

"I'm not saying that other people involved were just standing there watching," Nathan said. "I mean, that doesn't make a lot of sense now, does it?" I took it as a reference to Duncan's willingness to implicate Nathan and throw him under the bus, but not vice versa.

"Well, we don't know."

"I'm just answering the question. I'm only copping to what I did. All right? You know, not like other people."

"Run it by us, Nathan. How many times did you stab him?"

"Twice, maybe."

"Twice, that you remember?"

"Yeah."

We had finally broken through. We knew Nathan was dramatically understating his actions. Ron was stabbed many more times than twice. But he had admitted it. It was an exhilarating feeling.

"You would've remembered if it was more, right?"

"I can't say I would or wouldn't."

"Did he piss you off, Nathan?"

"Yeah, I must have been pissed to … to …"

"To do that?"

"To do it, yeah."

"Do you remember what pissed you off?" I asked.

"No."

Garcia asked, "Did he say something about Diane? Because the reason I'm asking that, Nathan, is in your earlier statement you said he had said something about Diane that pissed you off, and you told him, 'I don't appreciate that.' That was earlier in the week or earlier that day or evening."

"It's possible, I think. I really, honestly, all bullshit aside, no more drama, I can't remember."

"Okay. Do you remember how many beers you drank that night?"

"I know we bought a couple twelve-packs. At least."

"What did you do with the clothes? Because you were pretty bloody afterwards. Is it the way it's said on the tape, that you threw them in the dumpster, in the trash can, the next day?"

"Probably."

"How about the knife."

"Same."

"Which knife was this now?"

"Duncan's knife."

"Which is what? What type of knife is it?"

"Just a knife. I mean..."

"It's a Marine Corps knife?"

"Yeah... Eight, nine inches long blade."

"Let me ask you something, Nathan. The calls that were placed to Mr. Baker's house. Did you tell Duncan to make those calls?"

"I didn't tell Duncan to do anything. Duncan did what Duncan did on his own."

"Okay. But the calls were placed. And the calls were made by Duncan."

"Well, I wasn't—I'll put it this way, because see, I'm not like other people. When the calls were placed, I was in the house by myself with Diane. Duncan was not there."

"Okay. Did you tell Duncan to make those?"

"I didn't tell Duncan to do anything."

"Anything?"

"Duncan was his own person."

"Was that part of the plan, the previous plan?" I asked. "We know about the kidnapping plan. Whether that had anything to do with Ron really getting killed, we knew about this ransom thing, all that kind of stuff."

"Yeah, that was—and that was not my idea, okay?"

Garcia asked, "But you guys went to the park with that kind of bullshit plan that you were going to kidnap him or kill him and then call Mr. Baker?"

"Well, killing wasn't part of the plan."

"That just happened?"

"It just happened."

"What did he do that pissed you off, Nathan?"

"I honestly can't remember. I honestly cannot remember."

"Let me ask you something, just for our edification. When you stabbed him for the first time, did you stab him in the back?"

"In the side."

"In the side? And how was the tussle inside... Did you go across the tracks?"

"What do you mean, 'across the tracks'?" asked Nathan.

"According to the blood splatters at the scene there, there's blood on... Okay, you're walking in the tunnel from where you were drinking beer, the first blood is on the left side. And then Ron winds up on the right side of the tracks. Do you remember crossing the tracks?"

"No."

"Or fighting across the tracks?"

"No."

"Do you remember getting on him and stabbing him after he went down?"

"No."

"Why don't you run by us what you do recall," I said.

"All I can remember is we were drinking beer. We were standing on top of the hill, talking shit to each other, and we started walking through the tracks, and boom. That's about it."

"And you stabbed him because he pissed you off, or do you remember that?" asked Garcia.

"I remember stabbing him."

"But do you remember him pissing you off?"

"You know, I had to have done it out of anger. I wouldn't do it calmly."

"Why did you take Duncan's knife?"

"That's a good question that I don't have an answer to."

"Okay," I said. "Then you go back to the car?"

"Yeah."

"What did you guys do about the blood all over yourself?"

"I don't remember... I don't really remember. I don't remember there being blood on me, but evidently there was, and I don't remember what was done about that, because there was none in the car."

"Okay," said Garcia.

"Who drove back?" I asked.

"Duncan."

"Are you sure?"

"I think so, yeah."

"Was he pretty shaken up?" asked Garcia.

"At that point in time, I don't remember him being shaken up."

"Were you shaken up?"

"I don't remember that either."

"Do you remember taking Ron's wallet?"

"No."

"So the ID wouldn't be found on him or nothing? Okay, the next day when you went back to the park, you guys went back to look for the body, right, to see if it was still there?"

"I would assume so, yeah."

"What were you going to do?" I asked.

"I don't know. This was not my idea. Once again, this was not my plan."

"To go back," said Garcia.

"To go back. Why go back?" said Nathan.

"Okay. So you go back and you go in the tunnel and the body's gone, right?"

"Duncan went in the tunnel. I didn't go in the tunnel."

"You didn't go in the tunnel?"

"No."

"You didn't want to see?"

"No."

"Getting back to the wallet, do you remember taking the wallet?"

"No."

"Do you remember Duncan taking the wallet?"

"No."

"And you said the calls were made and you weren't present."

"No, I was not present."

"And to your best recollection, Nathan, the clothes were dumped in the dumpster?"

"Yeah."

"Which dumpster would that have been?"

"The apartment dumpster, I suppose."

"Were they at the apartments next door or at your apartment?"

"I think it was at our apartment."

"With the knife?"

"Yeah."

"Do you remember the wallet being in there too?"

"No."

"Just the bloody clothes and the knife. Did Diane know anything about this, Nathan?" Garcia asked.

"Did you ever tell anybody?" I asked.

"On the streets, no," said Nathan.

We had covered all the topics we wanted to ask him about and, more importantly, secured the confession we had hoped to elicit.

Garcia explained to Nathan what would happen next. "We're going to present all this to the DA's Office. Probably file on you. What they file on you, we don't know, man... You know Rick and I aren't here to screw you. You know that."

I said to Nathan, "You had mentioned earlier... something about an attorney and then at some point you said, 'Hey, I just, I don't know what I want to do.' We said, 'Hey, that's up to you.' Do you want to continue talking to us?"

"I mean, I don't see what difference it makes, at this point in time, to delay what's..."

"What's going to come out."

"Yeah," said Nathan.

"How we doing over there, Rick?" Garcia asked me, in reference to whether we were running out of tape on the recorder that had been rolling since before Nathan had entered the room.

"Fine," I said.

"Oh, this is being recorded?" Nathan asked, only realizing it then.

"Yeah, well, that's for your—everybody's—"

"You could have at least told me, though."

"Well, we don't tell anybody anything. But it's just for everybody's benefit."

I thought of something we had touched on earlier in the interview, before the confession. I told Nathan, "Your hand, I think, did get scratched in the tunnel that night. You made a statement, and again, it's in one of the tapes."

Garcia said, "You had already laid out basically, Nathan, to Duncan, 'Hey, look. If they come back with the blood and the DNA and shit, I'm just going to tell them I was wrestling.' It was kind of like, 'Hey, if that happens, my story is going to be that we wrestled.'"

I paraphrased, "On tape, you guys talk about 'This is what we'll say, basically, if the blood comes back.' You said right in the first conversation you guys had, you said, 'Yeah, man, they came and took my blood... And I was sweating the whole time.' Then you go on to say, 'But you know what? If it comes back, we'll just say we wrestled all the time. We'll say this. We'll say that.'"

"That's true, though," said Nathan.

"Yeah, it is. But you know as well as I do that's not where you got it... Duncan, by the way, isn't AB blood... He's not. It's your blood," I said. I paraphrased, "Then there's another time where Duncan said something about you getting a scratch on your right hand, or one of your hands. 'You remember when you got scratched by him?' And you say, 'Yeah.' Then another time he says something about you getting all scratched up from the walls of the tunnel. You say, 'No, that's not from the walls of the tunnel. That was from him.' Do you remember getting scratched that night?"

"No."

"Duncan remembered it."

"I don't see how he could remember it."

"Because he saw it. You showed it to him. Again, the thing is, all you remember is starting to stab Ron. And you remember a couple times, but you don't remember whether it could've been more than that?"

"No."

Garcia asked, "Did he say anything to you, Nathan, when you stabbed him? Like, 'Why are you doing this?'"

I said, "I know it's a tough thing to go back and try to recall this, but it's important."

"He said something, I suppose. I really can't recall. I don't remember. I don't remember really hearing anything or anybody."

"Was he screaming? Or struggling with you? Obviously he was probably struggling with you."

"Yeah, obviously. I don't remember hearing anything. Nothing, at all."

"Obviously you're much bigger than he is. You had pretty good control of him?"

"That's a trick question," Nathan said. He apparently thought we were trying to get him to admit to something that would hurt him legally.

"Well, no. I mean, obviously it doesn't matter really, if you think about it. I mean, he's dead, and you stabbed him. I mean, whether you had control, I'm just trying to find out as much as I can that happened." In my mind, we were already way beyond trying to get Nathan to incriminate himself. He had incriminated himself in multiple ways already.

"I guess. I don't know. If there was a struggle, I couldn't have had that much control."

Garcia said, "Let me ask you something, Nathan. What did you do with the knife immediately after the stabbing? Did you wipe it off? Or did you just continue to carry it with you?"

"I don't remember. I really don't remember." Nathan's lowered tone of voice and resigned body language signaled defeat.

I told Nathan it made no sense. "That was what Frank and I had problems with. You guys were roommates. And even though Duncan and Ron were close, and you and Duncan were close, you and Ron weren't that close. But still, you were roommates, and there wasn't any great animosity, was there?"

"I guess. I don't know. This was an idea or concept that was brought to me, okay?"

"By Duncan?" asked Garcia.

"Yeah."

"To kidnap Ron for money?"

"Exactly."

"So that was the plan that night, to take him up there and try to get some money?"

"Yeah."

"Did you think he would have any money?" I asked.

"Who, him?" Nathan said, referring to Ron.

"His parents?"

"According to what I was told by other people, yes."

"Who else told you they had money?"

"The person who gave birth to the plan."

"Duncan? Had there been discussion of kidnapping anybody else?"

"Not that I can recall."

"You just decided on a roommate. See, that's what was hard for us to understand, how something like this could happen to Ron when he was your roommate... Even though there was a lot of evidence that pointed toward you guys, it didn't make a lot of sense from our point of view. Do you understand what I'm saying?"

"Yeah."

"How did it get into the Ron area, as far as being your victim?"

"I don't know."

Garcia said, "Nathan, can I ask you something?"

"Sure."

"Feel better now?"

"Uh, not really."

"I mean, telling us that should take some weight off you."

"I'm in a total abyss right about now."

"I think you feel a little better. I think you should, because this one's going to get settled. You don't have to live with it for the rest of your life, because when you get out of here—"

"Oh, boy, that's a joke, man," said Nathan, laughing. He seemed aware of the dire straits he was in, legally, and the length of the prison sentence he could expect for murder.

"No, you know... It's something that you got to deal with."

I said, "Let me ask you this. Do you remember slitting his throat?"

"No."

"Were you in some kind of—at some point, did you become euphoric? Or in a state of—"

"I don't remember. I honestly do not remember. And that's the truth."

"But you remember stabbing him," said Garcia.

"Yeah. But not a whole lot of times. I don't remember stabbing him a whole lot of times. I just remember stabbing him, like—"

"Well, you did," I said. I likened it to a phenomenon I'd seen in shootings. A shooter insists they remember firing only twice, but the evidence shows they in fact emptied their gun. "Especially if he's still struggling. He was still struggling at that point... With the slashed throat, it was a pretty, pretty deep cut. Pretty deep."

"So, what am I looking at here?" Nathan asked.

"We don't know that," said Garcia.

I said, "That's up to the DA, Nathan. I mean, that's up to the DA to file. This is all going to be determined by a judge or jury, if it goes that far. It may not go that far. That's up to you and your attorney... I'll tell you what we're going to do... Rather than try to prolong you wondering what the hell's going to happen, I will probably write up everything that's happened, take it to the DA, who's already been apprised of the case. We've talked to the DA about the case. We don't have a warrant for you at this point."

"Do you really need one? I mean..."

"Well, at some point we're going to have to—"

"What Rick's telling you, Nathan, is it'll be written up," Garcia said. "It'll be presented to the district attorney, probably early next week. They're going to file a case on you. What they're going to file, we don't know. You know as well as I do that a filing does not mean that that's what you're going to get convicted of. It doesn't mean that's what you're going to get tried for. What happens then is a warrant is obtained, because you're in custody here. They send the warrant to Tehachapi. And they put you on a bus and send you back to LA

County Jail for arraignment on the charges, okay? You'll probably stay at LA County Jail pending the preliminary hearing on this case. After that, I really don't know, Nathan, whether they'll send you back here pending the trial or what the hell will happen. We don't know. But we've been up front with you. We laid out everything we got on you. And we appreciate you talking to us."

I said, "Let me ask you something else, Nathan. I kind of feel I already know what the answer is, based on a lot of things. Based on what we've talked about today, mostly based on your conversations that are on tape, it appears that Duncan never stabbed Ron. Is that true?"

"I can't say he did. I can't say he didn't."

"Because you don't remember?" asked Garcia.

"I don't remember."

"Did he ever talk about doing anything like that?"

"He never talked about really what he did. What *he* did," said Nathan, emphasizing the "he," meaning Duncan. "You understand what I'm saying?"

"Mm-hmm," I said.

"It was always about the shoe being on another foot, so, you know—I can't say he did or he didn't."

"Okay... Is there anything else you can think of that you want to tell us?"

"No."

"Anything you want to tell us to clear up anything that maybe isn't clear at this point?" asked Garcia.

"I wish I could tell you enough to clear the whole thing up, but I can't, so I can't recall anything."

We asked Nathan if he had any questions about what would happen next. He said he didn't.

I told Nathan, "You'll probably hear, but I don't know how long. We'll file the case next week. You're going to get charged. They'll file a murder, obviously."

"Obviously," said Nathan, another seeming acknowledgment of his dire situation.

"Yeah, that's what they're going to file... As far as how it's dealt with in the courts, that's between you, if you ever get that far in the system or as far as a trial, your attorney, and then the District Attorney's Office. Our job is to investigate and present the facts and that's kind of it."

"Thanks for your candor, Nathan," said Garcia.

"That concludes the interview. It is 1257 hours," I said, before I stopped the recording.

Driving back to Los Angeles, Garcia and I were elated.

There had been many moments in the case when I wasn't sure if we would ever get here. At one point, Nathan had seemed unbreakable, "the coolest motherfucker," as Garcia once described him.

But we had not given up, and it had paid off. Although Nathan had minimized some key aspects of his role in the murder, such as only stabbing Ron twice, it was a solid confession. I had no doubt Duncan's recorded conversations with Nathan were the key reason he had confessed.

For more than a year, it had been a closely kept secret that Duncan was cooperating in the investigation. Nathan now knew that Duncan had turned on him. For Duncan's safety, it was important I notify him and his family of Nathan's awareness.

I had conducted many intense interrogations through the years. They could be mentally as well as physically taxing. It reminded me of a feeling I had known as a kid after playing baseball for hours on hot summer days. I had felt exhausted but also exhilarated to be doing what I loved.

I felt similar emotions with having broken the case wide open. Equally spent and gratified.

There was more work ahead of me, I knew. But Garcia and I had accomplished our mission that day, together.

CHAPTER 19

"A HUGGING CIRCLE"
(February 22 to June 10, 1993)

DETECTIVES AND PROSECUTORS ARE different creatures.

A homicide detective's job is to solve murders. Their method of getting to the truth is to collect evidence, whether physical, testimonial, or circumstantial, that incriminates or exculpates a suspect.

A prosecutor's job also entails getting to the truth, but by other means. They use the amassed evidence to prove in court that the right person stands accused of the crime, and that they are indeed guilty.

Despite their different roles and approaches, detectives and prosecutors must work together in the interest of justice. Ideally, it is a collaborative effort, but things do not always pan out that way. In any given case, the detective-prosecutor relationship can become strained.

Prosecutors are responsible for gauging the quality of police investigations. Prosecutors must ensure that everything has been done in a thorough and ethical manner, and that there is enough evidence to prove the suspect's guilt beyond a reasonable doubt.

Detectives and prosecutors sometimes disagree in good faith on issues in an investigation. The most common cause for discord is whether there is sufficient evidence to charge a suspect with a crime, also known as filing a case. Typically, a detective might feel there is more than enough evidence to support charges, while a prosecutor, looking at the same evidence, might feel more is needed.

With Nathan's confession, I knew there was more than enough for a prosecutor to charge him for Ron's murder.

I requested a meeting at the District Attorney's Office. In the months since November, when Duncan met with Deputy DA Ernie Norris and Norris's supervisor, Michael Montagna, there had been a change of leadership in the DA's Special Trials unit. Montagna had been replaced by a new head deputy, David Conn.

I knew Conn from prior cases we had worked together. He had long been considered a rising star in the DA's Office. Conn's approach as a prosecutor was quietly aggressive. I had heard others describe him as a "Clark Kent type," a nod to his eyeglasses, style, and understated manner.

I met with Conn and briefed him on the Baker case, including Nathan's confession and Duncan's dual roles as participant and informant. We also discussed the still-unresolved question of whether Duncan should be used as a witness against Nathan.

Conn's instinct was not to allow Norris to use Duncan as a witness. Conn also told me he opposed letting Duncan walk away with just a slap on the wrist for his role in the murder. He asked for some time to consider his options on charging Nathan and what to do about Duncan.

In the meantime, there were a few loose ends pertaining to the case that I wanted to follow up on.

One concerned the call I had received in December from the University of Utah Police Department. A university fraternity advisor named Doug Christiansen had reported disturbing statements Duncan Martinez had made about his connection to an LA murder.

I decided to contact Christiansen directly. We spoke on the morning of April 28, and he confirmed that he'd had conversations with Duncan about the murder of a friend. He said Duncan had told him he witnessed the killing and did nothing to stop it. Christiansen had taken extensive notes on what Duncan and others had told him. He offered to send me a memo summarizing his investigation.

I received Christiansen's memo by fax the following day. It described a "unique situation" involving a Phi Delta Theta pledge identified as Duncan Gordon James Martinez.

In his memo, Christiansen recounted having heard a rumor that

"Mr. Martinez was in some kind of trouble with the Los Angeles Police Department. I was told that Mr. Martinez was being investigated as an accessory to murder."

Christiansen was alarmed by the rumor. He called the Phi Delta Theta pledge master, who told him Duncan had said he witnessed a murder but had nothing to do with it. Duncan also had said that "he was going to be charged with something to do with murder."

Concerned that fraternity members might be in danger, Christiansen decided he needed to meet with Duncan in person. They met that same night at the fraternity's chapter house. Duncan agreed to tell him what had happened in California.

Duncan said the murder took place in June or July 1990. Christiansen wrote, "He said prior to the murder he and a friend, the supposed individual who actually murdered the victim, were watching a *Dragnet* episode about kidnapping. He said he and his friend commented how nice it would be to kidnap somebody who was rich so they could get a high ransom ... Nothing more was said about this idea until a few months later when, Mr. Martinez said, he and his friend said they should kidnap and kill a third friend."

Duncan told Christiansen that later, on the night of the murder, the three of them went drinking. "After they had been drinking for a period of time, they had to go through a tunnel of some sort on the way back to the car. Mr. Martinez said his friend pulled a knife and repeatedly stabbed the other friend." Duncan then ran and said nothing to the police. "He said that he could not turn in one friend even though he had killed another friend."

Duncan told Christiansen he decided to leave LA because "it was too hard to deal with the police and the friends of the victim who were mourning." He ultimately ended up in Park City, began trying to clean up his life, and was now cooperating with the LAPD, Duncan said.

Christiansen wrote that he then called Detective Sherri Barnes. She had confirmed with the LAPD that Duncan was cooperating with an investigation and that he was not a threat to other students. She told him the LAPD said they were going to call Duncan and tell him to keep quiet for his own protection.

Christiansen arranged a meeting with fraternity officials and apprised them of the situation. After "careful consideration," it was decided that Duncan would be asked to resign as a pledge to Phi Delta Theta. Among the reasons cited was "the fact that this could be a potential public-relations nightmare for Phi Delta Theta, the entire Greek System as well as the University of Utah. It was felt that Mr. Martinez had been too free with this information with active chapter members as well as Melissa Bean, president of Pi Beta Phi Sorority."

Christiansen convened a meeting with fraternity officials and Duncan. They explained to Duncan that he could not continue as a pledge and would be asked to sign a letter of resignation.

Upon arriving home that night, Christiansen received numerous phone calls from active chapter members and pledges, expressing their concern that Duncan was being unfairly forced out. Christiansen agreed to attend an all-chapter meeting later that same night at the fraternity house.

At the meeting, Christiansen felt tension in the air. He asked Duncan if he was comfortable telling the entire group what he had told him the night before. Duncan said he was and proceeded to tell his story.

After Duncan finished, Christiansen added that Duncan had four or possibly five different names and had been convicted of passport fraud. Duncan clarified that he had used only three aliases.

The meeting went on for a couple of hours, Christiansen recounted. As it was breaking up, he observed Duncan crying. "It was very difficult for him to do, but he publicly resigned his pledgeship. This was a very moving experience to all in attendance. Pledges as well as actives were crying at the loss of Mr. Martinez as a pledge. Many of them started comforting Mr. Martinez. There was a group of about twenty young men standing around Mr. Martinez in a hugging circle."

The story Christiansen told in his memo was zany but, given my familiarity with Duncan, unsurprising. After hearing from Detective Barnes in December that Duncan had been talking indiscreetly about Ron's murder within his fraternity, Garcia and I had called Duncan and warned him this was technically a violation of his King for a Day agreement, and not to do it again. Christiansen's memo provided more details on Duncan's statements, but it did not merit another warning.

The other reason I took no action after receiving the memo was that

Duncan's status as a witness and potential criminal defendant was still up in the air, pending the DA's decision on how to proceed.

The meeting with the DA's Office was held on the afternoon of Monday, May 17. In attendance were Ernie Norris, who had handled the Baker case to date; Norris's supervisor, David Conn; and two representatives from the DA's upper management, Bill Hodgman and Frank Sundstedt. The LAPD contingent consisted of me; my new part-time detective partner, Mike Mejia; and our new supervisor at RHD, Lieutenant Danny Lang.

Since Garcia's retirement, I had been promoted to Detective III, to assume leadership of the team Garcia and I had worked with. A replacement for Garcia's position had not yet been selected.

The meeting with the DA's Office did not take long. Two major questions were up for discussion and final resolution. I was there to offer my input, but the decisions would rest with the DA's representatives.

First, how should the case against Nathan move forward?

There were two options. The more common route was for the DA to file criminal charges. After filing, California law required a preliminary hearing to be held to determine if the evidence was sufficient to go to trial. The other, lesser-used route was to seek an indictment through a grand jury. If the grand jury decided there was probable cause to believe the suspect committed the crime, an indictment would be issued.

One advantage of going to a grand jury is that it would streamline the court proceedings. In some murder investigations, it can take a year or even longer just to reach a preliminary hearing. When a grand jury indicts a suspect, it bypasses the preliminary hearing requirement. Following a grand jury indictment, the next stage of the case is the trial.

Conn said the evidence and testimony incriminating Nathan would be presented to the LA County Grand Jury. Conn expected no difficulty with a grand jury returning an indictment against Nathan for first-degree murder, along with a special circumstance of "lying in wait," one of several potential special circumstances specified in the California Penal Code. Special circumstances are aggravating factors that, if proven true in court, mean a stiffer sentence for the defendant. A conviction for first-degree murder with special circumstances could bring only one of two possible sentences: death or life without the possibility of parole.

"Lying in wait" does not necessarily mean the defendant waited somewhere for the victim to arrive and then killed them. If the defendant concealed their purpose from the victim and took them by surprise, that meets the criteria. In this case, Nathan and Duncan had lured Ron to the tunnel with an intent to kill, based on the plan the two had hatched together.

The other key question on the agenda was whether Duncan should be used as a witness against Nathan. The issue had been simmering for months. A decision needed to be made.

Norris was the only person in the meeting in favor of using Duncan as a witness. Everyone else, including me, was opposed. The way I saw it, why would we choose to use a witness with so many potential drawbacks when the evidence was sufficient without his testimony? I could not understand how a veteran prosecutor like Norris would even contemplate using Duncan under these circumstances.

Conn ultimately decided that Duncan's testimony would not be used. He gave three reasons. First, Duncan had severe credibility issues. Second, given the recordings and Nathan's confession, Duncan's testimony was completely unnecessary. Third, Duncan would want a reduced sentence in exchange for his testimony. Considering his role in planning Ron's murder and his actions afterward, Duncan was undeserving of such leniency.

Conn was most adamant about this last reason. He felt Duncan was much too culpable in the case to receive a "sweetheart" plea agreement and a light sentence. Conn said he would rather let Duncan remain a free man and move on with his life for now. Conn felt something might surface later that would allow him to be charged equally with Nathan.

Conn assigned Norris to be the prosecutor to take the case to the grand jury. He directed Norris to schedule the case to be heard by the LA County Grand Jury as soon as possible.

Unlike regular court hearings, which are open to the public, grand jury proceedings are conducted in secret. Neither the suspect the DA wishes to indict nor their defense counsel are there. Nor is the investigating detective, except when they are asked to testify. Only court staff, the prosecutor presenting the case, the witness giving testimony, and the grand jury members are permitted to be present. Witnesses are instructed not to share or discuss their testimony until an indictment is unsealed.

The grand jury's finite time, combined with the sheer number of criminal cases in Los Angeles, means only a tiny percentage of prosecutions begin with an indictment, as opposed to charges being filed. In fact, before Ron Baker's murder, I had never had any case I investigated brought before a grand jury. Nor did I have another for the rest of my career.

The evidence that Nathan Blalock murdered Ron Baker was presented to the grand jury over three days, from June 8 to 10, 1993.

Although I was not privy to the actual proceedings, I knew from Norris that he planned to call six witnesses.

The first was Gayle Baker, Ron's father. He would provide background on his son and give his account of the two ransom calls he received.

Next was one of the two Devonshire Division homicide detectives who initially handled the case. They would testify about the crime scene and the condition of Ron's body.

Third was a representative from the LA County coroner's office, ideally the medical examiner who performed the autopsy. They would testify to the autopsy results and cause of death.

Then there would be a criminalist from the LAPD's crime lab, who would testify about the analysis of the blood found under Ron's fingernails. Their testimony would also detail the ABO blood results for Ron, Duncan, and Nathan, including that only Nathan's blood matched the type under Ron's nails.

Fifth was Diane Henderson, Nathan's ex-girlfriend. She would testify about the events of June 21, 1990, in particular before the three roommates left the apartment and what she was told about their plans for the night.

The final witness was me. I would testify to the overall, multiyear investigation, as well as introduce the recordings of the three conversations between Nathan and Duncan, excerpts of which the grand jury would hear. Finally, I would discuss the confession Nathan gave to me and Garcia, before that recording also was played for the grand jury.

After Norris had questioned all the witnesses, his presentation concluded on June 10 with a closing argument. Norris asked the grand jury to indict Nathan Blalock for first-degree murder, with the special circumstance of "lying in wait."

Later that same day, the grand jury returned an indictment against Nathan for the charge and special-circumstance allegation Norris had requested. The indictment was sent to Department 100 of the LA Superior Court. There, it was read in open court by the judge, who then issued the arrest warrant.

Nathan, sitting in a state prison cell in Tehachapi, more than a hundred miles away, had no idea that he was now charged with his former roommate's murder. The first he would know about it was when a prison official informed him the warrant had been received. I doubted Nathan would be surprised. He knew we had the damaging tape recordings of him and Duncan. He also knew he had confessed. Nathan would soon be transported to LA County Jail to await his trial.

Meanwhile, in Utah, Duncan Martinez was living life as a college student. On the day of Nathan's indictment, the temperature in Salt Lake City peaked at a balmy 78 degrees. Duncan's hopes of becoming a Phi Delta Theta fraternity brother may have been dashed, but he was free to take the classes of his choice, party with his friends, and enjoy the beautiful soon-to-be-summer weather. His circumstances and prospects were immeasurably less grim than those of his former friend and co-suspect Nathan.

Nathan was staring down a trial that, if he was convicted of the charges, could end in only one of two ways: a sentence of death or life without the possibility of parole.

CHAPTER 20

"A MURDER THAT SOMEONE ELSE DID"

(June 30 to July 16, 1993)

ON THE MORNING OF June 30, I learned that Nathan Blalock had been transferred from the state prison to LA County Jail. This was as a result of the arrest warrant issued three weeks earlier. Nathan was now in place to be prosecuted for the murder of Ron Baker.

Later that afternoon, I headed to the county jail to meet briefly with Nathan. My purpose was administrative rather than investigative. Nathan's right-hand fingerprints were required on one of the pages of his arrest report, which I needed to complete.

At the jail, Nathan was summoned from his cell and escorted to meet me.

I explained to Nathan why I needed his prints. His demeanor was, as usual, cordial and agreeable.

While I took Nathan's prints, he told me that he wasn't the one who had killed Ron Baker. He added that he was now ready to tell the story of what happened and identify the person who had. He said he had not been ready to tell the entire story previously.

I assumed Nathan was referring to Duncan. Nathan had said during his confession that he and Duncan were the only people in the tunnel with Ron. I expected that Duncan would be Nathan's new fall guy and that Nathan would try to recant as much as possible about his own involvement.

Since I was not prepared to interview Nathan, I told him I would schedule a time with jail personnel and return the next day to hear his story. In actuality, I wanted to have with me the murder book to refer to, as well as a tape recorder to document the interview.

The next morning, I called the jail's liaison unit and requested a private meeting room in which to conduct the interview. LA County Jail is the busiest, most populated jail facility in the country. Without making an advance request, law enforcement visitors ordinarily had to use one of several Plexiglas booths in a communal room for attorney-client visits. Talking with Nathan while dozens of people sat around glaring at one another would not have been an optimal setting.

The interview room I was given was small and windowless but provided no distractions for Nathan. When he walked in, my tape recorder was already running.

I wanted it on the record why I was there to re-interview him. I said to Nathan, "Yesterday, when I came over to fingerprint you, you indicated that you were kind of willing to talk about Duncan's aspect of it... I'd like to hear what you have to say. When we were up in Tehachapi, I asked you some stuff and you kind of bounced around the Duncan issue. If you want to lay out what you recall now about Duncan's involvement, I'd be willing to listen to you. It's up to you."

"Yeah, I don't see why not," he replied. "It might shed a little clearer light on this whole situation here."

I explained that since he was in custody, I had to advise him of his constitutional rights again before I could hear him out. I read Nathan his rights and he agreed to waive them.

"Okay, run by me whatever's on your mind," I said. I had decided I would give Nathan the floor and just let him tell his story. I didn't plan to challenge him, other than to ask some questions to clarify whatever information he wanted to give me.

"Well," Nathan said, "anytime you have a roommate, there's always problems." In their case, he explained, there were always financial disputes among the three of them, in particular between Duncan and Ron. "Duncan is also known as a compulsive liar, as we found out later on. Anyway, but the night of the murder, we had all went out to the park... To cut through the thick of it, when I said before that I stuck Ron by accident, it was one time, I think, by accident. Ron was pushed into me from the front, and I heard Ron say, 'Ow.' But when he said, 'Ow,' it wasn't like he screamed in pain or anything like that. So that's when I thought, after thinking about what happened, maybe I did stick him, but it was not deliberate. It was an accident."

I knew Nathan was trying to downplay what he had confessed to me and Garcia, in order to minimize his criminal culpability as much as possible. I expected the Duncan-bashing information to come next.

"Who pushed him?" I asked.

"Duncan was in front of us. Duncan was leading us through the tunnel... Ron was in front of me... And I was walking last." Nathan said it was too dark to tell how far apart they were.

"Could you even see a figure? Could you even see figures in there at that time of night?"

"Barely. The deeper you go into the tunnel, the darker it gets. I dropped the knife, and the only reason why I had the knife is because this is, quote, unquote, Charles Manson Park, and there's crazies up there and everything else... Before that, when we were drinking beer, Duncan and Ron had been talking about something, some money or something like that, and kind of got into, not a real shoving match, but you know how buddies push around and play? Stuff like that."

"Okay. That was while you were drinking beer?"

"While we were drinking beer. But then again, we always play like that anyway... You wouldn't really think it was a fight or anything like that... Now, in the tunnel, after I heard Ron say, 'Ow,' I dropped the knife—"

"You had the knife in your hand?"

"Yes."

"It was out?"

"Yeah."

"And it was out because...?"

"Just because for safety reasons, you know. It had not been the first time that we had done something like this. The entire group would go up there. As a group, you always stay together in a group. But when there's only small numbers, you get a little leery."

I asked Nathan if he knew if Ron was pushed, or if Ron could have just stopped walking.

"I would assume he was pushed. But then again, it's hard to say, because when he said, 'Ow,' it was like if you were to jam your knee on this table or something, you know? It wasn't like a real painful 'Ow.'" He said he wasn't sure if Ron stopped and he walked into him or if Ron was pushed backward into the knife.

"Okay, so then he says, 'Ow,' then what do you do?"

"Then I dropped it. Well, first I asked him what happened, and I don't remember hearing a response. I dropped the knife because I thought I had stuck him. I was like, 'Are you okay?'"

I asked Nathan whether he dropped the knife accidentally.

"I dropped the knife on purpose, because I didn't know what had happened, and it was dark. I dropped the knife, and I heard a scuffling sound. And then I remember seeing flashes, like either a flashlight flash or a lighter flash or something along those lines."

"You heard scuffling right in front of you?"

"In the immediate vicinity, yeah, I would say."

I asked Nathan if the scuffle had sounded like wrestling.

"At that time it did not sound like a wrestling match. It sounded like *Okay, let's find whatever we dropped and keep going.* That's what it sounds like to me."

"More like someone on the ground looking for something? Is that where it was?"

"Yeah. And then I remember, like I said, it was either a flashlight or a lighter flashing... I don't remember if I struck a lighter or if Duncan struck a lighter, but at that point in time, when the light came up, when the light was flashed, I saw Duncan over Ron... I just remember a flash."

"Okay. Was it a quick flash or did it last for a while?"

"It was, I would say, about thirty seconds."

Thirty seconds seemed remarkably long for a flash, but I let Nathan continue with his story.

He went on: "At that point, I saw Duncan over Ron."

"Standing over him?"

"Kneeling down with him," he said. He described Ron lying on his back, with Duncan kneeling next to or over him. "And at that point, it was pretty much like panic hit suddenly... I don't know if Duncan was really panicked. I wouldn't say he was as panic-stricken as I was. My goal was *Well, let's get out of here. This is not good,* you know? And so we left."

I noted that Nathan had made no mention of actually having seen Duncan stab Ron. This struck me as unrealistic. Nathan not seeing any stabbing felt too convenient.

I asked him how Duncan seemed, if not panic-stricken.

"Not then, not at this point, but later on he seemed kind of jazzed or hyped."

"What was the condition of the body?"

Nathan said he didn't know. "I don't remember seeing him move or nothing like that."

"How long did this scuffle last?"

"For a few minutes... Somewhere between three and five minutes, I'd say. Then at this point in time, there's no real sense of time."

"Okay. Any words being said? Any yelling, any screaming, anything?"

"No, I can't remember any."

"Did you see any wounds on Ron?"

"No, not that I really focused in on."

"Any blood?"

"I do think I saw faint signs of blood, but not a lot. I mean, it was dark."

"Okay. But when the light went on, I'm talking about."

"Even then, yeah, maybe a little," he said. Given the severity of Ron's stab wounds and blood loss, this seemed doubtful to me as well.

"Did Duncan have any blood on him?"

"I didn't notice any at that time. But when we got back, it was a different story. When we got actually to the car." There, he saw a little blood on Duncan's hands and some on his shoes, Nathan recalled.

I asked if when they returned to the apartment Diane saw them walk in.

"Yeah, she did," he said. "I'm pretty sure she did. She couldn't help it." Without my prompting him, Nathan described his state of mind at the time. "My main thought here is, first of all... I'm thinking I have to cover myself, you know, because no matter what, I'm going to be implicated in this. And I'm going to get the time behind it, because I'm dealing with a racial thing here. You see what I'm saying? So I'm trying to think of a way that—and I'm thinking at the same time, *I didn't really do this*. But then Duncan and I are friends. And he came up with the idea that 'You know what? You don't tell on me, I won't tell on you.' And we made the pact. And that, in the phone conversation, was part of the plan that you heard me talking about. 'We had a plan. Let's stick to it.' That was the plan. 'You live your life, and I'll live my life.'"

"So you made a pact or a plan not to tell on each other?"

"Yeah."

Nathan explained that when Ron's father first phoned them, after the initial kidnapping call, Duncan wasn't there. "Me and Diane was there, and I was talking to Ron's father... When I was talking to him on the phone, then Duncan came in, and he was a little bit out of breath."

"When you guys had talked about this kidnapping thing, this story you guys had come up with earlier, that was part of the deal, right? To put a call in to whoever's parents, correct?"

"Yeah."

"Did Duncan tell you when he was going to go make that phone call?"

"No, I didn't know anything about that... I didn't know he was going to do it then."

"You knew he was going to do it at some point, but he just disappeared, and did it then without telling you specifically at that point?"

"Correct. He was—if I remember correctly—he was going to get some beer."

"When you guys had first talked about doing this kidnapping thing, this plot you guys had come up with, you said that was Duncan's idea, or was it your idea or what?"

Nathan implied the ransom was Duncan's idea. Nathan said he had never met Ron's parents before the murder. "I met them after all this had started. I never met his parents before then. I didn't know if they had money or not."

"Had you guys talked about who you could kidnap, when you guys were talking?"

"Not that I remember."

"Had you proposed anybody else other than Ron?"

"I don't remember personally proposing Ron. Although his name—I guess it came up. But see, not being from California, I don't know anybody. So how could I propose anybody's name?"

Nathan said he didn't know how long before Ron's murder the kidnapping plan was first discussed. "I never took it seriously, but it was somewhere close to then... Close to when he was killed... I would say within days."

"What was the purpose for taking Ron to the park?"

"Okay, as I found out, Duncan told Ron—he told me too—that we were going to meet some girls. That was the whole purpose of leaving. Even though, yeah, Diane was there, still a guy's a guy. You know what I'm saying?... That was the whole motive and how we were led to leave the house in the first place."

"Okay, but there were no—no girls were going to be there."

"When we got to the park, I didn't see any, yeah."

"Oh, so at that time you totally thought that there might be girls? That's righteously—"

"Yeah, we were going to meet girls. That's what I'm thinking." Nathan said the plan and all the talk about the girls came from Duncan. "Duncan came up with this elaborate story that he told his girlfriend... He was trying to line up jobs for he and I with Sony Corporation for megabucks as security guards and stuff like that too. Later on, I found out that's where, if things would have gone the way he wanted them to go, when the money came, that would've been our alibi. So he had already given me an alibi, a way to explain how I get all this money. It was my new job."

"What money is that?"

"The money that he would have gotten for doing whatever."

"The kidnapping thing?"

"Yeah... He told me afterward that that was the cover-up, for why I have all this money."

"For the ransom?"

"Yeah."

"Were you guys going to split it?"

"I would assume, you know, but—"

"It seems fair," I interjected, just going along with the conversation.

"Yeah, it seems fair. But once again, I never thought, first of all, it would be Ron and, secondly, it was even a serious idea. Because at the time, my job wasn't the greatest in the world, but I was working."

So far, I found Nathan's story not to be credible, but I kept my opinion to myself and allowed him to continue telling it as he thought best. If his case ever went to trial, it would be the responsibility of his future defense attorney to try to weave a cohesive explanation from what he said in this interview versus in his earlier recorded confession. Were Nathan to take the stand in his own defense, I imagined a prosecutor would have a field day pointing out the many contradictions in various accounts.

I asked Nathan if Duncan had his own knife that night.

"I don't know if he had one or not," he said. "No, no—the knife I was carrying was Duncan's... He had it first, and I got it from him."

"When did you get it from him?"

"Before we even got out the car."

"You took the knife from him?"

"Yeah, and I don't know if he had another knife or not. That, I don't even know."

"What was used on Ron, then?"

"I can only assume, once I dropped the knife. Duncan never said what was used or nothing like that, but he did have the knife that I dropped."

"When did he have it?"

"When we got back to the car, he had it... I don't know if he used that on him or not. But once again, thinking of myself, I go, in my head, *I got to get rid of this. Because if shit ever does blow up, it's going to look bad on me.*"

I asked Nathan whether Duncan ever said his knife was the one he had used to stab Ron.

"No... The incident wasn't even spoke of. It was like it never happened."

I asked Nathan a few more questions about Duncan's clothes and the knife.

Nathan said he tossed them in the dumpster the next morning

around sunrise. Duncan was not there when he threw them away, he said. Nathan also said he couldn't recall what happened to Ron's wallet, which was not recovered after his death.

"Did you ever see Ron's wallet?" I asked.

"I remember his checkbook... I think it was in the house."

"What about it?"

"Duncan wrote checks in it."

"How many? Do you recall?"

"I think one or two. I'm not sure how many for sure. I mean, he cashed them at the check place right up the street." Nathan said Duncan did not tell him he was going to forge Ron's checks.

"How do you know he did it?"

"I saw him... I watched him."

"Did he say why?"

"He said that Ron owed him money."

I decided to change direction and asked Nathan if Duncan had ever said why he stabbed Ron. I knew Nathan's answer, in some form, was going to be "No." In my mind, I was certain it was Nathan and not Duncan who had stabbed Ron, but I wanted to see what Nathan would say.

"It was never really discussed again," he replied. "And then when it was all over and whatnot, like I said, we had already made the deal where we'll still stay friends and everything... Basically, 'You live your life. I live my life.'"

"Both going your own way?"

"Exactly, because I didn't want to really be caught up in this, and that's when I pretty much moved to Lake Elsinore with Diane." Nathan and Diane came back up to LA and saw Duncan once, when he was staying in Hollywood at Lydia's house, he recalled.

"Did you guys discuss anything there?"

"Only what he had been doing since all this happened. He said he had a new job. He was going to buy a new car. And this, that, and the other. The next thing I know, I hear he's disappeared. That was the last time I heard from him up until I went to the county jail."

I asked Nathan if he was drunk when they were drinking in the park on the night of Ron's murder. Nathan said he could have driven and was under the legal limit.

"How about Duncan?" I asked.

"I would say he had a few too many, and Ron, who rarely drinks, two beers is enough to get him drunk."

"Was he pretty drunk?"

"He had had at least three or four, yeah."

"Did he act drunk?"

"If you consider laughing, joking, and having a good time acting drunk, yeah."

"Nothing happens to get anybody irritated out there, other than you mentioned a little bit ago that there was a discussion about money, or a little argument about money?" I asked.

"Yeah, not that I can really recall."

"Okay. When you guys were drinking, where was the knife?"

"For part of the time we were drinking, Duncan had it, and I took it from him while we were drinking."

Nathan had told me differently earlier in the interview. "I thought you said you got it when you got out of the car."

Nathan stuck by his new version. "No, I think I took it from him while we were drinking… I'm pretty sure."

"What'd you say? 'Give me the knife' or did he hand it to you or what happened?"

"I just kind of, like, took it from him. He had it, playing with it."

"When did you first take it out?"

"About maybe fifty, sixty feet before the tunnel, when we were still outside the tunnel."

"How far was everybody in front of everybody, when you're walking in the tunnel?"

"When we first walked in, we were at, I would say, ten-foot intervals, at least. But then once you get in the tunnel, it's dark, you start slowing down, and chain reaction. The first man slows down, the back keeps moving quicker. Next thing, we're all kind of, like, bunched together."

I asked Nathan to describe how he was holding the knife inside the tunnel. He said waist-high and in front of him, with the blade pointed slightly upward.

"Okay. He gets poked. The knife is dropped. You dropped the knife immediately. Then you hear a scuffling in front of you?" I asked, summarizing what he had told me earlier.

"In front of me, yeah," he said. He estimated the scuffle was within an eight-foot radius of him, but not so close that he was getting hit himself.

"Did you get involved in doing anything at that point?"

"No." Nathan said the next thing he knew, he saw a flashing light. He couldn't remember if it was his lighter or Duncan's.

"Then at that point you see Duncan on his knees, crouching or kneeling over Ron, and Ron—you don't recall him moving at all?"

"No, I don't."

"What does Duncan do or say?"

"I don't remember hearing anything. At that point, life itself, just like I said, there really was no time frame. Life just was, like, in slow motion, pretty much."

"You panic?"

"Yeah."

"Duncan, at that point, seems cool?" I asked.

"I guess call it, like, adrenaline flow, or whatever. It could have been panic, I don't know, but I've seen people panic, and for a panicking person, he was really cool and calm about it."

"Okay. What's the next thing you guys do?"

"We left."

"Who said, 'Let's take off,' or did you not say anything? You just walked out?"

"I think we just left."

"Ron was left where he was?"

"Yeah."

He and Duncan returned to the park the next morning. It was Duncan's idea, Nathan said.

"For what reason?"

"Duncan said to destroy the body. I wasn't really all that comfortable with that idea. Too much TV says, 'Never return to the scene of a crime.' But he had this idea to go back to the park."

I asked Nathan to describe where the scuffle took place in relation to the train tracks. He said he thought they were walking on the tracks when Ron fell into him. After the scuffle, Ron ended up to the side of the tracks.

"You guys don't move him?"

"No, I didn't touch him."

"The next day, when you went back, did you go in the tunnel?"

"I think I stood at the opening, and Duncan went in the tunnel, and came back and said that he wasn't there."

"Where did the idea first come up, about this kidnapping thing?"

"I think we were sitting around one night, and Duncan just came up with it. Out of the blue."

"Was there no motivation for it? Nothing that you guys did or saw or read or anything that sparked this thought?" I remembered Duncan had told me and Garcia the plan was first hatched after they watched an episode of *Dragnet* about a botched kidnapping.

"Not that I can recall."

"Duncan throws it out first?"

"Yeah, I think so."

"What do you remember being discussed?"

"First, we were talking about money, and he was talking about he needed to come up with some money, whatever, quick or soon... He needed to come up with some money for his insurance or something mundane, something like that. We just got into this conversation... It just came up."

"So then you guys start talking. Did you guys kind of think about the perfect crime, how it would be played out?"

This was something Duncan had suggested, that their original intent had been to improve upon a botched crime plan from the TV show, to the point that they would get away with it.

"No, I don't even think the conversation went that serious. It was more or less laughter along with it. It was never... I don't remember it going that serious."

"Okay. But at some point there's a, quote, unquote, kidnapping story that you guys think of. I mean, we've discussed that before."

"Yeah. Yeah."

I asked Nathan to describe the scenario they came up with. "What was the story? How was it supposed to go down?"

"Kidnap somebody and call their family, their house, their husband or wife, whatever, and run it down to them that 'We have your whoever, and this is how much money we want,' and that was basically the way it was supposed to roll. Duncan told me about a park that we could pick up the money in... There's like a lot of trails or something through it, and it's supposedly a really big park. What he was going to do was have the money dropped off at one trail, because he was a long-distance runner or whatever. He would run through the park, or whatever, and I would pick him up on the other side, stuff like that." Nathan said he never took the idea seriously.

"Did you guys talk about actually doing it?"

"I don't remember really talking about really doing it," he said. He likened it to boasting about doing something totally out there and implausible, versus reality. "A lot of people talk about things they'll never do in their life, like flying to the moon or driving in an Indy 500. You'll never do it in your life, but at the time, you talk about it... But then you laugh it off, and that's it. You know you'll never do it... This was one of those conversations. It was a one-in-a-million chance of it ever, ever happening, and I never took it serious. At that time, I was in love, and kidnapping was the furthest thing from my mind."

"Did Duncan have any injuries at all that you saw later?"

"I don't remember any."

"Okay. Never talked about what happened or why he did this?"

Nathan said no. He also made a point to deny again that Ron scratched him, despite his blood type being found under Ron's fingernails. "Somewhere in this story, there came up a comment about me being scratched. I still to this day do not remember being scratched anywhere, but the three of us did wrestle a lot," he said.

He additionally denied that the murder had anything to do with a statement Ron had made about Diane that Nathan supposedly had taken offense to. "The comment that he made about Diane, or whatever, was so, so stupid, it was more or less a joke. Because she had cooked us dinner, or whatever, and he made a comment about it... It was not the kind of comment that a person goes off and commits murder about... I mean, more people have said worse things about me as a kid coming up than what he could have ever done that really pissed me off... I've heard every racial joke there is, and I would think any of those jokes would be a lot more to offend me than what he said about Diane... So it was no big deal at all."

I had no more questions, and Nathan seemed to have gotten off his chest everything he wanted to tell me.

"Okay," I said. "I'll write it up, turn it over to the District Attorney's Office. I guess that's it. You think of anything else?"

Nathan said not really. He told me, "I've been thinking about it, and I really just don't want to take a life sentence, with a possible death over it, for a murder that someone else did. Even though I know with the evidence against me, even if I don't get charged with the murder, I can still get charged with accessory, which carries the same amount of time, basically. But still, there's a difference in, on your jacket, having an accessory and having actual murder."

"Jacket" was slang for a person's criminal record. It could also refer to a reputation for snitching.

I told Nathan that after he'd said the previous day that he wanted to set the record straight, he deserved the opportunity to do so.

"All right," he said. "I hope it helps."

"Okay, we'll see. It's not in my hands," I told him. This was the truth, and I didn't want to give him any false hope. For better or worse, Nathan's fate now rested in the hands of the DA and the court system.

"Thanks for just coming to hear me, though."

"No problem. I'll talk to you later, man. Take care," I told him.

"You too," Nathan replied, before he returned to his jail cell.

On Monday morning, July 15, two weeks after Nathan's attempted retraction of his confession and my jailhouse interview with him, he was arraigned in Los Angeles Superior Court for Ron Baker's murder.

Later that day, the LAPD put out a short press release that read, in part: "Today, Nathaniel Blalock, 25 years of age, and a roommate of Ron Baker at the time of his murder, was arraigned on a Grand Jury indictment charging him with Baker's murder and alleging special circumstances of lying in wait, which could qualify him for the death penalty."

At my request, the press release also noted: "The investigation did reveal that the killing was not in any way cult-related." I had pushed for this language for a few reasons. First, it was the truth. Second, I knew it would provide some comfort to the Baker family by publicizing that Ron's murder did not result from his interest in Wicca. Finally, I hoped it would put to bed some of the more lurid media speculation about Ron's murder and the motive behind it.

I was sure the local media would pick up on the press release, or at least the print media. How the story would be framed, I would not find out until the following day.

Sure enough, a story ran in the next day's *Los Angeles Times* about the case and Nathan's arraignment. I was gratified that it included a quote from Kay Baker, Ron's mother, who had told the paper, "We're pleased that this thing is finally coming to a conclusion... It's been a long time. And we're definitely relieved that it's not cult-related." The Baker family had already been told that privately, by me, but I sensed they appreciated that the information was finally reaching the public.

The indictment of Nathan Blalock marked another significant advance in the investigation. With his arraignment, the three-year-old case of Ron Baker's murder could be formally closed, under the official designation "Cleared by Arrest."

As with any case I worked, it was a relief to have someone held accountable for a crime they had committed. This one felt especially good, probably because for the first few years of the investigation, Garcia and I had our doubts we would ever reach this point. For so long, the suspects seemed almost within reach yet always somehow just beyond our grasp.

The technical closure of the Baker case was reason to exhale, but it did not mean the job was done. Nathan's trial still needed to be won. It was too soon to say when the trial might take place, and I knew it could be as long as a few years away.

Duncan's situation also remained unresolved, a dilemma never far from my mind. Like Nathan's fate in the courts, what happened to Duncan from a legal standpoint appeared to be out of my hands. Would he continue to live his life as Joe Citizen, unpunished for his role in Ron's murder?

As things stood, I saw no obvious path to being able to charge Duncan in the case. We had insufficient admissible evidence even to put him in the tunnel on the night of Ron's murder, let alone prove him guilty beyond a reasonable doubt.

To my frustration, it appeared that Duncan held the winning cards in his hands. He was in total control, free to live out his life however he wished.

PART III
THE THIRD BETRAYAL

CHAPTER 21

THE BURGLARY
(December 13, 1993 to March 4, 1994)

THE MESSAGE ON MY desk said to call Salt Lake City Police detective Jim Prior.

It was late on a Monday afternoon in December, five months after Nathan's arraignment.

Given where Prior was calling from, my first thought was *Duncan Martinez*.

Duncan's status had not changed. We did not have sufficient evidence to charge him. His prior statements to me and Garcia about Ron's murder could never be used against him. As things stood, Duncan was beyond the reach of the law.

I immediately called Prior back. He informed me that Duncan had been arrested for committing a burglary the previous Friday night. Prior recounted the basic details. He later sent me the complete police report on the incident.

Just before midnight on December 10, Salt Lake City officers responded to a burglar alarm at a sporting goods store named Wasatch Touring. The officers discovered a broken store window.

An initial search of the premises found no one inside. An officer then noticed a ladder to an upstairs storage area. He climbed the ladder and observed a man, later identified as Duncan, hiding. He was taken into custody. Duncan's leg had been cut by broken glass in the window he had entered through, but he declined medical assistance. Although the arresting officers did not ask him any questions, Duncan repeatedly stated he wanted to speak to a detective about the incident.

Duncan was found in possession of several items of merchandise from the store, including a $198 cycling jacket he was wearing when he was arrested. He was patted down for weapons, and none were found. Near Duncan's hiding place, however, officers discovered a plastic but authentic-looking replica of a Beretta 9-millimeter handgun. Duncan admitted he had brought the toy gun into the store and, before being arrested, had tossed it.

After Duncan was advised of his rights, and waived them, he told officers that he had entered the store intending to take a mountain bike. Once inside, he had moved one bike to the store's front entrance. Officers found the bike where Duncan had abandoned it.

Duncan told officers the reason he wanted to speak with a detective was that he had been forced to commit the burglary by an acquaintance named Emile.

After Duncan was transported to the police station, Detective Prior was called in to interview him. The interview began shortly after 2 a.m. Prior took notes but did not tape-record it.

Duncan told Prior the same story about having been coerced to commit the burglary by an acquaintance. He said Emile had demanded he steal a mountain bike for him, and if he refused, Emile would inform university officials of his involvement in a homicide investigation in California. Duncan feared Emile's exposure of his past could lead to him getting expelled from the university, he told Prior.

Duncan had no ID on him when he was arrested, but he gave Prior his true name. He told Prior he had been arrested only once before, for providing false information on a passport application.

When Prior ran Duncan's name to confirm his identity, the criminal history indicated that "Duncan Gordon James Martinez" was an alias for a person named "Jonathan W. Miller." Duncan explained that the Miller name was really the alias. Duncan told Prior he'd used that name when he attempted to get a passport so he could leave the country.

Duncan recounted for Prior the events leading up to his burglary arrest that night. He said he and a friend had shared a couple bottles of wine and then went to a party. When he returned to his apartment, Emile had been waiting there for him. Duncan said Emile told him, "You're going to help me out or I'm going to let the people at the university know what happened in California. You're going to get me a mountain bike from the business next door," referring to Wasatch Touring. Inside the apartment, Emile saw a plastic toy gun on a desk. Duncan said Emile had told him to take it with him.

Duncan then described how he broke a window and climbed through it to enter the store. He estimated he was in the store for less than ten minutes when police responded.

Prior asked Duncan to explain more about Emile's threat to expose him. Duncan said that about three years ago he had witnessed a homicide in California and had fled the area to escape from having to testify against the person responsible for the murder. As part of this attempt to flee, he had tried to obtain a passport under a false name.

Prior asked how Duncan knew Emile and how Emile knew about the California homicide case. Duncan said they had worked together at a restaurant in Park City. He explained he had told a few people at the restaurant about his problems in California. He said Emile must have heard about it through one of them.

After Prior finished questioning Duncan, he asked for permission to enter Duncan's apartment to retrieve his identification. Given what he had seen of Duncan's record, including his past use of an alias and his passport fraud conviction, Prior felt uncomfortable taking Duncan's word that he was who he claimed to be.

Duncan agreed, then asked Prior an unorthodox favor: He had a pet rat at his apartment that he had neglected to feed earlier. Since he was not sure when he might be released, and Prior was going to his apartment anyway, would Prior mind feeding the rat while he was there?

Prior ultimately decided to take Duncan with him. He gave the rat food and water. He then found identification for Duncan in the form of a Utah ID card, a student ID, and a Social Security card. He additionally viewed Duncan's photo in his high school yearbooks. Prior also spotted an LAPD business card for Detective Rick Jackson, Robbery-Homicide Division.

Prior wanted to know from me if there was any truth to the crazy tale Duncan had told him. He also wanted to make sure that Duncan wasn't wanted for anything else.

I told Prior that Duncan wasn't wanted, but his story was basically true. I added that the information Prior was passing on was phenomenal. My mind had already grasped that Duncan's statements to Prior were admissible evidence that could be used against him.

Prior's call was game-changing and startling. Then again, I'd learned already with Duncan that the unexpected could be expected.

True to form, Duncan had done it again. This was the precise scenario Head Deputy DA David Conn had envisioned might happen: Duncan getting in trouble again and talking too much.

I was highly skeptical of Duncan's story about the extortion-like plot initiated by the man he called Emile. It struck me as the latest in a long line of bizarre, dramatic, Duncanesque concoctions, stretching from his purported military assassination missions to his faked kidnapping.

I felt Prior needed to go for more right there and then. I asked if his interview with Duncan had been recorded. He said it hadn't.

I recounted for Prior the basic details and status of the Baker case. I advised him more evidence was needed to potentially move forward with charging Duncan for murder. I also explained Duncan thus far could not even be placed at the crime scene with admissible evidence.

I asked Prior if he would phone Duncan, but this time record the conversation. Duncan had already been released pending his court hearing in the burglary case. I told Prior to tell Duncan he had tried to call me but could not reach me. I suggested he say he was a bit confused about the murder part of the story Duncan had told him and ask Duncan to go through it again.

Prior and I discussed that since they would be on the phone rather than in a custodial setting, Miranda did not apply. There was no requirement that Prior read Duncan his rights or ask him to waive them before any questioning.

Prior agreed to call Duncan and give it a try. He said he would record the conversation and get back to me.

I called Deputy DA David Conn, now the assigned prosecutor on the Baker case, as it moved toward the trial of Nathan Blalock. Conn had taken over from Deputy DA Ernie Norris, who had obtained the grand jury indictment against Nathan six months earlier.

The reason for the change, as far as I knew, was internal politics within the DA's Office. Two years earlier, Norris had run in the 1992 election for Los Angeles County district attorney and finished a distant fourth in the primary. The winner of the general election had been another high-ranking deputy DA, Gil Garcetti. Norris had remained with the DA's Office but made it known he intended to challenge Garcetti in the next election. It wasn't long before Norris was transferred out of the DA's high-profile Special Trials unit.

David Conn, current head deputy of the Special Trials unit, had assigned himself the Baker case and assumed responsibility for its prosecution moving forward. This included both the yet-to-be-scheduled trial of Nathan and the unresolved decision on how to proceed with charging Duncan, if the opportunity presented itself.

I told Conn about Duncan's arrest and the statements he had made regarding his involvement in the murder. I also told him about my request to Prior to call Duncan and ask him to go over his statement again while recording it. Conn was wholeheartedly behind the strategy.

I thought it was ironic that I was calling Conn, of all people, about Duncan's latest escapade. During the debate about whether to use Duncan as a witness against Nathan, it was Conn who had been most adamantly opposed, since it would have forced his hand to offer Duncan some reduced sentence. Conn believed, as Garcia and I did, that Duncan was just as culpable as Nathan in the plot to kill Ron Baker. At the time, Conn had even said that he hoped Duncan would screw up down the road, which might result in clearing the hurdles to charge him.

It looked like the time for clearing those hurdles might have arrived.

I heard back from Prior two days later. He said he had called Duncan the day before, December 14, and re-interviewed him about the LAPD murder story. As requested, he had recorded the conversation. He mentioned that some of the details Duncan had told him were pretty graphic and shocking. He'd mail me a copy of the recording as soon as possible.

Based on Prior's account of the call, even before I heard the recording, I was elated. With Conn helming the case at the DA's Office, I knew it was likely Duncan would be charged, whether via a grand jury or by the traditional filing of charges and obtaining an arrest warrant.

I received a mini-cassette with the recorded conversation between Prior and Duncan when I returned to the office after the holidays. I sat down and listened to it immediately.

The call began with Duncan returning a message the detective had left for him.

"Burglary, this is Prior," he answered the phone.

"Yeah, this is Duncan Martinez."

"Duncan, hey, thanks for calling. What I'm trying to do is track down a little information on Emile," Prior said. He asked Duncan if he had any idea how to get ahold of Emile or a friend of theirs in common.

"I don't, actually. I can try and figure that out. I have no idea."

Prior said he was just trying to check over his notes. He asked Duncan how he was doing.

"Doing all right. It's been a rough weekend," Duncan said, referring to the burglary and his arrest a few nights earlier.

"Well, yeah, no kidding," said Prior.

"A very rough weekend," he emphasized. I couldn't help but roll my eyes.

Prior asked Duncan about his pending court case.

Duncan said he hadn't been given a court date, but he had spoken with court personnel. "I also spoke to the gentleman at Wasatch Touring," the owner of the store he had burglarized. "I wanted to start off with paying for the window, just because I don't think it's fair that they should have to do that... I already gave them some money. I gave them what I had. And I should get some more money in the next couple days."

Prior reminded Duncan he had been very willing to talk to him previously about the burglary. "You don't have to talk to me," he said, "you don't have to answer any questions about this. I'm still trying to track some things down on this Emile character."

Duncan said okay.

Prior asked him some questions about events leading up to the burglary, including his encounter with Emile.

Duncan said of Emile, "The big question I have is how he figured out where I live. Because I really haven't lived here that long... Not really many people know where I live. And Park City—I really haven't hung out in Park City for a long time... I'm wondering if he happened to run into somebody through the U or something."

"Is he a student at the U, do you think?" asked Prior.

"No, I highly doubt it... He's not the student type at all." Duncan said he would look into getting a phone number, "or at least figuring out Emile's last name." He said when he and Emile worked at the same restaurant in Park City, he was a waiter and Emile was a cook.

"I'm trying to find out, you know, run down what kind of hold this deal would've had on you. You know, the thing—your problems in California."

"Have you—I don't know if you've spoken to anybody in California or not," said Duncan.

Prior told him he had tried to call me but hadn't been able to get in touch. That obviously was untrue, but Prior was under no legal obligation to tell Duncan the truth. "Can you fill me in on what happened?"

"Yeah," Duncan said.

"I mean, again, you don't have to talk to me. Just for my interest to find out, by golly, what kind of hold this guy has on you."

"Did we talk about this at all the other day?"

"You just mentioned briefly that you'd been involved in an incident... In essence, that you'd witnessed an incident in California."

"Suffice to say, this is now about six months ago or eight months ago, was the initial problem. I'm going to say this first, just to explain a little bit. I was involved with a fraternity. I found out bad news about—or what was potentially bad news about—what was going on in Los Angeles. I told a couple of fraternity brothers, and it went everywhere. I mean, it ended up being phone calls to everybody. It turned into this huge rumor that caused me all sorts of problems in LA. I know that they don't really want things to be hyper-publicized. The only reason I say that is because I didn't say that last time and everything went everywhere. And it got me in trouble in LA or it got them pissed off at me in LA. I just say that so that this is between you and me here, as far as that goes."

"Okay," said Prior. He had no legal obligation, either, to inform Duncan their conversation was being recorded.

"Basically," Duncan said, "I witnessed my best friend kill my best friend. And I didn't know what to do."

"You lost me, man. You witnessed your best friend kill your best friend?"

"Yeah. It was my two best friends... Best friend is a—it's an interesting term... When I was in elementary school or something, you had your best friend and it was one person. And then as you get older, there's several guys."

"I understand. People you're very close to friendship-wise."

"Right. And I mean, there were extenuating circumstances. There were things that were talked about beforehand," Duncan said. I thought his reference to "extenuating circumstances" was quite an understatement, considering his previous admission that the whole thing was planned.

"What do you mean?"

"Well, to the extent that the gentleman that did it had even talked about it and related it to something that we talked about when we were drunk one day. It's a very messed up thing." His reference to the store owner as a "gentleman," and now Nathan as well, struck me as weird, and classic Duncan. It seemed like Duncan thought that by referring to others that way, he would come off as more genteel himself.

"What would you have talked about?" Prior asked.

"I mean, I can go through the whole thing," offered Duncan. "We sat around drinking one day and both of us were having trouble making ends meet and stuff, and money was a big problem. And we were drinking. I was out of school. I was kind of in a bad part of my life. I was supposed to have a bunch of scholarships or was expecting a bunch of scholarships out of high school, for track, and I never got them. And I got kind of mad... So we were drinking and we're fairly messed up. A TV show came on about a kidnapping, and we started talking about how stupid they were in the TV show and what we would do differently. We basically set up this little scenario. It was, you know, just something you do when you're drunk."

I shook my head at Duncan's last statement. Never once when I was drunk had I planned a murder. Nor did I know anyone who had.

Prior asked, "Trying to think of the perfect crime? Well, not perfect crime, but just playing 'what if'?"

"Right. And we talked about it, and that was that. And it was brought up again later on... The three of us lived together. Ron was the gentleman who was murdered. Ron was a really good friend. And he said to me one day, 'We're going to do it, but we're going to do it with Ron. And I was like, 'Yeah.' You know, first off, this thing was never serious anyway. And then secondly, he's saying we're doing it with Ron. I didn't believe a word. All of a sudden we were hanging out and he did it. I didn't know what to do. I covered for him for—I think I was still in LA for two weeks. I didn't say anything to anybody, and I couldn't deal anymore. I was being questioned by the police every day. I couldn't not tell the police, but I couldn't tell the police."

"Because you didn't want to rat out your buddy?"

"But it wasn't just that I didn't want to rat out my buddy. It was that I had hung out with all my friends for the two weeks after this happened. Everybody wanting to know what happened. And I had been the shoulder that everyone cried on. I was everyone's crutch getting through this. I don't know exactly where it came—"

"Did they all know that you actually witnessed it happen?"

"No, no one had a clue. I don't know. I think about this a lot. I don't know where I had the strength to do that, but I was everyone's crutch. How can I turn around and say, 'Okay, I was there'? 'We've been talking about this for two weeks and I haven't been able to tell you because I haven't had the, you know, gonads to say.' And I mean, I know that sounds really weak, but considering the state of mind, you know, that I wasn't in a real positive state of mind to start. It was a bad part of my life. It was a really bad part of my life."

Prior asked who the friends were that Duncan was talking to during those two weeks.

"I was hanging out with the group of friends that me and Ron had... It was about, I don't know, between ten and twenty people that I consistently hung out with for two weeks. And I haven't talked about this in a while. It's kind of—I was everyone's crutch."

It was the third time in about a minute that Duncan had described himself as "everyone's crutch." I thought it was a bizarre metaphor, considering the circumstances. Duncan seemed intent on praising himself for helping his friends through a difficult time, while taking no responsibility for being the cause of those tough times.

Duncan went on: "I was there and then I couldn't tell anybody, so I took off. I lived in Boston for a little over a year, about a year and a half, under a fake name."

"Would that have been the name you'd had on that passport?"

"Well, the funny thing about that is, and I've tried to explain it. I tried to explain it to the FBI when I was first incarcerated, a little over a year ago. The name that I used most of the time I was gone was not Jonathan W. Miller. It was James Lee Atkins... Jonathan Miller was the name I picked up right before I left Boston... I really wanted to call home. Basically, I didn't talk to anybody for the entire time I was there."

"How long were you in Boston?"

"Like I said, about a year and a half, something like that. I really wanted to call home. I healed myself as much as I could, but I couldn't heal myself enough that I could pick up the phone. The longer you wait, the harder it is to call."

Prior asked Duncan the name of his friend who committed the murder.

"Nathan."

"Nathan?"

"Blalock," Duncan said.

"So you and Nathan had gone out and partied, watched a TV show, and said, 'God, what if? How could this have been done better?'"

"All I remember is, 'My God, that is so stupid. What were they—' I mean, it was like an old *Dragnet*... I remember the two of us going— both of us have been in the military. And I think that was even what sparked the conversation, was 'Oh, man, anybody that's been in the military wouldn't have done that.' And it might have even been a military person that did it in the TV show. I don't even remember. I just remember that's what sparked the conversation. Like I say, it was just something we talked about over beer. And when it was brought up the second time, it was a conversation over beer. When it was brought up the second time, it was kind of like, 'Oh, we talked about this before. We'll talk about it again.'"

"Who was the instigator in that second conversation, concerning the incident?"

"It was Nathan...Anyway, my situation right now is that LAPD isn't quite sure what they're going to—what they want to do with me. Because I, you know, failed to assist them at the beginning, and I ran, and I knew of things beforehand...But because I've helped them so much since then, and basically done everything they wanted. I mean, every time they've asked me to come down and do something, I've gone. Every time they come around here and ask me to make phone calls, I've made them. But that's basically the situation there."

"What I'm trying to do, Duncan, as I've indicated, is I'm trying to find out what kind of hold this Emile would've had on you, to make you do what you did."

"Right."

"That's the reason for the conversation."

Duncan blamed his drinking for why he did Emile's bidding and committed the burglary. "Honestly, I think it was that I was completely happy-go-lucky drunk. I don't even know for sure. This is just my thinking, because I can't see myself acting that way. I can't see myself not saying, 'Screw you,' when put in that situation. It doesn't seem like me to me. I think it just may have been *Oh, I can do anything* kind of drunk... *I'll do this real quick, get him out of my hair so I can go to sleep, so I can get up early to study.* That's the thing that really pisses me off the most."

"Had you been sober, you probably wouldn't have done it?"

"Oh, if I'd been sober, I would've told him—excuse my language—I would've told him to fuck off...I've actually, because of the incident in LA and stuff, I've spoke to the gentleman at Wasatch Touring, and I said, 'There's two reasons I did this: (a) my future and (b) my mother.' Because I'm telling you, I can't call my mom."

"Why is that again?" asked Prior.

"My mom went through so much when I was gone for a year and a half in Boston. I didn't speak to my family for a year and a half. It destroyed my mom. She went through counseling the whole time ... She's just gone through so much. And things have finally come together with me and my family. Everything's finally worked out."

"That's why you said things went well, when you went down for Thanksgiving?"

"Oh, man. You can't understand what 'well' means either. I mean, after a year and a half of being away, there's been tension in the family, and this is the first time that everything clicked. I mean, that's the thing that really ticks—"

"You had a happy Thanksgiving dinner, basically."

"Yeah, and I've had a happy—I mean, I've had a happy quarter. I've had a happy everything. Everything finally clicks together completely for me. And then this has got to happen."

"This" referred to the burglary he had committed. Duncan spoke of it like some misfortune that had happened to him and had ruined his self-described happy times, rather than an intentional criminal act.

Duncan asked Prior whether the charges could be dropped if he made good on an agreement to pay the owner of Wasatch Touring for the damages. Prior said he couldn't give Duncan legal advice and all charging decisions were made by the county attorney.

"I just don't want this to end up turning around and being the final decision in LA to say, 'Okay, well, let's screw this guy,' because I got screwed here. That just wouldn't be—"

"I don't know that ... This screwup here, I don't know how it's going to come into play in the incident in California. I'm not down there. I haven't been able to confirm, even get ahold of Jackson to confirm, what specifically their district attorney's going to want to do ... They're the ones that are going to decide how far they're going to want to press the issue, charge-wise."

Duncan said, "I mean, I don't know if this makes any sense, and I don't know if you can even do this. Can I make a statement to the city that I'd be willing to do this, this, and that if we just let it go?"

"You could try it, but I don't know how far—"

"I'm just asking. I mean, I'm not real experienced with all this," said Duncan, playing down his recent encounters with law enforcement over the past few years.

"I don't know how that would even happen," said Prior. He explained that Duncan would be notified when to appear for his arraignment. "That's basically the reading of the official charges that you, Duncan Martinez, have been charged with business burglary, a third-degree felony; and felony theft, again a third-degree felony. How do you plead? Can you afford to hire an attorney?" Prior said after that would come a preliminary hearing, where a judge would decide whether there's enough evidence to proceed with the charges and hold a trial. "Whether it gets that far, Duncan, that's up to the legal wizards to decide."

"Well, I think that there would definitely be enough evidence, since I was procured inside the establishment." I chuckled at Duncan's self-awareness about the strength of the evidence incriminating him. It was probably the most sensible thing he'd said in the interview.

"Yeah, well, it's—I don't want to say open-and-shut case... It's a really good case from our point of view, I believe."

"Right."

Prior turned back to the murder in LA and what Duncan had told him up to this point. "Again, scribbling in my notes, we were chatting a little bit earlier. You and Nathan were drinking, deciding, watching TV, what a boneheaded maneuver this is with the kidnapping, might even have been some military deal. Then a couple weeks had passed, you talked about it again, after he initiated the conversation, thinking maybe it could be done better. Is that right?"

"Yeah. It was just like... you're watching anything on TV, and you see them do something that just makes no sense. And it's like, 'What are they thinking?'"

"How long after these conversations did the incident actually happen?"

"That's the question that I've tried to answer for LAPD accurately... The first conversation was about two months before, and the second one was probably about a month before."

"Okay, so again, about two months before these conversations had taken place, you all had gone out partying?" asked Prior.

"Actually it wasn't out partying. It was sitting around the house drinking beer and it was daytime."

"Did it occur at a house?"

"No, no, no. Oh, you mean when the actual killing occurred?"

"Yeah."

"The actual killing occurred up at the park when we were up there drinking. I thought you meant when that conversation—"

"No, I'm sorry... I'm trying to decipher all this. So you go to the park to party?"

"Uh-huh," said Duncan.

"Then what happened?"

"We were drinking beer. It was just the three of us. I mean, I can go into detail on what actually happened in the killing, but I'd prefer not to, just because it's something I don't like thinking about."

"Well, yeah, it's not a pleasant thing. Just because I'm basically curious at this point... Cops are basically curious by nature, Duncan, that's why I'm asking that."

"Well, there's a train tunnel there at the park we were at. We used to always go either in the train tunnel or on the far side of the train tunnel to drink beer, because gentlemen like yourself"—meaning cops—"tend not to go that far, and we can get away with drinking beer there without getting in trouble."

"Why didn't you drink at the apartment?"

"Change of scenery," Duncan said.

I thought his answer was more palatable than the likely truth, that the park was a better place to kill someone.

He continued: "I mean, to be honest, back then, all we did was drink. And, you know, it's fun. We'd go out and we'd be outside. You could be loud and you could be crazy."

"Wouldn't have your neighbors complaining about you," said Prior.

"Right. Nobody would care. It's like a rock park and it's kind of out in the middle of nowhere. You have to walk—well, you don't have to, but it's, like, a hundred times faster if you walk through the tunnel to get there. I think it's a quarter-mile tunnel."

"Okay. It's a train tunnel?"

"Yeah. It's got, like, fifteen feet on each side of the tracks."

"So if a train came through, you wouldn't have to run like hell to try to make it out?"

"No, it's actually really fun to be in there when trains come through, because it's a sudden rush of light. That train tunnel is pitch-black at nighttime. You can't see. I mean, you can put your hand up touching your nose and not have a clue it's there, visually."

"I understand."

"And when we went to leave, I was walking in front. The two of them were walking behind. I was the, you know, quote, unquote, Marine. I always did that ... We walked probably about a quarter of the way, if that far—"

"Did you guys have lights?"

"No, nothing. You walk and you use the tracks to guide ... You can tell by the slats underneath the rails when it turns, or as it turns, because it's got a real slight turn to it. You can keep yourself centered by that if you're paying attention to it. Most people that would do it would either walk on the tracks themselves or walk right next to it ... We used to always bring a knife up there, because all sorts of—like, it was a real bad place to hang out at night sometimes. At least there's a lot of rumors, but we've never really had any problems. But we used to always bring a knife up. It was always me or Nathan that carried it when groups of us would go, because we were the two military guys. It made sense to everybody."

"You and Nathan?"

"Yeah, and Nathan happened to have it that night. He was walking back behind with Ron ... And Nathan slipped. And Ron made a comment. And I don't have the foggiest idea what the comment was. I just remember him saying something. It was really out of character for Ron too, which, I don't know, it's just something that really bugs me, because that was so out of character for him. And Nathan jumped him."

"Was it a derogatory comment?"

"I mean, kinda. It wasn't something like 'Oh, you stupid moron.' It was something to the extent like 'Oh, Army man slips.' I mean, something like that. I mean, it wasn't even like he fell down. You just heard his foot slip. And the only reason I know it was him was by Ron saying something.

"Nathan jumped him. I heard them slam back and forth between the walls. I was carrying the remains of the twelve-pack or case that we'd brought. I set the thing down in front of me and turned around and took a couple steps toward it, stopped and took a couple steps back. I'm just completely in shock.

"Ron was screaming, 'Help me, Duncan.' Nathan was screaming, 'No.' I didn't know what to do. I didn't know how to react. God, I hate thinking about this. And the next thing that happened—I'm not really sure how much of a time interval there was. Now if my phrasing in some of this stuff seems awkward, it's because I've been questioned on every aspect of it a hundred—I'm just explaining—a hundred times. And I'm just so used to throwing in every tidbit that generally gets questioned."

"Sure. Go ahead," said Prior.

"I don't remember how long it was between when it started and when the next major thing that happened, happened. But all of a sudden there was light. Nathan lit a lighter. Now, that's probably the most devastating thing that has ever happened to me, was there being a sudden infusion of light. Because suddenly it was something that was real. It wasn't something that could be a practical joke that was playing on me. It couldn't be something that was, you know, whatever. It was—it was real.

"Nathan was sitting on top of Ron. At this point neither of them was talking to me really anymore, I don't think. He had the lighter in one hand. He had the knife in the other. He had Ron pinned down, his knees on his arms. Ron was just struggling, trying to get him off him. 'Why are you doing this to me? Why are you doing this to me? What have I ever done to you?'

"Nathan had the look like, I mean, like a superhero on his face. I mean, when you see Captain America in the comic books, he's always got the perfect 'I am God' look on his face."

"Okay," said Prior.

"Lighter went out. A few more blows. Lighter came back on. And Nathan was in the same position, but this time Ron was—it was noise, but it wasn't Ron. I don't know if it was voluntary at this point. I mean, Ron was pretty destroyed. Nathan was in the same position. Ron's arms were flailing around—not like a coherent person but more like a convulsive person. Lighter went out again. A few more strikes."

"Strikes with the knife?" asked Prior.

"I believe so."

"Okay."

"You know, that's one thing that really bugs me about watching movies now, is I remember that sound," Duncan said, apparently referring to the sound of Ron, grievously wounded and breathing his last breaths. "And I always expect, when I see something in a movie where somebody gets stabbed or something, to hear that sound... To be honest, and even though I think that every time I watch a movie, I really hope I never hear that again."

"Yeah."

"I mean, even if it's in a movie or something and somebody happens to get it right, I really don't want to ever hear that again."

"Yeah, I know," said Prior.

"I think he—Nathan got up. And you know what's weird, and I've explained this a couple times before, is I can remember kind of being able to see at this point. And there's no way you can see, because it's pitch-black... Because I have pictures of things, and I don't know if it was Nathan relighting the lighter... My brain having shut down somewhat, that I don't really remember. But Ron was making a lot of noise. I mean, there was, like, gurgling and stuff. You could hear movement. It was unbearable.

"I told Nathan, 'Dude, you've got to finish him off or something, because you can't leave him like that.' I don't remember exactly what I said right now, because I haven't talked about this in a really long time and it's really kind of tearing me up. And so he slit his throat. I remember seeing the sparks as the knife came off the body."

Listening to the tape, I was stunned when Duncan said he asked Nathan to finish Ron off. Duncan had alluded to this in his off-the-record King for a Day interview, but he had not said it so blatantly. And this time his statement was admissible evidence.

I knew immediately that it was a hugely damaging admission, regardless of his purported intent to have Nathan alleviate Ron's suffering.

As shocking as Duncan's statement was, it also seemed so typical of him. He had twisted his ruthless suggestion to Nathan to frame it as a merciful act, when in reality it had been the polar opposite. Duncan spoke of Ron like he had been an injured animal, such as a horse with a broken leg that needed to be put down, rather than a human being. It was hard to believe what I was hearing. It turned my stomach to imagine Ron's helpless final moments.

Prior must have felt shocked when he heard Duncan say it. Prior then asked him, "You made a statement to him: 'Hey, you can't leave him here like that'?"

"Or I think I might have even said, 'Hey, you better cut his throat and finish him off,' or something. I don't remember what I said." Whether or not Duncan actually used the words "cut his throat" or said something else along those lines, he was leaving no doubt that his intent had been to end Ron's life.

Duncan went on: "So, basically, we left. And he became Superman out of it. And I was a quivering mess...I saw everybody in tears and dejected about this, over the next weeks...I guess maybe that's where I got the strength. It was something to do to help everyone else out."

It was another "crutch" statement from Duncan, patting himself on the back for his heroic strength and selflessness amidst a tragedy he had initiated.

Duncan also wanted Prior to know how much he had grown since the murder: "The person I was before I left LA wasn't the best person. I told you about my situation. I drank a lot, you know. I wasn't a real model citizen. And of course, I've gone a long ways since then. I mean, I've been in school for two years...I've done well. I mean, I've gone from—"

"You've been establishing yourself?" asked Prior.

"Well, I'm trying. And it's hard. I've got a lot of years of stuff to pay back for," he said. The debts to which Duncan referred were evidently not moral but financial. "I have, you know, all these credit card debts and stuff that I got when I was back in that state of mind...I just happened to find out that one of them that I thought was three thousand dollars is one hundred forty dollars. You know, that was Friday afternoon. I mean, that's like, *Hey, I'm doing good. Something finally went my way.* And then this," meaning the burglary he had committed.

Prior said, "Some of the items that were taken from the store weren't...Emile mentioned to you that he wanted you to get him a mountain bike."

"Right."

"Why all the other stuff?"

"I went to grab a mountain bike. I look at the front door. The front door was locked, dead bolt on both sides. You can't get out of a store with a mountain bike like that. I mean, the window I went through, a mountain bike is not going to fit through there. And my only thought was I'd just grab a bunch of random things and, you know, hand them to him. And hopefully it would appease him. It wasn't even like it was that rational... I wasn't somebody thinking with all his wits. If I had, I wouldn't have been there. I mean, it just—that's how it happened. It was, you know, *Let's just make this guy happy and get this over with.* I mean, my biggest thought was going to bed. That was why I left the party. I wanted to go home and sleep, and get home at a reasonable hour, so I could sleep off my drunkenness and be up early to study."

"How much of a problem do you have—do you still have—with alcohol?" asked Prior.

"Well, you know, it seems like every time I've ever had any problems, it's been because of alcohol. But I really don't drink that much... It's peer pressure that kills me. And I'm usually not very susceptible to peer pressure... The times that I get really drunk, it's usually, 'Hey, man, there's a party up at the house,' 'There's a party here. Why don't you come?'"

"Uh-huh," acknowledged Prior.

"'Nah, I'm going to do this, this, and that,' or 'I'm going to go do this.' 'No, no, come on.' All of a sudden, I've got, like, five guys that I, you know, haven't seen in a while begging me to come out, you know?"

Prior asked Duncan to try to get him some more information to help him find Emile. "If you can do that, you got my name and phone number... Give me a call when you find that information out. Again, you're under no obligation to do so. Your statements you made tonight have been, you know, made willingly. And I've not coerced them out of you or anything... I'm curious to find out what the heck is going on."

"Right... I appreciate talking to you, actually," said Duncan.

"Sure."

"You know, I hope that if you have any questions, if I can be of any assistance, please let me know. Because I want to take care of this in the best way I can. I don't want to be, you know, stupid about this."

"Right, I understand," said Prior. He thanked Duncan for the call, and they hung up.

The recording wildly exceeded my expectations. I knew it was a crucial, devastating piece of evidence even before I had reached the end of the tape. After first betraying Ron, and then Nathan, it appeared now that Duncan had betrayed himself.

The main reason Duncan had managed to evade any criminal charges for Ron's murder, thus far, was the lack of admissible proof that he had planned it and had been present when Ron was killed. Duncan had recounted to Prior how he and Nathan came up with the idea beforehand, as well as what he saw and heard inside the tunnel. By doing so, especially on tape, Duncan himself had filled in the biggest evidentiary hole in a potential murder case against him.

Even worse for Duncan from a legal standpoint was his damning admission to Prior that he had urged Nathan to cut Ron's throat and "finish him off." Together with the other circumstantial evidence pointing to Duncan's involvement, I believed we had enough to charge him as soon as he admitted to being in the tunnel when Ron was stabbed. However, the admissible statement that he had asked Nathan to finish Ron off put us well over the threshold to charge him. It made him an active participant in Ron's death, regardless of how he tried to couch it as a compassionate act. The law doesn't allow for someone to cut a person's throat and hasten their death just to put them out of their misery. With what was on the tape, there was no doubt in my mind that David Conn would ultimately charge Duncan, equally with Nathan, for Ron's murder.

I noticed several characteristics in Duncan's demeanor with Prior that reminded me of his dealings with me and Garcia as well as with others we had interviewed who knew him.

Perhaps Duncan's most recognizable pattern of behavior was his repeated "woe is me" efforts to elicit sympathy. For instance, the way he prefaced any discussion of Ron's murder by claiming that he didn't like to talk about it. I knew that Duncan actually had told many, many people about the murder during his travels, conversations that he had initiated, not them.

Another example was his emphasizing how well things had been going in his life until "this happened," the burglary. Duncan had made it sound as if breaking into a store was something out of his control that was dragging his life down unfairly, instead of a crime that he had decided to commit.

Playing up his trauma while at the same time minimizing his responsibility served Duncan's ultimate goal: to show himself in the best possible light, with the least possible criminal exposure.

Duncan's chummy tone with Prior also felt strikingly familiar. I could never forget his comment to me and Garcia that we would be a lot of fun to hang out with, if only we had met under different circumstances. I thought Duncan had talked to Prior more like he was a friend or a therapist than a police detective investigating him for a crime. He had overshared, confiding in Prior about his drinking, his choice of friends, and other impertinent topics. I sensed Duncan had been trying to buddy up to Prior, much as I'd seen him do with other authority figures in a position to affect his future. This had included me and Garcia, and later on, his university's fraternity advisor, Doug Christiansen.

As Duncan had done with us, he had presented himself to Prior as eager to help. This played into the same buddy-buddy dynamic, in which Duncan attempted to foster a good rapport and then leverage it to benefit himself. A prime example was Duncan's questioning of Prior about whether the burglary charge could be dropped if he reached a settlement with the store's owner. I found it astonishing that Duncan believed he could enlist Prior's help in diverting his burglary case away from the criminal justice system and resolving it instead as a private matter.

Moreover, Duncan appeared intent on trying to sweet-talk his way out of trouble from the beginning. Not many people in the act of being arrested say right away that they want to speak to a detective, as Duncan had.

I was not impressed with Duncan's finger-pointing, casting blame for his misdeeds on anyone and anything but himself. The burglary wasn't his fault; it was Emile's fault for making him do it. In addition to being Emile's fault, it was alcohol's fault, because according to Duncan, he never would have done it if he were sober. I didn't buy the excuses.

In my estimation, everything Duncan had said to Prior was part of his effort to get out of trouble and emerge from the situation unscathed. The ease with which Duncan deployed his various conversational tactics showed just how manipulative he was.

Immediately after I finished listening to the tape, I took the mini-cassette Prior had sent me and walked it over to SID. I requested several copies of the tape be made, knowing I would be taking a few to the DA's Office. I also asked that the original mini-cassette be placed in the crime lab's safe to ensure its preservation.

As soon as the copies were made, I delivered one to David Conn, who said he would review it. It was up to him to look at the entirety of the case and decide how he wanted to proceed. Would he file a murder charge against Duncan, or would he seek a grand jury indictment, as in Nathan's case? Either way, I felt very confident that Conn would be on board with prosecuting Duncan with what was on the tape.

Conn was still weighing how to proceed about two months later, in early March, when I next heard from Prior. He informed me that Duncan had pled guilty on his burglary case. The plea was to a third-degree felony burglary charge.

Duncan was given a prison sentence of one to five years, but that sentence was suspended by the judge. Instead, he was placed on probation and ordered to pay a fine.

Duncan had just racked up his second felony conviction in two years: first for passport fraud and now for burglary. Yet he had received no jail time for either one.

Was a third felony conviction, for the murder of Ron Baker, on the horizon?

If so, that conviction would certainly not carry a no-jail-time sentence for Duncan.

CHAPTER 22

DEPUTY D.A. MARCIA CLARK
(May 13 to June 12, 1994)

IN SPRING 1994, RESPONSIBILITY for prosecuting the Baker case changed hands yet again.

Earlier that year, the jury in the murder trial of Lyle and Erik Menendez came back deadlocked after a five-month trial. The DA's Office announced its intention to retry the brothers for the premeditated murders of their parents in the family's Beverly Hills mansion.

Head Deputy DA David Conn was tapped to be the lead prosecutor for the retrial. Knowing his efforts to prepare and retry the Menendez case would consume all his time, Conn had to hand off his other pending cases.

Conn chose a colleague in the Special Trials unit to assume the prosecution duties in the Baker case: Marcia Clark. Clark was regarded as an excellent trial lawyer, having been mentored by Harvey Giss, a legendary prosecutor in the DA's Office.

I'd worked with Clark before and been impressed by her dedication, diligence, and the amount of time she put into her cases. During her trials, she often worked late into the evenings, always making the extra effort to meet the night before with the next day's witnesses.

Shortly after Clark took the reins, I met with her in her office. Among the staidly decorated, cluttered offices of her Special Trials unit colleagues, Clark's office stood out for one reason: On one wall was an enormous framed poster of The Doors' Jim Morrison.

I briefed Clark on the entirety of the Ron Baker murder investigation and where things stood. This included the status of Nathan Blalock's pending trial and the latest twists in the bizarre saga of Duncan Martinez. Like me, Clark was galled at Duncan using Ron's murder to try to get out of a burglary he had committed.

Clark told me she thought she would take the evidence against Duncan to a grand jury. In most ways, her presentation would replicate the case that her onetime colleague Ernie Norris had made to a grand jury with respect to Nathan. The major difference would be her addition of the statements Duncan had made to Salt Lake City detective Jim Prior.

Clark made it clear that she believed Duncan was just as culpable for Ron's murder as Nathan, and that both should be charged and punished equally. Her position on that contrasted with Norris's but was aligned with David Conn's. Clark and Conn both felt that in multi-defendant cases, Norris relied too often on offering one defendant a light sentence in exchange for testifying against others, even when it was unnecessary to prove the case. As for me, I felt Duncan deserved some benefit for his earlier cooperation. Despite my disdain for him, I believed his assistance should count for something. But all those decisions would be made by the DA's Office at a later time, closer to trial.

Clark also picked up on one other thing. The original indictment of Nathan obtained by Norris alleged only one special circumstance, "lying in wait." Clark felt a second special circumstance, "murder for financial gain," applied and should be alleged as well. That way, Clark explained, should a jury be undecided on one, there was a backup allegation it could opt to find true. A jury finding either of the special circumstances true would mean the difference between a defendant never being allowed parole and that same defendant being eligible for parole in just over twenty years.

In light of her belief in their equal culpability, and her decision to add a second special-circumstance allegation, Clark planned not only to present to a grand jury the case against Duncan but also to re-indict Nathan, adding the second allegation against him.

Clark said she would begin her review of the case files immediately in preparation for the new grand jury hearing. She also said there were two things she wanted to do, outside the office setting, prior to the hearing.

First, she wanted to meet with Ron Baker's parents, both for introduction purposes and to let them know her thoughts on the case as it moved forward.

Second, she wanted to visit the crime scene and personally venture into the train tunnel. Clark said she needed to see it in order to visualize it clearly. This was the only way she would be able to describe the location to the grand jury members and to question the crime scene detective who would testify. I knew the visceral experience of being inside the pitch-black tunnel would also benefit her in knowing the emotions Ron must have endured on that terrible night.

I made an appointment with the Baker family for Friday afternoon, May 13. Clark told me she'd like to go up to the tunnel after our visit with the family. She had the evening open but definitely wanted to get there before sunset. She said she wanted the experience of being in the tunnel, but after reading about it in the case file, she preferred not to do it at night.

When we arrived for the meeting, Ron's sister, Patty, was also there. Clark explained she would be returning the case to a grand jury, this time for an indictment of Duncan. The Bakers were understandably thrilled. Clark also told the family of the additional special-circumstance allegation she would apply to both young men, the allegation of "murder for financial gain," which would be bolstered by Mr. Baker's testimony of receiving the ransom calls. Clark hoped to present the case in the next month or so, she explained, but until then, and until Duncan was indicted and taken into custody, it was essential they keep this information to themselves. Duncan had already demonstrated that he was a flight risk. We couldn't risk him finding out about his imminent arrest and attempting to flee again.

I was impressed with Clark's consideration of Ron Baker's family. She fully explained her strategy moving forward and freely answered any questions the family put to her. Later, Patty Baker told me she and her parents marveled at Clark's fire and determination. Patty especially appreciated when Clark told her she knew how Patty must feel, as Ron's sister, and promised she would make sure Duncan was prosecuted as well as Nathan. Patty said she would never forget that.

From the Baker home we drove to Chatsworth Park. Clark and I trekked up the hill to the tunnel entrance where the three roommates drank together before their fateful walk inside. I had brought along the murder book, which contained all the crime scene photos. The photos would help Clark establish where and how it all had happened, from the locations of evidence items to where the fight had started and, finally, where Ron's body had been left.

I could tell Clark was charged up when we walked into the mouth of the tunnel. Tentatively, we moved deeper inside, our path illuminated only by my flashlight.

Eventually we reached the area where Ron's murder had occurred. We could no longer see any light from the tunnel entrance we had walked in from. Without warning, I turned off my flashlight. Clark yelled something like "Holy shit!" although, knowing her, it may have been even more expressive than that. Whatever expletive she uttered, it was clear she got the full effect of what the tunnel would have been like on the night of the summer solstice in 1990. As we made our way out of the tunnel, she continued to remark on the eeriness of the place, and how it must have felt to be attacked in that pitch-black setting.

Clark began her grand jury presentation on May 18. She relied on the same witnesses Norris had in the original grand jury hearing, a year before. The only new witness was Detective Prior, who testified to the new information Clark and I felt certain would clear the threshold for the panel to return an indictment against Duncan.

Prior recounted for the grand jury Duncan's hijinks involving the Utah burglary and his attempts to shift blame for it. His testimony placed Duncan in the park with admissible evidence for the first time. He also detailed Duncan's admission that he had told Nathan to finish Ron off.

The following day, the grand jury returned indictments for both Nathan and Duncan for first-degree murder, including the two special-circumstance allegations, "lying in wait" and "murder for financial gain," that Clark had sought.

Based on the indictments, an arrest warrant was issued for Duncan. Because he was located out of state and would need to be extradited to California, some additional procedural hurdles had to be cleared before the warrant could be served. An extradition package with the necessary paperwork was assembled by the DA's Office. I considered it highly unlikely that Duncan, upon his arrest, would waive extradition and voluntarily return to California.

Clark and I made plans to travel to Utah the following week. Our top priority would be to meet Duncan at his probation office and take him into custody. While in Utah, we also wanted to conduct some additional interviews regarding Duncan's time there.

Clark and I flew to Salt Lake City on Wednesday, June 1. After checking into our hotel, we decided to drive to Park City for dinner. I had gotten to know the small ski resort town pretty well by then, having traveled there several times over the life of the case.

Following dinner and a few drinks, we stopped on a whim in downtown Salt Lake City to wander around Temple Square. We took in the beautiful architecture of the Salt Lake Temple, surrounded by its landscaped grounds. The irrigation sprinklers happened to be on, spraying water across the grass and onto the walkways we strolled along. Clark, who had a background in dance, did a playful rendition of "Singin' in the Rain," feigning a tap-dancing routine through the water drops hitting the pavement. The spontaneous moment was a refreshing contrast to the seriousness of the matters at hand.

It was getting late and time to call it a night. We had a long day ahead of us, beginning with our 10 a.m. appointment at the probation office. The next morning, absent any complications, Duncan would learn he was being prosecuted for his onetime best friend's murder. It had been almost four years in the making.

We arrived at the office of Duncan's probation officer in advance of the appointed time. The probation officer had instructed Duncan to be there at ten but had told him nothing about the LA authorities who would be there.

Duncan arrived on time and was escorted into the office. He looked surprised to see me and a woman he did not know.

Without any fanfare, I informed Duncan he was under arrest on the authority of a warrant from Los Angeles County. I introduced him to Marcia Clark. The three of us were led to an interview room that had been reserved by the probation officer, where Clark and I could speak with Duncan.

A tape recorder was already running. I explained to Duncan that a grand jury had indicted him in Ron's death, and as a result, a warrant had been issued. I told him that I wanted to run down for him and Clark the chronology of everything that had happened, and that Clark wanted to hear his side of the story. I said because he was officially in custody, I needed to advise him of his rights first. After I read Duncan his rights and confirmed he understood them, I asked him, "Do you want to talk to us?"

"What's the charge?" he asked.

"It's murder," I said.

"I think I should have an attorney."

"That's up to you."

Duncan broke down and began to cry, something he would continue to do on and off throughout the interview. He sobbed for about thirty seconds, with no words exchanged, until he was able to regain his composure. "Relax," he told himself aloud. Except for some deep breaths, he was silent another ten seconds. Then he said, "Okay. I don't know what I should do. You know, I've always been completely open with you and I'd like to talk to you. I don't know if I should." Again he broke down. He said nothing for another fifteen seconds but made some histrionic noises that sounded like he was stifling an urge to scream.

As this continued, I finally said, "That's up to you, Duncan. Basically, like I said, what I want to do first, I want to go through some things and explain some things." I knew that Duncan had not "always been completely open" with us, as he had claimed. But I let that remark slide.

"Okay, well, why don't we do that," he agreed.

"Okay. Let me explain another thing ... We'll start off. If you want to waive your rights, that's completely up to you. If you don't want to, if you want to talk with an attorney, that's up to you ... If at any point during the interview you decide you want an attorney, you say, 'I want an attorney now.'"

"Let's do that."

"Is that what you want to do?"

"Yeah, that's fine."

"You sure?"

"Uh-huh," he affirmed.

"Okay," I said. I felt I was on relatively solid ground, with respect to Miranda, to proceed with the interview. After Duncan's initial statement that he thought he wanted an attorney, he had indicated his openness to continue talking without one. I'd had similar situations in other cases, in which the courts had deemed a suspect's statements admissible and not a violation of their rights.

"It's probably going to take me a minute to cope," he said.

Only then did I begin to explain to Duncan, "I'm not going to be asking you really any questions. I just want to go through some stuff, partly for your benefit, partly for my benefit, and partly for Marcia's benefit. The first interview we had with you, that first interview when you were in Salt Lake with Jim Barnes and Frank and me, right in that interview, we told you that nothing you told us in that interview could be used against you."

"Right... But isn't that being used against me already? I mean, isn't it?" He still sounded on the verge of tears.

I told Duncan that we hadn't said yet what was being used. I kept my tone matter-of-fact.

"I'm sorry... I'm just really freaked right now."

"That's okay," I said. "Then, any subsequent cooperation that you gave us in getting statements from Nathan Blalock could not be used against you. Remember that, okay? And any other cooperation you gave us, like the time you went out and bought the knife, things like that, any of that cannot be used against you."

"Right."

"That was the agreement, right? Okay. However, you were also told that you could be prosecuted if other evidence came up that had nothing to do with what you told us when you were cooperating with us.

Correct?" The point I was making was that Duncan had never been promised or given formal immunity.

"I don't remember that, but I believe you."

"Okay. All right... Let me ask you this. At one point there was a possibility of a plea agreement, where if you were ever used to testify against Nathan, you may have been allowed to plead to a voluntary manslaughter. You remember that? And then later I told you that the DA's Office didn't want to do that."

"I thought when you told me that, that you said that they didn't want to do that unless they needed me to testify."

"Right... In other words—"

"So I take it he pled guilty," said Duncan, referring to Nathan.

"No."

"Okay."

"No. I think what I told you is that they opted not to use you as a witness."

"Oh. I didn't understand it that way. That's all right... I'm sorry. It's going to take me a while."

"Okay. I understand. All right," I said.

Again Duncan struggled to control his emotions, which seemed to be a mix of anger and frustration. He made more histrionic noises and stomped his feet, as if trying to keep a tantrum at bay. "I was so happy this morning..." he said, but then he melted down in tears.

I waited for him to regain his composure, then forged ahead. I reminded him of the incident in December 1992, when he ended up speaking to Doug Christiansen, the fraternity advisor. I asked him if he remembered that.

"Mm-hmm," he affirmed.

"And that came to my attention. And we had a phone conversation shortly thereafter, where I told you, 'Duncan, talking to people independent of us, it's something that can be used against you.' I told you then."

"I don't remember that, but again, I trust you."

"No, I told you that. We spoke," I said.

"What I remember is that you advised me not to because it might be a problem. I don't remember you saying that it could be used against me. It's all right."

"All right. Okay. After that, after I told you that, you subsequently spoke to Jim Prior about it, here in Utah. Right?"

"Mm-hmm," said Duncan.

"First in a face-to-face conversation and then later in a telephone conversation."

Duncan nodded yes. He seemed to grasp the gravity of what he had done by talking about Ron's murder to Prior, and that it was the reason why he was now being charged.

Clark wanted him to acknowledge verbally his conversations with Prior. Speaking up for the first time, she said, "Duncan, I see you nodding your head up and down. Do you remember that?"

"Oh, I remember talking to him, all right," he answered, his tone mildly condescending.

I ignored his demeanor. "You laid out some of the stuff about the case," I said. "Do you understand where I'm coming from now?"

"Uh-huh."

"And that was all outside of any kind of agreement that we had, Duncan. I explained that. The Christiansen thing was outside the agreement as well. And even after—I explained that."

"I didn't understand it that way and it's my fault for not understanding it that way. But go ahead."

"That's the scenario of what's happened. I think you see exactly what has happened over the last few years and how it's gotten to the point it's gotten to now. This was all submitted to the grand jury, and they returned the indictment."

"Okay."

"And that's it. That's the deal."

"I just want to talk to my mom," Duncan said.

I told him he could, in a little bit.

Duncan's emotions again overcame him. Seemingly to himself, he blurted out, "Ahhhh! Why couldn't this happen a week ago? Why? Why did you have to wait until I let everything down? God!" Perhaps realizing it sounded like he was placing blame on us personally, he quickly clarified to me and Clark, "I'm not coming down on you."

"I know," I told him. Duncan's anger genuinely seemed directed inward, not at us.

"It's just at myself. I let myself down," he said, crying.

"It's been something that's been eating at you for what, three years now?" I asked.

"Well, it's been eating at me since the night. But I've been letting myself get a little happier and a little happier in the last couple years. I always told myself, 'Don't let yourself get completely happy, because that's when everything is going to come down.' And it finally did. And I was right... It drives me nuts. I got a great apartment. I've got a great girlfriend. I'm doing great in school. Everything is going really well in my life. I screwed up once in the past year, and you know, I think that's because everybody kept pointing a finger at me, telling me I was a bad guy. I just—I let myself get happy. How could I do that?" He resumed crying, then said, "I'm sorry. You guys don't need to hear me go off like this."

"No, no, it's understandable," I said.

"I just don't understand. I tried so hard to do everything I could with this, and I've been hurt by this for so long, and now..." He had trailed off. "So what level murder am I being charged with? What degree?"

"Charge is first degree and special circumstances," said Clark.

"Does Barnes know about this at all?" asked Duncan, referring to Jim Barnes, his onetime criminal defense lawyer.

I said no.

"I just thought when I was supposed to be arrested, it was supposed to go through his office or something," he said.

"No. I think that relationship seemed to have ended a long time ago. I've talked to him several times over the years... He's never said anything that he had any conversation with you. I've told him several times that we were going to come up and see you, or you were coming down, and he never questioned anything... But do you want an attorney? It's up to you, Duncan."

Clark said, "Duncan, you can stop talking whenever you want. Question is, do you want to stop?"

"Are you guys trying to get me to talk to screw me over? Or are you trying to get me to talk for some other reason? I mean, honestly. I mean—"

"Well, all I can tell you—" I started to say.

"I've always been open with you. Be open with me, please."

"No, I'm being honest with you... You're in custody and we've already told you. Things you say can be used against you in court."

"Okay, then I should get an attorney," said Duncan.

"I'm not saying everything will be... It depends on what's said. And the attorney thing is completely up to you. I'm not going to sit here and tell you, 'Don't get an attorney,' if that's what you want to do. And I think Marcia would agree with me on that."

"Well, I don't have a problem. I guess I should get an attorney. I don't know what I should do. I don't know what to do." He broke down in tears again. Between sobs, he said, "I just want to cry. I want to call my mom so my mom can tell me what to do. Because I don't know. Okay? Can I call her?"

I told Duncan that if he wanted to call his mother, we would let him.

"I mean, I just—I need somebody to tell me what to do, right now, because I can't..." He lost his composure once more.

I told Duncan I needed to handcuff him in order to take him to a phone. I asked him to stand up and turn around. He cried and whimpered as I cuffed his wrists behind his back.

"And as far as getting somebody up to my house?" he asked. "Can—"

I told him we would take care of that and notify his girlfriend of his arrest.

"Okay, because I've got to talk to her too, or have her know." He resumed crying. "It's so hard," he said between sobs.

Since the formal interview was over, I turned the tape recorder off. I escorted Duncan to a phone the probation officer said he could use to call his mother.

Mrs. Martinez answered, but Duncan was too emotional to speak with her. I took the phone from him and explained to her what was happening, that Duncan had made statements to some people about the case and a warrant had been issued for his arrest. While I was speaking with Mrs. Martinez, Duncan began talking to himself. He was rambling, but I heard him say, "I knew I wasn't supposed to talk to anyone, but I thought it was okay."

Duncan eventually managed to compose himself enough to speak with his mother.

After the call, Duncan asked if he could write a note to his girlfriend, Stephanie Glezos. I agreed and said I would deliver it, but only after I read the note in his presence, I told him. Whatever Duncan wrote to his girlfriend was not privileged. I also wanted to ensure he was not instructing her not to discuss with me or Clark what he had told her about Ron's murder.

We returned to the interview room. Duncan began writing on a small notepad he had on him. When he ran out of notepad pages, he switched to blank pages from a pocket-sized daily planner. In the end, his letter ran twenty-six pages long. Duncan handed it to me and I read it in front of him. He also gave me an earring he was wearing that he asked me to give to Stephanie, which I said I would do.

Duncan devoted much of the letter to professing his feelings for Stephanie, along with asking her to do an array of chores he needed help with. These tasks included talking with people to whom he owed money, what to do about his apartment lease, and contacting his professors about his grades. Duncan also revealed in the letter his state of mind at this moment of intense upheaval in his life. Most striking of all, however, was the self-centered way Duncan framed his current predicament as something unfair that had happened to him and that he deserved pity for, rather than the consequence of his own extremely poor decisions and voluntary actions.

I found one part of Duncan's letter especially ironic, and frankly disgusting. Duncan had written to his girlfriend, "Why, why are they doing this to me, what did I ever do that was so bad that they have to do this to me? WHY ARE they doing this to YOU!!" Whether inadvertently or subconsciously, Duncan had quoted nearly verbatim the words he had said Ron Baker yelled in the tunnel when Nathan was stabbing him: "Why are you doing this to me? What did I ever do to deserve this?" It was sickening to me that Duncan had used such similar phrasing about his self-inflicted situation.

Before we left the probation office, Jim Barnes, Duncan's attorney, called. I presumed Barnes had been notified by Mrs. Martinez. I explained the indictment to him and said that I was there with Deputy DA Marcia Clark. Barnes asked to speak with his client. Barnes then advised Duncan not to speak to me or Clark.

Duncan was subsequently booked into the Salt Lake County Jail on a "fugitive from justice" charge, with the underlying authority being the murder indictment from Los Angeles County. Whether Duncan would voluntarily waive his extradition to California or fight the case in court to prevent his return remained to be seen. In my experience, extradition challenges were far more likely to slow the process than actually succeed, but that didn't mean Duncan wouldn't try to delay the inevitable.

Clark and I drove to Duncan's apartment, where he had told us his girlfriend, Stephanie, would be. We wanted to ask her what Duncan had told her about the murder and his role in it. Anything he had said to her was outside of the King for a Day agreement and potentially could be used against him.

Stephanie was a petite white woman and a fellow student of Duncan's at the University of Utah. When Clark and I arrived, she appeared to have been crying. It was obvious someone, perhaps Duncan, had called her with the news. Also there at the apartment was Jim Purpura, Duncan's former roommate. Jim stayed outside, on a back patio, while we spoke with her.

Stephanie remained emotional throughout the interview, which I tape-recorded, as was customary.

It was completely understandable to me why she would be upset. Her boyfriend had just been arrested, seemingly out of the blue.

"Why has he been arrested?" Stephanie asked me.

"There was a warrant issued for his arrest."

"Why?"

"For murder."

"Why?" she repeated.

"Well, I'm not going to give you all the details of the case," I said.

"He said that he was supposed to be waiting to see if Nathan was going to plead guilty or not … Why did they just suddenly decide to put out a warrant and arrest him?"

"Some new evidence came up, which we did not have a couple years ago … As far as what happened, we need to hear from you what he's told you."

"I don't know what happened."

"What has he told you?"

"I don't know what happened."

"Okay, but that's not what I'm asking you. What has he told you about what happened?"

"Nothing."

"He never told you one thing?" She obviously was lying. "How did you know about Nathan?" I asked.

Stephanie realized she was caught and didn't answer my question. "I really don't want to do this," she said. She asked if she could get in trouble if she refused to say anything.

"You could. I'm not asking you to say anything other than what the truth is."

"Well, I don't know what the truth is because I wasn't there."

"Okay. What were you told? Whether it's the truth or not."

"I can't tell you what I was told because I can't tell this story. Because I don't know everything that happened."

"I'm not asking you to tell me every single thing. I don't think anybody that we've talked to, Stephanie, has told us every single thing, because they don't know the whole story either." I explained that Duncan had already told us about the murder, plus given us the names of several people he talked with about it, so we could verify his account.

"Well, he just called me and told me not to tell you anything," she said.

"Oh, he did? Why is that?" I asked.

"Because when the story goes along, it gets mixed up. And so whatever I tell you, it's not necessarily what he said to me."

"Well, I'm asking you the way you recall it. What you recall." I asked how long she had been Duncan's girlfriend and known him.

She said since January, which was about six months.

"So, what he's told you is fairly recent," I said. "And it's something that's a little bit out of the ordinary. I know he's talked to you about it."

"Look, I just found out that my boyfriend is on trial for murder. Can I please just go get a hug from my friend?" she pleaded. She was referring to Jim, outside on the patio.

"Do you want Jim to come in? I don't want you asking advice from Jim. Jim's not the person to be asking advice from," I said. I explained that Jim was one of the other people we had interviewed who had recounted what Duncan had told him.

"I couldn't tell you the story that Duncan told me because he's told me different things at different times. I can't put them all together for you." She seemed on the verge of tears.

"Well, try your best."

"No," she answered defiantly.

"Why?"

"Because I don't want to do this right now."

It was obvious Stephanie had relevant information but was holding back. I felt a bit frustrated with her, but also frustrated with myself, because I thought I wasn't doing a good job interviewing her.

Clark, also a trained interrogator, asserted herself to break the impasse. She said, "So Duncan has told you one thing at one time and different things at other times?"

"It's not been different things. It's just been different parts," answered Stephanie.

"Did he tell you who the fellow was that got killed?" asked Clark.

"Yes."

"Did you know it was his roommate?"

"It was his best friend," said Stephanie. I noticed she was less defensive and slightly more open with Clark than with me.

"Right," said Clark. "Did he tell you who he did it with?"

"He didn't do anything," Stephanie insisted.

"Did he tell you who he was at the park with?" I asked.

"Yes."

"Okay. And that's the man you already mentioned, Nathan. Correct?"

"Yes."

"Did he tell you what the plan was, Stephanie?" asked Clark.

"There was no plan... He didn't have a plan. He didn't plan on doing anything."

"He didn't tell you anything about talking to Nathan about a kidnapping for ransom?"

"He told me about joking around with his friends," said Stephanie. The phone in the apartment began ringing. "May I answer the phone?" she asked.

I said it was up to her.

Stephanie picked up. We could only hear her side of the conversation, a series of yes and no answers. "It's not happening to me, it's happening to you," she said into the phone, before she hung up. I suspected it was Duncan who had called, but I said nothing.

Clark continued to lead the questioning. She asked Stephanie, "He said he was joking around with Nathan about being able to do a kidnapping for ransom? Do you remember that?"

"Vaguely, something like that. I don't know exactly what he said... I'm sorry."

"That's not the truth," I said. "Did he tell you who made the phone call? The ransom call?"

"I don't remember exactly what he told me."

"What did Duncan just tell you on the phone now?"

"That he missed me. That he was sorry that he was doing this to me—"

"Did you tell him that we were here?" asked Clark.

"—and if you'd given me a letter yet," she said. I had not yet given her Duncan's letter.

"You told him that we were sitting with you now?" asked Clark.

"I just said you were here. You heard everything I said."

"Did he ask if we were asking questions?" I said.

Stephanie started to answer but was interrupted by Jim Purpura coming back inside from the patio. Jim had a cordless phone in his hand. He held it out to Stephanie and said, "Steph, Duncan wants to talk to you." He handed her the phone. Then Jim announced, "Duncan would prefer Stephanie not talk to you, until he's advised by his lawyer."

"That's not up to Duncan," I told Jim.

"Well, that's up to Stephanie, isn't it?" he answered.

Clark and I said it was.

"Okay," said Jim. "Well, I'm sure she'll feel the same way."

Stephanie ignored us and carried on talking with Duncan.

Knowing we had gotten all we were going to get, I told Stephanie, "Tell him we're leaving, so you don't have to worry about us anymore. As a matter of fact, he can call you back in a couple of minutes and you guys can talk as long as you want."

Stephanie told Duncan we were leaving and asked me if I had his letter. I handed it to her along with the earring he had asked me to give her, before Clark and I left.

The next morning, we met with another University of Utah student, Melissa Bean. I had seen Melissa's name in the memo produced by Doug Christiansen regarding Duncan's fraternity fiasco. Christiansen had written that Duncan was "too free" in sharing information about Ron's murder with, among other people, "Melissa Bean, president of Pi Beta Phi Sorority."

Melissa's mother, Mary Louise Bean, had accompanied her to the interview. Clark and I had no issue with allowing Mrs. Bean to sit in.

Melissa, in contrast to Stephanie, was cooperative and not protective of Duncan. Her manner was friendly, and she had a self-deprecating sense of humor. I liked her immediately. "It's good to know that I have such good luck in my past dating partners," she joked as we began the interview.

"Oh, did you date Duncan?" I asked. Christiansen hadn't mentioned that in his memo.

"Oh, yeah...I dated him. Got him thrown out of his fraternity. I mean, it was a trauma year for me. He ruined a lot of my life."

I explained that Duncan had been arrested on a warrant from Los Angeles, charging him with murder, and was in custody. "I don't want to give you a lot of particulars about the case, because I don't want that to influence anything you tell us. I want to hear what he told you."

Melissa said she had heard some things from Duncan, but also from other people, secondhand. "So I've heard kind of different versions and information through the years...They're very different stories. One implicates him, one doesn't," she explained.

"Okay. And obviously his is the most beneficial from his point of view, right?"

"Right. Actually, as people started to find out information about him—that he wasn't quite who he was saying, and that there was something going on in California—he started telling different things, or adding information, I guess, to make him sound a lot like a victim. He had originally said that he had witnessed a murder and that he had left Los Angeles."

"When did you first meet Duncan?" I asked.

"Fall of '92. He was a pledge with the Phi Delta Theta fraternity, where I spent a lot of time... That's how I met him. He was obviously very recognizable... He had a pierced nipple that he could light your cigarette with."

"Well, he's a charmer," opined Clark.

Melissa explained: "He'd put a safety pin through it and matches at either end of the safety pin, light those, and light cigarettes. It was pretty impressive. He was definitely a wild rebel man... someone I should have brought home to Mom and Dad."

"I would have loved to have met him," Melissa's mom said.

"We could probably arrange that if you still want to," I joked.

Mrs. Bean said no thanks.

Melissa told us she really started getting to know Duncan at the end of fall quarter. "I would say November, December. He had flown down to Los Angeles at one point during that fall to meet with people, I believe from the Los Angeles Police Department."

"Did he tell you that when he went down there or later on?" I asked.

"He told me when he went down. It was pretty hard to keep any kind of secret in the fraternity house because there was one main phone. So anytime a call came through, people knew about it... So I knew something was going on."

Melissa continued: "He had told me that he had witnessed a murder in Los Angeles. That it was down by the train tracks and that they had all been drunk. It sounded to me as if it was something that had gotten out of hand that he had witnessed. He told me that he had left town to go to Boston because he was in such shock of seeing a friend murdered. Which to me was a little bit fishy, but yeah, he's a great storyteller."

Melissa recalled talking to some fraternity members and telling them, "'Oh, it's really funny. I started seeing someone and he's involved in this murder case in LA.' Which, of course, they were very concerned about, and they had him thrown out of the fraternity, which did not endear me to Duncan... They were very concerned about having someone who may have legal problems, who might bring a certain amount of, I don't know, unsafety to the house... To tell you the truth, I felt awful about it. I thought, *This is a guy trying to turn his life around. I've done a terrible thing.* I felt really bad about that. We kept in touch, and he was very nice about what had happened." By midwinter, Duncan moved out of the fraternity house, she recalled.

Clark asked Melissa why it was believed that Duncan had legal problems if he was just a witness to a murder.

"Because he was flying down, back and forth. I don't think people believed what he was saying, that he had just witnessed a murder. People knew that he was already serving probation for living under a fake alias. People had heard stories about how he had gotten illegal plane tickets to come out here from Boston... People were starting to wonder about the truth to the story. I think a lot of people knew that Duncan was a bullshitter, and that he would sell you down the river if he thought that it was going to get him somewhere."

Melissa said Duncan still came by the fraternity house to hang out, even after he moved out. "He had been really well-liked. I always liken it to kind of a Charles Manson, David Koresh following that he had. And so he'd come by and party with the boys, and I'd go by with my guy friends who were older, and we'd see Duncan and try and be cordial. I know that one night he was telling us these stories about he had been this football star back home, but his parents couldn't know that he was playing football. So although he was on the front page of the paper, and he had done this, his parents never knew."

I asked whether the name she knew him by was Duncan Martinez.

"Doofus O'Reilly was his nom de plume up at the university," she told us. "That's what he loved to go by. He signed everything 'Doofus O'Reilly.' I know that he went as Jake, I guess, back east. But everyone knew that his name was Duncan Martinez. He hated being called Duncan, because I guess that's his father's real name, so he didn't like being called that. So he had people call him Doofus, which was very appropriate."

Clark asked Melissa if Duncan told her any more specifics about the case when she was friendly with him back in November 1992.

Melissa said that at one point later, around Christmas or January, she asked Duncan what had really happened. "He had said that there had been a kidnapping with a roommate from college. That there were three of them that were friends, and he and another friend had gotten drunk one night. And just, I guess in this drunken moment of epiphany, decided to kidnap their other roommate and hold them hostage for ransom from their father, who was supposedly very wealthy. What he told me was that they had gone down to the train tracks and gotten drunk, and it had gotten out of hand. And his—the other friend—had killed this boy while he watched it."

"So those are the two variations?" I asked.

"Right. I originally heard just that he had witnessed a murder. I later heard that it was a planned kidnapping, that they were going to try—"

"And this is from Duncan you heard this?"

"From Duncan. He explained that it was kind of a drunk, spur-of-the-moment 'Let's do this. This will be crazy. We'll get some money. Why don't we just kidnap him?' He rests very heavily on the fact that he was drunk and wasn't necessarily thinking."

"Did he tell you that they took him to the park for that reason, in order to kidnap him for ransom?" asked Clark.

"I never heard a park. All I knew was that it happened at the train tracks...in LA. That's all that I knew."

"Did he tell you how he knew this person? Or who he was?"

"It's been a while, but I thought that they had all been friends. I can't remember, but I'm thinking they had gone to high school together, or they had known each other for a while...That they were friends and this was not necessarily a malicious, getting-back-at-someone sort of thing."

"They were all acquaintances—you definitely remember Duncan telling you that?" I asked.

"Oh, yes. They all knew each other. Apparently he was very close friends with the individual who supposedly killed the boy. He was very good friends with him, and apparently good drinking buddies."

"And is this all the stuff that specifically Duncan told you?"

"Yes."

"Did anybody else tell you this specific information?"

Melissa said the specific information she'd heard from other people was that the body was knifed twenty-eight times and that it was in a car for two weeks.

"That's not from Duncan? That's from other people?"

"Right."

"But this other stuff, about the roommates, the kidnapping plot, the drinking, things got out of hand or whatever, that stuff... That was all specifically from Duncan?"

"Yes."

"And the train tracks, that was from Duncan?" asked Clark.

"Absolutely."

"What got him started telling you about this? Do you remember?"

Melissa explained that she chiefed the judicial system at the university and knew the people responsible for overseeing the Greek system. At some point, she offered to see what she could do to help Duncan obtain university housing, whether at the fraternity house or a dorm.

"Were you his advocate, then? Because you kind of liked him, he was—"

"Duncan, you know, he can totally spin a yarn. He can totally make you feel like a wonderful person."

"So you want to try to help him," said Clark.

"Oh, yeah, he's a star at doing that."

"So what brought him to your attention?"

"What brought him to my attention, when I first met him, was he had this great rebel, really evil James Dean kind of look. And I thought this was just amazing to see in Utah. And to a certain point, he really pissed me off, because he had these stories that I thought, *This has got to be bullshit, and I want to be able to call him on this someday, because I know this guy is bullshitting all of us.* And so I kind of started hanging out just because I was entertained by the stuff that he would tell, and his great parties, and how he had done all these amazing things."

Melissa said she would always ask Duncan about his family and why he hadn't been back to California. "I'm a prying sort of sorority girl. I was like, 'Well, what are you doing here if your family's in California? And why were you in Boston? And why are you on probation here?' Because he told us about the probation. I think he boasted about it more than anything else. And so he kind of started talking about how he had witnessed something that had happened.

"And I think, at the time, he probably felt very close to me. I think he thought that I was his ticket, probably, to a lot of security within the fraternity and within the system. I was the president of a sorority. I was a chief justice of a judicial system. I was an honor student. And I think he thought maybe, by hanging out with me, that would give him some credibility to what he was telling and to the way he was acting."

"So you're kind of like his social entrée?"

"Oh, very much so."

"So he can get on your good side, impress you. And so him telling you about this was partially to brag and impress you?"

"Partially I'm sure a little shock value, probably to see how I would handle it," Melissa told us. "And eventually it really backfired, since my big mouth opened up and he got thrown out of the fraternity."

Following our interview of Melissa Bean, Clark and I flew from Salt Lake City back to Los Angeles. The flight, on a small commuter plane, experienced severe turbulence for an extended period. Upon landing, a relieved Clark told me to check in with her the following week, to discuss our next steps on the case, in anticipation of Duncan's extradition.

On June 9, the day before I was to leave on a long-planned family vacation, I received a call from the Salt Lake County Sheriff's Office. A detective informed me that he had been in court with Duncan the day before. He said Duncan was attempting to get a bail reduction and would appear in court again the following week. Duncan had refused to waive extradition, meaning he planned to challenge in Utah his return to California to face charges. The detective suggested I begin the formal extradition process, should Duncan continue to refuse to voluntarily return.

I did not see any judge granting Duncan bail on a first-degree murder warrant, especially given his history of using multiple aliases and two prior felony convictions. Also, if Duncan continued to fight extradition, the process would likely take a few months.

Before I left the office that day, I called Marcia Clark, updating her on Duncan's status and the need for the DA's Office to begin formal extradition proceedings. I told Clark I would see her upon my return in a few weeks.

Three nights later, on the evening of June 12, Nicole Simpson and Ronald Goldman were viciously stabbed to death outside her Brentwood condo. Upon the discovery of the victims' identities, detectives from RHD were called to the scene to handle the investigation. It would prove to be one of the most infamous and consequential murder cases in Los Angeles history.

Within days of the killings, before I returned from vacation, Marcia Clark was tapped to be the lead prosecutor on the case that ultimately led to the arrest of O. J. Simpson.

As soon as I heard about Clark's new assignment, I knew she was out as the prosecutor for Ron Baker's murder. Another deputy DA had bitten the dust. Following Norris, Conn, and Clark, I would have to brief another prosecutor on the now four-year-old Baker investigation.

Little did Clark realize at the time how drastically her new case would affect her life. And little did she know that it would be her final case as a prosecutor, a calling that she loved and had excelled at for years.

CHAPTER 23

GOVERNOR'S WARRANT
(June 20 to November 14, 1994)

AS THE BAKER CASE entered its fifth year, there was a brand-new legal cast of characters.

Anne Ingalls, a deputy DA in the Special Trials unit, was assigned to take over from her colleague Marcia Clark as lead prosecutor.

Duncan's previous criminal defense lawyer, Jim Barnes, was replaced by another private attorney, James Gregory. Barnes, I knew, had been retained and his services paid for by Duncan's mother and stepfather. I assumed the same was true of Gregory.

Nathan, still awaiting his trial, was assigned a public defender, Laura Green, as his attorney.

I knew Ingalls personally but had never worked with her prior to Baker. She had been a deputy DA for ten years, the last two in Special Trials. To be selected for that elite assignment after only eight years as a prosecutor was extremely rare. Ingalls had proved her mettle and distinguished herself over several years in the DA's Hardcore Gang unit, where she prosecuted homicides and other serious crimes. I thought highly of her abilities and demeanor, which was low-key but palpably strong.

Change was also afoot at RHD. Since Garcia's retirement, more than a year earlier, I had been working with a series of temporary partners, but eventually I was paired with a detective named Mike Berchem.

Berchem was five years younger than me and had less time on the job, a dynamic similar to Garcia and me when I had first joined RHD. Before Berchem arrived at RHD, he had spent nine years investigating gang-related murders and assaults on the west side of the city, which included Hollywood and Venice, among other areas.

Our lieutenant, Danny Lang, had supervised Berchem in his previous assignment and had successfully advocated for him to be brought into RHD. Lang liked Berchem's work ethic, which was reflected in the high percentage of his cases he had solved.

I did not know Berchem before his first day at RHD. I learned he was a personable, down-to-earth guy. He was originally from Green Bay, Wisconsin, and, unsurprisingly, a huge fan of the Green Bay Packers. His childhood home was only two blocks away from Lambeau Field, the team's legendary stadium. On game days, fans had paid to park their cars on his family's front lawn.

Berchem set up his desk, immediately adjacent to mine, in Garcia's old spot. I noticed the unusual-looking penholder he placed on it: a pile of dried cow manure that had been shellacked and inset with a metal cup. Obviously I had to ask him about it. Berchem explained that it was a "cow pie" and a gift from his mother, who had said it would remind him where he came from. Wisconsin, of course, is known as America's Dairyland.

Duncan had a court hearing in Salt Lake City on Monday, June 20. He was asking that bail be set for his release, as he continued to fight the extradition process. An account of the hearing ran in the next day's edition of the local newspaper, the *Salt Lake Tribune*.

Duncan was represented by his Utah defense attorney, Robert Booker, and also had numerous other supporters in the courtroom. According to the *Tribune*, "At a Monday bail hearing, Booker showed up at 3rd Circuit Court with two U. professors, a former employer of Martinez's, three former roommates, a girlfriend and a half dozen other friends and supporters ready to vouch for Martinez. All were willing to have Martinez released into their custody while the extradition is worked out."

Booker's appeal for Duncan to be released on bail was unsuccessful. The *Tribune* reported:

> Judge T. Patrick Casey refused to set bail because of the gravity of the charges. A hearing to review Martinez's fugitive status is set for July 7.
>
> Booker said the murder charge is frustrating because the case is sealed, and he has been unable to learn upon what information it is based. He said Martinez would resist extradition until Los Angeles police prove they have evidence against him and that they are proceeding properly.
>
> Marcia Clark, the Los Angeles prosecutor handling the Martinez-Blalock case, was busy Monday with the double-murder arraignment of O. J. Simpson and was unavailable for comment.
>
> Booker believes something has gone wrong with California's case against Blalock, and are looking for a scapegoat.

I had absolutely no idea where Booker had come up with that theory. It was untrue. It sounded to me like a defense attorney posturing about a case he knew little about.

On July 12, I spoke with a detective in the Fugitive Section of the Salt Lake County Sheriff's Office. He told me Duncan Martinez had been in court the day before and was still challenging his extradition. He remained held without bail, and the court had granted him a thirty-day extension on the governor's warrant procedure.

A governor's warrant is a process by which a fugitive can be compelled to return to a state where a crime was committed if they refuse to return voluntarily to face charges. The local authorities in the state where the charges are filed must submit the necessary paperwork to its governor. The governor must then sign a document that attests to the charges and evidence connecting the suspect to the crime. After the governor from the charging state signs, it is sent to the governor of the holding state. In the Baker case, the charging state was California and the holding state was Utah. Once both governors have signed, the fugitive is finally ordered to be returned to the charging state.

Executing each of these steps is time-consuming, and the process can drag on for months. But in practice, it is pretty much foolproof. I had never had a request for a governor's warrant denied in any of my cases. Nor had I heard of a coworker's request for one ever being denied.

The next day, I called the Extradition Section of the DA's Office. I advised them of the update and confirmed the governor's warrant process for Duncan's extradition was on track.

On August 4, I received a call from James Gregory, Duncan's new defense attorney. He introduced himself and said he wanted to clarify some things regarding his client's cooperation agreement and pending extradition from Utah.

Gregory asked me if anything Duncan had told detectives from that point on was still protected under the original agreement Duncan had made with the police and the DA's Office. I explained the agreement was no longer valid and that I had made that clear to Duncan at the time of his arrest in Utah, in June. I told Gregory that I did not plan to further question Duncan because he had invoked his rights and was represented by counsel.

Gregory and I also discussed Duncan's safety, once he was extradited to California and held at Los Angeles County Jail. I told Gregory that I already planned to request a "keep-away order" from jail personnel that would, in theory, guarantee Duncan and Nathan would be totally isolated from each other. The reason for concern was obvious, given the potential for retaliatory violence when one inmate was known to have provided incriminating information on another, especially if both were being held in the same facility.

In my personal life, it was a melancholy time. I had lost my father four months earlier, and August 8 would be his first birthday after his death. We had always celebrated his birthday with some nice family gathering that included my mother, my two sisters, and the four grandchildren. My father had enjoyed more than anything just being around his grandchildren. It was the only birthday gift he would have needed.

Work was a welcome distraction for me.

On August 9, Deputy DA Ingalls and I flew to Salt Lake City. There were more witnesses to interview whose names had surfaced regarding Duncan's time in Utah. Among them was a onetime roommate of Duncan's from his Park City days. Given how many other people Duncan had spoken to about Ron's murder, I had zero doubt he also had talked to the roommate about it. Anything Duncan had told him about Ron's murder was fair game to use at trial.

That evening, Ingalls and I drove to Park City to interview the former roommate, Gago Avaneszadeh.

I showed Gago a photo of Duncan. Gago identified him as Duncan Martinez but said he generally had called him "Jake."

Gago explained they met in the spring of 1992, when they were coworkers at a Park City restaurant. At the time, Gago was looking for a place to live. Duncan said he knew the owner of a vacant house in Park City and told Gago he could arrange for them to rent the place. Duncan later said he had finalized a lease with the house's owner and asked Gago for $230 as his share of the first month's rent. Soon after, the owner of the house returned and was surprised to find strangers living in it, including Duncan, who had supposedly arranged the lease. Gago said Duncan's scam tanked their friendship and they went their separate ways.

Gago said, too, that Duncan told him about witnessing a murder in Los Angeles. Duncan said it happened in a tunnel in Chatsworth Park and involved two other people, a "Black kid" and a "rich kid." He watched the Black kid stab the rich kid but did nothing to intervene.

Duncan also told Gago that he went to Los Angeles to work with the LAPD and even wore a wire into the jail to see if he could get the Black guy to talk. Duncan said the Black guy asked him if he was wearing a wire and he replied, "What do you think?" Gago described Duncan as cool and unemotional when they discussed it.

Gago couldn't recall how their discussion of the murder started. He didn't ask Duncan many questions about it. Duncan just told him, Gago recalled.

Duncan told Gago he was attending the university and that it would make a good impression on the LAPD. Duncan also implied he was "home free," or felt that way, and wanted to keep impressing the authorities.

Gago said Duncan spoke freely about the murder. "Lots of people knew about it and everyone basically thought it was a joke." Gago said he believed the story but that it didn't make sense to him that Duncan wasn't involved. He even told Duncan he thought he was bullshitting him and was involved in it.

Gago's statement that "lots of people knew about it" made me wonder just how many others Duncan had blabbed to about the murder. Each time he told someone his account of what happened in the tunnel, it was a violation of our King for a Day agreement and its cardinal rule: Do not talk to others about the murder.

On the University of Utah campus alone, there were several dozen he had told. How many others out there had crossed paths and heard tall tales from the man variously known as Duncan Martinez, Jake Atkins, Jonathan Wayne Miller, and Doofus O'Reilly? It seemed like Duncan believed that if he spoke his version of events enough times, to enough people, he could convince himself it was the truth and somehow rewrite the facts of the case.

For the next few months, into the fall of 1994, the Baker case was mostly dormant. Nathan was biding his time in Los Angeles County Jail, awaiting a trial that had yet to be scheduled. His counterpart, Duncan, was sitting in the Salt Lake County Jail, making what efforts he could to prevent his return to Los Angeles.

I did not have any concerns over Duncan's eventual extradition. I believed the evidence against him was more than sufficient to keep a Utah judge from blocking his return. The governor's warrant procedure, meanwhile, continued to inch along.

In early November, I received notification that the governor's warrant had been signed by both Governor Pete Wilson of California and Governor Mike Leavitt of Utah. Duncan Martinez was available for release to the LAPD.

Berchem and I flew to Salt Lake City on Thursday, November 10. The following morning, we took Duncan into custody at the Salt Lake County Jail and flew with him back to Los Angeles.

The custom when transporting an in-custody suspect and flying commercial was to inform the gate agent, who would then allow us to board first, before all other passengers. We generally placed the suspect in a window seat, with my partner and I in the aisle and middle seats of the row. I always allowed the suspect's hands to be handcuffed in front of them during a flight, primarily for their comfort. It also allowed them to eat and drink during the flight.

Duncan gave us no trouble on the flight. In contrast to all of our previous encounters, there was little conversation between us.

Upon landing, we drove straight from the airport to the LAPD's Jail Division downtown, where Duncan was booked on the murder warrant. Since it was a Friday, he would not go to court until Monday and would remain in LAPD custody over the weekend. This meant he was safe for at least a few more days from crossing paths with Nathan, who was incarcerated in a different facility, the LA County Jail.

Not until after his initial court appearance would Duncan be transported to the county jail. I told Duncan that I would be requesting a keep-away order with the LA County Sheriff's personnel who ran the jail system, so he and Nathan would be placed in separate housing facilities. I also instructed Duncan that if he should see Nathan, he should advise deputies immediately of the keep-away order.

Duncan's safety awaiting his trial was a priority regardless of my personal opinion of him. I had discussed as much with Duncan's attorney, James Gregory, three months earlier, and I intended to honor the assurances I had given him then, as well as the ones I gave Duncan more recently.

First thing Monday morning, I called the jail's liaison unit. I explained that Duncan would be getting processed at the jail following his court appearance that day and the need for a keep-away order between him and Nathan.

Duncan was now officially "Defendant Martinez, Duncan Gordon James, AKA Miller, Jonathan Wayne, Case No. BA095512, Booking No. 4189014." He would be held without bail on a warrant signed by Judge Lance Ito, who would soon become a household name as the presiding judge in the as yet still pending trial of O. J. Simpson.

I called my former partner, Frank Garcia, who by then had been retired for almost two years. I let him know Duncan was back in California, for the first time as a charged defendant. Garcia and I agreed it felt good that we had gotten the case to this point. For so long, we had been apprehensive that it might never happen.

CHAPTER 24

THE PASSPORT INVESTIGATOR
(November 28, 1994 to February 26, 1996)

DUNCAN'S INITIAL 1992 ARREST in Utah, on a warrant for submitting a fraudulent passport application, was perhaps the pivotal moment in the case.

If not for that warrant, things might have turned out very differently. Duncan might have gone on living under his assumed name, Jonathan Wayne Miller, forever. Without the legal pressure of the passport charge weighing on him, Duncan might never have come forward and said who had killed Ron. Without Duncan's cooperation, Nathan might never have been arrested. There was not enough evidence otherwise at that time to prosecute anyone. Ron's case, like so many others, could easily have gone unsolved, with no one ever held accountable for his murder.

Yet despite it being a crucial turning point in the Baker investigation, I knew relatively little about Duncan's passport fraud, besides that he was arrested under the name Jonathan Wayne Miller and later pleaded guilty to providing false information on a passport application.

I did have one related lead I wanted to follow up on, now that Duncan had been extradited to California. A few months earlier, I had tracked down Emile Monette, the acquaintance Duncan had claimed blackmailed him into burglarizing Wasatch Touring. When I called Emile, I identified myself as an LAPD detective and said I would like to interview him. He immediately replied, "Does this have something to do with a guy named Duncan Martinez?"

Once I spoke to Emile, it was easy to clear him of any involvement in Duncan's burglary. His employer's records confirmed he could not have been in Utah when the burglary was committed. Emile's last contact with Duncan had been more than a year before the burglary.

I did learn something unexpected during my interview with Emile. Duncan had talked with Emile not only about the murder but also about how he had obtained a false identity for his passport application. Emile said Duncan told him he "went through the newspaper, picked out a dead baby, and got his Social Security number." This was tantalizing information.

In advance of Duncan's trial, it was important to delve deeper into his passport crime. Who was the real Jonathan Wayne Miller? Was he a living victim? Or was Miller dead, as Duncan had suggested to Emile? How had Duncan gone about stealing and establishing his new fake identity?

Learning the nitty-gritty of the passport case was key for a few reasons. The story would be powerful evidence at trial of Duncan's consciousness of guilt. Applying for a passport in someone else's name is not something an innocent person does. Additionally, if Duncan chose to take the witness stand and testify in his own defense, the lies he told on his passport application could be used on cross-examination to hammer his credibility. In order for prosecutors to be able to tell the jury the story effectively, it was necessary first to know the facts.

I wanted to obtain a copy of the fraudulent passport application Duncan had filed as Jonathan Wayne Miller, along with the case file of the associated investigation. I also hoped to interview the federal officials who had handled the application and ultimately rejected it.

I began my quest on November 28 by calling Agent Ken Crook in the FBI's Salt Lake City office. It was Crook who finalized the passport case and had Duncan prosecuted. I told Crook what I needed and my belief that it could be helpful evidence in Duncan's upcoming trial. Whether Duncan would go to trial or accept some kind of plea deal was still to be determined.

Crook said I would need to make my request to the FBI in Boston. He explained that even though Duncan's case had started with his passport application in Delaware, Boston was the lead office in the matter. He suggested I contact Agent Neil Cronin in Boston for assistance.

Cronin returned my call the following week. Without hesitation, he offered to send me a copy of the fraudulent application, as well as a set of all the investigative reports in the case.

When I received the FBI records, I realized the person I really needed to speak with was a man named Duncan Maitland.

Another Duncan, I thought.

Maitland was the fraud program coordinator in the State Department's Boston Passport Agency. It appeared he had tenaciously dug into the dubious application filed in Miller's name.

I called Maitland on December 14. It was news to him that the subject of one of his fraud cases had been charged with an LA murder. Maitland told me he clearly recalled the individual who had posed as Miller. Maitland said he was agreeable to meet regarding his work on the case.

Pretrial court proceedings for Nathan and Duncan continued intermittently into 1995. There was no imperative for me to travel to Boston to interview Maitland immediately. It could wait until Duncan's case moved closer to trial.

Maitland and I eventually agreed to meet on November 3, 1995, at the Boston Passport Agency. My latest detective partner, Dennis Kilcoyne, would join me on the trip.

Maitland greeted us and led us to an interview room. He was about my age and outwardly mild mannered but not meek. He came across as studious and professional. He also had an inner intensity that, over time, came to remind me of a bulldog.

Maitland told us he remembered the case well, despite that it happened four years earlier. He recounted that his investigation in this case centered on two individual passport applications, one for a James Purpura and the other for a friend of Purpura's, Jonathan Wayne Miller. I knew Purpura as Duncan's friend from Boston and later his roommate in Park City, Utah.

Both applications were initially submitted in early November 1991, Maitland said. Miller's application was submitted first and Purpura's a

Duncan Maitland and US secretary of state Colin Powell, 2003 (courtesy of Duncan Maitland)

few days later. Both were mailed from a post office in Dover, Delaware, and both applicants used the same Dover return mailing address.

Maitland explained that all passport applications submitted in Dover were forwarded to the Philadelphia Passport Agency for processing. Personnel there noted that both Miller and Purpura had used Delaware IDs as proof of their respective identities. According to Maitland, Delaware ID cards were known to be easily obtained. As a result, passport officials in Philadelphia sent questionnaires to Miller and Purpura, requesting additional documents to verify their identities.

On December 2, Purpura appeared in person at the Philadelphia office. He showed his photo in his high school yearbook, which was accepted as satisfactory proof of his identity.

Purpura then spoke to Mike Persons, the fraud program coordinator in Philadelphia, the same job as Maitland's in Boston. Purpura said he wanted assistance expediting the issuance of a passport for his friend Jonathan Wayne Miller. Purpura had brought with him Miller's completed questionnaire, along with a letter, purportedly written by Miller, which gave Purpura permission to act on his behalf. Purpura also presented various other forms of identification in Miller's name. These included photocopies of a Social Security card, a Massachusetts learner's permit, a Boston University student ID, and a voter registration card from Revere, Massachusetts.

Persons told Purpura that Miller would have to appear in person to continue with his application. Persons said Miller should bring with him the originals of his identification documents, plus additional documentation such as school records. Purpura's passport was issued late that afternoon and he was able to walk away with it.

The next day, Purpura returned to the Philadelphia office, again by himself. Once more, he spoke with Persons. He provided copies of two W-2 tax statements in Miller's name as well as a copy of Miller's transcript from Bartlett High School in Webster, Massachusetts.

Persons reiterated that Miller still had to appear in person. Purpura said that was impossible because Miller was in Massachusetts preparing for their trip. Persons told Purpura that Miller could go to the Boston Passport Agency and apply there. Persons gave Purpura Duncan Maitland's name as the passport employee Miller should ask for in Boston.

Maitland told us that Persons called him after his meeting with Purpura. Persons briefed him on the situation and advised him that an applicant named Miller might be coming into the Boston office. The fact that Miller never appeared at the Philadelphia Passport Agency himself, and his application was submitted instead by a third party, made Persons suspicious. Just based on what Persons told him, Maitland was also skeptical.

Persons faxed Maitland copies of the passport applications submitted by Purpura and Miller. Maitland alerted all of the counter personnel he worked with that Miller might show up to reapply in Boston.

Around ten the following morning, December 4, 1991, three people appeared at the Boston Passport Agency. They spoke to counter employee Andrew Dumanian, who recognized the name of one of the three people, Jonathan Wayne Miller. The other two individuals with Miller were identified as James Purpura and Tim Vaum, Miller's roommate in Revere.

Maitland said that when he was advised of Miller's presence, he instructed Dumanian to have Miller complete a new application.

According to Maitland, this would give the Boston office jurisdiction in the passport investigation.

Miller completed his new application, which was given to Maitland by Dumanian. Maitland compared the signatures on the new application with the one completed in Dover. They matched. This confirmed to him that he was dealing with one and the same person.

In support of his new application, Miller presented originals of the Delaware ID card, Social Security card, Massachusetts driving learner's permit, and Massachusetts voter registration card he had submitted copies of earlier. He also provided two passport photos and photocopies of the same W-2 tax statements and Bartlett High School transcript he had submitted with his first application. Miller presented some new documents as well. These included an original computer-printed letter from the Social Security Administration dated November 8, 1991, a few weeks prior, and original airline tickets for himself and Purpura to Paris, France, departing Boston that night.

Dumanian asked Miller about the Boston University ID card he had submitted a copy of through Purpura in Philadelphia. Miller said he had left it at home.

It was only after Miller filled out the required paperwork, and Maitland reviewed all the submitted materials, that Maitland went out to meet with him.

Maitland was direct with Miller. He told him point-blank that he needed a blood relative to come in and personally verify his identity. The relative would then be required to complete an affidavit, under penalty of perjury, attesting that Miller was who he claimed to be.

Miller insisted that was not necessary since he had Purpura and Vaum there to verify his identity. Maitland replied that was insufficient. Miller had listed both of his parents' names on his questionnaire. At least one would have to come in and complete an affidavit, Maitland told him.

Maitland recalled that Miller kept trying to circumvent the system. Miller claimed he was continually abused as a child and that both his parents were alcoholics. He said he left home and school in 1985, having completed only eighth grade, and since then had spent time in

California, Delaware, and Massachusetts. He said he had gotten mixed up in drugs but had straightened himself out. The trip to France he and Purpura were scheduled to leave on that night was to reward himself, he told Maitland.

Maitland said there was still time to issue a passport for him to make the trip that night, but the requirement that a blood relative come in was in his case nonnegotiable. Maitland pointed out that Miller had also listed an eighteen-year-old brother in the family-members portion of his questionnaire. Maitland suggested Miller ask his brother. Miller seemed hesitant about his next step and asked Maitland for his phone number. He told Maitland he would think about the situation and get back to him. Miller and his two friends then left.

Maitland received a call from Miller later that same day. He told Maitland he had nothing else to provide. Maitland asked about the Boston University ID Miller had earlier told Dumanian he left at home. Miller admitted he was not a student there. Miller said he went to the university to check on getting a GED as a substitute for completing high school. Miller explained that while he was there, he talked someone who worked at the university into issuing him a school ID. Purpura then got on the line. Purpura told Maitland he could not make the Europe trip alone and asked if something could be done. Purpura said Miller's family wanted nothing to do with their son. Maitland was unswayed. He repeated that only a blood relative's in-person affidavit would suffice for the issuance of Miller's passport.

Miller returned to the passport office in person a few hours later. Once again, he spoke with Andrew Dumanian at the counter. He told Dumanian he wanted to cancel his passport application and wanted his two passport photos back. Dumanian went to Maitland, who instructed him to make copies of the two photos and only give Miller the copies. Maitland also told Dumanian to ask Miller to write out a letter requesting cancellation of the application. When Dumanian returned to the counter, Miller was gone.

Miller came back in one last time that day. Dumanian was there, but Maitland was out of the office on a break. At Dumanian's request, Miller wrote out a letter stating he wished to cancel his passport application. Dumanian also gave Miller the copies of his passport photos.

It had been a long and trying day for the man who had presented himself as Jonathan Wayne Miller. It had also been a busy day for someone else: Duncan Maitland.

But Maitland's work on the case was not over. In fact, it was just beginning.

Maitland had suspected fraud in the case from early on. Someone in Maitland's position who was less dogged and conscientious might simply have dropped the matter once the application was denied. After all, the passport sought by Miller was never actually issued.

Maitland, however, began digging into the matter. Despite Miller canceling his application, it was a felony crime to submit a fraudulent passport application in the first place. If fraud could be established, then Miller had committed the crime on November 1, when he submitted his initial application in Dover, Delaware. He had exacerbated the situation by submitting a second fraudulent application in Boston in early December.

Maitland then walked us through many of the investigative steps he eventually took to determine if Miller's application was indeed fraudulent.

Maitland called the Massachusetts high school Miller had provided a transcript from. The transcript indicated Miller had completed seventh grade in the 1983–84 school year and eighth grade in 1984–85.

Maitland spoke to a counselor who had worked at the school for twenty years. The counselor said official records were only retained for five years. Maitland read the counselor some of the courses listed on the submitted transcript. The counselor informed Maitland that two of the classes, English 1 and English 2, were for freshman ninth graders and sophomore tenth graders. Maitland told us he realized immediately that this information did not match Miller's questionnaire, which stated he only completed the eighth grade.

Later, while examining the transcript more closely, Maitland noticed at the bottom of the page, printed in very small type, a line that read, "Honors Courses in English & Social Studies are rigorous programs limited to students with a Calif. Ach. Test score of 94% or better." The document submitted by Miller was a blank California school transcript that had been altered to appear as one from Massachusetts, with the addition of Miller's name, identifying information, courses, and grades.

Maitland also looked into the Social Security numbers Miller had provided on his applications and the identity verification documents he had supplied. Maitland noticed that Miller had submitted several documents with one particular Social Security number, including his 1990 W-2 statements. The problem, Maitland realized, was that Miller's Social Security number was not issued until November 1991. This was an obvious indication to Maitland that the W-2 statements, and the other documents dated before the issuance of that Social Security number, were falsified.

On December 5, Maitland telephoned the Massachusetts Registry of Vital Records and Statistics, which happened to be located just a few blocks from his office. Maitland spoke to a supervisor named Harold Leonard. Maitland gave him the name, date of birth, and place of birth given on the passport application. He also told Leonard the names of Miller's parents, as they were listed on the application. Maitland said he suspected the applicant could be using an "IDI," shorthand for an "infant death identity." Maitland asked Leonard to check into the birth and death records for anyone with the name and identifying information he had provided.

When Maitland and Leonard spoke again later that day, Leonard said he had belatedly remembered a young man who came in and identified himself as Jonathan Wayne Miller. Ordinarily, the Massachusetts state registry's official birth and death records were not available for members of the public to review. The originals of the records were preserved in "stacks" of bound volumes. Leonard said that Miller told him he was conducting genealogical research about his family, and Leonard allowed Miller access to the stacks. Leonard had found the sign-in sheet on which the young man hand-printed his name and signed it for admittance.

Leonard then told Maitland he searched and found a record of Jonathan Wayne Miller's birth in Webster, Massachusetts, on September 27, 1972, matching the information Maitland had provided. Next, he checked for death records and learned that a Jonathan Wayne Miller had died in Worcester, Massachusetts, on April 7, 1974, at one year of age.

An Index of Deaths between 1971 and 1975 indicated that the official record of Miller's death could be found in the stacks in Volume 109, as page 279. Leonard pulled Volume 109 for confirmation. He was shocked to discover that the page between 278 and 280 was missing. It appeared that page 279 had been sliced near the volume's inner binding and removed. Page 280 and a few subsequent pages had been partially sliced as well but remained barely attached to the binding. Leonard reported to Maitland that it was obvious some type of sharp implement, whether an X-ACTO knife or a razor blade, had been used.

Maitland was unsurprised that the real Jonathan Wayne Miller was dead. He already suspected as much. But the calculated removal of Miller's official death record showed the lengths to which the man posing as him was willing to go, and actually had gone, to make it seem Miller was still alive. It also demonstrated the seriousness of the man's intent to obtain a passport under false pretenses in a name other than his own.

Maitland called the Worcester City Clerk's Office, which would have a secondary copy of the death certificate on file. Maitland eventually obtained a copy. The birth date and parental information were the same as on the passport application, Maitland found.

Within days of Maitland's investigative discoveries and confirmation that the case involved an infant death identity, he submitted his findings to Agent Neil Cronin of the FBI's Boston office. The following month, Cronin filed a complaint and affidavit with a US magistrate judge. The judge in turn issued an arrest warrant charging "John Doe, a.k.a. Jonathan Wayne Miller" with the crime of making a false statement in support of a passport application.

Listening to Maitland's account of his investigation, I was struck by how essential a role he had played in the eventual apprehension of Duncan Martinez. If not for Maitland's diligence and persistence, the other Duncan would have gotten away with passport fraud and quite possibly much more.

Based on what Maitland told me, I decided I wanted to see for myself the official ledger of deaths with the missing page removed.

I walked over to the Registry of Vital Records and Statistics, the same office Duncan had visited four years earlier, and asked to see the bound volumes for the years of Miller's birth and untimely death.

Just as Maitland had described, in Volume 109 nearly all of page 279 was gone. All that remained between pages 278 and 280 was a thin stub of paper, perhaps a quarter to a half inch long, the left margin of the missing page that was not completely excised. The six pages that followed page 279 also showed evidence of having been sliced. Duncan obviously had applied a bit too much pressure with his blade when he cut it.

Once I saw the volume and the damaged pages, I knew I had to request the Boston Police Department photograph it for evidence. I was already thinking ahead to Duncan's trial and what the jury would make of the images. I felt they should hear how Duncan, in his efforts to become Jonathan Wayne Miller, had stolen the identity of an innocent toddler who had died due to a horrible accident more than twenty years earlier. I believed it was the kind of information that would weigh heavily on a jury and reflect very poorly on Duncan.

Massachusetts Vital Records and Statistics Volume 109, missing page 279 (courtesy of Boston Police Department)

Upon returning from Boston, I called the Worcester City Clerk's Office myself. I told the woman who answered why I was calling, to obtain a copy of the true Jonathan Wayne Miller's death certificate. As I explained the bizarre circumstances of the case and what Duncan had done, I could sense over the phone her outrage at his theft of a dead child's identity. Her reaction confirmed for me what I believed future jurors would feel when weighing Duncan's guilt.

Two days later, I received a faxed copy of the death certificate. The certified copy arrived in the mail soon after. The death certificate indicated Miller's cause of death, tragically, as accidental ingestion of Drano.

As the calendar turned to 1996, Nathan's and Duncan's long-awaited courtroom reckonings loomed. The court ruled that they would be tried separately, in front of different juries. Although it was one murder, the evidence that would be presented against them was significantly different. Holding two trials would simplify the court proceedings. Because Nathan was arrested earlier, he would be tried first. The court scheduled Nathan's trial to begin in mid-March.

I had a few more interviews to conduct ahead of Nathan's trial. I wanted to talk with some of Ron's friends in the group that, before his murder, had visited the tunnel above Chatsworth Park together. Among them were two young women, Debbie Armstrong and Adriane Tomlinson.

The focus of my interest was Duncan's claim that whenever they went there, he or Nathan always carried a knife. Nathan had additionally claimed that on the night of the murder, when they walked through the tunnel, he had held the knife out in front of him for self-defense.

The idea that someone would carry a knife in the manner Nathan had described struck me as unrealistic. Would someone really brandish a knife in the dark if, as both Duncan and Nathan had admitted, there was no actual, specific threat to their safety? It seemed more likely to me that Nathan, by saying that, had been trying to set up a defense that he "stuck" Ron accidentally. Since I anticipated this might be an issue at Nathan's trial, I wanted to question others regarding whether they had seen Duncan or Nathan with a knife on their previous trips to the tunnel.

On February 22, I made separate phone calls to Debbie and Adriane.

Debbie told me that they went to the park as a group only one time. "The talk that we went up there regularly is not true," she said. If anyone did go there regularly, she was unaware but felt she would have known.

Debbie said they mainly went to watch a train go through the tunnel and had heard it was neat. She also recalled that they "got kind of harassed" by a group of five or six guys who asked if they were devil worshippers. "There was no fight, though," she told me. According to Debbie, no one had a knife there that she was aware of, and definitely no one pulled a knife out.

I spoke with Adriane later the same day. She said she had been to the tunnel on prior occasions but only once as part of a larger group that included Ron, Nathan, and Duncan. Her most vivid memory of that night was that Ron threw up from drinking too much, and Nathan had to carry Ron down from the tunnel and put him in Duncan's car.

Adriane said that the one time she was there with Nathan and Duncan, they didn't pull out a knife, echoing what Debbie had told me. Adriane didn't think they even had a knife. She had never known anyone she was with at the park to pull out a knife when they went into the tunnel, she said.

My final task in preparation for Nathan's trial also involved the knife used to kill Ron.

In late February, I met at the coroner's office with Steve Dowell, a respected criminalist who specialized in examining toolmarks—the cuts, scratches, or impressions left on a body when it makes contact with a harder object. By comparing a toolmark to a particular object, it is sometimes possible to determine whether that mark could have been made by that object.

In this case, the toolmarks were the various knife wounds received by Ron and documented in his autopsy report. The tool for comparison was the Marine Corps–style KA-BAR knife Garcia and I had purchased, a duplicate of the model Duncan had said Nathan used on Ron. I had asked Dowell to analyze the exemplar knife and determine, if possible, whether it was inconsistent with Ron's injuries.

When Dowell notified me he had completed his report, I offered to pick it up in person so I could go over it with him. This was my standard practice because it allowed for a better back-and-forth, question-and-answer session than over the phone.

Based on Dowell's review of the autopsy report and photos, he had divided Ron's knife wounds into two categories.

The first category Dowell addressed in his report were "defense type wounds to the hands and forearm, and cutting wounds to the lower extremities." These could only be evaluated in general, Dowell noted. Slashing or slicing defense wounds inflicted on a victim's flailing hands, arms, and legs could have been produced by the sharp edge of any number of different knives. Ron's defense wounds were all consistent with having been caused by the exemplar knife. In other words, the KA-BAR could not be ruled out as having produced these injuries.

The second category of injuries were Ron's stab wounds, those caused by the knife penetrating his body. Dowell indicated all of the stab wounds were consistent with having been produced by a single-edged, rather than a double-edged, knife. The KA-BAR was single-edged.

Dowell additionally noted, "The autopsy report includes measurements for the length and depth of several of the stab wounds. By plotting the length vs. depth of these measurements, a profile of the actual knife blade may be determined."

Dowell's report concluded, "The overall pattern of the stab wounds as described and depicted are consistent with having been produced by a knife with the same or similar features as the submitted knife." The slash and stab wounds to Ron's neck were also consistent with the exemplar knife, although they could have been produced by other knives besides the KA-BAR.

After we finished discussing the report, Dowell made a comment that summed up, in just three words, my primary takeaway from his expert analysis. "No wounds inconsistent," he said.

Dowell's point was that there was no evidence to show that multiple knives had been used. The murder weapon was either the type of knife Duncan had indicated or one with similar dimensions.

It also supported the likelihood that there had been just one stabber. There were a few other possibilities, at least theoretically. Nathan and Duncan could have taken turns stabbing Ron, after he was incapacitated by the first stabber. Nathan could have handed Duncan the knife to finish Ron off by slitting his throat. Two knives of the same type or similar dimensions could have been used to inflict Ron's wounds. My personal belief was that only one knife had been used, and that it was of the brand and model Duncan had identified.

Leaving the coroner's office that day, I reflected that my meeting with Dowell was likely to be one of the last things I did on the case before Nathan's trial, the beginning of which was just a few weeks away.

Here I was, in the same building where Frank Garcia and I had started our investigation of Ron's murder almost five years earlier. Back then, neither of us had a clue as to what a strange, convoluted journey the Baker case would take us on—an odyssey that finally appeared to be nearing its end.

CHAPTER 25

JUDGMENT DAY
(March 18 to 29, 1996)

IT ALL CAME DOWN to this:

What price, if any, would Nathan and Duncan pay for their roles in planning and carrying out Ron's killing?

Would Duncan avert a trial by negotiating a plea deal with the DA's Office, agreeing to plead guilty to some lesser charge in exchange for a lesser sentence?

If both Nathan and Duncan went to trial, would a jury convict either of them, or both of them, of first-degree murder?

A guilty verdict was by no means guaranteed. Less than six months earlier, on the same floor of the same building where Nathan and Duncan would face trial, a Los Angeles jury had astonishingly acquitted O. J. Simpson of murder, despite overwhelming evidence of his guilt.

The Simpson verdict had sent shockwaves through all of American society, but for the LAPD and the LA County DA's Office, it had been especially jarring.

In the span of just a few years, Los Angeles and its criminal justice system had become ground zero for the country's racial divisions.

First had come the videotaped beating of Rodney King by four LAPD officers, which had ignited public outrage over police brutality and the unequal treatment of Blacks versus whites. That had been followed by the acquittal of the officers who had beaten King, a verdict that had set off six days of rioting. The disconnect between what the world had seen the officers do on tape and what they had been convicted of—nothing—had only reinforced the perception that the entire system was biased, soft on whites and unjustly tough on Blacks.

Next had come the LAPD's sensational arrest of Simpson, and his even more sensational and polarizing trial. The O.J. case had dominated the news and national consciousness for months on end, throughout most of 1995.

I attributed Simpson's acquittal to the distrust across racial lines that had been building for years. Suddenly, it seemed like it was not enough to rely solely on the facts of a case and the evidence to be presented in court. The Simpson jury's perceptions, whether or not I considered them well-grounded, could not be ignored.

As Nathan's and Duncan's trials approached, I had concerns.

I strongly believed that they were equally culpable for Ron's murder. I felt it was just and appropriate that the grand jury had indicted them for the same crime: first-degree murder. It remained to be seen what leniency Duncan would be offered, and if he would accept it. But there was a good chance that, for his cooperation, Duncan would receive a lesser sentence than Nathan.

The jury in Nathan's trial would hear nothing about Duncan's status in the case. In fact, the judge would instruct the jurors that Duncan's fate was not their concern and should not be taken into consideration. Even though Duncan had been charged equally, the jury would never know that.

They would hear Duncan's voice on the damning recordings, but they would not lay eyes on him. I worried that despite the judge's instructions, Duncan's absence would be so conspicuous that the jurors couldn't help but be suspicious. Why wasn't Duncan in the courtroom, either as a codefendant with Nathan or as a witness subject to cross-examination? Would they assume that Duncan had gotten away with a light sentence, or even had received immunity and no punishment at all?

Would a racially mixed LA jury accept that race had nothing to do with why Duncan and Nathan potentially faced unequal legal consequences? Despite appearances and public sentiment at the time, this was not another example of the criminal justice system treating the white guy with kid gloves while the Black guy, accused of the same crime, had the book thrown at him.

Would the racial divisions stoked in recent years, coupled with reservations over our case strategy, have a cumulative impact on the jury's decision? Or would the jurors be able to look strictly at the evidence presented and not allow any misgivings they had about Duncan's possibly favorable treatment to factor into their vote?

I could only hope it was the latter.

Part of what made me uneasy was how much was out of my hands. Unlike earlier in the case, when I controlled the pace and direction of the investigation, my influence over the trials and pretrial proceedings would be considerably more limited. I would testify as a witness to various aspects of the investigation. But other than that, my role now would more closely resemble an interested observer rather than a direct participant.

After Nathan's and Duncan's indictments, responsibility for moving their cases along rested with the courts. Additionally, any potential plea deal for Duncan was subject to negotiations solely between his defense attorney, James Gregory, and the DA's Office. In that regard, my position was similar to that of the Baker family. I had the prosecutor's ear and was free to speak up, but I had no power to shape, approve, or veto any plea agreement.

Prior to Nathan's trial, the DA's Office announced its decision that it would not seek the death penalty against him or Duncan. This guaranteed that if a jury found them guilty and found either or both of the alleged special circumstances to be true, their sentences would be life without parole.

I agreed with the DA's decision, based on my experience with many other potential death-penalty cases. Among the reasons the death penalty was not appropriate in Ron's case was that Nathan and Duncan were relatively youthful offenders, and neither had a criminal record at the time of the murder.

That Ron's killers would be spared the death penalty also seemed fitting, if for no other reason than when Ron was alive, he was vehemently opposed to capital punishment and had campaigned for its abolition. We knew from Ron's family about his heartfelt involvement with Amnesty International, writing many letters in support of banning the death penalty worldwide.

* * *

Nathan's trial began on Monday, March 18, in the courtroom of LA Superior Court judge Edward Ferns. Deputy DA Anne Ingalls, having overcome the rotating-prosecutor curse that sidelined her three predecessors assigned the case, would represent the "People of the State of California" at trial. Deputy Public Defender Laura Green would represent Nathan.

In homicide cases in Los Angeles, it is customary for the investigating detective to attend every day of the trial, which I did. Nathan's trial lasted two weeks, including deliberations.

Throughout the trial, Ron's parents and sister, Patty, were also a regular presence in the courtroom. Among the witnesses called to testify for the prosecution was Gayle Baker, Ron's father, who recounted the ransom phone calls he received on the night of his son's murder.

Alison Ochiae, a criminalist from the LAPD's crime lab, testified to the results of ABO blood testing she performed on fingernail scrapings from Ron Baker and blood samples taken from him, Nathan, and Duncan for comparison. The blood under Ron's nails was type AB, the same as Nathan's blood type. Ron and Duncan were both type A, which ruled them out as potential sources. Ochiae testified that the scrapings were an insufficient sample size for any DNA analysis.

Ingalls also called to the witness stand Diane Henderson, Nathan's onetime girlfriend, to testify about her recollections of the same night. Diane recounted that before Nathan, Duncan, and Ron went out that night, they all appeared to be getting along, with no arguments or uncomfortable feelings apparent between them. She described Nathan's and Duncan's demeanors as "normal" both before they left with Ron and later that night, after they returned home without him. Diane did not sense that Nathan and Duncan were in a disagreement or wanted to stay away from each other after they got home. Their relationship seemed normal, like they were friends, she recalled.

Diane also testified about a phone call she overheard that night, and what Nathan told her about it afterward. Because she heard Nathan say, "Mr. Baker," she understood the caller to be Ron's father. She heard Nathan answer some questions, but he never put the phone down to check if Ron was in his room, nor called out to him that his dad was on the phone, before they hung up. Nathan explained to Diane that Mr. Baker had called to see if Ron was at home. Nathan also said Mr. Baker had told him about a prank call he had received, about Ron being kidnapped and a demand for money. Nathan's demeanor while he was recounting this was normal and calm, Diane testified.

The final witness the prosecution called to testify was me. My primary role was to introduce for the jury the recordings of Nathan's surreptitiously taped conversations with Duncan, along with the recording of Nathan's confession to me and Garcia at the state prison in Tehachapi.

After the prosecution rested its case, Nathan's attorney, Laura Green, called him to the witness stand to testify in his own defense.

As a matter of legal strategy, most criminal defendants opt not to take the stand at trial. The prosecution bears the burden of proving a defendant's guilt beyond a reasonable doubt, and the Fifth Amendment protects a defendant's right against self-incrimination. Choosing to testify exposes the defendant to cross-examination by the prosecution, a potentially risky proposition. For that reason, defense attorneys generally advise against testifying in one's own defense unless it is absolutely necessary.

The fact that Nathan took the stand was therefore a telling indication of the strength of the evidence against him. If he and his attorney believed there was not sufficient evidence to convict him, the safer course would have been for Nathan to remain silent and not testify.

Nathan's predicament was that he was stuck with the variations of the story he had previously told, recordings of which the jury had already heard, prior to his testimony.

In his three recorded conversations with Duncan, Nathan did not deny stabbing Ron and said nothing to suggest that Duncan stabbed Ron as well. In his confession to me and Garcia, Nathan admitted to stabbing Ron twice but told us he could not say what Duncan did or didn't do. Later, in an effort to retract that confession, Nathan told me he initially stabbed Ron by accident, after which Duncan picked up the knife and attacked Ron.

In court, Nathan offered yet another version of events.

Under questioning by Green, Nathan testified that he invited Diane, whom he had known for a few weeks and was dating informally, to visit that day. Nathan said he initially planned to stay home with Diane that night, until Duncan reminded him of a job interview he had arranged for them at Sony. Nathan told Diane that he and Duncan would need to go to the job interview later that night.

Once Diane arrived, his plans with Duncan changed again, Nathan testified. "Martinez came to me in private after Diane had gotten in and told me that he had met some girls, and he had lined up three girls for the three of us, and we were to meet them at the park," Nathan said, referring to himself, Duncan, and Ron. "I questioned him momentarily about Diane being there, and he told me the Sony thing will cover it," so Nathan agreed to go along.

Green asked Nathan if, prior to that evening, he and Duncan had any discussion of "some kind of hypothetical kidnapping plot." Nathan said they had. "Several weeks in advance, we were reading the newspaper and watching television or something, drinking beer, and Martinez had mentioned it, yes... He stated that if the two of us were ever to do a kidnapping, we could do it better than that. It had some reference to what we were watching or something. I don't really remember." Nathan said he didn't take the discussion seriously at the time, and there was no talk at all about killing the victim.

"Let's get back to the park that evening," said Green. "When you arrived at the park, what did you guys do?"

Nathan said they parked, then hiked up the hill to the tunnel entrance. They had with them a few six-packs of beer. Unbeknownst to him, Nathan said, Duncan also had a knife. "Once we made it to the top of the hill, Martinez pulled out a knife and was basically playing with it, throwing it to the ground."

Nathan testified that Ron and Duncan got into a discussion about some money Ron owed. The conversation "started off kind of jokingly" but ended with "slight hostility."

At some point while they were drinking outside the tunnel, Duncan threw the knife into the ground and Nathan took it. "I picked it up and started playing with it, and then I put it away," Nathan said. He was wearing a hiker's fanny pack and stored the knife inside.

"Now, did any girls ever show up?" asked Green.

"No."

"And what was your mood like at that point, before you went in the tunnel?"

"After sitting there for so long and the girls not showing up, I was kind of pissed off a little bit, because I had pretty much screwed up my evening...I could have been at the house with Diane." Nathan said he told Duncan they'd wasted enough time and should leave.

It was Duncan's idea to walk through the tunnel, Nathan recalled. "Martinez said the quickest way back was through the tunnel because of where we had parked."

Once they were in the tunnel, "the attention of the discussion turned toward me and my personal family life." Nathan said both Ron and Duncan made prejudicial comments about his adoptive family. "The gist of the conversation pertained to...I was adopted. My family is mixed...My family is made up of Hispanic, Black, and Asian."

Green asked Nathan how that made him feel.

"I am real defensive about my family, and I was already pissed off. I got a little angrier."

"What happened after that?"

"I jumped out and basically jumped on Ron."

"When you say you jumped on Ron, do you mean you attacked him or you literally jumped on him, or what did you do?"

"I jumped on him as in a fighting mode...In the darkness I threw a couple swings, and he basically from what I remember turned on me and tried to attack me back. I remember that I had the knife, and I drew the knife, and I stabbed him." Nathan said he did not know where on Ron's body he stabbed him, because it was too dark. "I can recall one stabbing and one slash," he said.

"What happened after that?"

"Baker hollered for Duncan because I was fighting with him. He moved away from me. I dropped the knife...Duncan flashed his lighter to see what had happened, and we saw Ron bleeding. Ron started complaining about the bleeding...That he was in pain. He was hurt."

"And what is the next thing that happened?"

"Martinez started hollering at both of us, basically, 'Shut the fuck up,' you know, 'Everyone just chill the fuck out for a minute.' I grabbed my lighter... Martinez had the knife, and he was basically diverting himself toward Ron because Ron was really complaining at this point in time." Nathan recalled Duncan saying, "'You've always been a whiner. You're always fucking crying about something.' And he attacked Ron."

"What did you do while Martinez was doing that?"

"It was dark. I really could not see... I just stood there."

"Did you go to either of their aid?"

"No, I did not."

Sitting in the courtroom watching Nathan testify, I did not buy his story. Given what I knew of Ron's ideals, it was hard to visualize him taunting Nathan in a bigoted manner. I felt Nathan by claiming that was trying to elicit sympathy and mitigate his attack on Ron. I also felt Nathan was tiptoeing through his testimony to account for the different versions he had told in his previously recorded statements. He was boxed in by what he had already said and could not veer too far from it. Yet in front of the jury, more than ever before, Nathan depicted Duncan as the primary aggressor and attacker of Ron. It was apparent to me that Nathan's goal was to minimize his criminal involvement to the jurors. But I doubted they would buy his story either.

That said, I could not know for certain what impression Nathan was making on the jury. As usual, he was composed and, at least in his delivery, fairly convincing. I wondered how he would fare under tougher questioning, during his upcoming cross-examination by Anne Ingalls.

Green, meanwhile, continued with her direct. She asked Nathan what happened next.

Nathan testified, "I flashed my lighter again, and I saw Ron laying there. I told Martinez, 'Let's get the fuck out of here.'" Nathan said he couldn't tell what shape Ron was in and whether he was still alive.

Nathan said he and Duncan left the tunnel. While they were climbing down the hill, Duncan told him they could implement the kidnapping plan they previously discussed.

"Is that the first that you had heard about this kidnapping thing that evening?"

"That evening, yes."

"Was there any real discussion about that, or did he just say it?"

"He said it. My mind was elsewhere."

Green asked Nathan what his state of mind was when they left the tunnel.

"I was kind of in shock. I'd never seen Duncan, as long as I have known him, do anything like that. My main thought, too, was that I had been involved in this, to the degree that I was."

After they got to their car, Nathan recalled, they drove to a school that Duncan said he had gone to near their apartment. Duncan found an outdoor water spigot and washed off his hands and arms.

"At that point, was there any discussion about what had happened in the tunnel?"

"There was. I asked him basically, 'What are we going to do?' And that's when he gave me the story about the bus stop thing. It already had been pretty much told to Diane."

"What do you mean he gave you the story about the bus stop thing? What did he tell you?"

"He told me if anyone inquires of what happened, if we both tell the police that we dropped him off at the bus stop, then no one could protest to that... The main discussion was what we were going to tell the police... Basically we came to the agreement that I would never say nothing if he never said anything. Each had our own personal reasons. It was pretty much the gist of the conversation." Nathan said when they said it, he meant it, and he believed Duncan meant it as well.

Green asked Nathan about his state of mind after they got home and he saw Diane.

"At this point in time, I was rather afraid for myself, actually. I did not want her to know what had happened and that was pretty much it. I was just kind of, like, out of it, so to speak."

"Was it your intent to cover up what had happened?"

"Yes, because of the involvement that I had with it. That is why I didn't want her to know."

Green asked about the call that night from Ron's father, and why Nathan didn't tell Mr. Baker what he knew.

"Again, because I was afraid of the possible charges that could be brought up against me for being involved in that situation. So I went along with what Martinez and I had discussed."

Nathan testified it was Duncan's idea to go back to the park at sunrise the next morning. Nathan said Duncan told him he wanted to go back and destroy the body. They climbed to the top of the hill and Duncan went inside the tunnel. Nathan remained outside.

"What was your frame of mind at that time?" asked Green.

"That we really shouldn't be here. *This is a bad idea*," Nathan said. Later, he also told Duncan he thought the ransom calls to Mr. Baker were a bad idea. "I told him what he was doing wasn't too cool, and I really didn't want to have a part with it. He told me don't worry about it. He's got it under control."

"Did you then stick with the original story with the police, every time they interrogated you up to that point?"

"Yes, I did," said Nathan.

Green elicited from Nathan the fact that he was convicted of robbery in July 1992 and, as a result, placed in custody. Nathan said he had no idea at that time where Duncan was.

"At some point while you were in custody, did Duncan Martinez get in touch with you?"

"Yes, he did."

"When he contacted you, when he saw you face-to-face, that was actually in the jail, right?"

"Yes, it was."

"What did you think Duncan wanted when he was talking to you?"

"At first, I really thought he was going to be a friend, to see how I was doing, the situation I was in. And my next thought was that he was trying to ensure our deal was still a deal...That I hadn't spoken to the police about what happened, and he hadn't either."

"Now, there were times in the course of that conversation that you made reference to the fact that 'Don't use my name. This may not be secure.' What did you mean by that?"

"The topic that he was talking about, the murder itself, I did not want to be implicated in. So I was asking him not to use my name."

Green asked whether, during that conversation, Duncan made statements that were untrue.

Nathan said yes.

"And why didn't you respond to those statements?"

"At that point, the last thing I actually wanted to do was get in a long verbal thing with Martinez about what happened."

"And why was that?"

"Because of what my part—what I had done."

"And what had you done?"

"I had had the fight with Ron and stabbed him."

"Was there anything else that you did?"

"No," testified Nathan.

Green next asked about his subsequent phone call with Duncan, while Nathan was in custody in the state prison in Tehachapi. "During that conversation, did Duncan Martinez say things to you about what had happened that night that simply weren't true?"

"Yes, he did."

"And at that time did you respond to those things?"

"No."

"During either of those conversations, did you ever accuse Duncan Martinez of doing what he had actually done? In other words, say, 'You're the one that killed him. What are you talking about?'"

"Not outright, no."

"Why didn't you do that?"

"Because I was still believing that we were keeping the deal that we made... I would never say anything as long as he never said anything." Nathan said he was also concerned about the security of the phone lines at the state prison, and that their conversation might be monitored.

"Then, at a later time, the police came to Tehachapi to interview you... That's the conference that you had with Detectives Jackson and Garcia... Is that right?"

"Yes."

"What was your state of mind at the point in the interrogation that they played the tapes to you?"

"When they played the tapes, I got scared. I felt kind of betrayed. I was confused... I kind of couldn't believe what was going on."

"At that time, you did tell the police you had stabbed Ron Baker two times. Is that right?"

"Yes, I did."

"Now, why didn't you tell the police at that point that Duncan Martinez is the one who had dreamed up, had actually been the one who had planted the kidnapping idea, and he was the one who had killed Ronald Baker?"

"Because again, where I was, was not a good place to get a jacket or a label, so to speak, and I still could not believe that Martinez was doing what he was doing."

"When you say it was not a good place to get a jacket or label, what are you talking about?"

"Being incarcerated, again, if someone overhears or someone discovers that you snitched on someone or told on someone, your own life can be in jeopardy."

"Now, at a later time than that, did you have a conversation with Detective Jackson at the LA County Jail?"

"Yes, I did."

"At that time you told Detective Jackson that you had only stabbed Ronald Baker once accidentally. Is that correct?"

"Yes, I did say that."

"And is that true?"

"No, it's not."

"You also told Detective Jackson some other things that were not true during that particular conversation. Is that right?"

"Yes, I did."

"Why is it that you made those statements to Detective Jackson if they weren't true?"

"At that point in time, I was rather afraid that being the only minority, that when this thing hit the fan, it was all going to blow up on me anyway. I was trying to protect myself and let Detective Jackson know what I had done without still implicating anybody else."

Green ended her direct examination of Nathan by asking him about his military service.

Nathan told the jury he was in the military from 1985 through 1988, during which time he was stationed in Korea.

"During military training, did you have any combat training or anything like that?"

"Yes."

"If you were to set about deliberately killing somebody, would you do it in the manner that Ronald Baker was killed?"

"No, I would not," testified Nathan.

"I have nothing further," said Green.

Deputy DA Ingalls began her cross-examination by asking Nathan, "How would you go about it, to deliberately kill someone?"

"That is a very good question, one I can't answer," said Nathan.

"You're not sure how you would do that?"

"I would not do that."

Ingalls asked Nathan some questions about the knife and when he took it out that night.

Nathan said it was right before or during the time he and Ron got into a fight.

Ingalls asked, "When you said you jumped on Ron Baker, that means that you were the one that assaulted him first. Is that correct?"

"Correct."

"It was pitch-black. Is that correct?" asked Ingalls.

"It was very dark, yes."

"At what point did you take the knife out of your hiking pack?"

"After Ron and I got into a confrontation, he attempted to defend himself. That's when I drew it."

"So you jumped on Ron Baker and started hitting him first, correct?"

"Yes, but there were no solid connections made... I just from behind threw a couple of swings at him."

Ingalls asked Nathan if he could tell where Ron was, in the darkness. Nathan said yes.

"And you jumped on him because he had said something to you?"

"Yes. We had a verbal confrontation between the three of us."

"What was the nature of the verbal confrontation?"

"We were talking about, as I said earlier, my family, things I had done. Things of that nature."

"Things that you had done and 'things of that nature.' What is it that made you jump on Ron Baker?"

"I was already upset from pretty much wasting my time following

Martinez up the hill in the first place, to meet someone who never showed up, and the extra aggravation upset me more."

"So you were aggravated at Duncan Martinez for wasting your time?"

"Yes."

"And being aggravated at Duncan Martinez, you jumped on Ron Baker, correct?"

"After the verbal confrontation started, yes."

"The verbal confrontation... Did that occur in the tunnel?"

"On the way in and in the tunnel."

"And the verbal confrontation was about what exactly?"

"My personal life."

"And was something wrong with your personal life?"

"I am defensive about my family. As I said earlier, I have been adopted. I have got a lot of stuff in the past, racial prejudice toward myself and my family."

"So these were things that Ron Baker was saying to you?"

"Yes."

"So he was saying things that aggravated you so much that you waited until you got in the tunnel and attacked him?"

"That is when it hit the highlight point, yes."

"What was it that threw you over the edge, Mr. Blalock?"

"The simple fact that we were talking about my adoption at that point in time, if I remember correctly."

Ingalls asked Nathan a series of questions about his size and physicality, as compared to Ron. On direct, Nathan had said he studied jujitsu and tae kwon do while he was in the Army. Nathan testified he didn't know if Ron was learning any martial arts at the time of his murder. "I didn't know him that long," Nathan said.

"After you jumped on him and he tried to defend himself, did you do any of the things that you had learned, whether it was in the military or while you were in Korea, the tae kwon do?"

"No, I did not."

"But you were able to think clearly enough to take the knife out of your fanny pack, take it out and stab him. Is that correct?"

"It was not a thought. It was an instinctive reaction."

Ingalls questioned Nathan about the discrepancies between his testimony that day and his earlier statement to me, that he took the knife out before they entered the tunnel. "You're saying that that was a lie?" she asked him.

"Yes."

"That you did not have the knife out? You instead had it in your fanny pack?"

"Yes."

"The only reason you brought it out was to stab Ronald Baker after he tried to fight back?"

"Yes."

"Now, for some reason you dropped the knife. Is that true?"

"Yes."

Ingalls asked Nathan some questions about where on Ron's body he stabbed him. Nathan said he could not tell because it was dark.

"After you stabbed him twice, what did he do?"

"He screamed out to Duncan."

"Were these significant stabs? ... You're a powerful man. Did you hit him good?"

"I wouldn't say that."

"What would you say, Mr. Blalock?"

"I would say I used enough force to bat the person off of me."

"Does that mean that you kind of went in a little bit with the knife, where you sunk it in?"

"I don't know, however it went in."

"You were mad, though."

"Yes, I was."

"And you were maybe enraged. Is that correct?"

"I won't say 'enraged.'"

"But you were mad enough to attack him in the dark. Is that correct?"

"Yes."

"And you were mad enough to take out that big old knife and stab him a couple of times. Is that correct?"

"Yes."

"But you're sure that you didn't just plunge the knife as deep as you could?"

"I'm pretty sure, yes."

"You just maybe nicked him a little bit?"

"I wouldn't say 'nicked.' I did not attempt to drive the knife into him to the hilt, if that is what you're referring to. No, I did not do that."

Ingalls reminded Nathan, and the jury, of his previous statement to me that he initially stabbed Ron accidentally. "And again, that was a lie?"

"Yes."

"You were doing that to protect yourself?"

"Yes."

"To put yourself in the best light?"

"I won't say 'the best light.' I would say protecting myself."

"You're kind of stuck with some of the things that Duncan Martinez said to you that you did not deny. Is that correct?"

"Yes."

"So you needed to minimize your conduct in this matter. Is that correct?"

"I did not want to be charged for something that I did not do."

"And at that point you thought the best thing to do was to say that you accidentally poked Ron Baker. Is that correct?"

"Yes."

Ingalls asked Nathan if he dropped the knife on purpose, after he first stabbed Ron. Nathan said he did.

"And at some point somehow Duncan Martinez picks it up?"

"Yes."

"So you're saying that Duncan Martinez, in realizing the opportunity here because you have already stabbed Ron Baker, then goes and gets the knife … and proceeds to stab him the other thirteen times?"

"Only after Ron was basically complaining about the injuries that I had done to him."

"And Duncan Martinez says, 'I'm so sick of you complaining and whining,' picks up the knife … and proceeds to stab Ron Baker thirteen more times?"

"Not in that particular order. But yes."

"So you're saying it was Ron Baker complaining about your stab wounds that irritated Duncan Martinez, to the point that he decided to kill Ron Baker?"

"In essence, yes."

"Now, you didn't actually see Duncan Martinez stab Ron Baker, did you?"

"No."

"You didn't turn on your lighter?"

"I had it on, and it got hot, and I let it go out."

"So during the time you had it on, what was occurring?"

"I was trying to get near Ron, and Ron moved away from me."

"And what were you going to do, go and help him?"

"In essence, yes."

"So after stabbing him and trying to beat him up, you were saying, 'Jeez, I wish I hadn't done that'?"

"Basically, yes."

"Did you say anything to Ron, 'I'm sorry about that,' or not?"

"I asked him, 'Let me help you.'"

"And he said, 'No, stay away'?"

"Yes, basically."

Ingalls asked Nathan what he understood Duncan to mean when he said they could implement the kidnapping plan. "You knew what he was talking about?"

"I had only assumed that he was speaking about what was spoken about several weeks in advance."

"And you didn't say anything at that time?"

"I was not in agreement, no."

"Did you indicate that you were not in agreement?"

"I believe I did. I believe my main concern was getting away from the scene, though."

"This was a horrifying experience to see somebody killed like that?"

"Yes."

"And to see somebody that you lived with killed. Would you agree with that?"

"Yes, I would."

"And Duncan Martinez's cold-bloodedness in seizing this opportunity to kill Ron Baker for being a whiner and a sniffler was a shock?"

"It was a shock to me. I had never seen him do anything like that."

"Did you feel differently about Duncan after this happened?"

"Yes."

"Did you look at him and say, 'I don't know if I know you. You're kind of evil. You're not the man that I knew'?"

"I would say I looked at him in a different light, yes." Nathan said from then on he didn't associate with Duncan and tried to stay away from him. "I told him to go his way and I'll go my way," he testified.

"Yet when you came back to the apartment, you guys still interacted as friends, correct?"

"We interacted, yes... The next day we went to play basketball because I told him not to make harassing calls anymore."

"You thought that was kind of a dirty thing to do, kind of a mean trick to play on Mr. Baker?"

"I wouldn't use those exact words, but yes."

Ingalls circled back to the subject of the kidnapping plan and when he and Duncan discussed it. Nathan said he believed they talked about it at least two weeks before Ron's murder.

"Did you actually discuss doing it to Ron Baker?"

"No."

"What was it that you guys discussed?"

"Somewhere there was an article or a TV show or something, and someone had been kidnapped, and he asked me if we were to ever do a kidnapping, that we would do it better than that."

"That you could do a better job?"

"Yes."

"What was it you were watching that you thought could have been improved?"

"I don't recall. At the time, we were drinking." Nathan estimated the conversation lasted about a minute. "It was very vague."

"You didn't talk about how to pick up the money or how to make the phone calls, anything like that?"

"Yes. Martinez said because of his long-distance running skills that there was a park he knew about that he would have the money dropped off in... I think that's pretty much it."

"Was a certain amount indicated?"

"Not that I can recall at that time."

"There was no discussion whether or not Mr. Baker, Ron Baker's father, could raise a hundred thousand dollars?"

"Not at that time… Only after it happened. Only after the murder happened."

Ingalls asked when after the murder they discussed that Mr. Baker could raise the money.

"Martinez never told me that Mr. Baker raised a hundred thousand dollars. He only told me that he was going to do it."

"He told you he was going to what?"

"Make the calls."

"He indicated to you that he was going to implement the kidnapping plan?"

"Yes."

Ingalls asked Nathan some additional questions that highlighted various discrepancies between his testimony that day and what he told me and Garcia previously.

"When Detective Garcia asks you, 'What did he do to piss you off, Nathan?' You say, 'I honestly can't remember. I honestly can't remember.' You were not being honest then?"

"No, I was not."

"You knew that he had actually pissed you off and that's why you stabbed him?"

"Yes."

"They certainly gave you ample opportunity to try to get your version of the events, if there was something that, you know, made you mad or irritated you, something mitigating. They gave you that opportunity, didn't they, Mr. Blalock, during this conversation?"

"Yes."

"But you did not take advantage of that opportunity at that time?"

"No, I did not."

Ingalls continued asking Nathan questions about statements he made on one occasion that contradicted what he said on another occasion, or on the witness stand that day, or both.

"In the face-to-face conversation with Duncan Martinez when you indicated to him, 'It was a plan. We both know what the plan was.'… Do you recall that?" asked Ingalls.

"I recall hearing both those statements."

"And you said to him, 'Well, you know, like I say, it was a plan. We both know what the plan was.' Do you recall saying that?"

"Yes, I do."

"And that would indicate there was a plan to kidnap. Would you agree to that?"

"No."

"You would say that refers to something else?"

"Yes."

"And what would you say that something else is?"

"The plan to stick with the original story and not say anything to anybody."

"So when he is talking about 'I was scared, flipped out. People don't go and stab people like that.' And you talk about 'Oh, we planned it. It happened. That's the military. We both know what the plan was,' you are referring to the plan to stick to our stories?"

"Yes."

"You are not talking about the plan to stab him, kill him, and then call Mr. Baker?"

"No, no."

"Now, when you were speaking to Garcia and Jackson, you are talking about it being an idea or concept that was brought to you, referring to Duncan?"

"Yes."

"The kidnapping. And they say, 'To kidnap Ron for money?' And you say, 'Exactly.'"

"Yes … This is in reference to on the way down the hill when Martinez mentioned it to me again."

"So instead of you two planning this in the apartment a couple weeks beforehand, you're saying that this is something that was said to you as you're running down the hill after you guys killed Ron Baker?"

"Roughly, yes."

"Detective Jackson in that particular interview says, 'It appears that Duncan never stabbed Ron. Is that true?' And you say, 'I can't say he did. I can't say he didn't.' Do you recall making that statement?"

"Yes, I did."

"Are you saying that you can't say that he did, today? You don't know if he did or not?"

"I can say that he did, yes."

"Today you say that he did do it?"

"Yes."

"And you are doing that because your memory is better?"

"No, I remember at that point in time I did not want to implicate him."

"You did not want to implicate Duncan?"

"Or myself."

"By saying that Duncan also stabbed him, how would that implicate you?"

"It just makes the matter worse."

"How does it make matters worse when you already say that you have stabbed somebody?"

"We still had a plan. I still felt loyal to Duncan as far as not telling on him."

"So today you don't feel as loyal, so you can lay it out on him?"

"Well, after being confronted with the fact that everything has happened, yes."

Ingalls asked Nathan about the account he gave me when we spoke at the county jail. "You don't even tell him that you saw Duncan Martinez stab. Is that correct?" Ingalls asked.

"I'm saying now I did not see Duncan stab him. I can only go by what I heard."

"Well, did you hear him thrust the knife in there, into the body?"

"I could hear sounds that you could implicate that through, yes... It's hard to describe sounds... They're the sounds that something was going on."

"Well, there's a lot of things. You could have somebody crying in pain. You could have somebody—"

"There were cries and moans, so to speak, where I don't know if— there were just grunts and moans."

"Okay. So now you remember that it was moans. What kind of moans were they?"

"Moans of pain."

"Coming from Ron?"

"Moans from him, grunts from Martinez, yes."

Ingalls asked Nathan about the concerns he expressed, during his recorded phone conversations with Duncan, about the lines being secure. "You were worried about the cops listening, right?"

"To a degree, yes."

"So you were worried about the cops listening in on the conversation and hearing you being implicated in the conversation?"

"Yes."

"So thinking that the cops might be listening, you don't say, 'Hey, I didn't do anything. You did it'?"

"I believe at one point in time I did say that. Not those exact words, but I did say that."

"At each opportunity that Duncan Martinez takes to say, 'You were the executioner,' 'I can't believe you stabbed him so many times.'… He goes on and on like that. Would you agree?"

"Those are hypothetical situations… Martinez presented them as hypothetical situations."

"Well, he on many occasions says, 'I can't believe, dude, that you did this. How could you do that? How could you stab him so many times?' It didn't sound too hypothetical to me. Did it sound hypothetical to you?"

"No."

"And thinking that the cops might be listening, you don't shout, 'I didn't do anything. I didn't stab anybody. I had nothing to do with this,' do you?"

"No, I do not."

Ingalls returned to Nathan's conversation with me, when he tried to retract his confession. "You told him that maybe you did stick him, but it was not deliberate, it was an accident?"

"Yes, I did."

"You were worried about—trying again not to implicate you, right?"

"No, I did not want to receive the full burden of this because I did not kill Ron. I was worried, more or less being the only minority between the three of us, you know, all this stuff would fly on me."

Ingalls quoted another exchange between Nathan and me, regarding the ransom money demanded of Mr. Baker. "Now, according to this conversation with Detective Jackson, you guys were going to split it. Is that correct? Split the money?"

"Martinez offered to split it with me, yes."

"And you agreed to that?"

"At that point in time, no."

"You did not agree to it? You said, 'No, I don't want any part of it'?"

"At that time, I did not disagree. I did not agree."

"You didn't say anything?"

"I said something, but not in disagreement or agreement."

"So where Jackson says, 'Were you guys going to split it?' You said, 'I would assume.' Jackson says, 'It seems fair.' And you said, 'Yeah, it seemed fair.'"

"It was a fair assumption, yes."

"To split the ransom money when it was Martinez's idea and he was doing all the work and he did all the killing. Why should you get any of it?"

"Because Martinez was basically going to pay me to keep silent."

"Okay, so he was going to blackmail you by giving you half of this money to keep quiet about what you observed in the tunnel?"

"I wouldn't say blackmail. I would just say pay me to keep quiet."

Ingalls closed her cross-examination by paraphrasing what Nathan told me, after I asked him how the kidnap and ransom plan was supposed to go down. "You say, 'Kidnap somebody and call their family, their house, husband or wife, whatever... We have your whoever, and this is how much money we want.' Do you recall telling Detective Jackson that?"

"Yes, I did."

Following Nathan's testimony, the defense rested its case.

Ingalls and Green presented their closing arguments on March 25, a week after the trial began. The case then went to the jury.

The jury would have to decide if Nathan was guilty of first-degree murder as well as whether the two special circumstances alleged, 'lying in wait' and 'murder for financial gain,' were true. The twelve jurors had to be in unanimous agreement. All it would take was one holdout, in either direction, for the jury to deadlock and a mistrial to be declared. In that event, a new trial would need to be held.

There was no way to know how long jury deliberations might take. Rather than sit vigil at the courthouse, I returned to the office. I had other murder cases that I needed to work.

The call that the jury had reached a verdict came on Friday morning, after more than three days of deliberations.

I walked the two blocks from police headquarters to the Criminal Courts Building. Waiting to learn the verdict on one of my cases was always a tense experience. So much rode on hearing either "guilty" or "not guilty." Even in cases that seemed like a sure thing, surprises were possible.

Once I knew a verdict had been reached, I was confident that Nathan would be found guilty. I felt there was no way twelve jurors who heard the evidence could all agree on a not-guilty verdict.

Inside the courtroom, the jury's verdict was read aloud by the court clerk. Ron's parents and Patty were present.

As we looked on, Nathan was pronounced guilty of first-degree murder. The jury also found both special circumstances to be true.

Nathan reacted stoically to the verdict.

His sentencing would take place at a later date. Because of the jury's findings with respect to the special circumstances, and the DA's decision not to seek the death penalty, it was a fait accompli that the sentence he would receive would be life without the possibility of parole.

I felt elated and relieved, mostly because of the responsibility I felt toward the Baker family. They had been waiting for justice for almost six years.

Finally someone had been held accountable for Ron's murder.

Would Nathan bear the full weight alone of what he and Duncan had done together? Or would Duncan's fate follow Nathan's?

It remained to be seen.

CHAPTER 26

EQUAL JUSTICE?
(June 3 to August 26, 1996)

DUNCAN'S TRIAL WAS SLATED to take place in the courtroom of Judge Edward Ferns, the same judge who had presided over Nathan's trial and conviction.

As is sometimes the case, however, pretrial proceedings were conducted by a different judge, Jacqueline Connor, a former deputy DA who was well regarded for her smart, no-nonsense courtroom demeanor.

On Monday, June 3, Judge Connor convened a hearing for a motion filed by James Gregory, Duncan's attorney. Anne Ingalls, the prosecutor for Nathan, reprised the role for Duncan.

Gregory's motion centered on the alleged promise of a lenient sentence for Duncan in exchange for his cooperation against Nathan. Gregory planned to call two witnesses.

The first witness was Jim Barnes, Gregory's predecessor as Duncan's attorney. Barnes testified to his early involvement in the case. He spoke about Duncan's initial King for a Day agreement and that nothing Duncan told us that day could be used against him. Barnes also testified about his discussions with Deputy DA Ernie Norris, the prosecutor on the case at that time, regarding some kind of plea agreement for Duncan.

I was shocked by the second witness Gregory called: Ernie Norris himself. The fact that Norris was still actively working as a deputy DA was not the only reason the situation was bizarre and, at least in my experience, unprecedented.

In the time since his replacement as lead prosecutor on the Baker case, Norris had run for district attorney and lost. He had also been transferred from his longtime post in the elite Special Trials unit, the same unit where Ingalls now worked. As if things were not awkward enough, it was Norris who had sponsored Ingalls's assignment to Special Trials. Now she would have to cross-examine him in public.

On the witness stand, Norris recounted his part as the original prosecutor on the Baker case. This included his role as the architect of Duncan's King for a Day agreement and, leading up to the interview, as the main conduit to Duncan's original defense attorney, Barnes.

Norris disclosed he had made a one-time offer to Barnes, in consideration of Duncan's prospective cooperation. According to Norris, the terms discussed were that if Duncan pleaded guilty to voluntary manslaughter, he would receive a sentence with a guarantee of no jail time.

I was stunned by the revelation that Norris had offered Duncan a no-jail-time sentence. Generally, this was something a deputy DA, especially a veteran one like Norris, would discuss with the detectives on the case. Yet Garcia and I had heard nothing about it from Norris at the time, or since, until his surprise appearance as a witness for the defense.

Based on the testimony of Norris and Barnes, Gregory argued that the DA's Office was bound by the terms of the offer and should not be allowed to renege on the purported agreement. Accordingly, the first-degree murder case against Duncan should be dismissed or at least substituted with a lesser charge, Gregory contended.

Gregory also alleged misconduct by Deputy DA Marcia Clark when she presented the case against Duncan to the grand jury, arguing Clark intentionally misled the grand jurors by not informing them of Duncan's cooperation with the police.

Ingalls responded by identifying the holes in Gregory's arguments. No matter what Norris had offered or agreed to with Barnes, for a plea agreement for murder to be valid and binding, it had to be approved at the highest levels of the DA's Office. Furthermore, the plea agreement had to be memorialized in writing. Gregory could offer no evidence either had ever occurred with Duncan.

Ingalls said the sole binding agreement made with Duncan was that his statements to the LAPD in Utah, with his attorney Barnes present, could not be used against him. That deal was never breached. It was only when Duncan tried to get out of a burglary charge by telling police there about Ron's murder that he provided enough evidence to indict him. "Otherwise, he would be back in school or finishing school or whatever else he wanted to do," she said.

Ingalls additionally argued that Duncan was not entitled to leniency because he was jointly responsible for Ron Baker's murder. Ingalls cited the fact that Duncan was present when Ron was killed, his knife was used to do the stabbing, and he participated in the plan to obtain ransom money from the Bakers. "He is as culpable as if he had stabbed Ron Baker," she said.

During his testimony, Norris seemed to agree with Gregory's assessment of Marcia Clark. He repeatedly addressed Judge Connor directly, a breach of courtroom decorum. He also said it was his obligation as an "officer of the court" to call attention to what he believed was prosecutorial misconduct by his successors in not honoring the plea agreement he had proposed to Barnes.

When Connor pointed out that Norris had no authorization from his superiors to offer that plea deal, he interrupted her and began to vehemently protest. The exchange between prosecutor-turned-judge Connor and prosecutor-turned-defense-witness Norris became more and more heated, to the point that I felt Connor was close to threatening Norris with contempt of court. Only after Connor sternly warned Norris to check his behavior did he finally relent.

Personally, the courtroom drama made me feel uncomfortable. Ernie Norris had been a highly respected prosecutor for decades. I considered him a friend of mine, although I have to admit I lost some respect for him, seeing how he handled himself that day. I knew he was citing his ethical beliefs, but I also believed Norris felt cast aside as the prosecutor on the Baker case by his supervisor, David Conn. Conn had had his own disagreements with Norris about how to proceed on the case and Duncan's fate. Conn had decided that Duncan would not be used as a witness at Nathan's trial, both because his testimony was not necessary and because his credibility was horrendous. I felt Norris was acting in retaliation for being sidelined on the case and ultimately transferred out of the Special Trials unit.

At the conclusion of the hearing, Judge Connor did not announce her ruling. Instead, she encouraged Ingalls and Gregory to meet and attempt to reach a plea agreement.

The parties reconvened in Connor's courtroom on Wednesday morning, June 5. Connor denied Gregory's motion to dismiss, on the grounds that Norris's offer to Barnes was never approved by the upper levels of the DA's Office. Accordingly, the first-degree murder indictment against Duncan would stand.

Connor then asked for an update on the plea negotiations.

Ingalls reported that the DA's Office was prepared to let Duncan plead guilty to second-degree murder, which carried an indeterminate sentence of fifteen years to life.

Gregory countered that Duncan would not accept an indeterminate "to life" sentence, only a determinate sentence of fixed length. Duncan was unwilling to plead guilty to second-degree murder because there was no guarantee that, after serving the minimum, he would receive parole and be released, rather than kept in prison indefinitely, potentially for the rest of his life.

Neither side was willing to budge in court that day. Connor urged them to continue talking prior to Duncan's trial, which they agreed to do. Gregory suggested Duncan was open to pleading guilty to voluntary manslaughter, lower than what the DA's Office had put on the table. Connor made clear that she felt a sentence without any prison time for Duncan was out of line.

The following week, on June 14, Nathan appeared before Judge Ferns for his sentencing. His first-degree murder conviction with special circumstances meant his sentence was predetermined. As expected, Ferns sentenced Nathan to life without the possibility of parole. Nathan was at that time twenty-eight years old. He would almost certainly spend the rest of his living years within an array of California state prisons.

A few days later, I received a call from Deputy Brittain with the LA County Sheriff's Department. Brittain worked as a liaison between the county jail system and local law enforcement agencies, including the LAPD. He told me he needed some background information regarding an inmate named Duncan Martinez. He said Duncan was currently housed at the Wayside Honor Rancho, a satellite county jail facility near Castaic, north of Los Angeles.

Brittain explained that Duncan had asked a supervisor at Wayside for an inmate status change to K-10, the code for inmate informants, or snitches, as they were often called. The K-10 designation was for inmates who perceived a danger from other inmates and felt they needed additional protective measures.

I told Brittain I had already requested a keep-away order for Duncan from his crime partner, Nathan Blalock. Brittain identified the supervisor at Wayside who Duncan had spoken with as a Sergeant Blake. Brittain said Blake would have additional knowledge of why Duncan had requested the status change.

I spoke with Sergeant Blake on the phone that same afternoon. He told me Duncan had approached him and said the murder case in which he was charged was in the news. Duncan also alleged that prosecutor Marcia Clark's conduct was potentially going to get her disbarred. Duncan had told Blake that *60 Minutes* was going to do a story on it, and therefore he wished to be placed in protective custody.

I gave Blake some background on the case, including the keep-away order I had already requested between Duncan and Nathan. Blake thanked me for the information but did not say whether Duncan's status change request would be granted. That would be the Sheriff Department's call, based on what Duncan had told them, what I had added, and any other follow-up inquiries they might make.

I was skeptical of Duncan's claim about *60 Minutes*. I also thought it was interesting, yet unsurprising, that Duncan had mentioned Marcia Clark. Duncan's lawyer, Gregory, had also invoked Clark's name, repeatedly, during the hearing before Judge Connor.

I found it ironic, not least because Clark had done absolutely nothing wrong. Her newfound fame post-Simpson had made her a target of attacks, even when it was totally unwarranted. I believed it was a ploy to attract media attention, as if the mere mention of Marcia Clark, combined with vague allegations of misconduct, would prove irresistible catnip for reporters. In my opinion, that Clark's name was seemingly the only one ever raised and bandied about proved my point.

* * *

Connor's dismissal of Gregory's motion cleared the way for Duncan's trial to begin. As the trial date neared, plea negotiations between the DA's Office and Gregory remained deadlocked.

The DA's Office insisted it would go no lower than its offer of a second-degree murder plea by Duncan. Gregory held firm that Duncan would not accept that deal. The defense's sticking point continued to be the indeterminate "to life" portion of the fifteen years to life sentence that would be guaranteed with a second-degree plea.

I had been working homicide long enough to know that policies in the criminal justice system never remained the same for long. The pattern often seemed like a pendulum swinging one way and then the other, toward leniency or severity and back again.

In 1996, when Duncan was preparing to go to trial, few inmates serving "to life" sentences for murder were being granted parole and released from prison. They would come up for a parole hearing, or even multiple parole hearings, only to be denied and returned to prison indefinitely, long after they had completed their minimum sentences.

For Duncan, a fifteen years to life sentence meant he would have to serve about 85 percent of the minimum, or just under thirteen years, before he would be eligible for a parole hearing to determine if he should be released. At the time, however, the odds of Duncan being granted parole and released right away seemed unlikely.

I believed Duncan deserved some benefit for his cooperation and assistance, albeit not to the degree that Ernie Norris had in mind. Norris's offer did not take into account that Duncan's motive for cooperating had been self-serving, nor that he had ended up breaking the terms of the agreement.

I felt Duncan should serve in the neighborhood of twenty years before his potential release.

Although I gave it a great deal of thought, my opinion about what would be an appropriate sentence for Duncan meant next to nothing. I was free to share my thoughts with Ingalls, but I knew the final decision would be made by the DA's Office, generally at levels well above hers.

If second-degree murder was the DA's best and final offer, which they claimed it was, and Duncan rejected that deal, then his case would go to trial. If he was convicted at trial of first-degree murder with the special circumstances, the sentence he was guaranteed to receive was not fifteen years to life but life without parole.

Going to trial struck me as a tremendous risk for Duncan. Considering the strength of the evidence, it also seemed to me like a potentially enormous mistake.

I strongly believed it was in Duncan's best interest to accept the second-degree plea offer.

I assumed the offer on the table from the DA had been conveyed to Duncan and his family. But I could not be certain they fully understood what was at stake if Duncan took the case to trial. My gut told me I should reach out to Jeannie Martinez, Duncan's mother. Her interactions with Garcia and me had always been amicable. I felt she would have her son's interests at heart.

I called Jeannie one day a few weeks before the trial was to begin.

When I said who was calling, she immediately replied, "I'm not supposed to talk to you."

I told her I wasn't calling to ask her any questions, only to relay some thoughts I had. Jeannie said nothing but did not hang up.

I explained that I just wanted to make sure she was aware of the DA's second-degree plea offer and what it meant in terms of Duncan's sentence. I warned her that the jury hearing Duncan's case would without a doubt despise him for his involvement in the kidnapping-for-ransom plot and for allowing his best friend to be murdered. I said that based on my experience and how Nathan had fared at his trial, Duncan would almost certainly be found guilty of first-degree murder with special circumstances, as Nathan had been. The evidence against Duncan was just as strong as against Nathan. If Duncan pleaded guilty to second-degree murder, he at least stood a chance of being released from prison one day.

I told Jeannie that I felt Duncan deserved some benefit for helping the police investigate Ron's murder. I promised her that if Duncan took the second-degree deal, once he served his minimum sentence and became eligible for parole, I would write a letter to the parole board detailing his cooperation and the important role it played in solving the case.

After I said my piece, we ended the call. Jeannie had heard me out, which was all I had asked of her. She did not tell me her thoughts or address mine. Nor did she let on what Duncan would choose, the plea deal or a trial, or which way he was leaning.

Whether my call would have any effect on Duncan's decision, I did not know. But I was glad I had made the call.

There was another call I felt compelled to make before Duncan's trial began. I had not been looking forward to it.

Nathan's trial had received a fair amount of media coverage, and I thought Duncan's would attract as much or more. Considering that Duncan had spent time in Massachusetts and Utah, I expected the news coverage could extend beyond California.

I was concerned that it would come out at Duncan's trial that, while he was on the run, he had stolen the identity of a long-dead child, Jonathan Wayne Miller. I did not want Jonathan's parents to be caught unaware and learn of their son's victimization that way. I knew it would be re-traumatizing to them no matter what but hopefully less so if they had been warned.

It was not hard to locate the parents. I had much of their identifying information from their son's birth and death certificates.

I called Jonathan's father, James, who was still living in Massachusetts, where his son was born and had died more than twenty years earlier. I explained that Jonathan's identity had been stolen and assumed by a man who was now charged with murder in Los Angeles. Mr. Miller was understandably upset that his son and his son's memory had been violated. He informed me that he and Jonathan's mother, Mary, had divorced many years earlier.

I called Mary later the same day. Like her former husband, she was shocked and upset.

My heart went out to them. They had already endured the most terrible tragedy a parent can know. I had disturbed whatever peace they had been able to find with the passage of time. During my career I had made countless death notifications, and I always found them harrowing and painful. This felt even worse. I would remember my calls to Jonathan's parents as among the most heart-wrenching moments I experienced as a detective. Years later, when I was in Massachusetts, I visited the graveyard where Jonathan had been laid to rest and paid my respects.

In the weeks between the hearing in Judge Connor's courtroom and the start of Duncan's trial, change was afoot in my own life.

I was coming up on twenty years with the LAPD, the minimum tenure to qualify for a pension at that time. Over the previous few years, my wife and I had visited New England several times. She had fallen in love with the region and wanted us to move there once I reached the twenty-year mark. I had agreed. It seemed only right, given the demands my job had placed on her and the family, especially when our girls were younger. So much had revolved around my work during the decade-plus I'd been working homicide. I felt it was time to put my family first.

In mid-July, I was offered a job in Boston by a major air shipping company that made deliveries nationwide. If I took the job, I would be responsible for all company investigations in the six New England states as well as Upstate New York. I decided to accept.

But as my twentieth anniversary with the LAPD neared, I began to get cold feet.

I would no longer be working the job I loved, the job that felt so entwined with who I was. Investigating murders had been my boyhood dream and lifelong calling. I would miss the excitement and fellowship of the detectives, crime lab personnel, and prosecutors I had worked alongside on so many cases through the years. I knew a job in the private sector would be a major adjustment.

On July 24, despite my apprehension, I signed my retirement papers. My final workday as an LAPD detective would be August 9. We would hit the road for a two-week cross-country drive, with sightseeing stops along the way, before reaching the home we had rented for our first year.

My quite sudden retirement meant I would be unable to carry out the responsibility of sitting through Duncan's upcoming trial, now scheduled for mid-August. My former partner Frank Garcia would have to testify to what had transpired during our investigation of Ron Baker's murder.

It was a bitter pill to swallow, not being able to see through to the very end the case that had consumed so many of my working hours over the past six years. But my new job called.

Duncan and the DA's Office proved unable to agree on a plea agreement acceptable to both sides. Through his attorney, Duncan rejected the DA's offer of pleading guilty to second-degree murder and a guaranteed sentence of fifteen years to life.

Duncan's decision to roll the dice at trial, and risk a life-without-parole sentence, was his choice to make. He had every right to challenge the DA's Office to prove its case in court. Juries can be unpredictable. But I found it hard to imagine any juror liking Duncan or feeling any empathy for him once they learned the extent of his culpability for Ron's murder.

It also bothered me that, in turning down the DA's offer, Duncan was essentially saying he deserved no prison time for his actions and role in Ron's death.

No incarceration time for discussing and planning the kidnapping and murder of his own friend. None for his abject failure to intervene and come to his friend's aid during or after the stabbing. None for calling his friend's parents and with a disguised voice demanding money, giving them false hope their son was still alive. None for lying and withholding for more than a year and a half his knowledge of what happened, until he felt it might benefit him to come forward.

The leniency Duncan was receiving for his belated cooperation was the opportunity to plead guilty to second-degree murder. That was two full rungs below what he had been charged with. The DA's Office was willing to bypass a possible sentence of life without parole, as well as a possible twenty-five years to life sentence for first-degree murder. I thought it was a very fair offer.

When Duncan rejected it, it extinguished any sympathy I had felt for him receiving no benefit for his assistance.

I was somewhere in the middle of the country when, back in Los Angeles, Duncan's trial got underway in mid-August.

The prosecution's case and evidence presented by Ingalls were largely the same as during Nathan's trial. The one major addition to the witness list was Salt Lake City detective Jim Prior, who testified to the grisly details of what Duncan had told him about Ron's murder.

Unlike Nathan at his trial, Duncan did not take the stand to testify in his own defense. That his attorney did not call him did not surprise me, given the obvious issues with Duncan's credibility as a witness. Duncan was therefore spared the adversarial cross-examination that Nathan had been subjected to at his trial. The jury would decide Duncan's guilt without hearing from him directly.

The jury returned its verdict on Monday, August 26. The verdict for Duncan was the same as for Nathan: guilty of first-degree murder, with both special circumstances, 'lying in wait' and 'murder for financial gain,' found to be true.

Duncan had gambled and lost. His sentencing, like Nathan's, would be a mere formality.

It had taken more than six years for the justice system to catch up to what occurred inside the Manson tunnel on the night of the summer solstice in 1990. The case of Ron Baker's murder could finally be closed.

In the end, two separate juries considered the evidence individually against Nathan and Duncan and reached the same conclusion. They were culpable for Ron's murder to the same degree and thus deserved the same sentence: life without any possibility of parole.

CHAPTER 27

MY RETURN TO THE SCENES OF THE CRIMES
(1996 to 2020)

SOON AFTER I STARTED my new private-sector job in Boston, I realized I'd made a big mistake.

I hated the new job.

My primary responsibility was investigating who was responsible for any packages within my territory that "went missing."

In most cases, the leading theory was that it was an inside job, a theft committed by a company employee at some point along the shipment's route. This meant the usual pool of suspects were fellow company personnel, mostly warehouse workers and delivery drivers. Anytime a package went missing anywhere in New England or Upstate New York, I was tasked with going there to investigate. Interviews and tracking numbers took center stage in these investigations.

It was a far cry from trying to solve murders and bring killers to justice.

The grueling commute to my office in South Boston, seventy miles from our new home, made going to work even more unpleasant. I knew the drive and traffic would only get worse when winter weather conditions set in.

I sorely missed my old work. Trying to identify who had stolen a shipped computer did not compare to the thrill of figuring out who had stolen a person's life.

The Ron Baker case was a perfect example. The work had been painstaking, the long hours exhausting, and the stakes and pressure high. But for me, no feeling compared to putting together the pieces to solve the murder.

I also badly missed the camaraderie of my former colleagues, as I had expected I would. I had always enjoyed working with a partner. In my new investigative job, I worked alone.

The pain I felt at having to leave my post at RHD and my misgivings about the new job began to affect my personal life. My wife and I had grown apart. Within a few months, we agreed to separate, and eventually divorced.

I quit my job and began looking for something else in the area. I had a pension, but only a twenty-year service pension. It was enough to hold me for a while, but not enough to sustain both me and my support obligations after the impending divorce.

I taught a criminal justice class at a local college, but that was only part-time. My search for a full-time job was not producing results.

In 1997, I received a call from a former LAPD detective colleague, also retired, named Bill Gailey. Gailey and I had worked together at both the Hollywood Homicide unit and RHD. He had retired before me and started what would become a very successful private investigation firm. He offered me a job as one of his investigators.

I had not worked for six months and decided to accept the offer. Taking the job meant returning to Southern California. Unfortunately, I would be returning alone. My ex-wife had no interest in leaving her new life in New England. Our daughters would continue to live there with her. The geographic separation from them would be devastating. I was heartbroken. But my ex-wife was now a resident of the state she lived in. I could not take the girls with me.

I moved back to Southern California and dove into my new job at Gailey's firm. In the back of my mind, however, I was already contemplating trying to return to work with the LAPD. I knew I legally could do it, as long as my application came within three years of my retirement.

There were several obstacles. I would have to pass a fairly rigorous medical exam, which would not take into account that I was in my late forties, rather than a twenty-one-year-old police recruit. In order to improve my uncorrected eyesight, I had to undergo laser eye surgery. Would I pass muster physically?

There were also many uncertainties within the police department. I knew if I was rehired I was guaranteed to return at a detective rank, since that was my civil service designation when I retired. But that did not necessarily mean I could resume working homicides or return to my old assignment at RHD. That would depend on the department's needs and where there were positions open, if and when I made it to the point of being rehired. What if I went through the entire rehiring process only to be offered a detective position working auto theft?

I submitted my application and waited for it to be processed.

In mid-1999, I received a call from Captain Jim Tatreau, the current commanding officer of RHD. I did not know him personally. Tatreau told me he was aware I was attempting to come back on the job. He said he had done some background on my career and planned to bring me on again at RHD the day I returned. I was overjoyed.

My first day back with the LAPD was December 20, 1999. I was assigned to RHD's Homicide Special Section. Like my former squad, Major Crimes, Homicide Special had citywide jurisdiction for the select murder cases that would come to RHD.

About two years later, I was tapped to join a brand-new unit being formed within RHD, the Cold Case Homicide Special Section. A former colleague at Hollywood Homicide, Detective David Lambkin, had successfully lobbied for the creation of a team of detectives dedicated exclusively to tackling the backlog of approximately nine thousand unsolved murders committed in Los Angeles since 1960. The idea was to leverage advances in forensic science (like DNA analysis) and technology (like computer databases of evidence and suspects) to try to solve as many cold cases as possible.

The Cold Case Homicide Special Section came into existence in November 2001. It consisted of Lambkin, myself, and five other detectives.

Faced with such an overwhelming number of cases, our strategy was to prioritize those in which there was physical evidence that was untested and appeared promising. In screening cases, we focused on sexual-assault murders and murders in which the victim and suspect had had close contact, for instance, stabbings and fatal physical assaults.

I was absolutely thrilled with my new assignment. I loved delving into cases from decades past. Working cold cases felt to me like having access to a time machine. I was also confident our unit would produce good results. The vast majority of the city's unsolved murders had not been reinvestigated since the emergence of DNA testing. As I saw it, the crop was ripe for picking.

Within a few years, the new Cold Case Homicide unit had solved over two dozen murders, including those perpetrated by serial killers whose prolific killings were previously unknown to be connected.

The process of working a cold case is different from working a fresh murder. It begins with a thorough review of the documentation, all of the reports compiled over the course of the original investigation. Next comes a search for what evidence and witnesses are still around, which, depending on how old the case is, cannot be taken for granted. Generally, the last step is to approach and question the suspect. Most of the DNA and other forensic analysis linking the suspect to the crime scene has already been completed. All that remains to be done is confront the suspect, who is typically unaware that the case has even been reopened.

It's an exhilarating and surreal experience to solve a decades-old case, walk up to the suspect's front door, and wait for them to answer. The door opens and suddenly I'm face-to-face with the killer, who likely long ago assumed they had gotten away with murder. "I think we need to talk," I might say, starting a conversation that usually ends with their arrest.

Another especially rewarding aspect of cold case work is providing answers to families who may have given up any hope of justice for their murdered loved ones. In more than one cold case I worked, even ones I unfortunately was unable to solve, I developed an enduring bond with the victim's surviving family members. Sometimes the bond even outlasted the resolution and formal closure of the case. I attribute it to the powerful mix of emotions produced by the reopening of these seemingly forgotten, but not forgotten, unsolved cases. Inevitably, old wounds were reopened, but at the same time, families were grateful that someone cared and was still carrying the torch after so many years.

I also kept in touch with the Baker family, through phone calls and at least one visit to their home. Gayle and Kay sought solace in their religious beliefs and church community, where they continued to serve as devoted volunteers. They kept Ron's memory alive by visiting his grave on his birthday and every Christmas. On these visits, Gayle always brought garden shears, which he used to manicure and lovingly care for Ron's burial plot. After Gayle and Kay passed, in 2010 and 2013 respectively, I continued to speak with Ron's sister, Patty, from time to time.

Even as life moved on and I worked on other homicide cases, Ron Baker's murder stood out as a singular case in my career. For one, I had worked on the Baker case for a long period of time: six years from start to finish. Never had I had a case with so many unexpected twists and turns, nor would I have another one like it. Duncan and Nathan were among the most interesting and memorable suspects I encountered during all my years working homicide.

Working cold cases, I sometimes had to visit various California state prisons to interview inmates, whether a suspect or a witness.

Twice while working on unrelated cases, I happened to visit prisons where Nathan Blalock was incarcerated, first at Salinas Valley State Prison and later at Mule Creek State Prison. Both times, I sought Nathan out and visited with him.

My visits were short, not more than ten or fifteen minutes, just long enough to check in on his life in the institution and ask how he was doing. Our interactions were always cordial.

Duncan, on the other hand, I never visited. It was not because I had any animus toward him. It was simply a matter of circumstances. I never had reason to go to the state prison where he was serving his sentence. I'm not sure how Duncan would have greeted me, considering we ended on worse terms than I had with Nathan.

For the final twelve years of my LAPD career, I worked nothing but cold case murders.

* * *

I retired my second, and final, time from the LAPD in October 2013, after a total of thirty-four years on the job. In the last twenty-eight years, I had exclusively investigated homicides.

In 2006, I reconnected with a childhood classmate, Debbie Halliday. I had always harbored a schoolboy crush on Debbie, but we did not start dating until much later in life. Following my retirement in 2013, I moved to Northern California to be closer to her, and we married the following summer, forty-nine years after we first met.

During my first few years as a retired detective, I did a lot of traveling and played a lot of golf. Still, I missed working cold cases and could not shake the feeling I had more left to give.

In 2016, I received a call from the chief of police in the city where I lived. I did not know him, but someone had given him my name and number. He had also been told I had a lot of experience investigating cold cases. He asked if we could meet and I agreed.

I met the chief at his office that same week. He explained there was a cold case from 1985, a sexually motivated homicide of a woman. The chief said it bothered him that the case had not been solved.

I spent a few days reading the file and came up with an investigative game plan. Since I was a civilian volunteer, with no authority to make crime lab requests, I had to partner with an active-duty detective. My new partner was Detective Charlene Jacquez of the Contra Costa County Sheriff's Office. Working together, Jacquez and I used DNA analysis, which did not exist at the time of the murder, to develop leads and eventually identify a likely suspect who had died years earlier. We exhumed his body to obtain his DNA profile, which matched the crime scene evidence. We had solved the case. It was a feeling I hadn't been sure I would ever get to experience again after leaving the LAPD.

And it didn't stop there. In 2017, I met a cold case investigator with the San Mateo County Sheriff's Office named Dave Tresmontan. He was also retired from law enforcement but had returned to work cold cases. Tresmontan said he currently was working without a detective partner. I saw him as a kindred spirit who, like me, had not had his fill yet of police investigations.

After Tresmontan and I discussed our backgrounds, he said I should come work with him. He introduced me to his boss, the lieutenant overseeing the Investigations Bureau. Within a few weeks, I was hired to work with Tresmontan. Our mission would be to reinvestigate and see if we could solve more of San Mateo County's unsolved murders. Since then, we have solved multiple cases from the 1970s through the 1990s.

I continue to work cold cases there to this day, trying to provide answers, and hopefully some comfort, to the families of homicide victims.

PART IV
THE FINAL BETRAYAL

CHAPTER 28

"BY VIRTUE OF THE AUTHORITY VESTED IN ME"
(June 21 to December 7, 2020)

JUNE 21, 2020, MARKED thirty years since the night of Ron Baker's murder. I thought of him and the crime every year on the anniversary of his death. The date was easy to remember: June 21, customarily known as the first day of summer.

The early summer of 2020 already felt surreal, tense, and uncertain. And that was before the late-breaking, knee-buckling curveball that soon upended the long-dormant Baker case.

The world was just a few months into the COVID-19 pandemic. In California, daily life had moved online to contain the spread of the virus. Face-to-face interactions that I had always taken for granted suddenly felt risky and were to be avoided. Personally, I was informed my cold case work with the San Mateo County Sheriff's Office was suspended until further notice. The sheriff had mandated that all non-essential duties were to be curtailed indefinitely. Evidently, this included decades-old unsolved murders. Their potential solving would have to wait even longer.

Less than a month earlier, in Minneapolis, Minnesota, a Black man named George Floyd had been murdered by a white police officer, as other officers stood by and failed to intervene. Disturbing video of Floyd's killing had emerged and ignited nationwide outrage and street protests. The eruption of anger had reminded me of the volatile, painful aftermath of Rodney King's beating by LAPD officers in 1991, only it had been even more intense. When I saw the Floyd video, it was apparent that if increased oversight of police and criminal justice reform had not yet taken hold, it was about to. Among the fallout from Floyd's death was a rise in politically progressive candidates running for district attorney in locales across the country, with California seemingly leading the way.

Such was the troubling and troubled state of the world when, just after 9:30 p.m. on Saturday night, June 27, my cell phone rang. I was already in bed, watching TV with my wife.

I did not recognize the number and I let it ring. They could leave a voicemail if it was important.

Within a few minutes, a voicemail notification appeared on my phone. I listened to it. The caller was Patty Baker Elliott, Ron's sister. It had been a few years since we last spoke.

Patty sounded unsettled and distressed. "I'm sorry for calling so late," she began her message. "I just saw a news article that says Duncan may possibly be released. He's going to appear before the Board of Parole. I just wanted to see what I can do, or what can be done... I don't know who else to talk to. I wanted to see if you had heard about it and what your thoughts were. I thought they were supposed to let family know if anything ever were to happen."

I was surprised and perplexed. I had heard nothing about Duncan potentially coming before a parole board, and it didn't make sense. Duncan had been sentenced to life without parole, a term of imprisonment a jury had handed down almost a quarter century before. Inmates serving LWOP are not eligible for parole hearings.

To my knowledge, the only way an LWOP inmate could become eligible for parole was if their original sentence was commuted. The only person with the power to grant a commutation was the governor of California, currently Gavin Newsom.

I was aware that the number of commutations granted in California had risen sharply in recent years, a trend that began during the administration of former governor Jerry Brown and had continued under Newsom.

But the idea that Newsom would commute Duncan's sentence struck me as implausible.

Why would Newsom intervene in the case of Duncan Martinez, of all people? And if what Patty had said was true, and Newsom had commuted Duncan's sentence, how could this be the first that I, and more importantly Patty, had heard anything about it?

I called Patty back the next morning.

She explained she had seen an online news article about several pardons and commutations Governor Newsom had just issued. She had skimmed the article for the inmates' names, as was her habit whenever she saw a list like this in the media. She never expected to see Duncan's or Nathan's name, since she knew they had both received LWOP sentences.

Patty was stunned when she read down the list and came to the name Duncan Martinez. She felt betrayed and heartbroken that she had never heard anything from Governor Newsom's office, or anyone else, that a commutation for Duncan was even under consideration. The article indicated the commutation had already been granted.

Patty didn't understand how it could be that she was given no opportunity, as the victim's lone surviving family member, to weigh in before a decision was made by Newsom. She'd always been told by the DA's Office that she would be notified if any such issue came up. After Nathan and Duncan were convicted in 1996, she went to the DA's Office and completed paperwork to register as Ron's next of kin. She provided her address at that time, where she still lived to this day. It wasn't as if she had moved and failed to update her address. They had her contact information.

It did not take me long to find the article online. It was on the website of KTLA, a local TV station known for its news coverage. The headline read, GOV. NEWSOM PARDONS 13 FORMER INMATES AND COMMUTES 21 SENTENCES, INCLUDING SOME FOR LIFE WITHOUT PAROLE. It was dated June 26, two days earlier.

The article listed in alphabetical order the inmates whose crimes had been pardoned by Newsom, followed by those inmates whose sentences were commuted to lesser ones than they'd originally received. For each inmate, there was a brief summary of the crime they had committed, based on information provided by the governor's office.

Regarding Duncan, it stated, "Duncan Martinez, 50, was age 20 when he helped kill his roommate in Los Angeles County. He was serving a life-without-parole sentence after the victim was found fatally stabbed in a train tunnel. Before his body was found, the victim's parents received calls demanding a $100,000 ransom payment. But Martinez said they were to cover up the fact that his accomplice already had fatally stabbed the victim for making a joke at his expense."

Reading this description of Ron's murder made me angry. It was not true that the ransom calls were intended to cover up Ron's stabbing. A jury had heard all the evidence and had determined the motive for the ransom calls and Ron's murder had been financial gain, a finding that supported a life without parole sentence. Nor was it true that Ron's murder had been motivated by a joke Ron had made. That made it sound, erroneously, as if Ron bore some blame for his own killing.

Reading the newspaper account also made me feel suspicious. The description sounded uncannily similar to how I'd heard Duncan talk about and frame Ron's murder, always minimizing his own role and responsibility for what had happened. The article mentioned nothing about the kidnapping plan that both Duncan and Nathan had admitted they concocted and enacted before luring Ron to the tunnel. Nothing either about how Duncan, in Ron's last moments alive, had encouraged Nathan to finish him off. Nothing about Duncan being a serial liar, or his lengthy history of manipulating the people around him to benefit himself.

How had Duncan's slanted, incomplete, preferred version of the story become the one parroted by Governor Newsom and offered to the media for public consumption?

I did some more digging online and found a tranche of the official pardon and commutation certificates signed by Newsom. Duncan's was one page long and read in full:

EXECUTIVE DEPARTMENT
STATE OF CALIFORNIA
COMMUTATION OF SENTENCE
Duncan Martinez

In 1990, Duncan Martinez's crime partner fatally stabbed their roommate and fellow college student, Ronald Baker. Mr. Martinez was present, helped cover up the crime, and stole from Mr. Baker. On November 22, 1996, the Superior Court of California, County of Los Angeles, sentenced Mr. Martinez to life without the possibility of parole for murder.

Mr. Martinez was 20 years old at the time of the crime and is now 50. He has been incarcerated for more than 25 years. He has expressed sincere remorse for Mr. Baker's murder.

While serving a sentence with no hope of release, Mr. Martinez committed himself to self-improvement. Mr. Martinez has maintained an exemplary disciplinary record while in prison. He has completed self-help programming and earned an associate degree.

Mr. Martinez has been commended by correctional staff, and the warden of his prison recommended him for clemency. Mr. Martinez has lived in an honor dorm since 2001. He has participated in Paws For Life, a dog training program, since 2014.

Mr. Martinez participated in a serious crime that took the life of Mr. Baker. Since then, Mr. Martinez has dedicated himself to his rehabilitation and becoming a productive citizen. I have carefully considered and weighed the evidence of his positive conduct in prison, the fact that he was a youthful offender, his long-term confinement, and his good prospects for successful community reentry. I have concluded that Mr. Martinez merits the opportunity to make his case to the Board of Parole Hearings so it can determine whether he is suitable for parole.

This act of clemency for Mr. Martinez does not minimize or forgive his conduct or the harm it caused. It does recognize the work he has done since to transform himself.

At the bottom of the page was Newsom's official decree "by virtue of the authority vested in me" to commute Duncan's sentence to twenty-five years to life. Beside the signatures of Newsom and Alex Padilla, California's secretary of state, the document was adorned with the Great Seal of the State of California.

THEREFORE, I, GAVIN NEWSOM, Governor of the State of California, by virtue of the authority vested in me by the Constitution and statutes of the State of California, do hereby commute the sentence of Duncan Martinez to 25 years to life.

IN WITNESS WHEREOF I have hereunto set my hand and caused the Great Seal of the State of California to be affixed this 26th day of June 2020.

GAVIN NEWSOM
Governor of California

ATTEST:

ALEX PADILLA
Secretary of State

California governor Gavin Newsom's commutation of Duncan Martinez's sentence, June 26, 2020

After reading the text of Duncan's commutation, I felt even more disgusted than before.

There was an embarrassing factual error in the very first sentence. Duncan was not a "fellow college student" with Ron Baker. At the time of the murder, Ron was the only one of the three roommates who was in college.

It was not just that referring to Duncan as a fellow college student was wrong; it was misleading. When Ron was killed, Duncan was working part-time and had recently received an Other than Honorable discharge from the Marines.

What also bothered me was, why mention it at all? What relevance did it have to the commutation of Duncan's sentence, whether he was in college when the murder occurred? I could not think of any relevance, other than to make Duncan seem more sympathetic than, in reality, he was.

Newsom had devoted all of two sentences to recounting Ron's murder. If the governor of California was going to say so little about the case, was it unreasonable to expect him, at the very least, to get those few facts right?

Maybe I shouldn't have been so surprised. After all, as I knew, none of the people who understood the case best had been contacted or solicited for their input. Patty never was. Nor was I. Nor, I learned later, was Anne Ingalls, the prosecutor on Duncan's case.

Another statement Newsom made in the commutation, that Duncan "has expressed sincere remorse for Mr. Baker's murder," troubled me as well. On what basis did Newsom judge and determine the sincerity of Duncan's remorse? Or did the governor just take Duncan's word for it? How could he have been certain Duncan wasn't manipulating him, as I'd seen Duncan skillfully manipulate so many other people in the past? For that matter: When, and to whom, did Duncan express remorse? The commutation did not say.

And once again there was no mention of Duncan's involvement in planning Ron's murder, which seemed like a glaring omission. Why did Newsom leave that out? By doing so, intentionally or inadvertently, he significantly understated Duncan's responsibility.

Was this because the governor was unaware of Duncan's full complicity in the murder when he was evaluating whether Duncan deserved clemency? Did Duncan play down his involvement on his clemency application? Or was Newsom informed of all the unsavory details but decided to commute Duncan's LWOP sentence anyway? By what process had the governor decided to grant Duncan clemency? What due diligence was done, prior to his decision?

Retired or not, I was determined to get to the bottom of it. An investigation was warranted.

Could it possibly be that Newsom and his staff had neglected to conduct any investigation before acting to commute the sentence of a convicted murderer? I wanted to believe that was impossible. But I had already seen enough to fear the answer.

I began my own investigation the next morning, Monday, June 29. I knew that Duncan's new minimum sentence of twenty-five years, and the time he had already served, automatically made him eligible for parole.

My first call was to the DA's Parole Division, the unit that dealt with preparing for and attending parole suitability hearings for inmates serving indeterminate "to life" sentences.

The hearings held before a parole board weigh numerous factors in deciding whether to recommend release or continued incarceration. Factors considered include the specifics of the crime; whether the inmate admits guilt and takes full responsibility for their actions; the inmate's disciplinary record and self-improvement efforts while imprisoned; and, in murder cases, the sentiments of the victim's surviving family members.

A recommendation from the parole board that an inmate is suitable for parole does not guarantee their release. The governor has the discretion to accept or reject the recommendation. But given that it was Newsom himself who had intervened to commute Duncan's sentence, I considered it unlikely he would reject a parole board recommendation that Duncan be released.

I spoke with a supervisor in the Parole Division, a veteran prosecutor named Donna Lebowitz. I told her I had been the lead detective on a 1990 murder case in which one of the defendants, Duncan Martinez, had just had his sentence commuted.

Lebowitz said she would check to see if any letters had been written by the DA's Office to oppose a sentence commutation for Duncan. Such letters are not typically available to the public. But as the investigating detective on the case and as someone who would be assisting with preparations for the parole hearing, I would be able to obtain them, she said.

Lebowitz subsequently sent me two documents she had found in the DA's files, each a single page long.

One was a form titled "Notice of Intent to Apply for Executive Clemency." It was completed and signed by Duncan and dated March 5,

2017, more than three years earlier. At the bottom of the form, a DA's representative had signed to acknowledge receipt on March 20, 2017.

The second was a letter dated April 16, 2018, from the LA County DA's Office to then California governor Jerry Brown. It read:

Dear Governor Brown,

> *The Los Angeles County District Attorney's Office has received notification from the Board of Parole Hearings that inmate Duncan Martinez has made a request for a grant of Executive Clemency in the form of a commutation of sentence. The Los Angeles County District Attorney's Office is opposed to such a grant. In this special circumstances murder case, the inmate and his accomplice lured a young college student to an isolated train tunnel, where they robbed and murdered the victim. Thereafter, the inmate forged the victim's identification and cashed a stolen check.*
>
> *Inmate Duncan Martinez's sentence of Life Without the Possibility of Parole is not disproportionate to his crime. The circumstances of the crime involve a high degree of dangerousness. The seriousness and manner in the way the crime was carried out demonstrates the inmate poses an unreasonable threat to public safety. Further, without the legal authority to review the inmate's record of institutional conduct, we are not able to effectively evaluate the inmate's risk of current danger. Therefore, the Los Angeles County District Attorney's Office opposes a sentence commutation.*

The letter was signed by Steve Frankland, head deputy of the DA's Parole Division.

My next call was to Frankland, who two years later still held the same position.

I updated him on Newsom's commutation of Duncan. Frankland said he would check if there might have been other correspondence between the governor's office or its investigators and the DA's Office subsequent to the 2018 letter.

Frankland called me back later that week. He informed me that Duncan's Notice of Intent to Apply for Executive Clemency from 2017 and the DA's letter opposing clemency from 2018 were the only communications the DA had on file regarding Duncan's clemency.

On July 9, two weeks after Duncan's clemency was publicly announced, I ran his and Nathan's names through the Inmate Locator database of the California Department of Corrections and Rehabilitation, or CDCR. The publicly accessible government database provides information on people who are currently in state prison custody, including their age, admission date, and which prison they are in. It also indicates their parole eligibility status, parole board hearing history, if any, and when they are scheduled for the next one.

Unsurprisingly, Nathan's and Duncan's listings indicated they were incarcerated at different state prisons.

Nathan's parole eligibility date was listed as "LWOP," along with the note "The inmate shown above is serving a sentence of life without the possibility of parole and is, therefore, not eligible for parole consideration at this time."

It was the same information I had seen on Duncan's inmate profile every time I had checked it.

Now I saw that Duncan's status had changed. It indicated he was eligible for parole hearings, although no specific date for one had been set as of yet.

In early August, I began the next stage of my investigation. I wanted to know what state agency was responsible for completing the reports on inmates who applied for clemency. Was it within the governor's office or the CDCR, the state prison system?

Through my research, I learned of a unit called the Offender Investigations and Screening Division. Organizationally, the unit was part of the Board of Parole Hearings, within the CDCR.

I began by calling the CDCR. I told the receptionist I needed to speak with the person who had completed the clemency investigative report on Duncan Martinez. I explained that I was the original detective on his murder case.

Later that day, I received a call from a man named Steve Hay, an investigator with the Board of Parole Hearings. I told Hay I wanted to inquire about the recent clemency granted by Governor Newsom to Duncan Martinez. I recounted to him my involvement in Duncan's case and my bona fides, having retired after thirty-four years with the LAPD.

I also asked Hay for a copy of the investigative report prepared by his unit regarding Duncan's clemency application, upon which the governor had based his decision to commute Duncan's sentence.

"If it was up to me, I'd give it to you, but I'll have to run it by my boss," Hay replied.

Just by that statement, I figured the odds I would be able to obtain the report on Duncan's prospective clemency were close to zero. My gut feeling was confirmed when Hay added that he had never known of one of those reports being released to anyone.

I asked if it was possible to have the person who authored the report call me, so I could discuss the matter directly with him or her.

Hay said there had been a major turnover of personnel in their office, and it was very likely the report writer was no longer there.

I explained the report had to have been written very recently, since the governor had commuted the sentence only five weeks earlier.

Hay told me he was not sure he could release the name of the investigator who prepared the report on Duncan Martinez.

I was shocked at how little information he was willing to share. I tried reasoning with him. I pointed out that it was incumbent on me, as a police detective, to be completely transparent about the work I did on investigations that made their way into a courtroom. The same was true of prosecutors. The governor and parole board should be just as transparent about their own work, I argued. Considering the stakes, the public should know what went into the governor's decision to commute one inmate's sentence, while denying clemency to countless others. How else could the public have any confidence the process was fair?

Hay said he knew that the investigators responsible for producing reports on clemency applicants "have sit-down meetings with the inmates, to see where their head was back then," meaning at the time they committed the crime. He also knew the inmate's records from their time in custody factored into any clemency decision.

I was not reassured to learn that the only interview seemingly conducted, prior to the governor deciding to commute an LWOP inmate's sentence, was with the applicant themself.

I told Hay I could not understand how the people most knowledgeable about an inmate's case could be totally ignored and not afforded an opportunity to provide their perspective. Was it just assumed that the inmate applying for clemency would be fully honest and forthright? It seemed like an unrealistic expectation and a reckless approach for the governor to take in making such a weighty, irreversible decision.

I informed Hay that Duncan Martinez was a pathological liar and one of the most manipulative people I had ever encountered during my thirty-four-year police career. I would have been able to provide example after example if I had just been asked, I said. So would have the deputy DA who handled his prosecution.

Hay explained that the investigators in his unit were so inundated with clemency report assignments from the governor's office that they'd had to hire additional staff to try to keep up. For reports in the past, the trial judge was often interviewed about the case details, but that was not done any longer.

I advised Hay that the victim's sister had found out the inmate's clemency had been granted from a news article she happened to read. Hay said that was very unfortunate.

Before we hung up, Hay said he would do some further checking regarding my questions.

Hay called me back two days later. He had spoken with his supervisors, and they had denied my request for a copy of the report. He apologized and said he and many other parole agents support my way of thinking. He said the clemency reports "were being cranked out one after another in a formula-like way."

I did not blame Hay personally. It was not his fault that his office was too short-staffed to conduct quality investigations, rather than one-sided ones. Governor Newsom was the person I considered to be most responsible.

I thought it was appalling that Patty had not been consulted or even given a heads-up that Duncan had applied for clemency before Newsom went ahead and commuted his sentence. The obvious shoddiness of the investigation into whether Duncan was a worthy clemency recipient offended me. Also inexcusable was the total lack of transparency around Newsom's clemency decision-making process.

Was Newsom aware that so little due diligence was being done regarding the candidates for clemency presented to him? Did he care? Or was he just credulous and content to sign whatever was placed in front of him?

But what was done was done, I realized, and had to be accepted. There was no possibility of appeal and no precedent for reversing a sentence commutation once it had been granted.

Notwithstanding that a jury had decided a quarter century earlier he should never receive one, Duncan was going to get a parole hearing.

Although the battle over Newsom's commutation felt lost, there was still a chance to prevail at Duncan's parole board hearing.

The hearing was scheduled for December 8 at California State Prison, Los Angeles County, where Duncan had been incarcerated for many years. His hearing, at 8:30 a.m., would be the first one held that day.

In mid-October, I wrote a letter to the Board of Parole Hearings. I mailed it immediately, to ensure it arrived many weeks before December 8. I wanted the commissioners serving on Duncan's parole board to have a chance to read it.

The position I took in the letter was in opposition to Duncan's release.

This was a different position than I had taken many years earlier in the case. In 1996, before Duncan's trial and conviction of first-degree murder with special circumstances, he was offered a plea agreement by the DA's Office because of his cooperation with us. If he agreed to plead guilty to second-degree murder, he would receive a prison sentence of fifteen years to life. Duncan rejected the offer.

Why Duncan turned down the deal was beyond my knowledge. Was the decision to go to trial totally his call? Was it his defense lawyer's recommendation? Did his parents influence his decision? Or some combination of these factors? I could not say.

At the time, I felt strongly that it was a good offer, and he should take it. If in 1996 Duncan had taken the deal, he would have been eligible for parole hearings more than ten years before Newsom commuted his sentence. Very possibly, he might already have been released from prison.

Given that back in 1996 I felt fifteen years was a reasonable sentence for Duncan, and he already had served longer than that, how could I justify arguing now that Duncan should be incarcerated even longer?

In my view, once Duncan chose to reject that offer, all bets were off. He refused to accept responsibility and passed up a sentence much lighter than what Nathan had received. Ultimately, the jury's verdict validated what I believed the evidence fully supported: Duncan was culpable of involvement in a reprehensible murder that merited an LWOP sentence.

In my letter, I wrote:

Dear Parole Board Members:

My name is Rick Jackson. I retired from the LAPD in 2013, having worked exclusively in the field of homicide investigation for the last 28 years of my career. I was the investigating detective throughout the Ronald Baker murder case, which resulted in the convictions of Duncan Martinez and Nathaniel Blalock. Two separate juries found Mr. Martinez and Mr. Blalock guilty of first-degree murder with two special circumstances: lying in wait and murder for financial gain. Both were sentenced to life without parole. Yet, here we are.

Ironically, when I heard in June that Mr. Martinez's sentence had been commuted, I was already well into writing a book on this very case. For the last few years, I have been going through the entire investigation, listening to the old interviews and speaking with witnesses once again. As a result, my factual knowledge of the case is as clear as when it was being investigated.

Almost every witness, both then and in recent discussions, had told me that Duncan Martinez is an extremely manipulative person and a compulsive liar. During my six-year investigation, I saw Mr. Martinez routinely display these same qualities. Mr. Martinez consistently sought to avoid responsibility for his actions by falsely minimizing his involvement and trying to blame others for his own decisions and criminal acts.

Governor Newsom's commutation letter states that "Mr. Martinez was present, helped cover up the crime, and stole from Mr. Baker," a description of the murder that minimizes and significantly understates Mr. Martinez's true role. This may be because the Governor and his staff did not have the complete facts and considered only information that Mr. Martinez himself provided. In light of his lengthy history of lying and manipulation, Mr. Martinez cannot be relied upon as the sole source of credible information, especially regarding his involvement in Ronald Baker's murder.

I urge the Parole Board to consider the following facts and additional context, which Governor Newsom's commutation neglected to mention:

- *Mr. Martinez plotted the murder equally with his co-suspect, Nathan Blalock. Mr. Martinez personally tried to contact a different potential victim, a former classmate of his, before he and Mr. Blalock settled on their roommate, Ron Baker, a longtime friend of Mr. Martinez.*
- *Mr. Martinez and Mr. Blalock also played equal roles in luring Mr. Baker to the remote tunnel where he was killed, on the false pretense of a pre-arranged meeting with some girls. This was part of an elaborate plan to establish and bolster their own alibi.*
- *Mr. Martinez was Ron Baker's closest friend and the only person with an opportunity to stop his murder. Mr. Martinez instead betrayed his friend, did not intervene while Mr. Blalock stabbed him, and after he survived the initial stabbing, directed Mr. Blalock to "finish him off." Mr. Blalock then slit Mr. Baker's throat twice. Mr. Martinez sought to justify this directive by framing it as an act of mercy, rather than murder.*
- *Later that same night, and again the following morning, Mr. Martinez used a disguised voice to make two ransom calls*

to Ron Baker's soon-to-be-grieving parents, whom he knew well and whose home he had visited several times.

- Although Mr. Martinez knew the truth about his friend's murder, since he had planned and witnessed it, he accepted a role as one of Ron Baker's pallbearers and even delivered a eulogy for him at his memorial service.
- After Mr. Martinez came under investigation for the murder, he staged his own kidnapping and fled Los Angeles to evade justice. While on the run, he used multiple aliases and filed a false passport application in the name of a child who years earlier had died tragically. As a result, Mr. Martinez was convicted of felony passport fraud.
- When Mr. Martinez resurfaced after two years and offered to cooperate with prosecutors, it was only because he had been arrested on the passport charge and he saw coming forward as a potential way to extricate himself from the investigation of Baker's murder. At every point, Mr. Martinez's cooperation with police and prosecutors was entirely self-interested.
- Although Governor Newsom wrote in his commutation letter that Mr. Martinez "has expressed sincere remorse for Mr. Baker's murder," he has never done so publicly. Nor has Mr. Martinez ever expressed any remorse privately to Ron Baker's family or friends, many of whom Mr. Martinez knew personally and betrayed, along with his friend Ron.

For all of the above reasons, I strongly oppose a grant of parole for Duncan Martinez and urge the Parole Board to continue his incarceration. Mr. Martinez planned and committed a cruel, senseless, inexcusable act of violence against his longtime friend. While on the run from that crime, he committed two additional felonies, both of which involved major acts of lying and deceit.

I truly suspect that if Governor Newsom knew all of the facts in this case, he would never have commuted Mr. Martinez's sentence. Although Ron Baker's family should have been notified and given an opportunity to contest Mr. Martinez's application *for commutation, they were never consulted and only learned of it via media reports. The two people most familiar with the facts, myself and the prosecutor who tried the case, also were never contacted for any information.*

I hope the Parole Board will take these facts under consideration at Mr. Martinez's parole hearing and deny his case.

*Sincerely,
Detective Rick Jackson (Retired)
LAPD / Robbery-Homicide Division*

A little more than two weeks after I mailed my letter, Election Day 2020 was held.

The incumbent LA County district attorney, Jackie Lacey, was defeated at the polls by George Gascón, the former district attorney in San Francisco.

Gascón campaigned on a platform of reforming the DA's Office and implementing a progressive policy agenda. Many in law enforcement felt Gascón's policies were much too progressive. Nevertheless, he won the election, an outcome I mostly attributed to the social and political forces unleashed by the killing of George Floyd earlier that year. Gascón's campaign was also helped by endorsements he received from several higher-profile politicians. Chief among the state officials who had endorsed Gascón for Los Angeles DA was California governor Gavin Newsom.

Ironically, considering Gascón's widespread unpopularity in law enforcement circles, he came from a police background himself. Gascón was an LAPD officer and eventually rose in the ranks to assistant chief. After leaving the LAPD, he headed the police department in Mesa, Arizona. In 2009, Gascón was hired as San Francisco's chief of police. San Francisco's mayor at the time was future governor Gavin Newsom. In 2012, Newsom's last act as mayor was to appoint Gascón as San Francisco's new district attorney. Gascón had a law degree, but prior to being named top prosecutor by Newsom, he had never tried a case.

Now Gascón was set to return to LA and take the reins at the DA's

Office. He would be sworn in on December 7, one day before Duncan's already-scheduled parole hearing.

I never fathomed that the ripple effects of Gascón's election might include Ron's case and Duncan's future.

On the Tuesday before Thanksgiving, I spoke with Deputy DA Julianne Walker. Walker explained that she would appear at Duncan's parole hearing on December 8. She had already spoken with retired deputy DA Anne Ingalls, who had prosecuted both Duncan and Nathan. Walker said from her review of the case, and talking with Ingalls, she would argue vehemently to the parole board that Duncan should be denied parole. Walker said she had also spoken with the victim's sister, Patty.

I spoke with Walker a few more times in the two weeks leading up to the hearing. I let her know that I planned to attend the hearing with Patty Baker Elliott. I also told her I intended to make some comments to the board. Walker said she planned to deliver her own statement and present to the board evidence of Duncan's failure to accept responsibility for his part in Ron's murder, and challenge his claim that he was wrongly prosecuted.

Walker informed me that Duncan's hearing would not take place within the prison, as parole hearings typically were. Due to the COVID pandemic, all hearings were being held via Zoom. Only the inmate and prison staff would be physically present in the hearing room. All other participants, including the board members, Duncan's defense attorney, and others who wished to make statements would participate remotely over the computer.

I understood why and the need for the protocol. But I couldn't help but feel a virtual hearing would benefit Duncan and disadvantage those who could not be in the actual room with him. This would be especially true of the victim's family, I thought. Being in the same room while they made their statement would heighten the power and impact of their words and emotions. Without experiencing in person their grief and feelings about the possibility of parole, I feared it would be much easier for the board members to discount their perspective and the gravity of the situation.

As the date of Duncan's hearing approached, I decided I would travel to Los Angeles for it, despite the fact it would be held over Zoom. I wanted to support Patty and be at her side during the hearing. We would watch together and participate in the proceedings over a shared computer.

I had already arrived in Los Angeles on December 7, one day in advance of Duncan's parole hearing. Early that evening, I received a phone call from Julianne Walker.

I was not expecting to hear from her, but it did not cause me any concern. The hearing was first thing the following morning. I assumed she was calling to discuss final preparations and what to expect at the hearing. At worst, I figured she was calling to notify me that Duncan's parole hearing was going to be delayed or rescheduled.

That was not why she was calling.

Walker told me that the newly elected district attorney, George Gascón, had been sworn into office earlier that afternoon.

Gascón immediately had issued a number of "special directives" to the roughly eight hundred prosecutors who now worked under his command. One of the edicts, Special Directive 20-14, was on the subject of resentencing. It included a section that pertained to lifer parole hearings, exactly the type Duncan was due to receive the next morning.

Walker explained that the DA's new policy, as established by the special directive, was that prosecutors under Gascón were forbidden from attending parole board meetings, effective the following day. She said it also meant she was barred from presenting to the parole board the documents she believed were strong evidence that Duncan should be denied parole. Nor could she share the documents with me or Patty. Unfortunately, they were only available to the DA and Duncan's defense attorney, if he had one.

Walker said she could share with me some of the information contained in the documents, but only verbally. I told her I wanted to hear it.

Walker told me about Duncan's "risk assessment," a report she said was authored by a Dr. Athans. The risk assessment was based on an interview Duncan had with Athans in October 2020, just two months before this parole hearing.

According to Athans's report, Duncan had told her he was legally innocent in Ron Baker's murder and that his conviction was unfair.

Duncan had also told Athans he was "morally responsible" but not legally responsible.

I was shocked Duncan would've said that, especially right before coming up for parole. Taking responsibility for your crimes is one of the key expectations of a parole board.

I told Walker I would bring this up during the hearing. I knew that without the actual document, however, I would be unable to point specifically to where it was in the report. Whether the parole board would discount my argument because of this, I could not say or control.

Walker sounded upset. She told me she felt horrible that at the last minute she had to place on me and Patty the burden of presenting the argument against Duncan's possible parole.

I was stunned, not least by the extraordinarily short warning. Duncan's parole hearing was only about fifteen hours away.

In my view, Gascón's new policy was not just dangerous and wrongheaded but immoral. It was an abandonment of those left behind by horrific acts of violence, the victims' surviving family members, who I believed deserved more support, not less. Under the new policy, they would be left to fend for themselves before the parole board.

I also couldn't help but think, *What a difference a day makes*. If Duncan's hearing had been scheduled for one day earlier, there would have been a deputy DA there to oppose parole in a professional, experienced manner. The same was true if Gascón had waited until his first full day in office to issue his directives.

Later, I obtained a copy of Special Directive 20-14. On page 1, it stated, "The new Resentencing Policy is effective immediately and shall apply to all offices, units and attorneys in the Los Angeles County District Attorney's Office."

With respect to lifer parole hearings, the directive declared, "We are not experts on rehabilitation. While we have information about the crime of conviction, the Board of Parole Hearings already has this information. Further, as the crime of conviction is of limited value in considering parole suitability years or decades later, the value of a prosecutor's input in parole hearings is also limited … This Office's default policy is that we will not attend parole hearings and will support in writing the grant of parole for a person who has already served their mandatory minimum period of incarceration... However, if the CDCR has determined in their Comprehensive Risk Assessment that a person represents a 'high' risk for recidivism, the DDA may, in their letter, take a neutral position on the grant of parole."

The fine print was even worse than I had imagined. No longer would the DA's Office decide on a case-by-case basis whether a particular inmate serving a life sentence was a suitable candidate for parole. For inmates who had completed their minimum sentence, regardless of the heinousness of their crimes, it was not even an option under Gascón for the DA's Office to oppose a grant of parole. To the contrary, the DA's official position in all such cases was that it would *support* the inmate's bid for parole. In one day, incredibly, the DA's Office had switched sides. The victim and their surviving family seemingly were no longer their concern.

The last sentence of the section on lifer parole hearings struck me as ironic, and a farce. It stated, "This Office will continue to meet its obligation to notify and advise victims under California law, and is committed to a process of healing and restorative justice for all victims."

The law being referenced, I believed, was the Victims' Bill of Rights, also known as Marsy's Law. It was approved by voters in 2008 and incorporated into the California Constitution. Supposedly, it guarantees certain constitutional rights to crime victims and their families.

Section 7 of the Victims' Bill of Rights provides victims and their families the following right: "To reasonable notice of all public proceedings... upon request, at which the defendant and the prosecutor are entitled to be present and of all parole or other post-conviction release proceedings, and to be present at all such proceedings."

Section 15 grants a victim the right "to be informed of all parole procedures, to participate in the parole process, to provide information to the parole authority to be considered before the parole of the offender, and to be notified, upon request, of the parole or other release of the offender."

Section 16 provides the right "to have the safety of the victim, the victim's family, and the general public considered before any parole or other post-judgment release decision is made."

There is no specific reference to the rights guaranteed to victims' families prior to a governor commuting a sentence. I'm not a lawyer, but it seems obvious to me that a commutation certainly qualifies as a "post-conviction release decision, or any proceeding in which a right of the victim is at issue," the language provided in section 8 of Marsy's Law. Even though commutations are not explicitly mentioned, exempting them from the broad obligation to include victims' families clearly violates the spirit of the law.

After Nathan and Duncan were convicted and sentenced in 1996, Patty and her parents requested notice through the proper channels at the DA's Office. This meant Patty should have been notified by the DA's Office in April 2018, when it was known Duncan had applied for clemency a year earlier. Yet Patty received no notice whatsoever.

Nor did anyone from Governor Newsom's office make an effort to contact or notify Patty before the governor unilaterally acted to commute Duncan's sentence.

It wasn't that somebody dropped the ball. Everybody dropped the ball.

It made me wonder whether the legal obligations spelled out in Marsy's Law were disregarded only in Patty's case, in other pardon and commutation cases as well, or possibly even—I shuddered to think—in all cases in which Governor Newsom had granted clemency.

Regardless, like I told myself after I learned Newsom had commuted Duncan's sentence, what was done was done.

CHAPTER 29

A SHALLOW DIVE FOR THE TRUTH
(December 8, 2020)

PATTY AND I MET early the next morning to "attend" Duncan's parole hearing together.

As we waited on Zoom for the hearing to begin, Patty seemed nervous but, at the same time, somewhat resigned. She was going to say her piece. She hoped it would resonate with the board and influence their decision, and that Duncan would remain in custody, at least for the time being. But Patty had already learned by this point that the outcome was beyond her control.

I was a bit nervous myself. I still felt stunned by the DA's abrupt, surprise withdrawal the night before. Throughout our preparations, the plan had always been that the deputy DA would do most of the heavy lifting during the hearing. Now, with less than a day's warning, Patty and I would brave the hearing with zero institutional support.

Duncan's parole hearing, inconceivable six months earlier, began shortly after 9 a.m.

The parole board panel consisted of two commissioners. The presiding commissioner was Michele Minor, who was appointed in 2014 by then-governor Jerry Brown. Minor formerly held several positions in the state's prison system. The other member of the panel was Deputy Commissioner Cristina Guerrero, a lawyer.

"This is the parole suitability hearing for Mr. Martinez," Commissioner Minor said. "Mr. Martinez is in the BPH Hearing Room at

California State Prison, Los Angeles County. All other participants are participating remotely by video conference."

Minor noted Duncan was under twenty-six when he committed the crime. "So the panel will give great weight to the youth-offender factors in deciding parole suitability today," she said.

Patty and I could see, on the computer screen in front of us, Duncan seated in a chair facing the camera. He was dressed in a light blue button-down collared shirt and dark blue sweatpants with CDCR PRISONER emblazoned in yellow letters down the right leg.

I had not laid eyes on Duncan since 1996, almost twenty-five years earlier. Now, at age fifty, his hair had turned silver. A pair of reading glasses peeked from his shirt pocket. Duncan looked relatively young for his age, despite the change in hair color. If I had encountered him on the street, I would have recognized him, even after all these years.

Duncan's attorney identified himself as Michael Beckman.

After all the introductions, Beckman asked, "Do we have a district attorney?"

I guessed Beckman had not yet heard about the DA's new policy, as of the day before.

"No, we will not have a district attorney from Los Angeles County," Minor informed him. She explained how the hearing would proceed. "The first thing I want you to know is that we are not here to reconsider the findings of the courts, and we are not here to retry your case. This panel accepts as true the findings of the courts. The purpose of this hearing is to consider your suitability for parole... I want to make sure that you know, Mr. Martinez, we expect for you to be completely honest with us today in this conversation. I'm going to swear you in."

At Minor's direction, Duncan raised his right hand and swore that his testimony would be the whole truth and nothing but the truth. I wondered how much the commissioners knew about Duncan's history of dishonesty. I could only hope that they had read my letter.

Minor explained the CDCR had compiled a "central file" that contained all records from the duration of Duncan's imprisonment. Minor also noted Duncan had the "risk assessment" completed by Dr. Athans, which Deputy DA Walker had described to me the night before.

Duncan's central file and risk assessment, despite their primary importance to the parole board's decision, were not public documents. Duncan's attorney had access to them, as did the DA's Office, but Patty and I were not allowed to see them. It was another hand-tying disadvantage for us, resulting from Gascón's directive.

Without being able to read the risk assessment, it was impossible to say or know how thorough it was and the totality of what it was based on. How much did Athans know about Duncan's involvement in the murder? Was Duncan her only source of information? Did she challenge his answers at all or just take them at face value? Did she make any effort to vet his claims? If not, how could she accurately gauge his honesty and the risks if he were released?

Minor referenced that Duncan had qualified as a youthful offender. She asked him, "Is there anything that you can go back to, in your childhood and upbringing, that'll kind of give us some insight into how you came to make the decisions that you made?"

Duncan talked about feeling abandoned and alone at many points in his childhood. His biological father left when he was two. His mother was young and often had to work, which meant he spent a lot of time alone. At school, Duncan said, "I was the smartest kid in class." Everyone expected him to get the answer when everyone else could not, he recalled. "If I got it wrong, it was a big deal, which made me go inside with everything. At the same time, I was being bullied rather severely at the apartment we were living in." When he went to his mother, she believed and sided with the bully, not him, which he resented.

Minor asked Duncan to explain how the abandonment and resentment he felt affected him.

"Well, I developed the idea that I needed to do everything... I had to figure things out myself. I didn't ask for help... I didn't understand that community was a team sport. When I was at school, I tried to do everything alone. When I was at home, I did everything alone. That became a way of existence for me for a long time... Because I felt like I couldn't fail, I started to self-deceive... And as I got older and the problems... got worse and worse, I had to lie to myself more and more to overcome those failures, because I felt like I couldn't fail."

Duncan continued: "By the time I got to high school, I was living a life where I didn't have any real friends, but I pretended like I did. I had friends, but I didn't have any true, close friends... Internally, I was really unhappy because I kept failing. And the more I failed, the more I had to lie to myself. That really was the crux of my problems moving forward, is I built these lies bigger and bigger and felt that I had to. The inability to fail was the huge driving thing at that point."

Listening to Duncan, I felt underwhelmed by the hardships he described. Lots of people raised by overworked single mothers never become murderers.

I didn't doubt what Duncan said was true, or that he experienced his own childhood as traumatic. But I was at a loss to understand how a lack of close childhood friendships led him to murder Ron. And what did it have to do with whether Duncan should be granted parole?

If an inmate's difficult childhood was a mitigating factor, growing up without close friends was in my opinion far less emotionally scarring than physical and sexual abuse, witnessing horrific acts of violence, and whatever else many other inmates endured as children.

Even without being able to see Duncan's "central file," it was obvious he had taken many self-improvement classes. I had nothing against such classes being offered to inmates, including Duncan. I imagine they help many inmates come to terms with who they are and what they did.

However, listening to Duncan say things like "community is a team sport" and use terms like "self-deceive" made me question if he was merely regurgitating catchphrases he had heard in group therapy sessions. It sounded to me like Self Help 101. Had Duncan truly bought into the principles taught in the classes? Or was he just parroting to the commissioners what he thought they wanted to hear so they would grant him parole? How could anyone say or know?

Minor noted Duncan had no juvenile arrests but asked about his arrest for passport fraud.

"That was after we murdered Ron," Duncan said.

Duncan's phrasing surprised me. Never before had I heard him describe his involvement equally with Nathan. Duncan had always minimized his role in comparison. I felt he was using "we" to play to the commissioners, to try to show he was accepting responsibility. However, saying "we murdered" directly contradicted his claim to Dr. Athans in the risk assessment that he bore no legal responsibility for Ron's death. How could Duncan have it both ways?

Minor asked Duncan about his burglary arrest and if the same factors played into that decision. "Was that part of the same thing, or just kind of your manipulation and what was going on because you were running?"

"I would say that it's both...The same problems persisted until the bike shop, which was the burglary...That was one of the turning points for me in realizing how bad I had gotten. And I was also on the run. Both factors apply."

I agreed that Duncan's burglary arrest was a turning point for him. But he made it sound like he had a moral epiphany. It was a turning point because it was the first time he was held accountable and paid a price for his actions. Until then, Duncan had never faced serious repercussions for any of his wrongful acts.

Also, it was untrue that Duncan was on the run when he committed the burglary. At the time, he had been working with us and living in Utah under his real name for almost two years.

Minor asked Duncan what had motivated Ron's murder. "Why did this crime happen?"

"I spent a lot of time thinking about this...and at times I've had different answers over the years. I believe that Nathan thought he had to do something like this to prove something to himself. From my perspective, I didn't want a crime to happen...If I had been a human being, I could have stopped the crime from happening."

I thought it was a total accountability dodge by Duncan, putting all the blame on Nathan.

Minor questioned Duncan about the plan to kill Ron and how it came to be. Duncan's answers were consistent with what he'd always said about the plan: It had been drunkenly discussed weeks before, and he never thought it was real and would happen. I wondered if the commissioners saw Duncan's explanation for what it was: another deflection of responsibility.

"When you walked into that tunnel, did you know that a crime was gonna occur?"

"No," answered Duncan.

Minor did not know that Duncan had once told us, during his King for a Day interview, "I knew what was going to happen, and when it was supposed to happen, or where it was going to happen." That statement showed how specifically he and Nathan had discussed where Ron's murder was to take place. Duncan's answer to Minor was a complete lie.

Minor said, "Okay. So when it did, why didn't you stop him?"

"Initial fear. I was in fear and shock when it started. I froze, and when Ron was calling out, 'Help me, Duncan,' Nathan was calling out, 'No,' and I froze. I was scared, and honestly, in that moment, all I cared about was myself."

"There's a statement where you said something about, 'Finish him off,' or something like that. Why would you do that at this point? I mean, you don't expect this to happen. It happens. A good friend of yours—they're both your best friends. Why do you say, 'Finish him off,' or what did you say?"

"I believe that I said, 'You can't leave him like that. You have to finish him off.'"

"Okay. Why did you do that?"

"Well, on the one hand, I didn't want him to suffer. Ron was my friend, and the sound he was making in that moment was horrible. On the other hand, I couldn't handle that sound. I was selfish. It was horrible, and I didn't want to hear that anymore."

Minor asked why Duncan didn't go get help, rather than tell Nathan to finish Ron off.

"I did not think there was any help at that point... I believed Ron was not gonna survive."

I felt it was a weak excuse. It was cruel and wrong for Duncan to frame what he told Nathan to do as an act of compassion. But neither commissioner called him on it.

Minor asked Duncan if it was true that he was a pallbearer and gave a eulogy for Ron.

"Yes."

"How did you do that, after you were a part of this murder? How were you able to do that? Again, we go back to these causative factors.

The abandonment, low self-esteem... You'd been bullied. You were powerless. How do you then step up and do that?"

"Well, I would say, first off, it wasn't stepping up. I—"

"Well, you did it, so—"

"What I mean by that is, I did everything in my power to not take any responsibility for what had happened. I lied to myself... In my head, I didn't have anything to do with this... I didn't want to think about the things that I hadn't done before he died. I ran away from them at every opportunity. Ironically, embracing things like that was another form of running away."

Minor asked, "You also faked your own kidnapping?"

"Yes."

"Did your mom believe you had been kidnapped at one point?"

"I believe so."

"So you affected a lot of people's lives, based on all of what you did. All of this manipulation. All of this deceit... As you look back now, how do you feel about what you've done to the victim's family?"

"Ron was a friend, and I betrayed that friendship. I was a horrible, horrible human being where it would have been easy to be a human being. I was anything but. I failed Ron and Nathan, and I failed their families. I failed my family. I failed everybody... It's an ongoing effect of pain that I can't undo. I can't go back and change it, but man, I wish I could."

"What are you responsible for?"

"Ron's death. Absolutely."

I saw this as another example of Duncan claiming to take full responsibility, although it contradicted his earlier statements to Dr. Athans that he was not legally responsible for Ron's murder and Nathan was to blame. Duncan knew, to win parole, he had to take responsibility for his crime before the parole board. It was a box that needed to be checked.

Minor asked Guerrero if she had any questions.

Guerrero pointed out a passage in Duncan's risk assessment and read it aloud. "'The chasm between his internal world and the face he presented to his peers and family continued to grow. He was profoundly lonely yet portrayed a fun-loving and well-put-together persona.' So my question is, it seems like you're living, like, a double life, correct? You're portraying somebody else on the outside, and internally you are someone else. Are you doing that today?"

"No. One of the core components of all of that was that I isolated myself from everyone. One of the things that I have worked really, really hard to do is to embrace community. Community is incredibly important." Duncan described his support network as "not just valuable but essential to all that I do."

Guerrero was not satisfied with his answer. She pressed him: "Today, are you portraying to be someone else, and internally you're still the same person you were? For example, the person that murdered Mr. Baker. Are you? Do you understand my question?"

"I believe I do. I don't know how to show it, other than to say look at my support network... I think that's an important thing. But no, I'm not living internally anymore. I refuse to do that."

I felt Duncan still hadn't answered the question, but Guerrero moved on. She asked him, "Tell us, when was the last time you were manipulative?"

"I guess the last time I was manipulative directly would be when I was coaching softball. I absolutely would try to push the right buttons with my softball team, to get the best out of the men. But I don't actively manipulate. I don't see a reason to do that. I don't think you win by doing that."

Duncan was describing motivation, not manipulation, and citing it as a positive example.

"Okay. Let's talk about manipulation in a negative way, criminal thinking. When was the last time you were manipulative?"

"Honestly, I don't remember the last time I was criminally manipulative. That's not to say that I don't have criminal thinking. I think we all have criminal thinking at times, but I do not remember the last time I was criminally manipulative."

Duncan again had not answered the question. But Guerrero just said, "Okay. Thank you," and shifted the focus to Duncan's prison records. She noted his consistent participation in academic, work, and self-help programming, and how many official plaudits for good behavior he had received in each of the last several years. Within the prison system, the plaudits are known as "laudatory chronos." Minor told Duncan, "You have a lot of laudatory chronos."

Later, after reviewing a transcript of the hearing, I added up the number of laudatory chronos Duncan had received year by year. According to the figures cited by the parole board, between 2003 and 2016 he received a total of sixteen, an average of just over one per year. From 2017, the year he applied for clemency from the governor, through 2020, he averaged over ten laudatory chronos per year, more than ten times his previous, long-established rate.

Was it because Duncan's behavior in prison suddenly improved in 2017, and from then on he acted much more virtuously? Or was it that Duncan, in anticipation of applying for clemency, began to encourage prison staff to document his good behavior? He knew his prison record would be a determining factor in whether he would be granted clemency and, later, parole. The more laudatory chronos he received, the more deserving of clemency he would appear. Was the tenfold increase proof he had changed? Or yet more evidence of Duncan the master manipulator at work?

Guerrero noted the commissioners had received many letters in support of Duncan being granted parole, along with my letter in opposition. Among the people who had written letters on his behalf were his parents and sister, prison staff, professors from Cal State LA whom he took classes with, and fellow inmates. She added that Duncan had offers of employment from two different dentists to work as a dental assistant if he was granted parole.

Guerrero said Duncan had written a "parole packet" that included "remorse letters written to Ron Baker, the Baker family, to your codefendant, Mr. Nathan Blalock."

This was news to me and Patty. She had never received any remorse letter written by Duncan to Ron or to her family. I later confirmed that Nathan had never received any remorse letter from Duncan either.

What was the purpose of a remorse letter that was never seen by the wronged party? Because Duncan's parole packet was not public, his remorse letters could only be seen by the board, his attorney, and possibly the DA's Office, but not Patty, the last surviving member of Ron's immediate family. Despite whom the letters were addressed to, their actual audience was solely the parole board. It felt to me like another box Duncan knew he had to check.

After Guerrero said she had no further questions, Minor again brought up Dr. Athans's risk assessment. Minor said, "The doctor noted, as you discussed the crime, that there was no minimization and found that—felt that you had taken full responsibility for your actions."

In my view, Athans's conclusion flew in the face of Duncan's statement, included in her own report, that he felt he was morally responsible for Ron's murder but not legally responsible.

Which prompted additional questions: How did the doctor, without knowing the details of the murder or consulting anyone but Duncan, determine he was not understanding his role and was taking full responsibility? Did Duncan tell the doctor about his involvement in devising the kidnapping plot? Or did he lay the blame on Nathan, as he did earlier in this very parole hearing?

It felt like the truth had been turned on its head. From the time of the murder through the present day, Duncan had consistently minimized his responsibility for Ron's murder. Now, suddenly, based on little more than Duncan's own word, the opposite had been declared true. Even worse, the false declaration carried the weight of a doctor's expert opinion.

I never imagined that experts could be so credulous and the system so easy to manipulate. Especially by someone like Duncan, who presented well and was backed by an experienced, and likely expensive, private attorney. It was scary and disillusioning to witness. I could only wonder how Patty felt, watching all this unfold beside me.

Minor continued: "Overall, the doctor found you to be a low risk of violence if you were to be released in the free community… The doctor, again I note, said, 'He has accepted responsibility for his role in the life crime, did not seek to minimize involvement or externalize blame, and has spent his time in custody wisely'… That was the assessment of the doctor." Minor asked Duncan, "Do you have any comments about the doctor's assessment at this time, sir?"

"No. I thought it was… I thought she did a really good job," he replied.

I would have said so too if I were Duncan.

After a short break, Duncan's parole hearing resumed with remarks by his attorney.

Beckman said, "I'm going to be very brief because the truth is that if it isn't clear from his record and his presentation before you today, Mr. Martinez has rehabilitated himself in prison and should be found suitable for parole, there's not much I can say that would change your minds. He meets all the suitability requirements. He's admitted guilt, taken responsibility for the life crime. He doesn't minimize his role in it... He's genuinely remorseful and empathizes at an emotional level of the harm done to the victim and his family. He's demonstrated that in victims' letters and by actual performance, showing remorse and desire to make amends."

I disagreed with several of Beckman's assertions. In reality, Duncan had failed to take complete responsibility for Ron's murder. He had consistently minimized his role in the killing, including earlier in the parole hearing. Beckman, however, had the floor. All Patty and I could do at that moment was wait for our turn to speak.

Beckman continued uninterrupted. He talked about Duncan's volunteer work in prison and his post-release plans, if he was granted parole. Beckman noted, "Dr. Athans found him to be a low risk of violence... There is ample evidence of subsequent growth and maturation."

My gut feeling was that if Duncan got out, he was unlikely to re-offend by engaging in another violent crime. But I did not think that should be the sole criteria for him to be released.

Beckman closed his remarks with an ad hominem attack on me, which was not surprising. I had spoken out against his client and provided facts and reasons why he should be denied parole. It was easier to attack me, the detective on the case, than Patty, the grieving sister.

"Before I finish, I'm compelled to respond to the letter written to you by retired detective Jackson," said Beckman. "First, his motives for writing this letter are questionable. He states in his letter he's writing a book about this case. Now, it should be obvious having Mr. Martinez still in prison and painted in the worst possible way would dramatically increase sales of that book."

I doubted that was true. Duncan being granted parole seemed likely to generate controversy and more interest in the case, rather than less. I knew my motive for sending the letter had nothing to do with book writing, let alone book sales. I had only mentioned the book in my letter to explain my immersion in the facts of the case and why it was so fresh in my mind.

Beckman said, "Second, his claim that Mr. Martinez is extremely manipulative and a compulsive liar is not correct. Yes, it was at the time, but as Detective Jackson well knows, Mr. Martinez gave him the truth about the murder. Without Mr. Martinez's statements and testimony at trial, Nathan Blalock, the actual killer, would have taken a plea for second-degree murder."

This I knew was untrue. Nathan was never offered a plea for second-degree murder. Duncan also never testified at any trial, his own or Nathan's.

Beckman referenced the many letters in support of Duncan. "These attestations to his character should carry far more weight than the self-interested statements of a retired detective turned crime writer.

"Third, Detective Jackson contradicts himself… He says Mr. Martinez planned the murder equally with Nathan Blalock, but then… he says Mr. Martinez betrayed Ron Baker because he did not intervene while Mr. Blalock stabbed him. If the murder was premeditated by Mr. Martinez, why would he intervene during the actual killing? The killing would have been exactly what Mr. Martinez wanted, so why would he want to stop it? It's not correct."

This misrepresented what I had written in my letter. Beckman made it sound like I believed Duncan's sole betrayal of Ron was that he did not intervene during the stabbing. It was always my belief that the betrayal began well before the stabbing. Duncan's failure to intervene was merely an additional bad act.

Beckman said, "Fourth, Mr. Jackson's assertion that Mr. Martinez's cooperation with the police was entirely self-interested is equally false… Detective Jackson actually gave Mr. Martinez signed paperwork that Mr. Martinez would plead guilty and not receive any jail time."

Again, what Beckman told the commissioners had no basis in fact. I never gave Duncan any signed paperwork that he would plead guilty and receive a no-jail-time sentence. I wouldn't have had any authority to do so, except as a messenger for the DA, which never happened.

Beckman said that when Duncan applied for clemency, which was in 2017, he provided the DA's Office with notice of his intent to apply for a commutation. Beckman claimed the DA "voluntarily chose not to oppose and offer commentary on the petition."

This was untrue. The DA did oppose Duncan's application for clemency, in a letter to then-governor Jerry Brown in April 2018.

Beckman continued: "And as you see, they're not here today to oppose parole, and that speaks volumes for Mr. Martinez."

It was galling enough that, thanks to the timing of Gascón's swearing in, the DA had bailed out on the hearing at the last minute. Now Duncan's attorney was using their absence as an implicit endorsement of him being granted parole.

Beckman closed: "Duncan Martinez is ready to go home. He's earned the parole. Amazingly, he actually earned the parole grant years ago, before it was even available to him. Please find him suitable today. Thank you."

Next to speak was Duncan himself.

Patty and I watched on our computer screen as Duncan put on his reading glasses. He remained seated and read aloud from a few pages he held up in front of him.

"Ron Baker was kind, smart, and one of those people who genuinely appreciated everyone around them... I met him working at Sears, and he approached me with kindness and immediate advice... We ended up as roommates.

"On the night of June 21st, 1990, I betrayed Ron completely, and because of that betrayal, he is dead. My failures as a friend and human being stole Ron Baker from the world... I was an uncaring, selfish, deceitful coward... For so long, all I cared about was what was happening to me. I saw myself as the victim. I was too much of a coward to take responsibility, to admit even to myself that Ron's murder was my fault... I ran from everything.

"With a lot of struggle, a lot of growing, I worked to be better, to be who I thought I should've been all along... Finally taking responsibility for my actions, I started working to give back to others as I continued to work on myself. I went from a selfish, deceitful manipulator to a man who is humble, cares, and is not afraid to face up to what he is and has done... I am doing this because it is who I am now, who I want to be...

"Memories of Ron will constantly remind me of my purpose in life, making amends for my past... I want to work with animal shelters and rescues and to give back to the community like Ron did. I will be a positive member of society.

"Commissioner, Deputy Commissioner, I am so sorry for the harms caused on the night of June 21st, 1990. I take full responsibility for everything. Thank you for your time."

I thought Duncan did a very good job presenting himself to the panel, with both his words and his manner. I couldn't take that away from him. But was it real, or a performance?

After a short break, it was my turn to address the panel.

I aimed to give the sort of remarks the DA's Office might have delivered, had they been there. I reiterated many of the points I'd made in my letter, in particular Duncan's history of employing manipulation and deceit.

I tried to speak to Dr. Athans's risk assessment, which was difficult, considering I had not been allowed to read it. I challenged Duncan's claim to Athans that he was morally but not legally responsible for Ron's murder. "Accepting legal responsibility is the key issue here, because he was legally convicted of this murder. If he's just saying that he's morally responsible, no crime at all... That's a major issue, and if that's not minimization, I don't know what is."

I acknowledged that Duncan had helped us solve the case but argued that his motivation at all times was self-interest.

In closing, I told the commissioners, "I just feel he's still a problem... He's obviously gone to a lot of self-help things, and he knows how to word things. I think he maybe bamboozled Dr. Athans, with his abilities, his manner of talking. He's obviously well-spoken, but I feel there's a lot of underlying issues that make him definitely a risk to this day."

Patty was the last to address the panel.

She began her remarks by holding up to the laptop's camera, so the commissioners could see them, a series of photos of Ron, at different stages of his life. One showed young Patty and Ron in their pajamas, seated in front of the family's Christmas tree, her arm draped lovingly over her little brother's shoulders.

*Ron and Patty Baker Christmas photo, circa early 1970s
(courtesy of Patty Baker Elliott)*

She lowered the last of the photos. "It's really hard to even express the level of pain and heartache that my family went through… In our case, the pain did not stop with just dealing with Ron's death or the manner in which he was killed… For weeks after the murder, Duncan shared in our grief, all the while knowing exactly what had happened to Ron."

Patty noted that Duncan could have stopped his and Nathan's plan many times but never did. "At the point where he realized the act of killing my brother was actually going to happen, he could have yelled at Nathan to stop. He could have run and gotten help. When he heard my brother screaming, instead of doing any of these things, he told Nathan, 'You've got to finish him off because you can't leave him like that,' because he didn't want to hear the sounds of my brother screaming and the noise that he describes as something that will haunt him forever."

Patty recounted her family's ordeal beginning the night of Ron's murder, with the ransom calls her father received. "My father told me many times that those phone calls would haunt him, especially finding out later that Duncan Martinez had placed the phone calls after

Ron was already dead. The deception continued with Duncan being a pallbearer at the graveside service and delivering a tearful eulogy... We absolutely trusted Duncan. We didn't believe he was involved. My parents had seen him many times over the years... He even had an alarm code to the house."

Patty described how it affected them when Duncan suddenly disappeared, after staging his own kidnapping. "This put fear in all our hearts that possibly the same person had gotten to Duncan that had killed Ron. That is what Duncan wanted us all to believe, when in reality he was trying to escape, taking no responsibility for being involved in the murder."

Patty talked about her love for her brother and what might have been. "Ron was one of my best friends. He was such a kind person yet had a brilliant, inquisitive mind... Although my parents lived good lives, there was always a part of them that was missing with Ron gone. Our lives forever changed. We will never be able to hear Ron's infectious laugh or see what he would have become. My own family will never know their uncle, and he would have been a great uncle... But Ron was denied a chance because Duncan Martinez and Nathan Blalock had a plan and decided my brother would make a good victim."

Patty said she believed Duncan had no remorse for his involvement in Ron's murder, only remorse that he was caught. "He may not appear to be a violent person, but he is a manipulator, which in a way is worse. His manipulations of everyone—including his accomplice, Nathan Blalock—are some of the most disturbing actions I've ever witnessed," she said. "I am asking you to see through his current manipulation, and current self-preservation, and deem him a current unreasonable risk to society today, and to not grant parole. Thank you."

The two commissioners, Minor and Guerrero, recessed to deliberate.

They returned less than thirty minutes later.

Minor stated for the record the question they were to decide and the criteria they were bound by law to consider. "The panel must determine if the inmate continues to pose an unreasonable risk to public safety. A denial of parole must be based on evidence in the record of the inmate's current dangerousness. The law requires us to give great weight to the mitigating effects of the diminished culpability of youths as compared to adults... and any subsequent growth and increased maturity... We did consider the following evidence... the inmate's central file, the comprehensive risk assessment, all written responses received from the public, the testimony of Mr. Martinez," and all the victim impact statements made, including mine and Patty's, she said.

Minor then announced their decision.

"Based on the legal standards and evidence considered, we find today Mr. Martinez does not pose an unreasonable risk to public safety and is, therefore, suitable for parole."

My heart sank for Patty, sitting beside me.

Minor continued: "We did look at factors that aggravate his risk, when we looked at the crime. This was a crime that was committed in a heinous—this was a horrible crime. This was a crime in which the victim was vulnerable. He may have been under the influence. It was a crime carried out in a manner which demonstrates an exceptional disregard for human suffering. Mr. Martinez told his friend to finish him off. He was involved, I think just based on all of the information, and we are not here to retry the case, but I think he was a participant in putting this all together... The motive of this crime was inexplicable, and certainly after the crime, Mr. Martinez was manipulative in ways to avoid the law...

"But we find the factors aggravating his current risk are outweighed by factors that mitigate his risk. The comprehensive risk assessment determined Mr. Martinez poses a low risk of future violence... He has no extensive criminal history prior to the crime. No crimes of violence, and so his criminal and parole history was a mitigating factor... While he's been incarcerated, he has no rule violations, no serious rule violations. No violence while he's been incarcerated... It appears, based on the evidence in the record, that Mr. Martinez has changed...

"So based on the findings, we conclude today Mr. Martinez does not pose an unreasonable risk or threat to public safety. Accordingly, this panel find Mr. Martinez suitable for parole."

Minor explained the panel's decision was not final and would be reviewed by the full parole board. "That can take up to one hundred twenty days, for the review to be complete, followed by a review of the governor, which may take up to thirty additional days. You'll be notified in writing, Mr. Martinez, if there are any changes to this decision."

Moments later, the hearing ended. I felt like I had watched Duncan first maneuver his way out of a life without parole sentence and now potentially out of prison entirely.

Perhaps I shouldn't have been so surprised by the decision, given everything leading up to it. Duncan had benefited from a series of incredibly lucky breaks, from Newsom singling him out and commuting his LWOP sentence to Gascón taking office when he did, the day before Duncan's parole hearing.

In 1990, Duncan almost got away with murder by lying and conniving at every turn. But for our investigation, he might have succeeded. Ultimately, with Duncan's and Nathan's equal convictions and matching sentences, truth and justice had prevailed. At least that's how it seemed at the time. Perhaps naively, I believed that was how the story of Ron Baker's case would end.

Thirty years later, it appeared Duncan and the system had proved me wrong.

CHAPTER 30

AND IN THE END, THE LIFE YOU TAKE IS EQUAL TO …
(January 25, 2021 to April 26, 2022)

THERE WAS STILL A possibility the Board of Parole Hearings' decision could be reversed, either by the full parole board or Governor Newsom. If the board agreed that Duncan was suitable for parole, Newsom had three options. He could let the decision stand, in which case Duncan would be released; he could send it back to the Board of Parole Hearings to have them reconsider the decision; or he could overturn the decision and have Duncan remain in custody until a future parole hearing date.

Given that it was Newsom who had singlehandedly set things in motion by commuting Duncan's sentence, I did not see him overturning the board's decision. Doing so would imply that Duncan remained a threat to the public. That would call into question Newsom's original decision to grant Duncan clemency.

Still, I did not feel I could stand by and do nothing. I knew Patty felt the same way.

I wrote another letter, this time to Governor Newsom. I informed him of Duncan's involvement in planning Ron's murder and other bad acts, which, based on the text of his commutation, the governor knew nothing about. I also reiterated many of the points I'd made to the Board of Parole Hearings, including Duncan's compulsive lying, consistent minimization of his role, and history of blaming others for situations he got himself into.

I mailed my letter to Newsom on January 25, 2021, a month after Duncan's hearing.

Patty wrote her own letter to Newsom, asking him to not allow Duncan's release.

So did retired deputy DA Anne Ingalls, who included with her letter several documents from the case against Duncan. She wanted Newsom to read for himself the true extent of Duncan's culpability for Ron's murder and see more clearly his manipulative nature.

None of us received any response or acknowledgment from the governor, his office, or anyone associated with the state's prison system and parole board.

Governor Newsom ended up taking no action, letting stand the board's decision that Duncan was suitable for parole and should be released from prison.

On April 22, 2021, about four months after his parole hearing, and less than a year after his LWOP sentence was commuted, Duncan Martinez walked out of the California State Prison, Los Angeles County, where he had lived for most of the previous quarter century.

Patty was informed of Duncan's release. She in turn notified me.

All that remained of Duncan's debt to society was to complete a successful parole stint. During that time, he would have to comply with rules such as not committing any new crimes and attending regular meetings with his parole agent. Duncan's release conditions also forbade him from living within thirty-five miles of the victim's family, in this case only Patty.

Patty was told by parole officials that Duncan would remain on parole for three to five years.

On April 26, 2022, just one year after Duncan was released from prison, unbeknownst to me and Patty, Duncan was fully discharged from parole. He was a totally free man, no longer bound by any parole conditions and no longer under government supervision of any kind.

Patty and I were never told why Duncan's parole ended two years earlier than the minimum of three years she was previously assured he would serve.

I learned of Duncan's parole discharge by chance, a few months after it occurred, when out of pure curiosity I called the parole office to inquire about his status. I was informed that Duncan had completed his parole. I asked if I could speak with Duncan's last parole agent.

The parole agent agreed to take my call. I explained who I was and my involvement in Duncan's underlying murder case. He had no problem recalling Duncan from the many other parolees he had supervised over the years.

I said the victim's sister had been told Duncan would be on parole for at least three years. I asked why Duncan had been discharged early.

The parole agent could not give me a specific reason but said that throughout California early discharges from parole were happening much more frequently than in the past. He told me that prior to Duncan being discharged, he had strongly recommended his parole conditions be extended. He described the murder as particularly callous and Duncan as a "master manipulator," the same assessment previously reached by me and so many others.

He told me that unfortunately his recommendation that Duncan remain on parole had been disregarded. He said he thought it was interesting that many "prominent people," including "legislators and politicians," had called or written letters of support for Duncan. The parole agent declined to name any of these "prominent" supporters but said he was not surprised that his recommendation for continued parole had fallen on deaf ears.

I called Patty and asked her if she had heard about Duncan's change in parole status. She had not. I broke the news that he had already been discharged from parole.

Patty did not have much of a reaction. I think she may have lost the capacity to be shocked, due to the whiplash of Duncan's ever-changing and ever-more-lenient handling.

From time to time, I visit the CDCR Inmate Locator website and punch in Nathan Blalock's name. Nathan remains an LWOP prisoner, with no indication that he will ever have his sentence commuted.

Nathan was twenty-two at the time of Ron's murder, four years younger than the age cutoff for youthful offender status. Like Duncan,

Nathan qualifies as a youthful offender. However, inmates serving LWOP sentences in California have no legal right to a parole hearing, regardless of their youthful offender status.

Nathan, after he learned of Duncan's commutation, filed his own application for clemency with the governor. He, too, hopes for a reduction of his sentence from LWOP to twenty-five years to life. Should that happen, he would be eligible, like Duncan, for an immediate parole hearing. Until then, Nathan continues to live his life in Mule Creek State Prison in Ione, California.

Why has Nathan, unlike his crime partner, not received clemency from Governor Newsom?

One possibility is that Nathan's application is still being evaluated. Duncan had to wait three years after he applied for clemency before he received his commutation.

Another possible reason why Duncan has received clemency, but not Nathan, is that evidence shows Nathan was the sole stabber of Ron.

Was Duncan's cooperation with the LAPD a factor that counted in his favor? Without being able to see the reports and records reviewed by Governor Newsom, it is impossible to say.

The contents of Nathan's CDCR "central file" is another unknown. How does his disciplinary record in prison compare to Duncan's? Does Nathan have a similar track record of taking self-help programs, volunteering, and accumulating lots of laudatory chronos?

Lastly, could the disparity have anything to do with something Nathan had voiced concerns about more than once earlier in the case: that as a Black man, he would unfairly receive more blame and punishment than his white crime partner?

Was race at all a factor in the governor's decision to commute Duncan's sentence? I thought not, since at the time Duncan was under consideration for clemency, Nathan had yet to file his application.

This is not to say race played no role in Duncan being granted a commutation and recommended for parole. As in broader American society, the impact of race can be subtle and indirect, but no less real an injustice.

I believe a main reason Duncan was successful in seeking clemency was that he was represented by an experienced private attorney, someone skilled at presenting evidence and arguments that favored him. I saw firsthand at his parole hearing what a difference it made for him to have Beckman in his corner, especially with no prosecutor there to argue the other side.

Duncan evidently had a lot of family support, including financial backing to pay for an attorney, during his bid for clemency and release. Nathan, as far as I knew, did not have the benefit of any family support, financial or otherwise. The same was true when Duncan and Nathan had their trials. Duncan had a private attorney, and Nathan, a public defender. Was this discrepancy in support and resources a racial injustice? Perhaps not directly. But it still gave me pause and reason to wonder how emblematic it was of broader racial inequities in our criminal justice system.

Until Newsom grants Nathan the same clemency as Duncan, the fact remains that two people, one white and one Black, although both convicted of the same crime and given the same sentence, are being treated differently.

Did Newsom realize that by commuting Duncan's sentence he was creating a disparity? Due to the lack of transparency around the clemency process, I can't even say for certain if Newsom was aware that Duncan and Nathan are of different races.

Yet here we are. Again. The white man receives leniency. The Black man remains in prison, serving a sentence of life without parole.

The characters and circumstances may change, but not the troubling pattern and appearance of bias.

As a matter of fairness, should Nathan's sentence be commuted? The fact that Duncan is now out of prison might be Nathan's strongest argument that he should receive equal treatment and a chance at parole.

How would I feel if Nathan's sentence was commuted and he became eligible for parole?

It's hard to say.

In many ways, I respected Nathan as a person more than I did Duncan. Nathan also lied, but he was hardly as conniving and manipulative as Duncan. Nathan never did anything so disingenuous as speak at Ron's memorial service or shamelessly console Ron's family and friends, as Duncan had. Nathan never stole a dead child's identity.

Would I feel wrong opposing Nathan's parole, on the principle of equal justice among suspects? Or would I feel compelled, as I did in

Duncan's case, to try to convince the parole board that Nathan should not be released?

My gut instinct is that I would have to oppose Nathan's parole and release if things ever got to that point.

The way I see it, Duncan worked the system and managed to catch a big break, despite what, in my opinion, he actually deserved.

What it comes down to for me is that Nathan should not benefit from the fact that Duncan caught a lucky break. What the two of them did together was horrendous. Jointly, they took an innocent person's life and destroyed a close and loving family.

Since I believe that Duncan should still be incarcerated, then I feel that Nathan should still be incarcerated as well.

Time will tell whether Nathan ever gets the opportunity to make his case to a parole board.

In my decades of investigating murders, I have often wondered where my desire to keep working these cases came from, especially with having reached my seventies.

Granted, it is interesting work. But was that it?

I recently received a text message from a young woman I first met in 2002. She was a college student then.

Almost twenty years before, her mother was kidnapped and murdered. She was only two when she lost her mother. I met her when my partner and I were investigating the killing as a cold case, and our investigation eventually led to the arrest and conviction of the killer.

Her message to me read: "Rick! I was just thinking of you (as I often do around this time of year) with gratitude... Sending you a big hug and love!"

It was a very simple text. Yet it meant the world to me. It came nearly two decades after the conviction of her mother's killer, and forty years since the murder itself.

Her text reaffirmed the drive I had for my work, which has always been focused on those for whom I have sought to provide answers and, hopefully, some semblance of justice.

That will be my legacy from working a life of death.

ACKNOWLEDGMENTS

VERY SPECIAL THANKS: Detective Frank Garcia, my partner in crime; Matthew McGough, my co-writer in crime; Patty Baker Elliott, a fighter for the rights of victims' families; Duncan Maitland, my favorite passport-fraud coordinator; FBI special agent Neil Cronin (RIP); Melissa Bean, for your spirit and assistance; Christine Reyna, for your support and the education you provided in areas in which I was clueless; Detective Jim Prior, who helped to put us over the top; Phlash Phelps of SiriusXM, for your company and music during all of those early-morning West Coast writing sessions; Kathryn Busby, for your thoughtful contributions and insight; and Michael Connelly, for your friendship, inspiration, and assistance with this project.

Very personal thanks: Debbie Halliday, my wife; my daughters, Hillary Fitzgerald and Megan Sutton; my sons-in-law, Bob Fitzgerald Jr. and Rich Sutton III; my sisters, Dianne Jackson Kiser and Nancy Jackson Bevill, and my brother-in-law, Jim Bevill; my mother and father, Dorothy (RIP) and Matthew Jackson Jr. (RIP); my three grandparents, whom I longingly wished I'd known: Harry Wharton Jr. (RIP), Lizetta Beck Wharton (RIP), and Matthew McCoy Jackson Sr. (RIP); Nora Jackson, who once gave me an empty leather-bound book to fill with my words; my in-laws, Jay (RIP) and Dorothy Halliday Becker (RIP); Dr. Randy (RIP) and Cheryl Halliday (RIP), Dr. Larry Halliday (RIP), and Jim Halliday (RIP); Lorri Halliday; Vaughn Halliday (RIP); Nick McCann and Amber McCasland McCann; Ashley McCann Creen and Jeremy Creen; Alexa and Ethan Rudin; Jennie and Josh Dobies; my grandchildren, Noah Fitzgerald, Maddigan Fitzgerald, Ben Fitzgerald, Ellie Fitzgerald, McCoy Sutton, Ty Sutton, Jonah Rudin, Avery Rudin, Noelle Dobies, Colette "Coco" Dobies, Hazel McCann, and Oliver Creen; Linda Connelly; Jon Kiser; Stew and Doris Steckel; William McCann; special friends Bruce and Karie Frederick, Caitlin Frederick Myers, and Amanda Frederick; and John O'Loughlin. Finally, to Connie Hoban, my favorite English literature teacher; Jo Ann Kennedy McDonald, the ninth-grade teacher who inspired me; and Mary Seiersen, the fifth-grade teacher who introduced me to mystery books.

The writers from whom I have personally learned: Michael Connelly; Miles Corwin; Robert Ellis; James Ellroy; Tom Junod; Steven Keeva (RIP); Helen Knode; Michael Koryta; Michael Krikorian; Jillian Lauren; Sean Lynch; Kirk Russell; Joseph Schneider; and Joseph Wambaugh.

The LAPD coworkers who helped to shape me: Richard Aldahl; Dan Andrews (RIP); Addison "Bud" Arce; Ted Ball; Ernie Basset; Richard Bengtson; Michael Berchem; Larry Bird (RIP); Donald Bleier; Jim Bosse (RIP); Elizabeth Estupinian Camacho; Denis Cremins; Richard Crotsley; Fred Dahl; Tony Diaz (RIP); Marv Engquist; Peggy Fiderio; William Gailey; John Garcia; William "WOG" Gartland; Claude "Butch" Harris (RIP); Richard "Buck" Henry; George "No Make" Herrera; Doreen Music Hudson; Ron Ito; Gil Jones (RIP); Dennis Kilcoyne; Russell Kuster (RIP); Ewing "JR" Kwock; David Lambkin; Danny Lang (RIP); Tom Lange; Bill Lewellen; Dave Lovestedt (RIP); Tom Maioli; Tim Marcia; Otis Marlow; Charles Massey; Greg Matheson; Mike Mejia (RIP); Greg Meyer; Al Moen; Hank Petroski; George Reming; Don Riggio (RIP); Mitzi Roberts; Bob Rozzi; Jerry Stephens; Carl Supernor; Rick Swanston; James Tatreau (RIP); Mike Thies; Paul Tippin; Phil Vannatter (RIP); and John Zorn.

The deputy district attorneys: Marcia Clark; David Conn (RIP); Anne Ingalls; Ralph Plummer; and Sally Thomas. And I would be remiss if I didn't mention John Lewin, for his impressive body of work.

The honorable judges: Jacqueline Connor; Edward Ferns; Larry Paul Fidler; Kevin McCormick; Norman Shapiro (RIP); Stephen Trott; Michael Tynan; and Arthur A. "Andy" Wick.

Friends who have given strong support and encouraging words: Cynthia Amestoy; Steve Arrow; Dr. Jim Bagnall (RIP); John Barr; Roy Bissinger;

Michael Blashaw (RIP); Rick Buck (RIP); Joe and Joan Buonadonna; Lou Cheregotis; Craig Cleveland; Dan Daly; Roger and Dianne Ehlers; Bill Fenoglio; Miguel Ferrer (RIP); George and Lucia Foster; Reverend Dr. Dan Gibson; Joel Glick; Mike and Robyn Goodman; Lawrence Greenstein; Mike Gutierrez; Dr. David Hamill (RIP); Dr. Kim and Barbara Hannaford; Mark (RIP) and Patty Hannaford; David and Lynne Harr; Raphael Joson; Scott Klace; Tom Lederer and Terri Eggers; Debby Robertson Marchman; Mary Meronk; Helene Berkenwald Miller; Mike and Eulema Miller; Roger Mills; Tami Moore; Christine Nicoles; Blake Niehoff; Kyle Ogilvie; Laura Keefer Palmer; Jack Peisley; Dan Piraino (RIP); Dave Ramos; Debi Riordan Riley; Nancy Rove; Richard and Dawn Rove; Rob Schulman; Ken and Connie Scutari; Scott Sechman and Belinda Lucey; Troy and Sally Stanton; Joan Knothe Stein; Michael Steiner (RIP); Candi Haave Steinhauser; the Stevely Avenue gang, who have provided support for me for years; Mike (RIP) and Sue Stevens; Jaci Gieser Stirnaman; Jim Struble and Carol Wilcott Struble; Barbara Frowiss Taylor; Barbara Townsend; David Tresmontan; Reg Truman; Patty and Don Underwood; Lisa Waldman and the staff at Bridges Restaurant; Jack and Karen Wildvank; and Missy Verdin Wonacott.

The team at Mulholland Books / Little, Brown and Company: Josh Kendall; Liv Ryan; Karen Landry; Dianna Stirpe; Chloe Texier-Rose; and Kayleigh George.

Professional acknowledgments: Andrew Blauner, my literary agent; and Diane Golden and Sarah Lerner, my entertainment attorneys.

—Rick Jackson

Thank you first and foremost to my coauthor, Rick Jackson, whose invitation to collaborate on this book opened a new world for me. Thanks for trusting me to tell your story and for helping me understand how homicide investigations should be conducted.

Thank you to my wife, Kathryn, and sons, Hudson and Declan, for your support and for always helping me to keep things in proper perspective. I love you.

Thank you to my mother, Rose, whose dedication as a high school English teacher set an example in our family and helped lead me to a life in books, and to my sister, Sarina, and brother, Damien.

ACKNOWLEDGMENTS

Thank you to the entire team at Mulholland Books / Little, Brown and Company, led by Josh Kendall and Liv Ryan, whose work helped make this book a reality and bring it to readers.

Thank you to my literary agent, Andrew Blauner; my book-to-film agent, Jason Richman at UTA; and my attorneys, Alex Kohner and Ashley Briskman. I am lucky and grateful to have you in my corner.

Thank you to the friends who encouraged me during the writing of this book, in particular: Jeff Alexander, Tom Bissell, Wendy Burke, Michael Connelly, Rob Cucuzza, Jane Cha Cutler and R. J. Cutler, Julie Durk and Andrew Kevin Walker, Keith Eisner, Wayne Federman, Dan Josefson, John Ortiz, Matthew Thomas, David Wilcox, and Betsy Ross.

—*Matthew McGough*

AUTHORS' NOTE ON SOURCES

THIS BOOK IS A work of nonfiction.

We have endeavored to tell the true story of Ron Baker's case in a fair and accurate manner. Although much of it is told in the first person, we did not rely on memory alone to reconstruct the case details.

This account is based on a variety of sources, including investigative reports and notes; audio recordings; witness interviews and statements; photographs and diagrams; newspaper articles; and other research materials obtained by the authors. During the writing of this book, we also conducted additional interviews with several people involved in the original investigation.

Wherever in the book exact quotations are attributed to a person, that information comes directly from an audio recording, interview transcript or written statement, or court testimony given by that person. Some quotations have been edited lightly but solely for clarity and readability, not to alter the meaning of what was said.

—Rick Jackson and Matthew McGough

SELECTED BIBLIOGRAPHY

Associated Press. "Gov. Newsom Pardons 13 Former Inmates and Commutes 21 Sentences, Including Some for Life Without Parole." KTLA.com, June 26, 2020.

Associated Press. "U. Student Charged with L.A. Killing." *Deseret News*, June 21, 1994.

Connelly, Michael. "Slain Man Frequently Visited Site of Occultists." *Los Angeles Times*, July 7, 1990.

Connelly, Michael, and Steve Padilla. "Mysticism Fascinated Slain Man: Crime: The Introspective Student May Have Gone to a Park to Meditate. His Body Was Found There Near a Site of Occult Observances." *Los Angeles Times*, July 4, 1990.

Los Angeles Daily News Staff and Wire Services. "Student Killed on Solstice May Have Been Sacrificed." *Los Angeles Daily News*, July 4, 1990.

Williams, Timothy. "Inmate Pleads Not Guilty in '90 Stabbing Death of Roommate in Chatsworth Tunnel." *Los Angeles Times*, July 16, 1993.

INDEX

Page numbers in italics *indicate illustrations.*

Allen, Bryant, 139, 140
Amnesty International, 403
Arce, Addison "Bud"
   at Hollywood Homicide, 21, 26, 27
   on Kuster's murder, 134
   at Robbery-Homicide Division, 21, 28, 30, 139, 140, 141, 218
Archibald, Lydia, 38–41, 99, 112, 160, 162, 243, 259
   Duncan leaving stuff at house of, 171
   Duncan staying at house of, 61, 122
   Duncan's call to, about kidnapping, 97–98, 101, 103, 109, 110, 115–18, 172–73, 176, 177, 196
   on Ron and Wicca, 40–41
   at Ron's memorial service, 59
Armstrong, Debbie, 397–98
athames, 52, 63, 96, 119–20, 123–24, 127
Athans, Dr., 463–64, 468, 469, 471, 473, 476, 477, 480
Auerbach, Andrea, 100, 119
Auerbach, Jessica, 99, 100, 108, 119
Avaneszadeh, Gago, 382–83

Baker, Gayle, 13–14, *14,* 171–72, 466
   calls to Ron's roommates, 15, 43, 49, 56, 62, 64, 66, 74, 87, 90, 159, 160, 283, 320, 405, 409
   career of, 14–15
   church and, 14, 440
   Clark and, 357
   Connelly and, 83, 84
   death of, 440
   discovery of Duncan's "Things To Do" list, 132, 179
   frustration with investigation, 141
   at Nathan's trial, 404, 424
   police informing, about Ron's murder, 32–33, 34, 96–97, 104
   ransom calls to, 14–16, 21, 56, 84, 128, 159–61, 183, 194, 205, 357, 404, 410, 418, 481–82
   reaction to Duncan's possible involvement in Ron's murder, 133
   reporting Ron's possible kidnapping to police, 16–17
   on Ron and Mystic's Circle, 61–62
   visiting and caring for Ron's burial plot, 440

Baker, Gayle (*cont.*)
  as a witness in grand jury case against Nathan, 313
Baker, Kay, 13, *14*, 466
  on arraignment of Nathan for Ron's murder, 329
  career of, 15
  church and, 14, 440
  Clark and, 357
  Connelly and, 83
  death of, 440
  discovery of Duncan's "Things To Do" list, 132, 179
  frustration with investigation, 141
  at Nathan's trial, 404, 424
  police informing, about Ron's murder, 32–33, 34, 104
  ransom calls and, 15–16, 21, 129
  reaction to Duncan's possible involvement in Ron's murder, 133
  on Ron and Mystic's Circle, 61–62
  visiting and caring for Ron's burial plot, 440
Baker, Patty. *See* Elliott, Patty Baker
Baker, Ronald
  alcohol and, 46, 68–69, 72, 78, 88, 122–23, 125, 128, 187–88
  apartment of, description of, 38, *39*, 39–40
  athame of, 52, 63, 123
  blood type of, 404
  burial plot of, 440
  at Chatsworth Park prior to night of murder, 33, 42, 50, 52, 54, 57, 64, 85, 88, 128
  cigarette brand of, 167
  collection of license plates with Duncan, 107
  friendship with Duncan, 67, 74, 124, 130, 167, 189–90, 198, 262, 459
    after damage to Duncan's car, 64, 74, 88, 122
    beginning of, 41, 74, 479
    screaming for Duncan to help during struggle with Nathan, 157, 204, 219, 240, 243, 348, 472, 481
  funeral of, 55
  making dinner for roommates and Diane, 49, 73, 86, 89, 155
  memorial service for, 58–60, 460, 472, 482, 489
  murder of, investigation of. *See* Baker homicide investigation
  Nathan and
    arguments between, 164, 166–67, 185, 186, 190, 204, 240
    meeting each other, 50, 85
  opposition to capital punishment, 403
  personality of, 47, 53, 58, 72, 88, 130
  photographs of, *14*, 480, *481*
  sexuality of, 42, 53–54, 88
  Wicca and, 50, 51, 53, 54, 57, 58, 73
    introduction to Wicca, 17, 40–41, 55–56
    Mystic's Circle and, 15, 17, 18, *18*, 35, 41, 42, 46–47, 51, 61–62, 73, 74
    occult-related items in bedroom of, 18, *18*, 39–40, 61, 63
Baker homicide investigation
  assignment of Garcia and Jackson to, 21–22, 30
  autopsy report in, 11, 12, 19, 31–32, 46, 68, 398–400
  blood analysis in, 81–82, 96, 118–20, 136, 207–13
    on blood on athames, 96, 119–20, 141–42, 143
    on blood on broken beer bottle, 247–48
    of Nathan's blood sample, 208–11, 228–30, 237, 245, 255, 277, 284–87, 291, 295, 301, 313
    on Ron's blood-alcohol level, 68–69, 88, 122–23, 128, 187
    on Ron's blood type, 46
  contact with Baker family during, 32–34, 61–62, 96–97, 104, 105, 132, 141
  early stages of, basic tasks in, 45–46, 47
  forged checks and, 35, 45–46, 64, 68, 74, 79–81, 103, 104–5, 113–14, 125, 127, 453
  Duncan on, 161, 196–97
  Nathan on, 121–22, 323

Questioned Documents Unit on, 119, 120–21
identification of Ron in, 19–20
interviews during
  with Adriane Tomlinson, 397, 398
  with Christine Reyna, 50, 51–54
  with Debbie Armstrong, 397–98
  with Diane Henderson, 84–85, 89–91, 111
  with Duncan Martinez. *See* Martinez, Duncan: interviews with
  with Gago Avaneszadeh, 382–83
  with James Purpura, 180, 200, 203–5
  with Kathy Kritzberg, 40, 41
  with Lance Strickler, 55–57
  with Lydia Archibald, 38–39, 40–41
  with Martin Carr, 57–58
  with Melissa Bean, 371–76
  with Nancy Bradish, 205–6, 207, 218–20
  with Nathan Blalock. *See* Blalock, Nathan: interviews with
  with Roland Trevino, 47–48
  with Shirley James, 114–15
  with Stephanie Glezos, 367–71
  with Tewanda Nicholson, 111–12
  with Yasmin Fouda, 105–6
kidnapping plan and, 164, 167, 168, 192–93, 204–5, 219, 220, 242–43, 245, 309, 340–43, 345, 352, 374, 375, 406, 408–10, 417–20, 422–23, 448
  Duncan on, 155, 156, 159, 165–66, 171, 182–83, 184–85, 194, 202
  Nathan on, 283, 284, 290–91, 297–98, 303, 320–22, 326–27
media coverage during, 48–49, 65, 66–67, 83–84, 328
motive for killing Ron, 413–14, 448, 469–70
  Duncan on, 166–67, 186, 187, 190–91, 471
  Nathan on, 290–91, 293–94, 296–97, 298, 302–3, 323, 324, 327–28, 419
Mystic's Circle and, 15, 17, 18, *18,* 35, 41, 42, 46–47, 51, 61–62, 73, 74

polygraph examinations and
  Duncan's agreeing to take, 64–65, 69–70, 77–78, 82
  Nathan's refusal to take, 94
processing of crime scene, xiii–xiv, 7, 8–12, *10,* 32, 34
ransom calls and, 35–36, 46, 159–60, 161, 183, 184–85, 194, 195, 297
recordings of conversations in
  between Duncan and Nathan, 222–44, 249–66
  between Prior and Duncan, 333–37, 338, 349–50
Ron's toxicology screen report in, 68–69
search of Ron's bedroom during, 18, *18, 39,* 39–40, 61, 62–63
sixty-day summary of, 126–29
stabbing in, 244, 279–80, 287–92, 295–98, 302, 304, 315–19, 324–25, 340, 346–49, 405, 411, 412
  Duncan on, 156–58, 169–70, 179–80, 199, 239–40, 371, 372–73, 374–75
  Duncan urging Nathan to finish Ron off, 459, 472, 481, 483
  Nathan on, 407–8, 416–17, 420–22
walk through of crime scene at Chatsworth Park, 34–35, 37–38, 357, 358
See also Blalock, Nathan; Martinez, Duncan
Bank of America robbery, 207–8
Barnes, Jim, 364, 378
  advising Duncan not to speak with Jackson or Clark, 366
  advising Jeannie Martinez to cooperate with police, 107
  Duncan talking to, before going on the run, 163, 176
  on Duncan's possible kidnapping, 100, 101
  at Duncan's Salt Lake City interview, 149, 153, 161, 172, 181–82, 200, 361, 426
  on inquiries regarding Duncan being directed through him, 92, 94–96

Barnes, Jim *(cont.)*
  "King for a Day" agreement and, 150, 425, 426–27
  request for immunity for Duncan, 144, 145, 205, 428
Barnes, Sherri, 271–72, 309, 310
Bean, Mary Louise, 371, 372
Bean, Melissa, 310, 371–76
Beckman, Michael, 468, 476–77, 478–79, 488–89
Belushi, John, 268
Berchem, Mike, 378–79, 383–84
Blake, Sergeant, 429
Blalock, Nathan
  apartment of, description of, 38, 39
  application for commutation of sentence, 488, 489–90
  arguments between Ron and, 164, 166–67, 185, 186, 190, 204, 240
  arrest of, for murdering Ron, 314
  bank robbery and, 246, 249
    arrest for, 207–8, 213–15, 221, 227, 410
    sentencing for, 213, 220, 221, 222–23, 227–28
  blood sample provided by, 208–11, 228–30, 237, 245, 255, 277, 284–87, 291, 295, 301, 313
  cover story for night of Ron's murder, 49–50, 58, 66, 69, 85–87, 90, 91, 111, 122–23, 255–58, 264–65
  in Detroit at family reunion, 43, 62, 162
  Diane Henderson and, 86, 87, 89, 183, 263, 284
    breakup between, 208, 214, 237
    staying with Diane after Ron's murder, 66, 84, 162, 176, 323
    testifying at Nathan's trial, 404–5
  drug use of, 125
  Duncan's claim of writing remorse letter to, 475
  Duncan's fear of, 162–64, 172, 175, 177, 198, 240
  family of, 407
  on forged checks, 121–22, 323
  friendship with Duncan, 167, 189–90, 198, 219, 220, 262, 270–71
  going to Chatsworth Park
    after Ron was reported missing, 50, 85, 90, 128–29, 282–83, 292, 299–300, 325–26, 409–10
    with friends prior to Ron's murder, 50, 85, 128
  grand jury indictment of, for Ron's murder, 311–14, 328–29, 337, 356, 357, 358
  interviews with, 17–18, 43, 85, 91–93, 125, 126, 306
    in August 1990, 120, 121–25, 280
    in July 1990, 84–89, 90, 91, 280
    in June/July 1993, 315–28, 405, 412
    before leaving for Detroit, 49–50
    in March 1992, 208–10, 229–30, 237, 245, 255, 277
    at state prison in February 1993, 274–306, 411–12
    while in Michigan, 65–66
  Jackson's visits with, after trial, 440
  kidnapping plan and, 164, 167, 168, 192–93, 204–5, 219, 220, 242–43, 245, 309, 340–43, 345, 352, 374, 375, 406, 408–10, 417–20, 422–23, 448
    Duncan on, 155, 156, 159, 165–66, 171, 182–83, 184–85, 194, 202
    Nathan on, 283, 284, 290–91, 297–98, 303, 320–22, 326–27
  meeting Ron, 50, 85
  military service of, 50, 86, 412–13, 414
  motive for Ron's murder, 413–14, 448, 469–70
    Duncan on, 166–67, 186, 187, 190–91, 471
    Nathan on, 290–91, 293–94, 296–97, 298, 302–3, 323, 324, 327–28, 419
  pact with Duncan about Ron's murder, 320, 323, 407–8, 411, 419–20, 421, 423
  ransom calls and, 15, 43, 49, 62, 64, 66, 87, 90, 159–60, 161, 164, 194, 195, 205, 283, 320, 405, 409
    recordings of conversations between Duncan and

INDEX | 501

investigators' preparations for, 222–26, 249–51, 274–77
Nathan's concern about phone line not being secure during, 228–29, 232, 233, 261, 290
while Nathan was at Riverside County Jail, 227–44, 290
while Nathan was at state prison in Tehachapi, 249–66, 410–11
refusal to take polygraph examination, 91, 94
sentence of life without parole for Ron's murder, 428, 454, 487–88
in stabbing Ron, 244, 279–80, 287–92, 295–98, 302, 304, 315–19, 324–25, 340, 346–49, 405, 411, 412
Duncan on, 156–58, 169–70, 179–80, 199, 239–40, 371, 372–73, 374–75
Nathan on, 407–8, 416–17, 420–22
urging Nathan to finish Ron off, 459, 472, 481, 483
trial of, for Ron's murder, 347, 378, 404–24
decision of DA's Office not to seek the death penalty in, 403, 424
Green's questioning of Nathan in, 405–13
Ingalls's cross-examination of Nathan in, 413–23, 435
Jackson at, 403, 404, 405, 424
jury deliberations in, 423–24
jury verdict of guilty in, 424
at LA County Jail awaiting, 314, 315, 383
race and, 401–3, 407, 414, 422
witnesses testifying in, 403, 404–5
Wicca and, 56, 66, 85
Blatty, William Peter, 6
Blood Alcohol Unit, 69
Boden, Richard, 250
Booker, Robert, 153, 199, 379–80
Bordey, Reymond, 120–21
Bradish, Nancy, 181, 205–6, 207, 218–20
Bressler, Lewis, 9
Brittain, Deputy, 428–29

Brown, Jerry, 446, 453, 467, 479
Burnham, Chuck, 50, 103
Bush, George H. W., 70, 72

California Constitution, 465
California Department of Corrections and Rehabilitation (CDCR), 455, 465, 468, 488
Capote, Truman, 202
Carr, Martin, 40, 42, 46–47, 50, 51, 54–55, 57–58
Casement, Suzi, 50–51
Casey, T. Patrick, 380
CDCR (California Department of Corrections and Rehabilitation), 455, 465, 468, 488
Chatsworth Park, 4–5, 8–9, 18, 21, 31–44, 50, 52, 56–58, 63–64, 68–69, 85, 90–91, 122–23, 128, 146, 155, 166, 183, 192–93, 282, 358, 382, 397
Chemical Processing Unit, 46
Christiansen, Doug, 271–72, 308–10, 353, 362, 371
Clark, Marcia, 355–59, 378, 429
as prosecutor on Baker case, 355
at Duncan's arrest, 359–67
in grand jury proceedings against Duncan, 356, 357, 358, 360, 363, 426, 427
interviewing Melissa Bean, 371–76
interviewing Stephanie Glezos, 367–71
meeting Ron Baker's parents and sister, 357–58
reindictment of Nathan with second special-circumstance allegation, 356, 357, 358
visiting the crime scene, 357, 358
as prosecutor on Simpson case, 377, 380, 429
Cleary, Sergeant, 222–23
Clutter family, 202
Cold Case Homicide Special Section, LAPD, 438
Conn, David, 308, 311, 336–37, 338, 355, 356, 427
Connelly, Michael, xiii–xiv, 48–49, 65, 66–67, 83–84

502 | INDEX

Connor, Jacqueline, 425, 427, 428, 429, 430
COVID-19 pandemic, 445
Crocker, Ken, 9, 10, 18–19, 34–35, 36, 37, 129
Cronin, Neil, 388, 395
Crook, Ken, 146, 147–48, 387–88

Detective Headquarters Division of LAPD, 97, 112–13, 133
Dorn, Will, 141
Dowell, Steve, 398–99, 400
Dragnet, 182, 245, 309, 326, 342
Dulgarian, Rick, 112–13
Dumanian, Andrew, 390–91, 392–93
Durrer, Al, 9

Elliott, Patty Baker, 13, 17
　Duncan's claim of writing remorse letter to, 475
　at Duncan's parole board hearing, 462–63, 464, 467, 469, 476, 477, 479, 480–82, 483
　on friendship between Ron and Duncan, 67
　keeping in touch with Jackson, 440, 446–47, 487
　lack of notification from officials about Duncan, 446, 447, 451, 456, 460–61, 466
　letter to Newsom, 486
　meeting Clark, 357–58
　at Nathan's trial, 404, 424
　photographs of Ron and, *14, 480, 481*
　at Ron's memorial service, 59
Everything Audio, 72, 125
Exorcist, The (Blatty), 6

FBI, 142, 143, 146–47, 342, 387–88, 395
Ferns, Edward, 404, 425, 428
Fitzgerald, Sandra, 9, 10, 11, 12
Floyd, George, 445–46, 461
folie à deux murder cases, 202–3
Fouda, Yasmin, 105–6
Frandson, Phillip, 27
Frankland, Steve, 453–54
Franks, Bobby, 202–3

Gailey, Bill, 437
Garcetti, Gil, 337
Garcia, Frank, 21–24, 25
　assignment to Baker homicide investigation, 21–22, 30
　background of, 22
　Barnes and, 92, 94–96, 144, 145
　Christine Reyna, interview with, 50, 51–54
　contact with Baker family, 32–34, 61–62, 96–97, 104, 105, 132, 141
　at coroner's office, 31–32
　Diane Henderson, interview with, 84–85, 89–91, 111
　Duncan on the run, investigation of, 163, 172–73, 174–75, 194, 196
　Duncan's kidnapping, investigation of, 97–98, 99–100, 102–3, 106, 116
　calling Duncan's friends during, 136–37
　Jeannie Martinez and, 107–9, 110, 113
　Ralph Latham and, 109–10
　FBI contacting, about Duncan, 146–47, 148
　forged checks, investigation of, 104–5, 121–22, 161, 196–97
　getting handwriting sample from Duncan, 79–81, *80*
　getting murder book for Baker homicide investigation, 36
　interviews with Duncan
　　"King for a Day" interview in Salt Lake City, 148–50, 153–200
　　in May 1992 in Park City, 214–18, 220
　　at station, 63–65
　　during visits to apartment shared with Ron, 38–39, 41–43, 63, 162, 172
　interviews with Nathan, 65–66
　　in August 1990, 120, 121–25, 280
　　impression of Nathan from, 91–93, 125, 126, 306
　　in July 1990, 84–89, 90, 91, 280
　　in March 1992 for blood sample, 208–10, 228, 229–30, 237, 245, 255, 277

at state prison in February 1993, 274–306, 411–12
Jackson and, working relationship between, 22, 28–30, 385
James Purpura, interview with, 180, 200, 203–5
Kathy Kritzberg, interview with, 40, 41
kidnapping plan, investigation of
  Duncan on, 155, 156, 159, 165–66, 171–73, 176–77, 182–85, 194, 196
  Nathan on, 283, 284, 290–91, 297–98, 303
"King for a Day" agreement with Duncan, 150, 180, 268, 272, 310, 361–62, 425, 472
knife used to stab Ron, investigation of, 168, 173, 177–78, 192, 287, 290, 295, 296, 297, 299, 300, 302
LA Riots of 1992 and, 212
Lance Strickler, interview with, 55–56
LAPD career of, 22–23
Lydia Archibald, interview with, 38–39, 40–41
Martin Carr, interview with, 57–58
media and, 48–49, 65, 66–67, 83–84
motive for killing Ron, investigation of
  Duncan on, 166–67, 186, 187, 190–91
  Nathan on, 290–91, 293–94, 296–97, 298, 302–3, 419
Mystic's Circle, investigation of Ron's connection with, 46–48, 50, 51–54, 61–62
Nancy Bradish, interview with, 205–6, 207, 218–20
Naval Criminal Investigative Service and, 96, 118
Norris and, 247, 248–49, 269–70
obtaining Duncan's "Things To Do" list, 132–33, 179
polygraph examinations and Baker homicide investigation
  Duncan's agreeing to take, 64–65, 69–70, 77–78, 82

  Nathan's refusal to take, 94
ransom calls, investigation of, 46, 159–60, 161, 183, 184–85, 194, 195, 297
recording conversations between Duncan and Nathan
  while Nathan was at Riverside County Jail, 222–44
  while Nathan was at state prison in Tehachapi, 249–66
request for coroner's office to seal Ron's autopsy file, 68
response to Kuster's shooting, 134, 135
retirement from the LAPD, 30, 273, 274, 275
Rodney King beating, investigation of police officers involved in, 139–40
Roland Trevino, interview with, 47–48
search of Duncan's car, 81–82
search of Ron's bedroom, 39, 39–40, 61, 63
sixty-day summary of Baker homicide investigation, writing, 126–29
stabbing of Ron, investigation of
  Duncan on, 156–58, 161, 164–70, 178–80, 192–93, 199, 211
  Nathan on, 279–80, 291–92, 295–97, 298, 302, 304, 405
testifying as a witness at Duncan's trial, 433
Tewanda Nicholson, interview with, 111–12
walk through of crime scene at Chatsworth Park, 34–35, 37–38
Yasmin Fouda, interview with, 105–6
Gartland, William O., 29, 139, 225, 226, 275
Gascón, George, 461–62, 463, 464–65, 469, 479, 484
Gates, Daryl, 139, 212
Giss, Harvey, 355
Glezos, Stephanie, 366, 367–71
Goldman, Ronald, 377

Gourley, George, 69–79, 80
  administering test to Duncan, 77
  compiling list of questions for Duncan, 69
  questioning Duncan after revealing polygraph results, 77–79
  questioning Duncan prior to polygraph, 70–77
governor's warrant process, 380–81
grand jury indictments, advantage of, 311
Green, Laura, 378, 379, 404, 405–13
Gregory, James, 381, 384
  deadlock in plea negotiations, 428, 430–31, 434
  pretrial motion for Duncan, 425–26, 427, 428, 429, 430
Guerrero, Cristina, 468, 473–74, 475, 482

Halliday, Debbie, 441
Hay, Steve, 454–56
Helms, Freddie, 139–40
Henderson, Diane, 58, 227, 228, 313
  at apartment on the night of Ron's murder
    Diane on, 89–90, 287, 404
    Duncan on, 41–42, 64, 86, 154–55, 174, 327–28
    Nathan on, 49, 86, 87, 91, 238, 256–57, 286, 297, 319, 320, 321, 327–28, 405–6, 409
  Duncan's call to, to find out where Nathan might be, 214–18, 220, 244
  interviews with, 84–85, 89–91, 111
  lack of knowledge about Ron's murder, 183–84, 237, 300
  Nathan and, 86, 87, 89, 183, 263, 284
  breakup between, 208, 214, 237
  staying with Diane after Ron's murder, 66, 84, 162, 176, 323
  Ron's dinner for roommates and, 49, 73, 86, 89, 155
  search of property after bank robbery, 208
  as a witness at Nathan's court appearances, 313, 404–5

Heuser, Eva, 19
Hickock, Richard, 202
Hodgman, Bill, 311
Holliday, George, 137, 201
Hollywood Division of LAPD, 25–26
homicide detectives and prosecutors, different roles and approaches of, 307

In Cold Blood (Capote), 202
Ingalls, Anne, 378, 462
  interviewing witnesses in Salt Lake City, 381–83
  lack of notification from officials about Duncan, 451, 461
  letter to Newsom about Duncan, 486
  as prosecutor in Duncan's trial, 434–35
    deadlock in plea negotiations, 428, 430–31, 434
    response to Gregory's pretrial motion to dismiss, 425, 426–27, 428
  as prosecutor in Nathan's trial, 404, 413–23
    on kidnapping plan, 417, 418–20, 422–23
    on motive for jumping on Ron, 413–14
    on pact not to say anything about Ron's murder, 419–20, 421, 423
    on stabbing Ron, 414–17, 419, 420–22
Ito, Lance, 384

Jackson, Rick, 490
  approach to witnesses, 138–39
  Arce and, 21, 26
  assignment to Baker homicide investigation, 21–22, 30
  autopsy report, analysis of, 46, 398–400
  background of, 24–25
  Barnes and, 94–96, 100, 101, 366
  belief in Nathan and Duncan as equally culpable for Ron's murder, 402
  Berchem and, 378–79, 383–84

briefing Clark on Baker case, 355–56
Christine Reyna, interview with, 50, 51–54
Clark and
  arresting Duncan, 359–67
  interviewing Melissa Bean, 371–76
  interviewing Stephanie Glezos, 367–71
  meeting with Baker family, 357–58
commutation of Duncan's sentence, investigation of, 446–57
Conn and, 308, 311–12
contact with Baker family, 32–34, 61–62, 104, 132, 141, 357–58, 440, 446–47, 487
contacting Duncan's mother regarding DA's plea offer, 431–32
at coroner's office, 31–32
Diane Henderson, interview with, 84–85, 89–91, 111
Duncan on the run, investigation of, 114–15, 142–43, 163, 172–75, 194, 196
Duncan's kidnapping, investigation of, 97–103, 172–73, 176–77, 196
  calling Duncan's friends during, 136–37
  Duncan's father and, 112
  Jeannie Martinez and, 110
  tracing location of call to Lydia, 103, 107, 109, 110, 115–18
efforts in preventing Duncan's parole, 486–87
  letter to Newsom, 485–86
  letter to the Board of Parole Hearings, 457, 458–61, 477–78
  at parole board hearing, 462–64, 467, 469, 477–80, 483
Emile Monette, interview with, 386–87
forged checks, investigation of, 63, 104–5, 113–14, 119, 120–22, 125, 161, 196–97, 323
Gago Avaneszadeh, interview with, 382–83
Garcia and, working relationship between, 22, 28–30, 385

getting handwriting sample from Duncan, 79–81, *80*
getting murder book for Baker homicide investigation, 36
Gregory and, 381
helping solve cold cases after retirement, 441–42, 445, 490
Ingalls and, 381–83
interviews with Duncan
  at arrest, 360–65
  "King for a Day" interview in Salt Lake City, 148–50, 153–200
  in May 1992 in Park City, 214–18
  at station, 63–65
  during visits to apartment shared with Ron, 38–39, 41–43, 63, 162, 172
interviews with Nathan
  in August 1990, 120, 121–25, 280
  impression of Nathan from, 91–93, 125, 126, 306
  in July 1990, 84–89, 90, 91, 280
  in March 1992 for blood sample, 208–10, 228, 229–30, 237, 245, 255, 277
  at state prison in February 1993, 274–306, 411–12
investigation into how Duncan obtained a false identity for his passport application, 387–96, 396
James Purpura, interview with, 180, 200, 203–5
Kathy Kritzberg, interview with, 40, 41
kidnapping plan, investigation of
  Duncan on, 155, 156, 159, 165–66, 171, 182–85, 194, 202
  Nathan on, 283, 284, 290–91, 297–98, 303, 320–22, 326–27
"King for a Day" agreement with Duncan, 150, 180, 268, 271–72, 308–10, 349, 361–62, 363, 425, 472
knife used to stab Ron, investigation of, 168, 173, 177–78, 192, 287, 290, 295, 296, 297, 299, 300, 302, 317, 318, 322–24, 397–400

Jackson, Rick (cont.)
  LA Riots of 1992 and, 212
  Lance Strickler, interview with, 55–57
  LAPD career of, 25–29, 45, 311, 437–40
  Lydia Archibald, interview with, 38–39
  marriages of
    first, 55, 135, 433, 434, 437
    second, 441
  Martin Carr, interview with, 57–58
  media and, 65, 67, 328
  motive for killing Ron, investigation of
    Duncan on, 166–67, 186, 187, 190–91
    Nathan on, 290–91, 293–94, 296–98, 302–3, 323, 324, 327–28, 419
  Mystic's Circle, investigation of Ron's connection with, 46–48, 50, 51–54, 61–62
  Nancy Bradish, interview with, 205–6, 207, 218–20
  at Nathan's trial, 403, 404, 405, 424
  Norris and, 247, 248–49, 269–70
  notifying Jonathan Wayne Miller's parents about Duncan stealing son's identity, 432
  obtaining Duncan's "Things To Do" list, 132–33, 179
  opinion on appropriate sentence for Duncan, 430
  on parole for Nathan, 489–90
  photograph of, 30
  polygraph examinations and
    Duncan's agreeing to take, 64–65, 69–70, 77–78, 82
    Nathan's refusal to take, 94
  preparation for Nathan's trial, 397–400
  Prior's recording of conversation with Duncan for, 333–37, 338, 349–50
  ransom calls, investigation of, 35–36, 46, 159–61, 183–85, 194, 195, 297
  reaction to Duncan's rejection of plea offer, 431–32, 434
  recording conversations between Duncan and Nathan
    while Nathan was at Riverside County Jail, 222–44
    while Nathan was at state prison in Tehachapi, 249–66
  relationship with daughters, 21, 27, 36, 55, 106–7, 130, 433, 437
  requesting a "keep-away order" from jail personnel for Duncan, 381, 384, 429
  requests to Scientific Investigation Division (SID)
    to analyze evidence for any latent fingerprints, 46
    to analyze Ron Baker's fingernail kit, 118–19, 136, 212–13
    for DNA test of blood on Duncan's athame, 141–42, 143
    to test for Ron's blood type and compare it to the blood on his clothing, 46
  response to Duncan's request to be placed in protective custody, 428–29
  response to Kuster's shooting, 134–36
  retirement from the LAPD, 433–34, 436–37, 441
  Rodney King beating, investigation of police officers involved in, 139–40
  Roland Trevino, interview with, 47–48
  search of Duncan's car, 81–82
  search of Ron's bedroom, 39, 39–40, 61, 62–63
  Shirley James, interview with, 114–15
  sixty-day summary of Baker homicide investigation, writing, 126–29
  stabbing of Ron, investigation of
    Duncan on, 156–58, 161, 164–70, 178–80, 192–93, 199, 211
    Nathan on, 279–80, 291–92, 295–97, 298, 302, 304, 315–20, 324–25, 405, 412
  taking Duncan into custody, 383–84
  Tewanda Nicholson, interview with, 111–12
  visits with Nathan after his trial, 440

walk through of crime scene at
    Chatsworth Park, 34–35, 37–38,
    357, 358
  as a witness at LA County Grand
    Jury, 313–14
Jacquez, Charlene, 441
James, Duncan, 112, 113, 114–15,
    193–94
James, Shirley, 112, 113, 114–15, 122,
    125, 193–94
Johnson, Mark, 59
Jordan, Mike, 213

Karner, Roland, 3–4, 5, 7–9, 34, 35
Kennedy, Robert F., xiii
Kilcoyne, Dennis, 388
King, Rodney, 137–38, 139–41, 201,
    211–12, 401–2, 445–46
Kritzberg, Kathy, 38–39, 40, 41, 106
KTLA, 447–48
Kuster, Russ, 136
  as homicide coordinator, 21, 26, 27,
    28, 29
  murder of, 133–36
Kwock, J. R., 139, 140, 141

LaBianca, Leno, 142
LaBianca, Rosemary, 142
Lacey, Jackie, 461
Lambkin, David, 438
Lang, Danny, 311, 379
LAPD
  Communications Division of, 98
  creation of Cold Case Homicide
    Special Section, 438
  Detective Headquarters Division of,
    97, 112–13, 133
  Hollywood Division of, 25–26
  Robbery-Homicide Division (RHD)
    of, 16, 20, 28, 29, 36–37
  Rodney King beating and, 137–38,
    139, 201, 211–12, 401–2, 445–46
  SID. *See* Scientific Investigation
    Division (SID)
  Sound Lab of, 97
Latent Prints Unit, 121
Latham, Ralph, 109–10
Leavitt, Mike, 383

Lebowitz, Donna, 452
Leonard, Harold, 394–95
Leopold, Nathan, 202–3
Litton Federal Credit Union, 104,
    113, 119
Loeb, Richard, 202–3
Los Angeles, xiii
  deadliest decade in history of, 6, 26
  Gascón's Resentencing Policy for,
    463, 464–65
  homicide trials in, investigating
    detectives at, 404
  LA Riots of 1992 in, 211–12, 401
  perception of LAPD officers in, after
    beating of Rodney King, 137–38,
    139, 201–2, 211–12, 401–2
  Simpson's acquittal and, 402
Los Angeles Daily News, 19, 48, 66
Los Angeles Times, 48, 65, 66–67,
    83–84, 329
Lowery, James, 207–8, 213

Maitland, Duncan, 388–89, 389,
    390–92, 393–96
Manson, Charles, 5, 6, 142
Manson Family killings, xiii, 5, 6
Manson tunnel, 5, 7, 12, 435
Marko, Bela, 134, 135
Marsy's Law, 465–66
Martinez, Duncan
  allowing investigators to search
    Ron's bedroom, 61, 62
  apartment of, description of, 38, 39
  on arguments between Nathan and
    Ron, 164, 166–67, 185, 186, 190
  arrest of, for murdering Ron, 359–67
    Barnes advising Duncan not to
      speak with Jackson or Clark
      after, 366
    calling Stephanie Glezos after,
      370–71
    fighting extradition to California
      after, 376, 379–81, 383
    flying back to Los Angeles with
      Jackson after, 383–84
    notifying mother about, 363, 365
  background of, 469–70
  blood type of, 211, 234, 247, 404

Martinez, Duncan *(cont.)*
  burglary in Salt Lake City
    arrest for, 471
    on being forced to commit, 334, 335, 336, 338–39, 343, 350, 353
    discussions with Prior after arrest for, 334–35, 338, 350–51, 353
    notification of Jackson about, 333–34
    pleading guilty to, 354
  cigarette brand of, 167
  collection of license plates with Ron, 107
  commutation of sentence of, 484, 488
    application for, 452–54, 455, 478–79
    Beckman's representation of Duncan in, 488–89
    clemency investigative report in, 454–57
    Jackson's investigation into, 451–57
    public announcement on, 446, 447–48
  as a compulsive liar, 456, 458–59, 485
    about military service, 53, 70, 72, 85, 106, 107–9, 125, 269
    Nathan on, 316
    at the University of Utah, 373
    while on the run, 106, 107–9, 112, 113, 114, 119, 122, 145, 269
  confiding in others about Ron's murder, 180–81
    Bradish, 181
    father and stepmother, 193–94
    fraternity, 271–72, 308–10, 362, 363
    Prior, 340–43, 345–50, 352, 358, 459, 481, 483
    Purpura, 180, 199–200, 204
    as violating his "King for a Day" agreement, 272, 310, 362, 363
  cover story for night of Ron's murder, 41–42, 58, 64, 69, 73, 86–87, 91, 111, 113, 122–23, 128, 255–58, 264–65
  drug use of, 125
  fear of Nathan, 162–64, 172, 175, 177, 198, 240
  forged checks and, 64, 68, 74, 79–81, 80, *103*, 104–5, 113–14, 119, 120–22, 125, 127, 161, 196–97, 323, 453
  friendship with Nathan, 167, 189–90, 198, 219, 220, 262, 270–71
  friendship with Ron, 67, 74, 124, 130, 167, 189–90, 198, 262, 459
    after damage to Duncan's car, 64, 74, 88, 122
    beginning of, 41, 74, 479
    Ron screaming for Duncan to help during struggle with Nathan, 157, 204, 219, 240, 243, 348, 472, 481
  going to Chatsworth Park
    after Ron was reported missing, 43, 57, 63–64, 68, 85, 90, 128–29, 197–98, 325–26, 409–10
    with friends prior to Ron's murder, 42, 50, 85, 128, 193, 397–98
  grand jury indictment of, for Ron's murder, 356, 357, 358, 360, 363, 426
  interviews with, 17–18, 43, 85
    at arrest, 360–65
    "King for a Day" interview in Salt Lake City, 150, 153–200, 268, 272, 310, 361–62, 363, 425, 472
    in May 1992 in Park City, 214–18, 220
    at station, 63–65
    during visits to apartment shared with Ron, 38–39, 41–43, 63, 162, 172
  as James (Jake) Lee Atkins, 113, 115, 194, 270–71, 342
  job at Everything Audio, 72, 125
  as Jonathan Wayne Miller, 194, 204, 334, 384
    arrest of, for submitting a fraudulent passport application, 146–48, 153, 194, 199, 207, 210, 334, 342, 379–80, 384, 386, 387, 460, 470
    investigation of passport application submitted by, 388–96, *396*

stealing and establishing fake
  identity as, 387, 432
therapy with Bradish as, 181,
  205–6, 207, 218–20
kidnapping plan and, 164, 167,
  168, 192–93, 204–5, 219, 220,
  242–43, 245, 309, 340–43, 345,
  352, 374, 375, 406, 408–10,
  417–20, 422–23, 448
  Duncan on, 155, 156, 159, 165–66,
    171, 182–83, 184–85, 194, 202
  Nathan on, 283, 284, 290–91,
    297–98, 303, 320–22, 326–27
lack of remorse expressed for Ron's
  murder, 460
life in prison, 449, 470, 474–75
manipulative traits of, 474, 482, 487
military service of, 70, 71–72
  administrative discharge from
    Marine Corps Reserve, 108
  Duncan's claims about, 53, 70, 72,
    85, 106, 107–9, 125, 269
  Naval Criminal Investigative
    Service on, 96, 118
motive for Ron's murder, 413–14,
  448, 469–70
  Duncan on, 166–67, 186, 187,
    190–91, 471
  Nathan on, 290–91, 293–94,
    296–97, 298, 302–3, 323, 324,
    327–28, 419
pact with Nathan about Ron's murder,
  320, 323, 407–8, 411, 419–20,
  421, 423
parole of, 446–47, 457
  Athans's risk assessment report on,
    463–64, 468–69, 471, 473, 476,
    477, 480, 483
  decision on, 482–84
  eligibility for, 446, 449, 452, 454
  full discharge from, 486–87
  Ingalls's letter to Newsom on, 486
  Jackson's letter to the Board of Parole
    Hearings on, 457, 458–61, 477–78
  Jackson's letter to Newsom on,
    485–86
  parole hearing for, 446, 462–64,
    467–84, 486
  Patty's letter to Newsom on, 486
  post-release plans after, 477
  support network and, 474, 475, 489
polygraph examination of, 67–68,
  69–79, 110
  agreeing to allow car to be searched
    after, 81–82
  agreeing to take, 64–65, 69–70
  answering Gourley's questions after
    results from, 77–79
  answering questions during actual
    test, 77
  answering questions prior to actual
    polygraph, 70–77
  failing, 77–79, 82, 91, 94, 96, 126,
    129, 145, 163, 189
ransom calls and, 16, 49, 56, 64,
  74, 87, 159–60, 161, 164, 183,
  184–85, 194, 195, 205, 240,
  459–60, 481–82
recordings of conversations
  between Duncan and Nathan,
    222–44, 249–66, 290, 410–11
  between Prior and Duncan,
    333–37, 338, 349–50
on religion, 258, 261–62
Ron making dinner for, 49, 73, 86,
  89, 155
at Ron's memorial service, 59–60,
  460, 472, 482, 489
on the run, 142, 163, 172–73,
  174–75, 196
  blocking out all emotions while, 220
  effect on mother, 343–44
  faking own kidnapping while,
    97–103, 109–10, 115–18,
    125–26, 129, 132–33, 172–73,
    176–77, 179, 196, 269, 460,
    473, 482
  in Inyo County, California, while,
    142–43
  leaving for Florida while, 112,
    113, 115
  staying at father's house while,
    112, 113, 114–15
  telling dramatic lies to people while,
    106, 107–9, 112, 113, 114, 119,
    122, 145, 269

Martinez, Duncan (cont.)
  sentence of life without parole for
    Ron's murder, 435, 446, 449
  in stabbing Ron, 244, 279–80,
    287–92, 295–98, 302, 304,
    315–19, 324–25, 340, 346–49,
    405, 411, 412
    Duncan on, 156–58, 169–70,
      179–80, 199, 239–40, 371,
      372–73, 374–75
    Nathan on, 407–8, 416–17, 420–22
    urging Nathan to finish Ron off,
      459, 472, 481, 483
    as a student at the University of
      Utah, 250, 271–72, 308–10, 314,
      372–73, 376
  trial of, for Ron's murder, 347, 425,
    434–35
    decision of DA's Office not to seek
      the death penalty in, 403
    jury verdict of guilty in, 435
    pretrial motion to dismiss,
      425–28, 430
    rejection of plea offer prior to, 428,
      430–31, 434, 457–58
    request to be placed in protective
      custody while awaiting,
      428–29
    witnesses testifying in, 433, 435
  trying to locate Nathan for
    investigators
    calling Diane Henderson, 214–18
    calling Nathan's father, 220–21
  Wicca and, 56, 63, 73
  as a witness at trial, credibility of,
    224–25, 269–70, 308, 311–12,
    337, 362, 427
  "woe is me" efforts to elicit sympathy,
    341–42, 350, 352–53
  on writing remorse letters, 475
Martinez, Jeannie, 99, 175, 473
  call to Nathan about Duncan's lies,
    122, 124
  Duncan telling Nathan police had
    been to house of, 228, 229, 230,
    251–52, 253–54, 265
  effect of Duncan being on the run on,
    343–44

  hiring Barnes as Duncan's attorney,
    150, 163, 205, 378
  interactions with Garcia and Jackson
    about Duncan's kidnapping,
    107–9, 110, 112, 113
  Jackson contacting, regarding DA's
    plea offer, 431–32
  notification of Duncan's arrest for
    murdering Ron, 363, 365
  picking up Duncan's box from the
    Bakers, 171
Martinez, Otto, 109, 110, 114, 378
Massey, Chuck, 29
Matheson, Greg, 141, 212–13
McCarty, Scott, 107, 108, 109
McPherson, Sergeant, 226
Mejia, Mike, 311
Menendez, Erik, 355
Menendez, Lyle, 355
Metoyer, Pat, 61, 62–63
Midsummer Night's Dream, A
  (Shakespeare), 3
Miller, James, 432
Miller, Jonathan Wayne
  deceased at one year of age, 387,
    394–96, 396, 432
  Duncan's use of identity of. See
    Martinez, Duncan: as Jonathan
    Wayne Miller
Minor, Michele, 467–68, 469,
  470–73, 474, 475–76,
  482–84
Monette, Emile, 386–87
Montagna, Michael, 268–70, 308
Moseley, Peggy, 9–10, 18–19, 34–35, 36,
  37, 129
murder book for each homicide
  investigated by the LAPD,
  overview of, 36
Mystic's Circle, 15, 17, 18, *18*, 35, 41, 42,
  46–47, 51, 61–62, 73, 74

Naval Criminal Investigative Service,
  96, 118
Newsom, Gavin
  commutation of Duncan's sentence,
    460, 466, 484, 488
    application for, 488, 489

Jackson's investigation into, 451–57
endorsement of Gascón for Los
    Angeles DA, 460
Ingalls's letter to, 486
Jackson's letter to, 485–86
Patty's letter to, 486
Nicholson, Tewanda, 64, 96,
    111–12, 281
Night Stalker. *See* Ramirez, Richard
Norris, Ernie, 426
    agreement with Barnes, 149–50,
        425, 428
    Conn taking over as assigned
        prosecutor on the Baker case,
        336–37
    decision to charge Nathan, 247,
        248–49
    grand jury proceedings against
        Nathan, 312–13, 314, 337,
        356, 358
    plea deal offered to Duncan, 426, 430
    on using Duncan as a witness in
        Nathan's trial, 269–70, 308,
        312, 427
    as a witness in Duncan's pretrial
        motion, 425–26, 427

Ochiae, Alison, 120, 404
Offender Investigations and Screening
    Division, 455

Pacific Bell, 35, 97, 99, 103, 109,
    115–16, 117
Padilla, Alex, 450
Padilla, Steve, 66–67
Paws For Life, 449
Perez, Vickie, 64, 96, 111, 281, 282
Persons, Mike, 389, 390
Petroski, Hank, 26–27
polygraph evidence, as an investigative
    tool, 67–68
Powell, Colin, 389
Prior, Jim
    contact with Jackson after Duncan's
        arrest for burglary, 333–37, 354
    recorded conversation with Duncan
        about burglary charges, 338,
        344–45, 350–51, 353

about Emile's hold over Duncan,
    338–39, 343, 350, 353
about Ron's murder, 336, 337–52,
    353, 356, 358, 363
as a witness
    at Duncan's trial, 435
    in grand jury case against
        Duncan, 358
prosecutors and homicide detectives,
    different roles and approaches
    of, 307
Purpura, James
    Duncan confiding in, 180,
        199–200, 204
    efforts to help Duncan get a passport,
        388–90, 391, 392
    interview with, 180, 200, 203–5
    Stephanie Glezos and, 367,
        368–69, 370

Questioned Documents Unit,
    119, 120–21

race, perceptions about
    after George Floyd's murder, 445–46
    after Rodney King beating, 137–38,
        139, 201, 211–12, 401–2, 445–46
    in gathering evidence, 201–2
    jurors and, 93, 401–3
    Simpson's acquittal and, 402
Ramirez, Richard, xiii, 6, 65
Reyna, Christine, 47, 48, 50, 51–54,
    57, 58
Rhudy, Craig, 17–18, 35, 43, 56,
    63–64, 85
Robbery-Homicide Division (RHD) of
    LAPD, 16, 20, 28, 29, 36–37

Salt Lake Tribune, 379–80
Sands, John, 165, 166, 182, 183,
    194, 248
Satanism, 5–6, 47, 52, 53, 55
Scientific Investigation Division
    (SID), 40
    Blood Alcohol Unit at, 69
    on blood on broken beer bottle,
        247–48
    Chemical Processing Unit of, 46

Scientific Investigation Division *(cont.)*
  inspection of police officers' uniforms for evidence, 140
  Latent Prints Unit of, 121
  photographs in Baker case, 9, 40
  Questioned Documents Unit of, 119, 120–21
  Serology Unit of. *See* Serology Unit
Scully, Vin, 82
Serology Unit
  analysis of Nathan's blood, 210–11
  analysis of Ron Baker's fingernail kit, 118–19, 136, 207, 210–11, 212–13
  testing for Ron's blood type, 46
  testing of blood on athames, 96, 119–20, 141–42, 143
  testing of reddish spots found in Duncan's car, 81
Shakespeare, William, 3
SID (Scientific Investigation Division). *See* Scientific Investigation Division (SID)
Simpson, Nicole, 377
Simpson, O. J., xiii, 377, 380, 384, 401, 402
Smith, Perry, 202
Spahn Movie Ranch, 5
Special Directive 20–14, 463, 464–65
Stallings, John, 100, 107, 110
Stephens, Jerry, 28
Strickler, Jenny, 41, 42, 50, 55, 85, 125
Strickler, Lance, 125, 259
  at Chatsworth Park, 42, 50, 193
  Duncan and Nathan living with, 41
  hosting Wicca classes, 55–56, 63, 85
  interview with, 55–56
  introducing Ron to Wicca, 17, 40–41
summer solstice, 3
Sundstedt, Frank, 311

Tate, Sharon, 5, 142
Tatreau, Jim, 438
Taylor, James, 135
Thies, Mike, 28, 273
Tisinger, Rita, 96
Tomlinson, Adriane, 397, 398
Tresmontan, Dave, 441–42
Trevino, Roland, 35, 46, 47–48, 50, 53, 58

UCLA Police Department, 47, 50

Vaum, Tim, 390, 391
Victims' Bill of Rights, 465–66

Walker, Julianne, 462, 463–64, 468
Wicca, overview of, 51–52, 57
Wilson, Mike, 40
Wilson, Pete, 383
Woodland Hills United Methodist, 14, 55, 58
Wright, Wilbur, 26

Yelchak, Mark, 103, 107, 109, 110, 115–16, 117

Zorn, John, 29, 67, 135, 139

ABOUT THE AUTHORS

Rick Jackson had a thirty-four-year career with the Los Angeles Police Department, the last twenty-eight of which he worked exclusively as a homicide detective.

Since his retirement, he has been featured in three true crime podcasts with author Michael Connelly. In 2024, he was an executive producer for and appeared in a four-part docuseries on MGM+, *The Wonderland Massacre and the Secret History of Hollywood.*

Jackson now lives in Northern California. Since 2017, he has worked part-time as a cold case homicide detective with the San Mateo County Sheriff's Office.

In his spare time, Jackson loves to travel and play golf, and he is an avid baseball fan.

Matthew McGough is an investigative journalist, a lawyer, and the author of two books, *The Lazarus Files: A Cold Case Investigation* and *Bat Boy: Coming of Age with the New York Yankees,* which inspired the CBS series *Clubhouse.* He is the recipient of two Southern California Journalism Awards from the Los Angeles Press Club for his reporting in *The Atlantic.* McGough has also written for television and was a writer and legal consultant for NBC's *Law & Order.*

He lives in Los Angeles with his wife and their two sons.